Transformation & Convergence
in the Frame of
Knowledge

Transformation & Convergence in the Frame of Knowledge

Explorations in the Interrelations of Scientific and Theological Enterprise

by

Thomas F. Torrance

Wipf and Stock Publishers
150 West Broadway • Eugene OR 97401

1998

Transformation and Convergence in the Frame of Knowledge
Explorations in the Interrelations of Scientific and Theological Enterprise
By Torrance, Thomas F.
Copyright©1998 Torrance, Thomas F.

ISBN:1-57910-107-0

Printed by *Wipf and Stock Publishers* 1998
150 West Broadway • Eugene OR 97401

ACKNOWLEDGEMENTS

The kind permission of several publishing houses has been granted for the reprint of essays published in their journals.

Pergamon Press, Oxford
'The Integration of Form in Natural and in Theological Science', from *Science, Medicine and Man*, vol. 1, 1973, pp. 143–172.
'The Open Universe and the Free Society', from *Ethics in Medicine and Science*, from vol. 6, 1979, pp. 145–153.
'The Place of Michael Polanyi in the Modern Philosophy of Science', from *Ethics in Medicine and Science*, vol. 7. 1980, pp. 57–95.

Convergence, Inc., New York
'Ultimate Beliefs and the Scientific Revolution', from *Cross Currents*, vol. xxx, no. 2, 1980. pp. 129–149.

Éditions Duculot, Paris-Gembloux
'Christian Theology in the Context of Scientific Revolution', from *Bibliotheca Ephemeridum Theologicarum Lovaniensium*, vol. xliii, 1976, pp. 295–311.

Cambridge University Press, Cambridge
'The Problem of Natural Theology in the Thought of Karl Barth', from *Religious Studies*, vol. 6, 1970, pp. 121–135.
'Newton, Einstein and Scientific Theology', from *Religious Studies*, vol. 8. 1972, pp. 233–250.
'Immortality and Light', from *Religious Studies*, vol. 17, 1981, pp. 147–161.

St Patrick's College, Maynooth, Dublin
'Truth and Authority: Theses on Truth', from *The Irish Theological Quarterly*, vol. xxxix, no. 3, 1972, pp. 215–242.

Contents

I have dedicated this book to *The Center of Theological Inquiry* recently established under the direction of Dr James I. McCord at Princeton, New Jersey. The aim of this institute is to sponsor advanced theological thinking, not least in the kind of dialogue advocated here between theologians and scientists, and thus to give a lead in the continuing transformation and convergence in the frame of knowledge.

Preface

The various essays which make up this volume have arisen out of a sustained engagement with the tension between Christian theology, as it has been renewed directly or indirectly through the great work of Karl Barth, and the general frame of thought that has dominated European culture for several hundred years. I have had constantly in mind the immense achievement of the Early Christian Church which set itself not only to communicate the Gospel to the Graeco-Roman world but to transform the prevailing frame of thought and culture so that the Gospel could take deep root and develop within it. It was soon realised that the Biblical doctrines of the Incarnation of the Word of God in Jesus Christ and the redemption of the creation through him conflicted sharply with the dualist modes of thought embedded in Greek philosophy and science, as well as religion, and could not be given adequate articulation and formulation unless the basic concepts of Greek philosophy and science were transformed under the creative impact of the Gospel. That is what the theologians of the Early Church undertook to do, and though it took several centuries they succeeded to such an extent that they not only gave a profound formulation of the Christian Faith within that transformed framework that has stood the test of time, but injected into the foundations of European thought the masterful ideas that were later to give rise to empirico-theoretical science as we now know it. That was a signal achievement which remains a challenge and an inspiration for every generation, for the Christian Faith must be brought to bear transformingly upon the whole frame of human culture, science and philosophy in every age.

It was certainly Karl Barth's aim to set twentieth century theology squarely back on its own proper ground in the revealed knowledge of God, and to reforge its inner bond with the foundations of the One Holy Catholic and Apostolic Church in the Nicene doctrines of the Incarnation and the Holy Trinity. And in so doing he restored the scientific integrity and grandeur of the theological enterprise. With him the pure science of theology took a giant stride forward, comparable to what took place in the fourth, fifth and sixteenth centuries under the controlling insight that what God the Father is toward us in his self-revelation through Jesus Christ and in the Holy Spirit he is inherently and eternally in himself as the living God, the Creator of all things visible and invisible. The rigour and power with which Karl Barth applied the same insight to the whole

spectrum of our knowledge of the ways and works of God led to a
profound shift in the epistemological structure of theology which
matched the radical change in our scientific understanding of the
God-given intelligibilities of the created universe that ranged from
the emergence of field-theory in the physics of Michael Faraday and
James Clerk Maxwell to the relativistic physics of Einstein and his
heirs. The significance and relevance of Karl Barth's theology in
this respect is best indicated by pointing to his doctrine of God.
With a quite herculean effort of thought he brought together the
Patristic emphasis upon the Being of God in his Acts and the
Reformation emphasis upon the Acts of God in his Being, thus
combining as never before the ontic and dynamic aspects of knowledge of God, thereby transcending the dualist modes of thought
which seeped back into Christian theology in East and West,
damaging Byzantine and Latin, Roman and Protestant, traditions
alike for many centuries. Hence it may well be claimed, with all the
appropriate differences taken into account, that Karl Barth's
achievement in theology anticipated the new way of thinking
which physicists have had to undertake in seeking to integrate the
corpuscular and undulatory theories of light, thereby transcending
the unsatisfactory dualism between particle and field which was
built into the fabric of classical physics by Newton and which still
troubles quantum theory.

Why is it, then, that now, some fifty years after his great *Church
Dogmatics* began to appear, Karl Barth is still far from being
understood or appreciated as he deserves, but instead continues to
provoke considerable resistance? The answer given must certainly
have to do with the fact that while Karl Barth's own theology
represents an advance far ahead of his contemporaries, the socio-
cultural frame of thought, within which theology continues to
function, remains largely unchanged. Bound up with this is the fact
that in his concentration upon the material content and inner
structure of Christian theology Karl Barth did very little to work
out the implications of what he was doing for the transformation of
the received frame of thought that is needed if the results of his
work are continually to be regained and appreciated. Karl Barth
was aware that such a transformation could take place only over a
long period of deep-seated engagement in dialogue between Christian theology and natural science, for in its own immense advance
natural science today is thrown into the same kind of conflict with
the prevailing frame of thought and is met with the same kind of
recalcitrance before the structural demands of radical change.

It must not be forgotten that in order to achieve his objective

Karl Barth had to cut theology free from the culture-conditioned framework within which it had become trapped and by which it had become severely compromised. He took his cue from the Reformers who found that they had to detach the formulation of Biblical and ancient Catholic Christianity from the framework of Aristotelian philosophy and science with which it had been synthesised, if they were to carry forward into the new age their understanding of the Gospel in a dynamic mode as well as in a theoretical form matched to its actual content. Unhappily post-Reformation theology soon became trapped within a 'modern' framework in which it was steadily accommodated to Cartesian, Newtonian and Kantian structures of thought and the brilliant European culture which they underpinned. Something like a new Reformation of theology was called for, but one in which there would be genuine appreciation of human culture without any reductionist subordination of Christian faith to an alien system of mechanistic concepts or time-conditioned socio-cultural patterns and institutions.

That is where Karl Barth came in, as one can see so well from his massive analysis of nineteenth century Protestant theology as it emerged out of the eighteenth century under the influence of Kant and then fell under the spell of Hegel. He demanded a consistent and rigorous scientific method in theology in accordance with which all unwarranted preconceptions and hidden assumptions and all antecedent conceptual systems are called into radical question during the course of *a posteriori* inquiry on the ground where God actually makes himself known to mankind, and in the compelling light of the objective content of what he reveals to us of himself and his relations with us in space and time. It was in that connection that Barth insisted on rejecting any and every form of an independent 'natural theology' regarded as an antecedent conceptual system to which all actual or revealed knowledge of God had to be schematised if it was to be accepted as 'rational'. In point of fact, as is shown in this volume, Barth, without realising it at the time, was doing in theology precisely what Einstein was doing in natural science, when he questioned the validity of schematising physics to the rigid framework of Euclidean geometry, that is of an independent and antecedent conceptual system detached from actual experience, and set about dismantling the rational superstructure of mathematical time and space which the Newtonian system clamped down upon the universe of bodies in motion and thereby distorted knowledge of it. Einstein's insistence that geometry must be incorporated into the heart of physics where it becomes four-dimensional, indissolubly bound up with the structure of physical knowledge as itself a

form of 'natural science', was paralleled by Karl Barth's insistence
that natural knowledge must be incorporated into the heart of our
actual knowledge of God where it is indissolubly bound up with its
epistemological structure and serves its scientific articulation and
formulation. However, what Karl Barth did not seem to appreciate
adequately, was the fact that since God makes himself known to us
in the created universe where he has placed us and therefore in and
through the spatio-temporal structures and intelligibilities of the
universe which, under God, are more and more disclosed to our
scientific inquiries, there are basic interconnections between
theological concepts and natural scientific concepts which have to
be brought to light, if we are to do full justice both to our
knowledge of God and to our knowledge of the created order. It
will be through dialogue between theology and science at that level
that we will be able gradually to transform the general frame of
human knowledge in such a way that will make for a reconciling
convergence of thought and a healing of the damaging splits in
human culture. So far as Christian theology is concerned, this task
is not an optional extra, for it is our inescapable obligation in Jesus
Christ not only to preach the Gospel to all mankind but to
evangelise the foundations of all human life and thought.

It is perhaps not sufficiently appreciated that the conflict that
arises between new ideas and the general frame of thought has to do
with an essential feature in all rational, and not least scientific,
knowledge, namely, the public element in what we call 'facts' or
'data'. We perceive things not just with our eyes but with our
minds, for, as we have discovered through the experimental use of
inverting spectacles, it is only when our visual and mental images of
things coincide that we can observe or apprehend them in any
intelligible way for what they really are. But the mental or conceptual component in 'facts' is influenced or slanted by the need for
publically accepted or generally accredited 'facts'. There is therefore
an inter-subjective, and in that sense an 'objective' element that
enters into our normal observations, so that the way in which we
'naturally' see and understand things is controlled rather more than
we are explicitly aware by habits of mind which we have acquired
and now share with others in our family or society. This applies
even to the culture to which we belong or the age in which we live,
for they acquire perspectives that are tacitly governed by subjective
or mental components which have been assimilated into their basic
stock of unquestioned assumptions. This applies no less to any
normal science with an established tradition which has come to
operate, not only with agreed principles and universally accepted

laws, but with unconsciously held outlooks and attitudes, latent beliefs and implicit assumptions which do not obtrude themselves for they have become assimilated into the scientific mind and for that reason exercise a regulative control over the critical discrimination of evidence and the formation of satisfactory scientific theory. When a long-accepted scientific tradition in the way things are to be regarded blends with the cultural tradition of the society in which that scientific tradition has arisen, then we have the establishment of a general frame of knowledge which is inevitably resistant to radically new ideas and the logical reconstruction of prior knowledge which they demand. The history of natural science is replete with conflicts of this kind, but mention may be made of the many decades it took for the kinetic theory of heat to gain acceptance over the caloric theory, or of the similarly long time it took for a relational and dynamical theory of the electromagnetic field to gain the ascendency over a mechanical interpretation, not to mention the rearguard action that is still being fought on behalf of mechanistic conceptions in several branches of natural and social science.

James Clerk Maxwell used to say that the most important questions in science have to do with what he called 'fundamental ideas', that is, with ideas that enter into and affect the basic structure of scientific inquiry and theory. In that case there can hardly be a more far-reaching conflict than that with an empiricist frame of thought which expels all 'metaphysics' in the claim that fundamental ideas of a philosophical or epistemological kind can have no place in natural science. A thorough-going empiricism of this sort, however, is already rabidly rationalistic, for it operates with an in-built dogmatic assumption of an *a priori* kind that observational 'facts' or 'data' are quite bare, without any intelligible component, and that ideas are abstracted from them by way of logical processes alone. It was with a general frame of scientific knowledge informed by rationalistic empiricism of this kind that Einstein found himself in sharp conflict in face of the fact that nature discloses itself to scientific inquiry as inherently intelligible. Consequently he rejected the positivist and empiricist dogma that ideas are deduced from experience, by showing that there is no logical bridge between ideas and empirical realities, and replaced the dualist way of relating theory to experiment by another, grounded on the recognition that empirical and theoretical factors inhere in one another in nature independent of our perceiving and conceiving of it and must be allowed to inhere in one another in our knowledge of it at all levels. Thus in reaching and developing relativity theory Einstein found himself compelled, in conflict with the prevailing empiricist and positivist frame of knowledge, to reconstruct the foundations of physics on a unitary basis in which form and being, structure and matter, were not allowed to be torn apart, but provided the spring-board for every new advance in discovery. What he achieved in this way has proved to be paradigmatic, not only for physical science in its progressively deeper understanding of the behaviour of nature, but for all human inquiry in the requirement to let empirical and theoretical factors interpenetrate one another in the establishment of our knowledge in accordance with their natural inherence and coherence in objective reality. In the structural kinship that arises in this way between our human knowing and what we seek to know, it is startling to find what a close relation there seems to be between the laws of nature governing the universe which God has created and the very different laws governing the operations of the human mind which God has created in such a way that we may have knowledge and communion with him the Creator of the universe.

In my own examination of the received frame of knowledge with which Western theology has tried to operate for centuries but with which it could not come to terms without severe loss of its own material substance, I have found at stake the same basic difficulties that physical science has encountered in carrying through the great transition of thought from Clerk Maxwell to Einstein. Hence in the process of my explorations, reflected in this volume, I became increasingly convinced that theological and physical knowledge, scientifically and rigorously pursued, have a great deal in common in spite of their very different objectives. They are closely allied in having epistemological problems that are basically similar owing to the framework of thought within which both have had to function and owing to their common conflict with dualist, phenomenalist and mechanistic habits of thought. Hence it should not be surprising that the elucidation of a set of problems in one field of inquiry may well assist the solution of a parallel set of problems in the other field of inquiry. Whatever natural science may have to learn or indeed unlearn in dialogue with theological science, I am convinced that theological science has not a little to learn from natural science in overcoming some of its persistent difficulties.

As I understand it, epistemological dialogue between Christian theology and physical science could be of genuine service to the Roman Catholic Church today in the strange impasse it seems to face after the Second Vatican Council. On the one hand, an immense advance has been registered in the clarification and deepening of the Church's understanding of the heart and substance of the Christian Faith, not least in respect of Christology and Soteriology and the way they affect the liturgy and mission of the Church. But on the other hand, the Roman Catholic Church remains trapped in obsolete dualist structures of thought which derive from mediaeval roots but still govern its epistemology and canon law. So long as the epistemological and canonical structures of dogma remain unreformed the immensely exciting renewal of the Church's theology will only meet with constant resistance and misunderstanding. This is evident in the thought of well-known theologians like Edward Schillebeeckx and Hans Küng, both of whom appear to be still tied to dualist and phenomenalist, if not also mechanist, habits of thought, and who therefore are unable to integrate empirical and theoretical ingredients in their understanding of Jesus Christ at the very heart of the Faith. But the problem is no less evident in the host of churchmen and theologians all over the world, who misunderstand the distinction drawn between the substance and the formulations of the Faith, and who have come to interpret the significance of the Council in terms of the relativism of all doctrinal formulations of our knowledge of God. That is to say, in tune with a misunderstanding widespread in the social sciences today, relativity is confounded with relativism. Misunderstandings of this kind could easily be clarified with the help of natural science, although that might only have temporary effect so long as the epistemological and canonical sub-structure of the Roman Catholic Church is not overhauled to match the great advance in theological insight and precision manifest in the Second Vatican Council. This illustrates the kind of benefit we can derive from steady dialogue between theological and natural science. And it is surely the kind of benefit God means us to have since in his providential ordering theologians and scientists both have to pursue their inquiries and establish knowledge within the same structures of space and time which are the bearers of all our creaturely rationality.

The dialogue between natural and theological science in so far as I myself have engaged in it has shown me that a profound transformation in the fundamental frame of knowledge has been taking place, often through a painful reorganisation of traditional habits of mind and accepted theories, but with very heartening results in the reconciling of differences, the healing of cultural splits between the sciences and the humanities, and a steady convergence of thought under the constraint of the unifying order of created reality.

It must be admitted, however, that while transformation and convergence of this kind are well advanced in the hard sciences, the social sciences on the whole still lag far behind. It is among them that resistance to dynamic field-concepts and reaction in favour of mechanistic concepts are often at their strongest. They have yet to work out how empirical and theoretical components in knowledge are continuously integrated in a realist and convincing way, although the road ahead has been remarkably opened up by the pioneering work of Michael Polanyi. The continued backwardness of the social sciences means that the transformation in the frame of knowledge being brought about by the physical sciences has not yet established itself within the paradigmatic habits of thought that characterise our socio-cultural life and its established institutions. And since it tends to be within the general framework they constitute that the Church has to fulfil its mission to people, Christian theology, in its determination to be faithful to the objective intelligibilities of God's creation and of his self-communication to us through Jesus Christ in space and time, is still deeply involved in the struggle for the mind of contemporary society. However, as I have indicated, theological science is far from being alone in this task, for it can count on powerful support in the changing structure that has been overtaking the physical sciences at a profound epistemological level which is bound to affect all human knowing. What has already been achieved is so full of promise that it is to the alliance of scientific and theological enterprise that we must look for a transformation and convergence of thought that will affect the whole range of human knowledge in the future.

I owe it to my readers to point out that this book now takes the place of another which I had projected under the title of *Integration and Interpretation in Natural and in Theological Science*. The composition of that book had to be changed as the chapters dealing with hermeneutics were taken out and published separately under the title of *Reality and Evangelical Theology*, but this has given me the opportunity to include several other essays in this volume which bear more positively upon the overall theme.

The Rev. Robert T. Walker of Edinburgh and the Rev. Douglas A. Trook of Madison, New Jersey, have generously helped me in the correction of the proofs. I am also much indebted to the typesetters, Mayne, Boyd and Son Ltd, of Belfast, who have matched the high standards of their professional service with signal patience and courtesy. I thank them all very warmly.

Edinburgh,
April, 1982.   Thomas F. Torrance

CHAPTER I

The Making of the 'Modern' Mind from Descartes and Newton to Kant

THROUGHOUT his many works Martin Heidegger sought to drive home the idea that the serious epistemological difficulties that persist in cropping up in modern philosophy and science must be traced back to the parting of thought from reality and the domination of abstract formalisation over nature.[1] That was not, admittedly, an altogether new story, for already in ancient Greece mind and being, *logos* and *physis,* were moving apart, but it was owing to the extension of abstract processes of thought that there took place a secession of reason from being in which the reason assumed the status of a law over being and operated by imposing abstract patterns of thought prescriptively upon being. Heidegger evidently took his initial cue for this argument from John Duns Scotus who reacted rather critically to the teaching of Thomas Aquinas and sought to establish a more realist epistemology in which room was made for a direct relation between mind and being as such without intermediary images of reality, and so called for a severe curtailment of abstractive processes of thought.[2] Heidegger did not discuss the fact, which seems to have had some influence on Duns Scotus, that the dualist detachment of thought from being was halted and reversed in the early centuries of the Christian era when patristic thinkers on the ground of Christian understanding of creation and the incarnation insisted that both the matter and the form of the universe were equally created out of nothing and are inseparably united in one pervasive contingent rational order throughout nature. Thus Christian theology rejected the determining presuppositions of Greek science and philosophy, a necessary relation between the world and God and the bifurcation between matter and form, and opened the way for a realist natural science in which faithful knowledge of the universe can be established under the objective control of its independent contingent reality and its divinely conferred inherent intelligibility. This Christian outlook upon the created universe had the effect of liberating the understanding of nature from the iron grip of necessary forms of thought extrinsically clamped down upon it, and called for an open empirical investigation of its intrinsic processes and their hidden patterns of order, together with the development of autonomous modes of scientific inquiry appropriate to the formulation of autonomous laws of nature.

The history of thought tells us that this radically Christian conception of the universe was given a very rough passage owing to the resurgence and persistence of the pre-Christian model of science, according to which the proper objects of rational investigation are necessary, timeless and universal, which had the effect of excluding anything of a contingent nature from the domain of genuine knowledge. Moreover, for nearly a millennium Augustinian and Aristotelian metaphysics combined to build into the controlling framework of Western theology and philosophy dualist modes of thought which, together with the axiomatic identification of the rational with the necessary, timeless and universal, obscured the understanding of nature and obstructed the emergence of empirical science. In view of this development Heidegger was surely justified in his critique of the extensively abstractive and disjunctive character of mediaeval scholastic philosophy and science, on the ground that due to the emphasis upon logical and formal processes of thought – in spite of all claims to the contrary- alien rationalisations were allowed to mould and structure the understanding of reality or being.

There is another side to this story, however, which must be taken into account if full justice is to be done to the development of Western thought in mediaeval times. This relates to the fact that the Christian conception of the creation and the contingent nature of its rational order persisted in the submerged substructure of scientific knowledge of the world, modifying the Aristotelian system of relating matter, form and causality in terms of the primacy of the universal over the particular and of the necessary over the contingent, and holding in check the impulse of a highly intellectualist notion of truth as the adequation of intellect and reality, in accordance with which correspondence of the human understanding with reality tended to slip imperceptibly into correspondence of reality with the human understanding. Such a passage from a mainly realist to a subtly idealist theory of knowledge was almost inevitable within a general framework of thought governed by a radical disjunction between the intelligible and sensible worlds linked in the human understanding through representative images and ideas in the middle, but it was held in check and modified under the constraint of the Christian doctrine of the creation of the world out of nothing and its endowment by the Creator with an inherent intelligibility of its own. However, in so far as the intelligibility of created realities was traced back to immutable rational forms in the mind of God, as happened in the Augustinian-Thomist tradition of thought, the full impact of the doctrine of creation of the world out of nothing was severely curtailed and the all-important concept of the objective contingent rational order of nature, which it implied, was smothered. Hence even when in the later Middle Ages genuine moves toward an empirical scientific understanding of nature were in evidence, they were deflected by severely formal and logical modes of thought concerned with the establishment of necessary universal truths of reason. Thus the tendency toward empirical realism could not shake itself free from the domination of abstract formalisations over nature.

It was not until the fifteenth and sixteenth centuries that there took place another decisive reorientation in the foundations of knowledge of sufficient power to give rise to empirico-theoretic science in the form in which we now know it, that is, one in which experiment and theory interact creatively and critically upon each other in discovery of the hidden laws of nature. This was a reorientation which through the Reformation was deeply indebted to the high patristic reconstruction of the foundations of knowledge but which through the Renaissance reintroduced into the stream of Western science classical Greek and not least Neoplatonic modes of thought, so that once again an ambiguous outlook developed in which damaging forms of dualism compromised a unitary grasp of the contingent rational order of the world. These difficulties were deepened through a combination of Aristotelian phenomenalism and Euclidean geometry built into the new approach to nature through Galileo. Nevertheless a renewed emphasis upon the creation of the world out of nothing, together with a rejection of the deistic detachment of God from the world latent in the Latin conception of God's immutability and impassibility, played a profound role in the development of an objectively grounded systematic understanding of celestial and terrestrial movement in the created universe. With a basic change in the doctrine of God the whole concept of nature changed, not without the help, however, of Renaissance humanism, with the result that a masterful form of experimental inquiry entrenched itself in natural science, in the course of which logically deduced static structures of thought were replaced by rather different structures, combining ontic and dynamic ingredients, which were empirically derived under the constraint of objectivities and intelligibilities found to be inherent in nature.

The effect of this new approach was to make primary a way of knowing in which people were determined to think as the facts disclosed through experiment compelled them to think, or to think strictly in accordance with the nature and activity of the given realities in the field under investigation. This was not arbitrary, speculative thinking, but thinking bound to its chosen field, but for that very reason thinking that becomes detached from unwarranted preconceptions and prejudices, thinking that acknowledges only the priority of its object and will not submit to any kind of external authority. This was a rigorously objective way of thinking which declined to take anything for granted in its determination to be faithful, and which operates by allowing the realities being investigated to disclose themselves in their own state and light, by penetrating into their inner connections, and by establishing knowledge of them in terms of principles and laws derived from those inner connections. Thus there grew up an empirico-theoretic science in which reality itself was respected as the ultimate judge of what is true or false in our understanding of it, and therefore a way of regarding positive advance in scientific knowledge, while securely built upon foundations laid in the past, as one that is always open to revision in the light of further disclosures from the hidden depths of intelligibility immanent in the universe.

There is, however, another factor, that is distinctively modern, which must be taken into account in understanding the development of the European mind. Precisely because of its stress on empirical inquiry, scientific knowledge of this new kind has to respect the agency of the human inquirer and make room for his rational judgment without detracting from the principle of objectivity. That is to say, the interaction of persons or rational agents with the world into which they inquire must be taken into account as an intellectual equation in man's understanding and interpretation of nature in its dynamic, self-ruling structures independent of him. This is an ingredient in human knowledge which arose out of Augustinian and Franciscan theology but which was injected into the rise of modern thought largely by John Calvin who insisted that knowledge of God arises only as mutual relations are set up between God and the human knower, which made paradigmatic the realisation that it is the human person who is the rational agent of objective operations.[3] Authentic knowledge, not only in theology, comes about only through a relation of fidelity (*fides*) to what we seek to know, and therefore proceeds by way of a voluntary obedience of our minds to what it has to tell us of itself, i.e. through a movement of the human reason in which it submits to the objective claims of reality and thereby serves its 'revelation' or disclosure to human questioning and understanding. This was precisely the notion that Francis Bacon transferred to natural philosophy in his account of the scientist as a 'servant of nature' and of the way in which he puts his questions to nature, following clues that nature is found, and sometimes forced, through observation and experiment to provide of its own inner mysteries and connections. The book of nature is not to be read and interpreted, and the kingdom of man or the dominion of science is not to be entered, he claimed, by dictating to nature but by following as a little child its own leading and by renouncing all antecedent conceptions of it as alien and distorting prejudices.[4]

Scientific procedure of this kind implies that a moment of the will enters into the active investigation of nature, for the scientist as rational agent is engaged in an advancing process of constructive inquiry and knowledge. In this sense he can be spoken of as *homo faber*, but as Bacon himself envisaged this activity, it is one in which man builds up his kingdom over nature through a willing or voluntary submission to its claims upon him. That is to say, this is a form of active inquiry in which the human subject engages, as a rational agent, in objective operations. However, when this understanding of the role of the human subject as the active agent of inquiry and as *homo faber* was allied to the Renaissance concept of the *autonomous reason,* which it resurrected from classical Greece, it became steadily twisted in another direction, in the isolation of the human subject over against nature, and thus in a split between subject and object and an ominous tension between reason and experience. In short, there developed what F. A. Hayek has called 'constructivist rationalism' which has affected not only the basic activity of natural science but has spread beyond it in the technological culture of modern society.[5]

Thus in spite of the immense advance in scientific understanding of the universe in the sixteenth and seventeenth centuries, and in the conception of science itself, different streams of thought emanating from the Reformation and the Renaissance combined to give the developing framework of European science and culture a damaging ambiguity, by injecting into it on the one hand a serious hiatus between reason and experience while trying on the other hand to coordinate theoretical and empirical ingredients in knowledge, which inevitably gave rise to a *rationalist empiricism*. Two fateful forces are then found to be at work shaping the 'modern' mind: *(a)* the transference of intelligibility to the human pole of the knowing relationship, with a corresponding lapse in the concept of the inherent intelligibility of nature; and *(b)* the encroachment of the masterful idea that we can understand and verify only what we can make and shape for ourselves.[6] That is the mentality of *homo faber* so characteristic of instrumentalist science and of western industrialist and technological society, which has permeated the whole range of modern culture, affecting theology, science, philosophy, and art alike, although of course in different ways. This is the ingrained assumption of our minds that it is we who, by our rational and scientific operations, clothe the universe around us with form and structure and thereby give it meaning for ourselves.

Our task now is to examine the making of this 'modern' mind in some detail. First we shall look at the foundational thought of Descartes and Newton who in different but complementary ways built into the fabric of western thought a fundamental dualism between subject and object on the one hand and between God and the world on the other hand. The confluence of these two forms of dualism had far-reaching implications. The effect of a detachment between subject and object, within a cosmological outlook in which mathematical time and space were given an absolute status independent of material existence but divinely containing and causally conditioning it as an inertial system, was to reduce the knowing subject to inner states of consciousness over against a determinate nature as object. Once again, however, something like the mediaeval notion of 'images in the middle' was forced forward, and a powerful doctrine of 'representative perception' or 'sense data' was allowed to control the relation between the subject and the object, with the result that there took place a steady retreat from the ontological claims of objective reality into the inner mental processes and consciousness of the human subject. Then we shall have to devote some attention to the way in which this impasse for natural science, exposed by the critical analysis of David Hume, was handled by Immanuel Kant in his valiant attempt to establish the grounds of epistemic objectivity through a transcendental reduction of the conditions of knowledge, and to bridge the deep hiatus between the theoretical and empirical factors of knowledge by means of the synthetic *a priori*. However, when phenomenalist dualism in Kant's argument took the form of a radical distinction between what things are in themselves, which is not open to our knowledge, and what they are as they appear to us, where only they may be known, he found that he could not make Newton's laws of motion intelligible to the human reason without a basic ingredient of construction in defining what is known and knowable. What is unknowable, he held, cannot be constructed and only what is constructible is knowable. Hence he was forced to conclude that the human intellect does not draw its laws from nature but on the contrary imposes its laws upon nature. In so doing, however, Kant established himself as the prophet of the 'modern' mind.

DESCARTES

Descartes' thought had two distinct roots. On the one hand, it went back to a revived Augustinian piety and philosophy, with its differentiation between knowledge of corporeal things which the mind gathers through the senses of the body and knowledge of incorporeal things which the mind gains through knowledge of itself.[7] This theory of knowledge had the effect of throwing the seeker after truth upon the depths of his own soul and of interiorising faith in God in such a way that it was detached from knowledge of the world. The projection of this Augustinianism out of the late Middle Ages into the post-Renaissance Roman Catholic thought, in which Descartes had been trained (at the Jesuit college of La Flèche in Maine), meant the carrying over into the new world of the old dichotomy between the sensible and intelligible realms in an even sharper form, as the cement of Aristotelian physics and metaphysics which had been brought in to hold the two realms together crumbled away in 'the age of reason'.[8] With Descartes this took the form of a clear separation of the realm of mind as 'thinking thing' from the realm of matter as 'extended thing'. On the other hand, Descartes' thought went back to the new scientific outlook that took its rise from Galileo's establishment of the mathematical structure of the universe, and from his phenomenalist approach to nature in which he sought to determine the principles and laws of the real measurable world governing the appearances of things in space and time. With Galileo this involved a clear distinction between 'primary' and 'secondary qualities', as they came to be called, i.e. between the constant characteristics of the experienced world (form, magnitude, motion, etc.) which are geometrical and quantifiable, and those which are merely the effects of these primary characteristics of nature on our senses and which are therefore subjective.[9] That meant, as E. A. Burtt has pointed out, a return to a more Platonic orientation in thought,[10] and it naturally fell into line with Descartes' Augustinian-Platonic distinction between the intelligible and the sensible. However, whereas Galileo was not concerned with these primary characteristics of nature in themselves so much as with their effects in the sensible world, that is, with the *how* of events or processes of motion, Descartes was interested in Galileo's new way of using mathematics as a tool of reasoning in relating theoretically drawn conclusions to the sensible world. Thus Galileo's concept of inertial force (later to be formulated as a law by Newton), together with his principle of relativity formulated for mechanical phenomena, opened up for Descartes the possibilities of a scientific method which brought a speculative and deductive mode of reasoning to bear upon experience.[11] Undoubtedly his own early training in, and his remarkable flair for, mathematics predisposed Descartes especially toward an appreciation of the theoretical component in the new science. This two-fold root in Augustinian and Galilean thought is reflected in Descartes' early resolve 'no longer to seek any other science than knowledge of myself, or of the great book of the world'.[12]

Dissatisfied with earlier handling of logic, geometrical analysis and algebra, and yet convinced in the face of the fluctuating and unreliable nature of sense perception, that certain knowledge is reached only through a pure unclouded act of understanding *(intellectio pura)*, Descartes developed *another method* (suggested by his application of algebra to geometry resulting in 'universal mathematics') which would have the advantages of traditional logical and mathematical reasoning without its defects.[13] This was a way of reaching certain basic and indubitable ideas, as few as possible and in the most general form possible, into the truth and self-evidence of which his mind could penetrate intuitively and independently of the conditions in which they were given, and then in the light of these ideas and by reference to them bring rational order and structure into the rest of human knowledge.[14] This involved the procedure of methodological doubt *(de omnibus dubitandum est)* which segregated the two ultimate ideas of self-understanding *(ego sum cogitans)*[15] and the existence of God *(Deus est)*[16], i.e. ideas of the most complete generality, and then from these, constituted into his unified theoretical basis, Descartes set out by intuitive-deductive reasoning to derive the basic concepts and relations of the particular sciences, reducing them to an order which they may not have had in their natural relations of antecedence and consequence.[17]

This method entailed a rejection of the Aristotelian principle that there is nothing in the understanding which was not previously in the senses, and a dismissal of the formalistic use of the syllogism as inapplicable to the investigation of the unknown and suitable only to the communication of knowledge we already have.[18] On the other hand, Descartes operated with the assumption that the relation of God to the universe has given it an objective intelligibility which makes it accessible to rational inquiry,[19] and indeed makes possible scientific attempts to grasp reality by pure thought apart from our observations, so that the observations *through* which the mind penetrates may themselves be judged for their truth or falsity in the light of that reality.[20] That is to say, Descartes was convinced that the basic theoretical concepts of science cannot be derived by abstractive or logical processes from sense experience. This must not be taken to mean that for Descartes science can be reduced to *a priori* reasoning, for we cannot do without empirical presentations of things to our senses, and indeed the more advanced our knowledge is the more necessary experiments are.[21] But it does mean that the empirical justification of natural scientific knowledge is to be sought not in detailed points of correspondence with experience so much as in the coordination of the whole theoretical structure with the empirical world, and even that coordination must be discerned by an act of intellectual intuition, not by a process of logical deduction.

Here Descartes has clearly anticipated modern theoretical physicists such as Eddington, Jeans, Milne and even Einstein, in at least two respects. *(a)* He was convinced that in scientific activity our primary conceptions are reached before and apart from our reasoning processes – hence his stress upon *meditation* as a basic scientific activity,[22] replacing attempts to derive concepts by abstraction from sense experience or to logicalise induction. *(b)* While rigorous deductive operations are properly carried out from conceptions reached in this way, there is no logical way of coordinating them with the system of our sense experiences. They are coordinated through acts of intellectual intuition which are not arbitrary but disciplined and coherent acts of insight into the intelligible structure of reality which prove themselves to be right in the processes of our scientific operations.[23]

It may well be objected that this is to give Descartes too generous an interpretation, for there is another side to his thought. His achievement in theoretic science was bought at the expense of a deep gulf between subject and object, 'thinking thing' and 'extended thing', that is, through a conception of mind entirely independent of bodily existence. 'I knew that I was a substance the whole essence or nature of which is to think, and that for its existence there is no need of any place, nor does it depend on any material thing; so that this 'me', that is to say the soul by which I am what I am, is entirely distinct from body, and is even more easy to know than is the latter; and even if the body were not, the soul would not cease to be what it is.'[24]

This posed for Descartes an acute problem: how material objects are known by an immaterial mind. 'His answer', as Kemp Smith has summarised it, 'is that material bodies through their action on the sense-organs and the brain generate images or duplicates of themselves. These images, existing not in outer space but only in consciousness, are mental in nature; and being mental they are, he would seem to conclude, immediately and necessarily apprehended by the mind.'[25] In other words, the immediate 'objects' of the mind are not things in themselves but what the mediaevals called *objecta mentis,* the elaborated 'images in the middle', yet these, insists Descartes, are only sense data or secondary qualities and have no real existence.[26] But if this is the case, do they represent something real beyond our consciousness? The fact that we cannot help but have certain ideas in sensory experience convinces us that they proceed from certain objects outside us which caused them in our consciousness.[27] But on analysis this does not stand up well to criticism, and Descartes was forced to rely on the existence of God to establish a connection between our sense experience and an objective causal order.[28]

God is not brought in, however, simply like a *deus ex machina,* for the necessity of God in his constancy and reliability for the objectivity of human knowledge is closely related by Descartes to the incompleteness of the mind's representative ideas.[29] They have 'objective reality' as the immediate 'objects' upon which the mind is directed, i.e. as 'modes of consciousness', but in order to be that they require relation to what has 'more objective reality' beyond themselves, just as the effect draws its total reality from its cause. The ideas of the mind, then, which arise through sense experience must have a 'formal or actual reality' beyond the kind of reality they have as mere representations which is a kind of artifact (*artificium objectum*).[30] This 'formal actual reality' Descartes relates to extension or space as the object of pure mathematics which the mind intuitively apprehends through presentations to the senses.[31] 'We must at least admit that all things which I conceive in them clearly and distinctly, that is to say, all things which, generally speaking, are comprehended in the *object of pure mathematics,* are truly to be recognised as external objects.'[32] Since this is the case, the reality of the corporeal or empirical world becomes reduced in the last analysis to the formal relations of extended bodies through which the mind by pure intellection apprehends universal and necessary truths.[33]

Such was the Cartesian dualism between a realm of material extension, essentially geometrical and mechanical in character, and a realm of unextended, thinking substance, which, as A. D. Lindsay put it, 'has had such a fatal influence on modern theories of knowledge'.[34] On the one hand, Descartes' identification of matter with extension or space, while allowing him to develop a concept of space as a three-dimensional coordinate system, because of his dualism, lent itself to a movement of thought in which space was regarded as superior to and detached from empirical objects, thus hardening the dualism.[35] At the same time Descartes' application of mathematics to space or matter, together with his conception of mechanism and his formulation of the general law of action and counteraction, is one of the main sources of the mechanistic view of the universe.[36] On the other hand, his dualism not only created such difficulties for European thought that it became obsessed with problems of perception, which have regularly bifurcated in idealist and positivist directions, but so exalted the status of the thinking ego that Descartes enormously advanced the Enlightenment concept of the ultimate end of man as the triumph of the human spirit over the forces of nature. Moreover, he helped to create its great tool, the instrumental reason, for the accomplishment of that end: that they might become 'the masters and possessors of nature'.[37] So far as Descartes himself was concerned, his profound faith in God and the central and necessary place for God in his whole system of thought, curbed the presumption of his reason, restraining it from trying to transcend its own limits and from trying to limit the possible or the real to the humanly conceivable.[38] But when scepticism, poised upon the certainty of the self-understanding, replaced his methodological doubt,[39] and God as the creative ground of objective intelligibility in the universe began to disappear out of the picture, rationalism and materialism entrenched themselves in European culture. The age of the autocratic reason, what Kant was later to call heautonomy, set in.[40]

NEWTON

Newton, even more than Descartes, was profoundly influenced by Galileo, not simply in respect of the new science of dynamics founded by Galileo,[41] but in his fundamental approach to the interpretation of nature. Speaking of the *total* impact of Galileo on Newton in science in general and in dynamics in particular, John Herival has written: 'Certainly the whole cast of Newton's thought, his humility before nature, his drive toward exact quantitative results, his delight in experiment, was altogether Galilean, and if he recognised any master in science apart from Archimedes it could only have been Galileo.'[42]

Both sides of Galileo's thought were important for Newton: his belief in the mathematical code of the universe and therefore in mathematics rather than logic as supplying the key to its interpretation;[43] and his conception of scientific method in which theory and exact experiment are connected together, especially in demonstration but also in exploration.[44] Of particular importance, however, was Galileo's habit of beginning with careful theoretical analysis of problems in their actual empirical context,[45] such as the analysis of the problem that had arisen in understanding the motion of a projectile, by thinking it out in the relatively simpler case of a falling body, which made it clear to Galileo that a very different notion of force than that which obtained in Aristotelian physics was needed; and then by putting various hypotheses to the test through comparing the consequences he deduced from them with the results reached in arranged experiments.[46] It was thus that Galileo came up with a new concept of force (in its relation to the change in velocity rather than to velocity itself) which laid the basis for the science of mechanics but at the same time undermined the foundation of Aristotelian physics. This matched in terrestrial mechanics the revolution which Copernicus had advocated in celestial mechanics, so that Galileo's discoveries raised questions which led to the overthrow of the Aristotelian separation *(chōrismos)* between celestial and terrestrial mechanics which had inhibited the advance of natural science for so long, and opened the way for Newton's reestablishment of the unity of nature.[47]

It was this remarkable opening up of the scope of empirical and theoretical science by Galileo, together with his demonstration that problems of motion could be reduced through analysis into quantitative relations and thus made amenable to mathematical interpretation and handling, that paved the way for Newton. On the other hand, Newton had also been deeply influenced by the empirical tradition in science which derived from Francis Bacon and had been considerably developed by some of his fellow countrymen, such as Gilbert, Boyle and Hooke.[48] It was the Baconian rejection of 'middle axioms' and 'anticipations of nature' that reinforced for Newton the importance of experimental investigation and demonstration and made him suspicious of 'hypotheses'.[49] At the same time, Galileo's distinction between primary and secondary characteristics and especially his corresponding distinction between knowledge, mathematically grounded in what is immutable and objective, and the illusory notions of sense, rooted in what is fluctuating and subjective, along with his theory of the atomic structure of matter and of the mechanical motion of material bodies, had a powerful part to play in Newton's thought. But here we must also take into account the place of Descartes in the background of his science, for it was through the Cartesian modification of some of these ideas that Newton came to develop his own system.

After careful examination supplied by Newton himself Herival has shown that in spite of Newton's considerable dislike of Descartes he was nonetheless deeply indebted to him. 'The arguments here advanced, if sound,' Herival says, 'point to a very important influence of Descartes on Newton in dynamics, direct in the case of the principle of inertia, circular motion, and collisions, indirect in the case of Newton's concept of force.'[50] Newton's main disagreement with Descartes in mechanics had to do with his concept of vortices and his identity of matter with extension in space, but behind that lay also his rejection of Descartes' rather rationalistic abstraction of mathematics and his method of argumentation from certain or indubitable positions reached by pure intellection. That is to say, Newton operated with a different and more realist conception of mathematics coordinated with experience. Reaction against Descartes at this point was to lead Newton into a stronger notion of causality and into a more rigidly mechanical conception of the universe. However, it was not simply in his mechanics but also in his metaphysics that Newton was indebted to Descartes, for he took over more or less uncritically the Cartesian development of Galileo's phenomenalism as something that belonged, almost axiomatically, to the new science which he championed and of which he became the supreme exponent.[51] Thus Newton accepted Cartesian dualism with its doctrine of subjective representations between the mind of the observer and the objective structure of nature, and its clear distinction of the independent realms of mind and matter; and, which is equally significant, he accepted the Cartesian idea of 'localisation' of the mind in the body,[52] but differed from Descartes in giving, rather like Boyle (yet not going so far as Boyle), secondary properties some place of reality in nature and in relating the human mind to material reality through the particular part of the brain which he called the *sensorium*.[53] Newton certainly held that the soul or the mind is lodged within the brain and has no immediate contact with the external world, but he had a stronger sense of the fact that the secondary qualities that arise in the sensorium are in some sense properties of nature, for they are sensations of motions or dispositions in the external world.[54] Thus while Newton operated with a closer relation between scientific concepts and sense experience, far from overcoming Cartesian dualism, he built it deeply into his whole system and thus into the fabric of western science.

In line with the classical tradition in patristic and mediaeval thought, and also in line with the views of Galileo and Descartes, Newton held strongly to the Christian understanding of the creation in accordance with which God has made the universe out of nothing and maintains it in such a way that it remains immutably and inherently orderly.[55] But he surpassed his predecessors in stressing the God-given mathematical structure of the created universe and the strictly causal and quantifiable character of its immanent relations, which call for empirico-mathematical interpretation. And so, writing in the preface to the first edition of his great *Mathematical Principles of Natural Philosophy*, Newton declared: 'I offer this work as the mathematical principles of philosophy, for the whole burden of philosophy seems to consist in this: from the phenomena of motions to investigate the forces of nature, and then from these forces to demonstrate other phenomena.'[56] Or again in a proposal for the Royal Society, he wrote: 'Natural philosophy consists in discovering the frame and operations of nature, and reducing them, as far as may be, to general rules or laws – establishing these rules by observations and experiments, and thence deducing the causes and effects of things.'[57]

Several aspects of this grand conception of natural science call for discussion. It has nothing to do with any 'occult qualities' but only with 'manifest qualities' of nature. That is to say, it does not inquire into hidden or occult causes but seeks to determine the causal inter-action between corporeal things in terms of 'manifest principles' which it derives from phenomena. In creating the universe God constituted it out of primitive durable and indivisible particles which have in them an inertial force *(vis insita, vis inertiae)* giving rise to passive laws of motion, and are moved by certain active principles such as gravity. Since it is through these forces that particles interact and cohere in regular patterns manifest in the universe, it is the proper method of natural inquiry to derive two or three general principles from them and then show how the properties and actions of all corporeal things follow from these principles.[58] The only hidden or occult causes that science may legitimately be concerned with are those which can be deduced from phenomena or 'manifest effects', for the only 'frame of nature' with which science operates is that which is necessarily connected with sensible objects. This rules out of order 'imaginary or hypothetical' or 'occult' causes such as the final causes and the entelechies adduced by Aristotelian science, for they are not 'mechanical'.[59] This implies of course that natural science cannot bring us, immediately at any rate, to knowledge of the first cause which is certainly not mechanical and is not related to nature by any kind of necessity, but it also means that when in its deductive movement from more compound to more simple causes it arrives at 'the most simple cause' natural inquiry can go no farther, for 'no mechanical account or explanation of the most simple cause is to be expected or given; for if it could be given the cause were not the most simple'.[60]

That is to say, natural science does not probe into the ultimate nature of causes, but taking them for granted (e.g. gravity) and leaving them to be discovered, seeks only to determine the principles or general laws of nature in accordance with which sensible objects or phenomena are as a matter of fact interconnected.[61] 'The business of true philosophy is to derive the natures of things from causes *truly existent* and to inquire after those laws on which the Great Creator *actually* chose to found this most beautiful Frame of the World, not those by which he might have done the same had he so pleased. It is reasonable enough to suppose that from several causes, somewhat differing from one another, the same effect may arise, but the *true* cause will be that from which it *truly and actually does arise;* the others have no place in true philosophy.'[62] Assuming, then, the objective stability and intelligibility of nature, physics is strictly an *a posteriori* science concerned with the causes of sensible effects; it is the mechanics of actual states of affairs manifest in the particulate structure of the universe.[63]

In consistency with this position Newton would have nothing to do with merely abstract mathematics or the 'pure mathematics' of the Cartesians: in the actual world mathematics is concerned with physical principles and quantifiable relations. Geometry, in particular, instead of constituting an independent *a priori* system of relations, is necessarily a branch of mechanics,[64] building along with experiment the heuristic and demonstrative method with which to 'unfold the mechanism of the world'.[65] In fact, mathematical mechanics has a double role to fulfil, in moving inductively (i.e. deductively through experiments) from observational phenomena to principles and propositions and then in relating them back again demonstratively through other experiments to observational phenomena.[66] It was precisely because nature, as Newton conceived it, was a mechanism operating according to natural law, that mathematics and experiments complemented each other so smoothly and effectively. Thus, as Einstein has said of Newton, 'Nature to him was an open book, whose letters he could read without effort. The conceptions which he used to reduce the material of experience to order seemed to flow spontaneously from experience itself, from the beautiful experiments which he ranged in order like playthings and describes with affectionate wealth of detail.'[67] Moreover, Newton claimed that by operating in this *mathematical way* he could avoid all questions as to the nature or quality of the forces being investigated and therefore the need for any merely hypothetical ideas, that is, for anything not mathematically deduced from phenomena.[68]

This is the significance of Newton's statement, *hypotheses non fingo* ('I frame no hypotheses'), originally made, as we have noted, with respect to the nature of gravity.[69] A mechanical account of the behaviour of notions in the universe does not need to penetrate into the ultimate nature of matters like gravity, but limits itself to the system of phenomenal connections set up by it or dependent on it. Nature is so uniformly mechanical in its structure that we can by experiment reveal its basic and simple relations, and then bring mathematics to bear upon them to convert them into the quantitative form, from which theory can then be derived by way of positive and direct conclusions.[70] This involves first mathematical analysis, in which certain principles are established in the course of experiments by rigorous argumentation from effect to cause, and then mathematical synthesis, in which those principles now assumed are tested for their explanatory power by comparing the phenomena which result from them in further experiments with the phenomena of nature from which they were originally deduced. Scientific operations of this sort by the rigorous nature of their mathematical connections leave no room for any speculative or hypothetical reasoning.[71]

Does this mean that Newton would accept as scientific concepts only those deduced from phenomena, or derived by way of abstraction from observations? A completely unambiguous answer to that question can hardly be given. It is certainly clear that he insisted on the rigid exclusion of hypotheses from his 'system', for the feigning of hypotheses, as he expressed it, is not relevant to mechanical explanation.[72] 'Whatever is not deduced from phenomena, is to be called an hypothesis; and hypotheses, whether metaphysical or physical, whether of occult qualities or mechanical, have no place in experimental philosophy. In this philosophy particular propositions are inferred from the phenomena, and afterwards rendered general by induction. Thus it was that the impenetrability, the mobility, and the impulsive forces of bodies, and the laws of motion and gravitation were discovered.'[73] On the other hand, that would appear to leave room for hypotheses wherever it is not possible to proceed by way of inference from observations, or when one is inquiring into the internal causes of phenomena (which Newton declined to do), and not just into the principles according to which things are causally interconnected. But if so, that cannot in the nature of the case be included within a mechanical system as such.[74] Nevertheless, it is also evident that Newton was prepared at times to advance speculative hypotheses in the service of scientific inquiry, as in his paper submitted to the Royal Society in 1675 on the nature of light.[75]

Further evidence for Newton's use of hypothesis is sometimes said to be found in the famous series of *Queries* as to the properties of light which are set out in the third book of the *Opticks*.[76] But if this is the case it only makes it clear that a scientific hypothesis for Newton was not an imagined assumption or a postulate advanced without empirical grounds but a *compound question* directed through theorems to the phenomena being investigated. Even if this involved what Newton called 'the inventing of phenomena' through skilfully arranged experiments,[77] its purpose was to determine the laws inherent in nature, and to avoid any possibility of imposing laws aprioristically upon nature.[78] This is quite consistent with the rules laid down in the *Principia* that scientific method admits no more causes of natural things than are true and sufficient to explain their appearances, and that since there must be a strict conformity between effect and cause no generalisation is permitted beyond the uniformity of nature. 'We are certainly not to relinquish the evidence of experiments for the sake of dreams and vain fictions of our own devising; nor are we to recede from the analogy of nature, which is wont to be simple and always consonant with itself.'[79] That is to say, scientific concepts reached by way of abstraction from appearances or the deduction of causes from sensible effects must be strictly controlled by comparison with the mechanical structure of nature as it is unfolded through experiments.[80] 'For Newton, then, science was composed of laws stating the mathematical behaviour of nature solely – laws clearly deducible from phenomena and exactly verifiable in phenomena – everything further is to be swept out of science, which thus becomes a body of absolutely certain truth about the doings of the physical world. By his intimate union of mathematical and experimental methods, Newton believed himself to have indissolubly allied the ideal exactitude of the one with the constant empirical reference of the other. Science is the exact mathematical formulation of the processes of the natural world. Speculation is at a discount, but motion has unconditionally surrendered to the conquering mind of man.'[81]

It is important to remember, however, that Newton's realist conception of mathematics, with its close nexus between geometrical and mechanical structure, implies that mathematics, when it is considered merely in itself, is incomplete and therefore requires to be developed along with scientific unfolding of the mechanism of the world.[82] Hence, as Stanley L. Jaki has finely said: 'For Newton, mathematical physics was always to be remodelled after the data of observation. Mathematics, to be sure, was only the idiom through which mechanics expressed itself, but the inner consistency of a mathematical function was not supposed to prejudice the facts. When it failed to accommodate certain facts it was to be revised or to be simply discarded.'[83] Such a point was reached in the problem of how to calculate the elliptical orbit of a planet and how to formulate exactly the discoveries of Galileo that 'the descent of bodies varied as the square of the time *(in duplicata ratione temporis)* and that the motion of projectiles was in the curve of a parabola'.[84] An expansion of mathematical instrumentality was needed, and Newton came up with what he called 'the inverse method of fluxions' in order to achieve a mathematical reduction of variations and changes in physical processes.[85] Thus by means of the differential and integral calculus and its algebraic mode of representation he was able to find a way of passing from the dynamic to the quantitative aspects of nature and vice versa, and so to establish exactly the connection between mathematical law and mechanical reality through 'the even flowing of a continuous function'.[86] That is what the *Principia* is about: he proposed an exact formulation of the three laws of motion, and proceeded to reduce the motions of bodies, the quantities and relations of the universe to a uniform mechanical system governed by universal gravity according to general differential law.[87] At the same time Newton was able to subsume Kepler's laws of planetary motion within his system by deriving them from the principles he had established. Newton followed the same method in the *Opticks*, which he summarily expressed in the statement: 'To derive two or three general principles of motion from the phenomena, and afterwards to tell us how the properties and actions of all things follow from those manifest principles would be a very great step in philosophy, though the causes of those principles were not yet discovered.'[88]

In view of all this it would seem clear that in spite of Newton's insistence that he framed no hypotheses but deduced his concepts and principles from phenomena, his use of an algebraical calculus (which he invented and did not deduce from observations, although they may well have suggested it to him) to determine the motions of bodies and make them mathematically intelligible and 'manipulable' within a coherent set of differential laws so that they could be given exactly their corresponding place within the physical mechanism of the universe, meant that he did erect in the *Principia* an essentially *hypothetico*-deductive system of mechanics – without of course any detachment from empirical grounds or experimental verification. That is to say, Newton's 'I frame no hypotheses' cannot be taken in its actual context to be as positivist as it has often been construed (e.g. by Laplace), for his basic scientific concepts were 'hypothetical' as well as 'physical', and yet so 'real' that they could not justly lend themselves to a conventionalist interpretation (e.g. by Mach). Yet this hypothetico-empirical character of his system is admittedly somewhat disguised by the fact that, although he apparently made his discoveries and reached his astonishing generalisation of physical theory through the instrumentality of the infinitesimal calculus, he translated what he had achieved into the kind of geometrical form which others would more readily understand.[89] This is perhaps most apparent in his equation of the laws of motion with 'axioms' in the classical sense, i.e. as fixed principles from which to engage in logico-deductive operations.[90]

This procedure also had another effect. By his interpretation of motion and change, as J. D. Bernal has rightly said, 'Newton established, once and for all, the *dynamic* view of the universe instead of the *static* one that had satisfied the ancients'.[91] Nevertheless, the fact that he presented the new understanding of the universe as a comprehensive mechanical system in the forms of classical geometry helped considerably to give that system a hard deterministic character built up out of originally *static concepts*. It was not indeed until there arose the concept of a *field of continuous dynamic relations and transformations*,[92] as initiated by Clerk Maxwell and developed in relativity theory and quantum theory, that scientific concepts could be fluid again. However, the static character of the concepts of Newton's mechanics goes back also to another primary aspect of his 'philosophy', in which, he claimed, 'we ought to abstract from our senses and consider things themselves, distinct from what are only sensible measures of them.'[93] This was the fruit of Newton's inheritance in Galilean phenomenalism and Cartesian dualism adapted and recast in the fateful distinction between absolute and relative time and space. It was a distinction between the mathematical and the sensible which had the effect of driving a deep bifurcation between science and common sense.

'I do not define time, space, place, and motion', Newton wrote, 'as being well known to all. Only I want to observe that the common people conceive those quantities under no other notions but from the relation they bear to sensible objects. And thence arise certain prejudices, for the removing of which it will be convenient to distinguish them into absolute and relative, true and apparent, mathematical and common.'[94]

This idea that there are two different types of concepts evidently has its roots in the kind of Augustinian-Aristotelian tradition as it was given a new slant by Galileo and Descartes, together with their postulatory mode of penetrating behind the illusions of sense to determine the real, quantifiable world, but it is also demanded apparently by Newton's mathematical method and his laws of motion.[95] It implies a distinction between the real content of nature, a system of bodies in motion governed by mechanical causation, and our relative, sensory observations, and so between true scientific concepts and merely observational concepts. However, in line with his repudiation of *a priori* hypotheses, Newton sought to derive the former from the latter, i.e. as 'propositions inferred by general induction from phenomena', while making them quite distinct from and independent of the latter, thus constituting them a reference-system by means of which the latter can be corrected and controlled (purged of 'certain prejudices'). In so far as they do effect that correction and control, and therefore afford a reliable and sufficient explanation of appearances, they must be regarded as physically verified, but apart from that kind of coordination with the world of our sense experience they must be treated as merely abstract. Thus behind this distinction between absolute and relative, true and apparent, mathematical and common, lies the need for objective, scientific validity irrespective of observers.

Newton's discussion of absolute, true and mathematical time and space over against relative, apparent and common time and space is set out in the all-important scholium which follows the eight definitions with which the *Principia* opens and immediately precedes the formulation of the three laws of motion. In it Newton summarised his profound analysis of the problems that face us in penetrating through the maze of our sensory observations to understand the motions of bodies in time and in space, with a view to achieving through mathematical synthesis a scientific system of the world. It is matched by the general scholium with which the *Principia* (in its second edition) concludes, and in which the world thus scientifically interpreted is related to its Creator.

Here, then, on the one hand, time and space are considered absolutely in themselves without relation to anything external, as homogeneous and isotropic, undifferentiated and unchanging, and as embracing all things within the universe while yet distinct from them.[96] That is to say, they constitute the one universal uniform inertial system which conditions all things that exist in time and space,[97] and therefore constitute the ultimate reference-system by means of which we may correct our observational notions of magnitudes in time and space and reach universally valid conceptions of them. On the other hand, time and space are also considered in terms of different particular systems which arise within the universe through coordination with sensible objects and bodies in motion, and which as such are 'movable dimensions' within immutable time and space while remaining relative to our observations in a part of space and in our common time. Since time and space in themselves are homogeneous and undifferentiated, they cannot be seen or be distinguished in their parts by our senses, so that we use in their stead 'sensible measures of them', that is, coordinate-systems within our observable world, which we commonly mistake for true time and space.[98]

It is from these sensible measures or observable magnitudes that we deduce true, mathematical time and space as 'measured quantities', but sensible measures are not to be confounded with those quantities themselves which are real, for they are essentially relative to our sense experience and are therefore only 'apparent'.[99] They are 'relative quantities' within mathematical time and space which remain constant in their parts and immutable in their order, for time and space absolutely considered are primary and relative only to themselves; they constitute that *in which* all things are placed, 'in time as to order of succession and in space as to order of situation'.[100] In other words, while we cannot but make use of observable geometrical magnitudes or coordinate-systems in determining our knowledge of objects in time and space, they are unavoidably prejudiced systems relative to ourselves as observers, and require to be corrected and interpreted by reference to absolute, true and mathematical time and space, if they are to have the kind of exact and universal character which we require in science. Hence, just as in analytical and synthetic ways Galileo corrected observational ideas of motion in terms of change and velocity, so Newton through a more concise development of Galileo's discovery,[101] sought to correct our observational ideas of space by reference to what we now speak of as the 'mass-point'.[102]

Since time and space, as we understand them, are bound up with the motions and changing velocities of bodies, Newton's argument hinges on his analysis of the dynamics of motion. Particular coordinate-systems, as we have seen, arise when a sensible body is used as a fixed point for determining position, but since there may actually be no body at rest in the universe, these coordinate-systems are to be thought of as movable systems in time and space.[103] But further analysis of the properties, causes and effects which distinguish absolute from relative motion seems to reveal that the concept of movable systems implies the concept of absolute space as the point of absolute rest to which they are referred as 'relative spaces'.[104] 'It is indeed a matter of great difficulty', Newton said, 'to discover and effectually to distinguish the true motions of particular bodies from the apparent, because the parts of that immovable space in which those motions are performed do by no means come under the observation of our senses. Yet the thing is not altogether desperate; for we do have some arguments to guide us, partly from the apparent motions; partly from the forces, which are the causes and effects of the true motions.'[105]

Newton is somewhat ill at ease here, for he does not completely succeed in establishing the connection between absolute and relative motion, and therefore between absolute and relative time and space which they imply.[106] That is to say, Newton is forced to bring in a theoretical component, independent of the empirical components, in order to do justice to the empirical components themselves. This is highly significant, for it indicates that he is unable purely by abstraction from observations to derive the axiomatic basis or reach the fundamental concepts needed for his physics and mechanics, but must in part at least outflank the sensible measures of common time and space, and so transcend the realm of their empirical verification.[107] Thus in the last resort what Newton did was to fall back upon his profound belief that the universe, far from being arbitrary, has been so constructed that in the simplicity and uniformity of its natural order it is accessible to our theoretical analysis and synthesis;[108] and then in the light of that conviction to posit concepts of absolute time and space, independent of the empirical processes that fall within their embrace, in order to provide those processes with the constant and regular framework which they require in order to be understood in terms of the mechanism which they prove to constitute in our experiments. This was of course a specific scientific and mathematical extension of the role that common time and space play in giving objective correlation and stability to our stream of sense perceptions and in pointing beyond to a permanent ground for the simplicity and uniformity of nature upon which we rely in all ordinary experience and rational behaviour.[109]

It was thus that absolute time and space appeared to Newton to be the simplest way of linking together the manifold features of nature and of combining the laws of motion with the general law of attraction to form a comprehensive system of the world that was logically coherent and complete. Certainly his astonishing success in offering a uniform and exact explanation of all motion in the universe, celestial and terrestrial alike, seemed to justify the theoretic basis which he set up. It was this success, however, as Einstein pointed out, which apparently blinded Newton's successors to 'the fictitious character' of absolute time and space, i.e. the presence in the theoretic basis of Newton's science of concepts which are 'free inventions of the intellect', and so misled them into thinking that all fundamental scientific concepts can be abstracted or deduced from sense experience.[110] This does not mean that the notions of absolute time and space were necessarily false because they had logically independent conceptual status which Einstein calls their 'fictitious character', for science cannot operate without at least a minimum of concepts of this kind to support its structure.[111] In any case, as Einstein argued elsewhere, although the notions of absolute time and space are to be rejected, Newton's introduction of them as independent concepts into his thought to give exact meaning to the principle of inertia and the laws of motion was 'one of his greatest achievements', while his decision to assign time and space 'an absolute role in the whole causal structure of the theory . . . was, in the contemporary state of science, the only possible one, and particularly the only fruitful one'.[112]

In the last analysis, then, there is an irreducible gap in the scientific structure of Newton's system of the world, between a minimum of theoretic concepts and the vast complex of empirical concepts deduced from appearances.[113] That minimum, however, comprising absolute time and space, is all-important, for absolute

time and space constitute the inertial system which causally conditions all material objects or events within the universe, while
remaining independent of them, and thus supplies us with the
objective intelligible foundation for the simplicity and uniformity
with which we operate in scientific inquiry as well as in common
sense experience, and without which neither would be comprehensible. In other words, absolute time and space gave expression to
Newton's firm belief in the ultimate and inherent intelligibility of
the universe, which allowed him to disregard questions or
hypotheses as to the specific nature of causes, e.g. of gravity, and
yet to unfold the complicated mechanism of nature by deducing its
causal interconnections.[114] But the absolute or independent role
assigned to mathematical time and space in this way, over against
all relative times and spaces, implied that there is a wide gap
between the way in which we explain the actual function of
mechanical causes within the universe, and the way in which the
mechanistic system of the universe as a whole is to be explained.
That is the point to which Newton gave explicit recognition in the
General Scholium to Proposition xlii at the end of the second
edition of the *Principia*,[115] twenty-six years after the publication of
the first edition. In it the independent ontological status of absolute
time and space, and therefore the objectivity and comprehensibility
of the universe, are finally grounded in the eternal and infinite God
who, 'by existing always and everywhere, constitutes duration and
space'. There Newton seems to have identified absolute time with
the eternal duration of God and absolute space with the infinite
presence of God, which together form that in which all things are
contained and moved.[116] In a similar vein, earlier in the *Opticks*,
Newton had related infinite time and space to the 'boundless
uniform sensorium' of God, within which he comprehends and
moves all things according to his will.[117] Thus Newton accounted
for the natural and immutable order of the universe, 'this most
beautiful system', by relating it not only to its original creation by
God but to the constancy and universality of his containing and
controlling presence.[118]

    The scientific significance of this way of relating the world to
God through infinite, absolute time and space, may be indicated by
pointing to Newton's claim that the mechanical causes which
operate within the universe, in terms of which we explain, for
example, the motions in the heavens, cannot be extrapolated to
account for the origin of its order. For that a different kind of
'cause' is required, the agency of will.[119] Expressed differently, this
means that the laws of nature do not apply at all to those creative

processes by which what is nature came into being, but only to those observable processes of nature that is already in being. In the ultimate analysis, therefore, the laws of nature in the universe as we know it are to be understood as having flowed from the creative and rational will of God.[120] That is to say, Newton insisted that the universe cannot be conceived to be a mechanical system complete and consistent in itself, for its immanent order is not completely explainable within that system, but the universe may be conceived as a consistent mechanism if it is related to the *counsel* of a *voluntary* and *intelligent Agent* beyond it, the living God who rules over all.[121] Neither chance nor necessity can provide a sufficient or intelligible explanation for the variety of things or the beauty manifest in the universe, far less for the most beautiful frame of the world itself.[122] We are thrown back upon the ultimate *will* of God the Creator who is the one source of all the stability and regularity of the rational order of the universe.[123]

On the other hand, this relation of the material universe to God, through the time and space constituted by his eternal existence and omnipresence, brings its own difficulty, for it is time and space thus conceived which constitute the ontological foundation for the laws of nature. How can God and the material universe be connected together in this way? The problem is particularly evident in respect of space. 'Since every particle of space is *always,* and every indivisible moment of duration is *everywhere,* certainly the Maker and Lord of all things cannot be *never* and *nowhere* . . . God is the same God, always and everywhere. He is omnipresent not *virtually* only but also *substantially;* for virtue cannot subsist without substance.'[124] The difficulty of linking the omnipresence of space with the omnipresence of God in this way is pointed up when we note that for Newton 'space must possess a kind of physical reality if his laws of motion are to have any meaning, a reality of the same sort as material points and intervals between them'.[125] Does this imply, then, some sort of synthesis between God, or at least the dominion of God, and the material universe, and thus seriously compromise the divine transcendence? Certainly Newton himself would have denied this, for he clearly intended to guard himself against such a charge. He explicitly wrote into the General Scholium that God is not identical with eternity and infinity, i.e., with infinite time and space.[126] And in any case he insisted that infinite time and space as constituted by God's existence and omnipresence are quite independent of the material objects and events in the universe, for they act on them only as an inertial system. 'In him are all things contained and moved, yet neither affects the other; God suffers nothing from the motion of bodies, bodies find no resistance from the omnipresence of God.'[127]

Granted, then, that God is related to the created universe through time and space, he still remains entirely independent even if only through the absolute role played by time and space in the universe, i.e., in containing material bodies which in no way exert reaction on them.[128] God is in no way affected by material reality, while material reality, which derived from God by way of creation, continues to be related to him only through the inertial conditioning of his containing and comprehending presence. But since through absolute time and space the universe is related to God as the point of *absolute rest,* by reference to which all relative time and space and therefore all natural order are determined, God is necessary to the universe, while the universe is not necessary to God.[129] There is thus a mutual, but not a symmetrical, relation of detachment between God and the universe, with considerable import for both theology and natural science. On the one hand, it implies that there is no way of reaching God even as the first Cause by deducing him from the connection of causes and effects within the universe: we cannot even determine the nature of causes or offer an account of the most simple causes through deducing them by analysis from phenomena.[130] The phenomena of nature, however, can raise the question as to the existence of 'a Being, incorporeal, living, intelligent, omnipresent, who in infinite space, as it were in his sensory, sees the things themselves intimately and thoroughly perceives them, and comprehends them wholly by their immediate presence to himself'.[131] On the other hand, it implies that while preternatural causes have no place in physics, and while God cannot be brought into any logical synthesis with mechanical causes (for he cannot be thought of as a mechanical cause), some discussion of God does have a rightful place in natural science.[132] And so Newton justified his reference to God in the General Scholium, even though he cut his discussion short. 'And thus much concerning God, to discourse of whom from the appearance of things does certainly belong to natural philosophy.'[133]

Neither in theology nor in natural science, therefore, can we operate with an immediate, logical or necessary connection between God and the world or the world and God. Here we face a 'logical gap' similar to that which obtains between the empirical concepts of physics and those few, simple theoretic concepts which ultimately support its basic structure as a science. In spite of such a gap, the concept of God is held to be scientifically required for a complete and consistent explanation of 'the frame of the system of the world'. It is when we ask how Newton conceived of that requirement that we become aware of the ambiguity of his thought.

God is required, in the deepest and most comprehensive sense, as the ultimate source and foundation for the intelligibility of the universe and for its objective stability, i.e. for the cohesion, uniformity and simplicity of nature, which make it constantly accessible to rational investigation and exact computation. The astonishing regularity or harmony that underlies and undergirds the variety in the nature of things is not finally explicable in terms of natural causes, or in terms of chance or necessity, but requires God as the absolute determinant of what it is. Certainly the very fact that we can determine with such astonishing exactness the interconnection of mechanical causes within the universe, without knowing the nature of the causes themselves, which must nevertheless be assumed in a mechanical system, indicates that we are concerned with intelligible structures which reach beyond what we can understand, so that we are justified in assuming that what extends beyond what we know or can know is in harmony with what we do know. But for Newton something else is implied here: without the factor of an absolute determinant, independent of our conceiving of it, without final causes or the divine contrivance of things, behind the system of second or mechanical causes, the universe would not be what it is in its regular motions, or be accessible to our orderly analysis and synthesis. As our scientific investigations unfold the mechanism of the world it is revealed not to be a mathematical machine complete in itself, for it involves the kind of order that results from the *choice*[134] of an intelligent and voluntary Agent, or the will of a Being necessarily existing, and that requires reference to him if it is to continue as such into the future.[135] As the universe cannot be thought of as self-originating, so it cannot be thought of as ultimately self-perpetuating. Hence, although natural science in its limitation to mechanical causes can tell us nothing about God, it may yield exact and coherent knowledge of things only in terms of an absolute reference-system constituted in the inertial conditioning of all things by God.

For Newton, however, God is also required on scientific grounds to fulfil certain functions within the immanent processes of the universe. Newton had in mind not only those features of nature which defy complete reduction to mechanical law, but certain 'irregularities' in the motions of the universe which, as he claimed, require constant divine intervention in order to preserve harmony and stability within the solar and stellar systems.[136] He was particularly impressed with the balanced proportion of distances, velocities and masses in the regular motions of the planets in respect of one another and of the sun. 'To make this system with all its motions, required a cause which understood and compared together the quantities of matter in the several bodies of the sun and planets and the gravitating powers resulting thence, the several distances of the primary planets from the sun and of the secondary ones from Saturn, Jupiter, and the earth, and the velocities with which these planets revolve about those quantities of matter in the celestial bodies; and to compare and adjust all these things together, in so great a variety of bodies, argues that cause to be, not blind and fortuitous, but very skilled in mechanics and geometry.' If God's power were not constantly deployed maintaining this balance and harmony within the solar system, 'considerable disturbance' would result.[137] Newton argued along similar lines in regard to the stellar systems, for the conservation by divine power of the proper intervals between them, which prevented them from 'falling upon one another'.[138] Thus Newton could speak of the relation between God and the universe as one in which God moves bodies within his boundless sensorium and is able 'to form and reform parts of the universe'.[139] That is to say, God is thought of as performing a *regulative* part within the systematic connections of bodies in motion in order to resolve recurrent irregularities.

Regarded from one point of view, this appears to reflect a rejection on Newton's part of complete determinism, that is, a view of the universe as a completely closed system of cause and effect, and that would certainly be consistent with his rejection of a universal mathematics, which we have already noted. From another point of view, however, it appears rather like calling in of divine or final causes to make up for the deficiencies allegedly found in the chain of mechanical causes, where those divine causes are made to operate in interconnection with and on the same level as mechanical causes. Newton, of course, would have repudiated such a charge. Nevertheless, he appears to have confused, or mistakenly run together, the all-important comprehending and containing role of God in relation to the creation of the universe and its continuance as an entire system, and the role of God in regulating the chain of mechanical causes and coping with the emergencies resulting from irregularities within the universe.

This ambiguity was to have important consequences in the history of European thought. It gave the impression that the relation of the world to God and of God to the world is to be conceived in connection with the gaps that open up in our scientific knowledge of the universe. Hence the more those gaps were reduced, the more the alleged irregularities in the system of motion in the universe yielded to mechanical explanation in accordance with Newton's laws, the less room there appeared for God in any human understanding of the universe. And so Laplace who developed the Newtonian system of the world to its most complete form, in apparently demonstrating the internal stability of the solar system according to completely self-regulating and eternal law, could insist that he had no need of that 'hypothesis' – 'God'.[140] That is to say, by doing away with the need for a divine role in regulating and harmonising mechanical connections within the universe, he imagined that the question as to the relation of the universe as a whole to God had also been answered. But that has not proved to be the case, for rigorous mathematics has not only shown Laplace's notion of the inherent stability of the universe to be ultimately deficient, but has also demonstrated the untenability of a system which is complete and consistent within its own limits.[141] Hence Newton's primary point remains: the impossibility of reducing the universe to a completely mechanical system, and therefore the need for a *non-mechanical agency* to be correlated with it in order to support it as an intelligible whole and provide sufficient reason for its accessibility to scientific investigation. This question is forced on us, Newton claimed, by the advance of science itself;[142] and that certainly appears to be more and more evident in our own day as the epistemological and cosmological dualism which has so long prevailed in European thought yields to the revolution associated with relativity theory.[143] In his own times, however, Newton's primary point, as we have called it, was undoubtedly very difficult to appreciate in the context of causal determinism as it arose out of the attempt to quantify all motion and subject the entire realm of nature to mechanical law. That was even more the case with Newton's heirs and successors as the concept of a mechanistic universe hardened into an unquestioned dogma and dominated the whole range of science.

In concluding this examination of the relation of the universe to God in Newton's thought it may help us to draw together certain aspects of it which in one way or another affected the direction of subsequent thought in shaping the general frame of understanding.

1. The notion of the presence and duration of God as constituting mathematical time and space implied what one might well speak of as a mythological synthesis between God and the universe. If all things are contained in God as their *place,* as Newton held,[144] then something like a *physical* connection is held to obtain between the universe and God. This is the point in Newton's notion of space

which Bishop Berkeley found to be pernicious and absurd. Unless space is only relative we are forced into the dilemma 'of thinking either that Real Space is God, or else that there is something beside God which is eternal, uncreated, indivisible, immutable'.[145] Leibniz also objected to Newton's synthesis of God and infinite space through his concept of the divine sensorium, on the ground that this was to lapse into 'materialism'. While agreeing that the world is a machine that wants to be continually influenced by its Creator, Leibniz held it to be derogatory to God to think of him as making something which was in regular need of mending in order to be set right.[146] Neither Berkeley nor Leibniz would have anything to do with absolute time or space, but the effect of their criticism upon those who accepted the Newtonian system was to force them into a deistic disjunction between God and the mechanism of the world, if not into open atheism. On the other hand, the profound dualism inherent in the Newtonian system between absolute time and space and the motions of bodies within them, or between volume and mass, probably inhibited monistic tendencies toward an outright identification of God with the order or rationality immanent in the universe.[147]

2. The role of an ultimate reference-system assigned to independent, immutable, isotropic and homogeneous time and space in the causal structure of Newtonian science, i.e. as constituting an inertial system conditioning everything that falls within its embrace, meant that the basic concepts of science were determined by the way they were thought out from a point of absolute rest. Even each coordinate-system as a sensible magnitude is determined through the relation of the observer to an immovable object, or at least to a relatively immovable object, such as the sun in our own solar system, as its point of absolute rest. Thus, together with the casting of the differential laws of motion and attraction into the axiomatic framework of classical geometry concerned with the interrelations of rigid bodies, apart from time, this had the effect of producing a hard mechanistic system of the universe built up of finally static concepts. There we have at least one principal root of the dogmatic imperialism of the positivism and scientism that ran from the eighteenth into the twentieth century.

3. Absolute, mathematical time and space form the boundless uniform sensorium of God which conditions all things in the universe without being affected by them, and as such are quite independent of their relation to any observer. Nevertheless, they are correlated in our knowledge of the universe with observational geometrical magnitudes located in relative, apparent or pheno-

menal time and space, or coordinate-systems relative to ourselves as observers and therefore varying from observer to observer. Thus, although mathematically defined time and space transcend our observation, and are not amenable to empirical verification, they are nevertheless introduced into the basic structure of science as the absolute reference-system, universal and everywhere the same, which is needed to correct the prejudiced notions derived from appearances in relative coordinate-systems, and thus out of varying, distorted, observational notions to produce mathematically precise concepts of the universal and objective kind (i.e. the same for every observer) with which we operate in exact science.[148] Hence, as F. S. C. Northrop has pointed out, Newton, following Galileo, had to reject the Aristotelian identification of the content of nature with what is sensed or (in Newtonian language) with what is observed in relative, apparent, sensible time and space, and develop a conception of nature as an atomic system of physical objects governed by mechanical causes and located in absolute, invisible, mathematical time and space.[149] In Newton's natural philosophy, then, it was the divine sensorium which constituted the ultimate framework of reference for the formulation of scientific and universal concepts; but when the synthesis of absolute time and space with God began to fade away, it was inevitable that the human pole of the knowledge relation should be thrust forward into the centre of reference, i.e. the sensorium of the earthy observer. And that was indeed the road taken by European thought from Locke, through Berkeley and Hume, to Kant.

LOCKE, BERKELEY AND HUME

With John Locke there arose an empirical approach to philosophy which seemed to be demanded by the new corpuscular physics and mechanics being established by Boyle and Newton, as its epistemological counterpart.[150] This was an inquiry into the phenomenalism implied by the new science in its attempts to explain 'the appearances of nature' or phenomena, in the conviction that it is sense experience alone that yields all the basic ideas upon which human knowledge is built up. 'Our observation employed either about external sensible objects, or about the internal operations of our minds perceived and reflected on by ourselves, is that which supplies our understandings with all the materials of thinking. These two are the fountains of knowledge, from whence all the ideas we have, or can naturally have, do spring.'[151] In the reception of these basic ideas the understanding acts for the most part passively, but then it proceeds to elaborate human knowledge through composition, comparison, and abstraction, i.e. through pure inductive operations.[152] In this way, Locke returned to a more Aristotelian approach to knowledge in reaction against the rationalist tendencies of Descartes, accepting the principle that there is nothing in the mind which was not first in the senses: 'there are no innate principles in the human mind, for, apart from interaction with the material world in sensation, the mind is 'a white paper, void of all characters, without any ideas'.[153]

Locke's epistemology represents a rather significant change, for in this approach he concentrated, not like Newton upon the objective orientation of appearances toward the atomic structure of the real quantifiable world, but upon their subjective orientation: the way in which objects appear to the observer. 'Appearances' are here understood as 'objects in the mind', or the 'determinate ideas' that arise within the mind under the impact of physical objects upon it.[154] Now since for Locke the interaction between physical objects and minds which this involves could not be construed in terms of mechanical causes that obtain among physical objects themselves, the human observer being treated merely like another physical object,[155] he was forced to draw a clear-cut distinction between 'material substances' (the atomic bodies in the system of nature) and 'immaterial substances' (minds or spirits). Like the former, immaterial substances are independent, indivisible and indestructible, but they are also 'thinking substances' capable of consciousness, so that when they are acted on by material substances they receive their effects as 'internal operations of the mind', as 'impressions and reflections upon them'.[156] Thus there arises, Locke maintained, the 'ideas and appearances' which God has fitted the mind to receive from things and thereby to know them.[157] Immaterial substances are thus epistemically suited to the material substances which constitute the physical system of the universe, and it is in their correlation with one another that the context is provided in which all human knowledge arises and all science is developed.

However, this dualist theory of material and immaterial substances accentuated the phenomenalist problem inherited from Galileo: how to cope with the misleading picture of the universe derived through our senses. Locke distinguished more sharply than Boyle or Newton between two kinds of qualities that characterise appearances and are projected by our senses as observational ideas: primary qualities which are modifications of matter in the bodies that cause perceptions in our minds, and secondary qualities which are the sensations produced in us by primary qualities. Our ideas of primary qualities are resemblances of the bodies that give rise to them, but our ideas of secondary qualities are not resemblances, although we project them upon the bodies we perceive as appearances.[158] Hence we never know things simply in accordance with what they are independent of our perception but only as they appear to us as observers, so that the world as known is conditioned partly by the atomic structure of nature and partly by the sensuous effects it causes in our minds. But since we can never get beyond our observations and everything known is relative to the particular observer, how are we able to distinguish what is universal for every observer and thus achieve objectivity? What is there that can play the role of a reference-system, always and everywhere the same, which is needed for scientific operations?

For answers to these questions we must look to Locke's doctrine of the nature and consciousness of the human observer as an immaterial substance acted on by material substances in the universe around him. The fact that immaterial substances are merely 'empty cabinets' makes them all equal, and always and everywhere the same, and so provides the epistemic condition needed for uniformity.[159] And the fact that they have ideas only as they are acted on by material substances 'extrinsical to the mind', and therefore that the simple ideas upon which all knowledge is built are forced on them, so that they can no more refuse, alter or obliterate the images produced in it by objects set before it, provides the epistemic conditions needed for determinacy, adequacy and objectivity.[160] Moreover, the fact that the consciousness of the observer which receives ideas as internal operations of the mind is the *consciousness* of a *substance,* immaterial though it is, i.e. a persistent, enduring subsistence, always identical with itself, which stands under or upholds it, giving permanent support for its ideas or appearances, provides the epistemic conditions necessary for stability and continuity in knowledge.[161] It is thus in the nature of the mind of the observer as an independent and continuous centre of consciousness, the thinking *self,*[162] an immaterial substance in fitted correlation with material substances, that Locke finds the centre of reference which may be assigned a role in observational knowledge similar to that assigned by Newton to the inertial system of independent, isomorphic and homogeneous time and space in his scientific structure. But since the mind of the observer is quite blank, before the activity of material substances upon it, and since the only conceivable alternative to Locke were *innate* ideas or principles (which were to be rejected), the scientific elaboration of observational ideas is carried out without the organising control of formal structures that are not themselves empirically derived. This inevitably entailed a retreat from the primacy of mathematics (unless of course an empiricist account of it could be offered), but also a depreciation of the purely theoretic component in scientific knowledge which had played such a decisive and important role in the advance of physics from Galileo to Newton. Thus, through the correlation of the consciousness of the observer strictly with appearances, through the union of thinking substance with sensed objects, Locke incorporated the subjective pole of human knowing into science in such a way that he laid the foundation for the inductive observationalism and empiricism of later times, yet it was an attempt to think through the epistemological implications of the Galilean principle of relativity.[163]

Influential though Locke's theory of knowledge was, however, it contained a deep contradiction that called for considerable rethinking. The impossibility of accounting for mathematics on the basis of appearances alone, or through the association of sense ideas, and thus the impossibility of accounting for the relation between the sensible measures of apparent time and space to the measured quantities of mathematical time and space which transcend observation, so fundamental for Newtonian physics, meant that knowledge of the universe must be given a broader and deeper foundation than that which could be supplied by sense experience alone. The contradiction in Locke's 'new way of ideas' became exposed through the analysis of Berkeley and Hume.

Assuming that all knowledge is grounded in the way Locke held it to be, upon the sense impressions that arise in the consciousness of the observer, and assuming also, with Locke, that the ideas we reach through introspection and reflection upon these impressions do not entail the existence of what is meant, then there are no observational or empirical grounds for assuming the existence of the material substances themselves which are said to produce these impressions and ideas in our minds. If there are material substances they must be known on grounds supplementary to those provided by sensation, but on Locke's theory of ideas, as Berkeley showed, the notion of material substances independent of our perception is meaningless.[164] Thus the logical implications of Locke's epistemology would be devastating for natural science as well as for theology: for both the inherent intelligibility as well as the objectivity of what is claimed to be known would be cut away.

Hume's analysis had much the same effect upon Locke's notion of immaterial substance, but this was even more damaging for it dissolved Locke's central point of reference by showing that the persisting and enduring self, the consciousness of the thinking substance, is nothing more than an association of particular, contingent, successive sense experiences.[165] Given, then, the empiricist epistemology advocated by Locke, it can be shown that not only do we have no empirical evidence for other minds, but we do not have empirical evidence for the independent reality of our own. Hence any belief in immaterial substances or independently existing selves would have to be justified on other grounds than the immediate impressions of the senses or our introspection of them. However, Hume carried the logic of this empiricism even further, in showing that the relation between one immediately observed fact and another is merely 'contingent'. Thus knowledge grounded upon the observation of the senses yields no evidence for necessary connections.[166] Here too, it would appear, if any belief in causal or necessary connection is to be maintained it must be traced to other than observational or empirical sources, for it is not reached inductively. 'Objects have no discoverable connection together; nor is it from any other principle but custom operating upon imagination, that we can draw inference from the appearance of one to the existence of another.'[167] Yet Hume's own position was not so sceptical as it might appear.[168] Just as we use reason to correct the senses, so we must use reflective thinking to supplement custom, while his view that in the last analysis reason ought to rest on 'natural beliefs' when we find ourselves unable to offer any satisfactory explanation of an all-important connection, indicates that he held knowledge to repose upon a wider and more deeply rooted foundation than that which we find in direct observations or perceptions. That is to say, immediate apprehension gives us only a limited range and depth of knowledge which does not prove adequate even for the foundation of what is given.[168] Nevertheless, Hume clearly had little place for a theoretical component in knowledge, which was not itself experimentally or empirically derived, either in controlling scientific inquiry or in providing support for the basic structure of science.[169] And this proved to be as big a difficulty for natural science as it did for natural theology, for the negative conclusions of Hume's empirical positivism, the failure of the natural reason to establish an intelligible connection between the universe and God, also revealed the failure of this whole approach to account for the inherent intelligibility of the universe which made it accessible to rational and scientific inquiry. The only future open to that kind of science is very unsatisfactory: a descriptive observationalism that lacks explanatory power, operating at the best with only a conventionalist notion of theory as a convenient arrangement of observational ideas for certain pragmatic ends.

KANT

The effect of David Hume's epistemological analyses created a serious impasse for the empirical approach to knowledge. If no intrinsic or necessary connection is perceivable between one observed factor and another, then some of the most important components of scientific knowledge, e.g. in Newton's system of the world, such as substance, relation, causality, are not reached through sense experience, and cannot be employed in inductive operations from phenomena. That was the shock that opened Kant's eyes to the inadequacy of a purely observational or empirical approach to knowledge. If all that we are left with after Hume's analysis are immediately apprehended particulars, then mathematics and physics are left without foundations upon which to build. But Newton himself had demonstrated that sense experience by itself yields only sensible measures from which we get no more that relative coordinate-systems of time and space, whereas an absolute reference-system of mathematical time and space is necessary for exact science. Hence it became apparent to Kant, himself a mathematician and an astronomer, that a new and more adequate foundation had to be laid in which theoretical factors, not observationally derived, played a basic role along with phenomenal data in the direction of scientific inquiry and in the essential structure of science. The importance of Kant in the development of European thought is located in his attempt to construct an epistemology in which the empirical contribution of Locke, Berkeley and Hume was combined with the more rationalist approach to knowledge of Descartes and Leibniz, in such a way as to show that purely theoretical *a priori* elements and empirical *a posteriori* elements operate together in all our knowing, in everyday life as well as in scientific constructions. The result of this was his famous *synthetic a priori*.[170]

However, Kant's reconstruction of the foundations of knowledge brought serious problems, which we shall have to examine, but at this point we must indicate the connections of his thought with that of Newton and Locke. Kant retained the 'absolute' or independent character of Newton's mathematical time and space, its character as an inertial system for the scientific determination of the atomic structure of nature, but he transferred it to the human understanding, that is, to Locke's centre of reference in the consciousness of the observer, to constitute the basic 'forms of sensibility' which are independent of experience but regulative of our spatio-temporal apprehensions. To these he added substance, relation and causality as formal structures of the mind, called 'categories of the understanding', likewise independent of experience, through which the observer organises everything apprehended in time and space as objects of human knowledge. It was the *a priori* status of these formal structures of sensibility and understanding that provided the condition for objective knowledge (the same for every observer), but their logical independence of experience forced Kant to posit a 'transcendental ego' (as his absolute centre of reference) correlated to the 'empirical ego' (Locke's centre of reference) of this or that observer, which could play the role assigned to absolute time and space in Newton's system and even the role of the divine sensorium.

The effect of this reconstruction was at least twofold. By tracing the theoretic components of knowledge to the structures of the mind which are independent of experience, and therefore not modifiable through experience, Kant built into the foundation of knowledge a disastrous ingredient of necessity or determinism. Since it is now the human understanding in its unchanging and uniform structures which becomes the centre of absolute rest, in accordance with which all knowledge of the universe is formalised, scientific concepts inevitably acquire a finally static and necessary character. Moreover, by grounding these theoretical factors in the human mind through which it shapes, regulates and controls everything we apprehend, Kant gave powerful philosophic form to the concept of the active, creative reason, and thus contributed in a massive way to the formation of the way in which modern people have tended to think.

In the introductory outline of this essay it was pointed out that behind the rise of rationalist empiricism in science and philosophy two fateful tendencies set in and steadily encroached upon European thought: an inversion of the knowing relationship and a constructivist mentality. We must now examine the bearing upon that development of 'the Copernican revolution' in Kant's reconstruction of the foundations of knowledge and assess his impact upon the making of what we have called 'the modern mind'.

1   The transfer of intelligibility to the human pole of the knowing relation, i.e. its attachment to the autonomous reason, was a
distinctive but paradoxical trend of the Enlightenment, for, in spite
of the insistent belief in a natural order of things accessible to
rational inquiry and formulation, it led to the view that the necessity upon which laws of nature depend is lodged in the mind and
not in things themselves. Along with that development the concept
of the inherent intelligibility of the universe began to fade away.
This change is particularly evident in the thought of Kant when he
claimed that instead of drawing its laws from nature the human
understanding confers them upon nature, for in our scientific
interrogation of nature we compel it to yield answers in accordance
with *a priori* principles we bring to it.[171] Since, as he held, it is this
prescriptive operation of the reason that makes knowledge of
nature possible, Kant was forced to conclude that 'the understanding is itself the source of the laws of nature, and so of its formal
unity'.[172] 'Although we learn many laws through experience, they
are only special determinations of still higher laws, and the highest
of these, under which all others stand, issue *a priori* from the
understanding itself. They are not borrowed from experience; on
the contrary, they have to confer upon appearances their conformity to law, and so make experience possible. Thus the understanding is something more than a power of formulating rules through
comparison of appearances; it is itself the lawgiver of nature.'[173]
Kant could speak of 'the systematic unity of nature as objectively
valid and necessary', for he found it difficult to understand how our
reason can operate in this legislative way 'unless we also presuppose
a transcendental principle whereby such a systematic unity is *a priori*
assumed to be necessarily inherent in the objects'.[174] Yet he clearly
conceived of this as 'only a projected unity, to be regarded not as
given in itself'.[175] Moreover, when he spoke of what is 'given' or
'objective', Kant construed that in a formal or regulative way:
'given' and 'objective' do not refer to any character of things in
themselves but to the synthetic and necessary form which appearances take in our cognition of them. His emphasis fell not on any
objects given independently, but on what he called 'the objective
unity of self-consciousness' which he held to constitute 'an objective condition of all knowledge'.[176] 'It is not merely a condition that
I myself require in knowing an object, but is a condition under
which every intuition must stand in order to *become an object for
me.*'[177] This implies a radical change in the very notion of 'object', as
referring, not to what is independently real, but to what is 'brought
into being' within the conditions of our experience, the pheno-

menal or the empirical object.[178] Kant's main point here has been tersely expressed by Gerd Buchdahl: 'The "objectivity" of the phenomenal object is not "objectively given" but "subjectively wrought".'[179]

What, then, did Kant make of the notion of intelligibility? He did not conceive of it as referring to any positive character in the real world: the intelligible is no more than a negative correlate of the sensible. 'Whatever in an object of the senses is not itself appearance, I entitle *intelligible*.'[180] There is, then, a distinction to be drawn between the sensible and the intelligible *(mundus sensibilis et mundus intelligibilis)*, or the phenomenal and the noumenal, but since, Kant claimed, we can have no knowledge except of what is drawn within the field of our sensible intuitions, 'the intelligible entities' *(Verstandeswesen)*, which doubtless correspond to 'the sensible entities', cannot properly be regarded as *intelligible objects*.[181] They cannot be thought of as determinate things in terms of distinctive inner predicates. Thus even when we find ourselves forced to postulate 'intelligible objects' upon which appearances, that are never self-grounded but always conditioned, may terminate, they are mere thought-entities.[182] 'The intelligible character' of empirical objects simply refers to their non-empirical, non-sensible ground, and must be taken in a *purely negative* and not in a positive sense.[183]

In other words, the intelligible or the noumenon is a concept without an object *(ens rationis)*; it is no more than a *limiting concept*, the function of which is 'to prevent sensible intuition from being extended to things in themselves, and thus to limit the objective validity of sensible knowledge'.[184] Thus Kant's critique of the pure understanding 'does not permit us to create a new field of objects beyond those which are presented to us as appearances, and so to stray into intelligible worlds; nay, it does not allow of our entertaining even the concept of them'.[185] Hence in spite of the fact that for Kant the empirical world was conceived as grounded in the non-empirical or the intelligible, that intelligible ground does not need to be considered in empirical inquiries which are concerned only with appearances which must be capable of complete causal explanation in terms of other appearances in accordance with natural laws. 'We have to take their strictly empirical character as the supreme ground of explanation, leaving entirely out of account their intelligible character (that is, the transcendental cause of their empirical character) as being completely unknown, save in so far as the empirical serves for its sensible sign.'[186] This follows, of course, from Kant's basic idea that the only way to make an object understandable *(verständlich)* is to bring it within the conditions of sensibility and so 'to the form of appearances', for it does not make sense to speak of objects outside the frame of phenomenal experience. [187]

It should now be clear that this Kantian rejection of any knowledge grounded positively in intelligible and determinate realities and controlled through steady reference to their inner relations, together with the devaluation of 'the intelligible' to what is essentially unknowable and even unentertainable, could not but have the effect of banishing the notion of intelligibility or understandability from any independent basis in the order of nature and of limiting it solely to the interconnection of appearances or observations. Further, if what makes things understandable or intelligible to us are, not any properties which they may have in themselves or as they are given to our perception, but the ordering and regulating concepts derived from ourselves as observers and knowers, then the notion of intelligibility in its positive sense becomes in fact transferred to the human pole of the knowing relation. [188] Moreover, since these concepts were regarded as arising through the forms of sensible intuition and the categories of the understanding which are *a priori*, i.e. independent of experience and therefore not open to modification by experience, this inevitably imported powerful elements of subjectivity and necessity into the structure of scientific knowledge. The implication was that scientific activity does not so much explore as shape nature, and does not so much discover as create reality.

2. The rise and development of the masterful idea that we can understand only what we can construct for ourselves now becomes a distinctive feature of the 'modern' attitude of mind. From the foregoing it will be evident that here too we must point the finger at Kant, with reference to his idea that an object *is* what it becomes in our cognition of it. Something only becomes an object for me through the objective unity of my self-consciousness, as it is brought within the synthetic self-activity of the *I think*. [189] It was especially when Kant turned to mathematics and geometry that he became convinced that construction enters as a constituent ingredient into what is known and regarded as knowable. 'To know anything in space (for instance, a line), I must draw it, and thus synthetically bring into being a determinate combination of the given manifold, so that the unity of this act is at the same time the unity of consciousness (as in the concept of a line); and it is through this unity of consciousness that an object (a determinate space) is first known.' [190] It was thus that Kant claimed to be able to make the laws of motion intelligible to reason, but he went on to hold that all

cognition of objects involves spatio-temporal construction. That is to say, we *construct* our concepts and empirical objects are for us *constructions* in space.[191] And so, to cite Gerd Buchdahl again, '"construction" becomes a basic ingredient in Kant's definition of possible cognitive experience'; 'Kant's insistence on the unknowability of the "internal nature" of bodies will now be expressed in terms of impossibility to construct.'[192] In other words, we understand and verify only what we can make and shape for ourselves.[193]

There can be no doubt that Kant made a very significant contribution to the concept of scientific knowledge as it developed from Galileo and Newton by showing that it operated through a constant coordination of the empirical and theoretic components of knowledge. 'Reason has insight only into that which it produces after a plan of its own . . . Reason, holding in one hand its principles, according to which alone concordant appearances can be admitted as equivalent to laws, and in the other hand the experiment, which it has devised in conformity with these principles, must approach nature in order to be taught by it.'[194] There Kant seems to be expressing rather faithfully the way in which scientific knowledge has consistently been advanced since Galileo and Newton, through theory-guided experiment and experimentally informed theory under the instruction or disclosure of nature itself. However, Kant took a wrong turn in the way in which he brought together the empirical and theoretical factors in trying to resolve the empiricist impasse, which has proved very unfortunate for the development of thought. On the one hand, he construed the theoretical component in scientific knowledge in terms of necessary and legislative concepts, while, on the other hand, he changed the question which Bacon had taught science to put to nature, in the character of a servant or pupil who listens to what he is told,[195] into the kind of question put by a judge who compels witnesses to answer the questions he himself has formulated and in accordance with the stipulations those questions impose, i.e. 'constraining nature to give answer to questions of reason's own determining'.[196] And so with reference to the geometer Kant wrote: 'The true method was not to inspect what he discerned in the figure, or in the bare concept of it, and from this, as it were, to read off its properties; but to bring out what was necessarily implied in the concepts that he himself formed *a priori,* and had put into the figure in the construction by which he presented it to himself. If he is to know anything with *a priori* certainty he must not ascribe to the figure anything save what necessarily follows from what he himself set into it in accordance with his concept.'[197]

There is certainly a profound element of truth here, the fact that in all our knowing there is a real interplay between what we know and our knowing of it. Man himself is part of nature and is so intimately related to nature that he plays a formative, and nature a productive, role in scientific inquiry, discovery and interpretation. This is everywhere apparent in the magnificent achievements of empirical and theoretic science, but the way in which Kant himself combined the theoretical and empirical components of the epistemic process has had grave consequences. It is certainly to be granted that we do not apprehend things apart from a theoretic structure, but if the theoretic structure actually determines what we apprehend, then what we apprehend provides no control over our understanding.[198] The one way out of that impasse requires a theoretic structure which, while affecting our knowledge, is derived from the intrinsic intelligibility of what we seek to know, and is open to constant revision through reference to the inner determinations of things as they come to view in the process of inquiry. But this is ruled out by the Kantian thesis that the theoretic structure is aprioristically independent of what we apprehend and that there is no possible knowledge of things in their own inner determinations or relations. While Kant was certainly concerned to show the limits of the pure reason, his theory of knowledge served to reinforce the Enlightenment doctrine of the autonomous reason (e.g. in its Lockean and Cartesian forms alike) and even to exalt it into a position beyond what had hitherto been claimed, where through prescriptive legislation it subdued nature to the forms of its own rational necessities. As F. S. C. Northrop has expressed it: 'For neither Locke nor Hume was the human person as knower a positively acting, creating being. With Kant the position is entirely changed. Apart from the knowing person, which Kant termed "the ego", the *a priori* forms of sensibility and categories of the understanding which this ego brings to the contingent data of sense, there would be no single space-time world whatever, with its public, material objects and knowers. In this fashion Kant transforms the modern man's conception of himself from a merely passive into a systematically active and creative being.'[199]

Kant's position cannot be appreciated adequately without regard to what he called *the practical reason* and its synthetic use, for it is from this perspective that the human reason is seen in its independence of determining causes of the world of sense and in its freedom in the world of understanding where it operates as itself a *causality*.[200] 'The will is a kind of causality belonging to living beings in so far as they are rational, and *freedom* would be this property of such causality that it can be efficient, independently of foreign causes *determining* it.'[201] Certainly a rational being must regard himself *qua* intelligence as subject to the laws of the world of understanding, but these are laws which have their foundation not in experience but in the reason alone.[202] Within this realm, therefore, the reason is autonomous and self-legislating, i.e. it must be conceived as practical or as giving effect to the object of the will. In this way, claimed Kant, the realm of the intelligible, which the pure reason could treat only as a limiting concept without any positive or knowable content, is now given *objective reality* by the practical reason.[203] Yet Kant took care to add that this does not mean any extension of our knowledge to the supersensible realm or any enlargement of our knowledge with regard to intelligible objects, for 'the objective reality' of this intelligible realm must be considered strictly from a practical or moral point of view – in terms of the ends or the objective of the practical reason.[204] In other words, by 'objective' here Kant referred to the *condition* under which practical laws are valid for every rational being.[205] And yet he did go so far as to speak of the practical reason as *producing the reality* to which it refers, or as *making objects,* arguing that their *existence* was required by the practical reason,[206] although in the realm of the understanding they are only heuristic concepts for the pure reason.[207]

One further point may now be noted. In order to account for the fact that empirical objects, which are brought into being and take shape within the synthetic activity of the knowing ego, are universally the same for different people, Kant correlated them with what he called 'the transcendental ego', a sort of 'common ego' exalted above nature where it constitutes an inertial centre by reference to which the universal and necessary laws of nature are worked out – laws to which every man as an empirical ego is subject. But since it was impossible on these 'empirical principles' of the theoretical reason to offer an adequate account of man as a free moral agent, Kant turned to the 'rational principles' of the practical reason, in accordance with which man as a rational being recognises himself to be subject to the world of understanding which not only presupposes but requires the idea of freedom.[208] The immediate upshot of this separation of the pure reason in its practical use from the pure reason in its speculative use was the segregation of morality and religion from empirical and scientific knowledge of the world. Kant was surely right in arguing that 'in practical philosophy it is not the reasons of what *happens* that we have to ascertain, but the laws of what *ought* to happen',[209] for in the former we are concerned only to lay bare the causal laws that control phenomenal sequences, whereas in the latter we are concerned with principles of action that do not rest on contingent grounds and are independent of the mechanism of nature.[210]

The consequences of this, however, are two-fold. On the one hand, it gives the practical reason a primacy over the theoretical reason, on the ground that it exhibits a law of causality, the determining principle of which is set above the conditions of the sensible world,[211] which tended to lead to functionalism and pragmatism in ethics, to a moral operationalism in theology,[212] and even influenced the development of empiricism toward operationalism and conventionalism in natural science.[213] On the other hand, it sheltered moral and theological propositions from the kind of critical questioning that arises in empirical and theoretical inquiry, which, to say the very least, is rather unhealthy, and which did in fact lead to a detachment of religion from its historical grounds and to the indifference of theology to metaphysics.[214] Professor H. B. Acton argued cogently that by the principle of autonomy Kant did not mean that through the practical reason the rational being is himself the source of the moral law, or that he is legislative in the sense that he *makes* laws, but that he is only legislative in the sense that he is obliged to acknowledge and enunciate universal laws that are *a priori* and unconditionally binding, upon himself and all others. The moral law is not arbitrary, merely relative to 'our reason'.[215] That is to say, then, such concepts as 'good', 'freedom', 'duty', 'God', and 'immortality', are not just private notions relative to individual persons or groups of persons. But in that event, as Northrop has pointed out, 'the same logic which took him (Kant) to a transcendental scientific ego to account for differing persons having a single concept of a public world would take him to a transcendental moral ego to account for differing persons having the same idea of "good", "freedom", "duty", "God", and "immortality".' He went on to say: 'When this happens, as it did with Fichte and Hegel, the freedom of the individual evaporates as quickly out of Kant's moral and religious philosophy as it did out of his scientific philosophy. In fact, the development of classical German thought from Kant through Fichte to Hegel and Marx is the story of this occurrence.'[216]

Enough has now been adduced to show the combined effect of Kant's critical and practical philosophy by which he gave a 'Copernican' twist to the slant of the modern mind. The theoretic reason cut off from objective control by the inner relations of things, and the practical reason with its stress on the primacy of the will over

nature, together reinforced the Enlightenment concept of the autonomous reason and made it into an *objectifying instrument* through
which man can subdue everything to his own understanding, and
thus achieve what Bertrand Russell called the supremacy of mind
over the non-mental universe.[217] This is the self-exaltation of the
active, creative reason which acknowledges as valid only what it
can conceive and master through the structures of its self-
understanding and subdue to the demands of the unconditioned
will of man through its principle of 'practical use'. Thus the two
main doctrines of the Kantian philosophy have profoundly influenced the development of an instrumentalist science and the
emergence of the masterful society. They come together today in
what we know as technocratic man and the technological society,
but it is at this very point that the deeply-ingrained anthropocentrism of the 'modern' attitude of mind has come under steady attack
from the advance of pure science and its profounder grasp of the
objective yet open structures of the finite but unbounded universe.
The more deeply scientific inquiry and theory have been able to
penetrate into the inherent intelligibility and inner structure of the
universe at all levels of its manifestation, the more it has been able
to grasp reality in its depth in such a way that it has had to shake off
the influence of Kant and give the really modern mind a radical turn
which has set it back upon God-given intelligibilities and objectivities of creation.

This is not to say that Kant can now be dismissed, any more than
we can dismiss Newton. But just as Newtonian concepts, reconstructed and modified as they are repossessed from Einsteinian
relativity theory, have their proper place in the foundations of our
science where they are treated as constituting a limiting case to the
concepts forced upon us by our new understanding of the universe,
so Kantian concepts arising out of the coordination of the theoretic
and empirical components of scientific knowledge, but now reconstructed and recast through controlling reference to the inherent
intelligibility of the space-time universe, may still have at least a
critical and indeed a healthy role to play in the philosophy of natural
and theological science.

As typical of the changed outlook which is indebted to Kant
while also differing rather sharply from him, we may conclude this
discussion with a citation from Max Planck: 'The fact which led me
to my science and filled me with enthusiasm for it, from my youth
upwards, and which is by no means self-evident, is that our laws of
thinking coincide with the lawfulness in the course of the impressions which we receive from the external world, so that man is

enabled to obtain enlightenment on this lawfulness by means of pure thinking. In this it is of essential significance that the external world represents something independent of ourselves, something absolute that we are facing, and the search for the laws that hold for this absolute seem to me the most satisfying task for the life's work of a scientist.'[218]

NOTES

1. Cf. M. Heidegger, *An Introduction to Metaphysics*, New Haven and London, 1959, p. 178f.
2. John Duns Scotus, *Ordinatio, prol.* n. 1.
3. John Calvin, *Institutio*, 1.1.1f. This is to be taken together with Calvin's reversal of the mediaeval order of asking the questions *quid sit, an sit, quale sit, Inst.* 1.2.1.
4. For references see my discussion of Bacon's method in *Theological Science*, London, 1969, pp. 69ff.
5. F. A. Hayek, *Law, Legislation and Liberty*, London, 1973, vol. 1, pp. 5f, 9ff.
6. Typical of this constructivist notion of truth is the thought of Giambattista Vico, *De antiquissima Italorum sapientia*, 1710, who argued that the rule or criterion of truth is to have made it, i.e. the concept of *verum et factum* with which he entitled ch. 2 of this work.
7. St Augustine, *De Trinitate*, 9.3.3; cf. also 8.6.9; 10.3.5, 5.7, 8.11f; 14.6.8; 15.12.21, etc.
8. See the discussion by N. Kemp Smith on the relation of Descartes' ideas to those of St Augustine, *Studies in Cartesian Philosophy*, London, 1902, pp. 3ff.
9. See E. A. Burtt, *The Metaphysical Foundations of Modern Science*, revised edit., Garden City, N.Y., 1932, pp. 72ff.
10. *Op. cit.*, p. 84.
11. 'The discovery and use of scientific reasoning by Galileo was one of the most important achievements in the history of human thought, and marks the real beginning of physics. This discovery taught us that intuitive conclusions based on immediate observations are not always to be trusted, for they sometimes lead to wrong clues.' A. Einstein and L. Infeld, *The Evolution of Physics*, New York, 1938, p. 6f.

12. R. Descartes, *Discourse on Method, The Philosophical Works of Descartes,* tr. by E. S. Haldane and G. R. T. Ross, London, 1931 edit., vol. 1, p. 86.

13. *Method,* 2, p. 91f; *Rules for the Direction of our Intelligence,* 4, pp. 7f, 13f.

14. See especially the *Rules* for the fullest account of this mathematical method, and also *Method,* 2, p. 92f.

15. For the Augustinian roots of this see *Soliloquia,* 2.1; *De vera religione,* 39.73; *De Trinitate,* 10.7.4, 10.14; *De Civitate Dei,* 11.26.

16. Cf. Frederick Broadie, *An Approach to Descartes' Meditations,* London, 1970, who shows the enormous importance of the existence of God for Descartes' whole system of thought.

17. R. Descartes, *Method,* 2, p. 92. The ultimate truths or axioms are not of course limited to God and the soul. Cf. *The Principles of Philosophy,* part 1 on 'The Principles of Human Knowledge', e.g. 49 and 75, pp. 238f, 252f.

18. *Rules,* 10, p. 32f; *Method,* 2, p. 91; *Meditations,* 6, p. 188.

19. See especially *Principles,* 2, art. 37 (not fully translated in the edition of Haldane and Ross, p. 267) in which 'the first law of nature' is related immediately to the immutability of God; cf. also *Principles,* 3, arts 1 & 3, pp. 270ff.

20. *Meditations,* 4, pp. 171ff; *Principles,* 1, 73: 'In truth we perceive no object as it is by sense alone, but only by our reason exercised upon sensible objects.'

21. *Method,* 6, p. 120; cf. further *Rules,* 12, for the interplay of the four faculties, understanding, imagination, sense and memory; and *Principles,* 3, art. 4, 'Of phenomena or experiments and what their use is in philosophy', etc. (Eng. tr. not supplied by Haldane and Ross).

22. *Rules,* 3, p. 7f; 4, p. 9f; 6, p. 24f; 9, pp. 28ff; 11, p. 33f, etc.; and *Method,* 2, pp. 91ff; 3, p. 98f.

23. See especially *Rules* 3 & 4 for the way in which Descartes combines *intuition* and *induction,* while recognising that no method can teach us how these operations are performed, for they are the simplest and most primary, pp. 5f, 9ff. Deduction of one thing from another is effected not by rules but by intuition, *Rules,* 10, p. 33. Coordination of this sort resembles what F. S. C. Northrop has called 'epistemic correlation', *The Logic of the Sciences and Humanities,* New York, 1947, ch. 7, and *Man, Nature and God,* New York, 1962, ch. 15. Cf. further pp. 26f, 90f.

24. *Method,* 4, p. 101.

25. N. Kemp Smith, *A Commentary to Kant's Critique of Pure Reason,* London, 1930, p. xxxix.

26. *Meditations,* 3, p. 161ff.

27. *Meditations,* 3, p. 160f; 6, pp. 186ff; *Principles,* 2, p. 254.

28. *Meditations,* 6, pp. 189ff; *Principles,* 2, p. 254f; 4, p. 301f. Cf. F. Broadie, *op. cit.,* pp. 59ff.

29. This was reinforced by the argument from the incompleteness of the thinking self, *Meditations,* 3, p. 165ff.

30. *Meditations,* 3, pp. 161ff, 170f; 4, pp. 171ff, 6, pp. 186ff. Cf. the definitions offered by Descartes in reply to objections (Everyman edition, p. 229f): 'By *objective reality of an idea* I understand the entity or being of the thing represented by the idea, in so far as this entity is in the idea; and, in the same manner, it may be called either an objective perfection or objective artifice *(artificium objectivum),* etc. For all that we conceive to be in the objects of the ideas is objectively in the ideas themselves. The same things are said to be *formally* in the objects of the ideas when they are in them such as we conceive them; and they are said to be in the objects *eminently* when they are not indeed such as we conceive them, but are so great that they can supply this defect by their excellence.'

31. *Rules,* 4, pp. 55ff, 61f; *Meditations,* 3, p. 164f; *Principles,* 1, p. 140f; 2, pp. 258ff, 260ff.

32. *Meditations,* 6, p. 191. In other words, Descartes insisted that what is capable of being grasped in mathematical forms is *real.*

33. *Principles,* 2, pp. 258ff.

34. A. D. Lindsay (Lord Lindsay of Birker), Introduction to Descartes, *A Discourse on Method,* Everyman edition, tr. by John Veitch, p. xix.

35. Descartes' concept of motion did supply a corrective by offering grounds for real and not just formal differentiation in matter, and so anticipated, as Einstein claimed, the notion of space which reconciles the geometric and kinematic points of view. Introduction to Max Jammer, *Concepts of Space,* New York, 1960, p. xiv; but, as Jammer shows, this was not taken up, pp. 38ff.

36. See the full text of *Principles,* 2–4, and the Eng. tr. of 4.188, p. 289.

37. Cf. J. D. Bernal, *Science in History,* Pelikan Edition, 1969, vol. 2, p. 447.

38. *Principles,* 3, p. 270f.

39. Cf. *Method,* 3, p. 98f.

40. Immanuel Kant, *Critique of Judgment,* tr. by J. H. Bernard, 1892, Introduction, sect. 5, p. 25.

41. Galileo Galilei, *Dialogues Concerning Two New Sciences,* tr. by H. Crew and A. de Salvio, New York, 1914.

42. John Herival, *The Background to Newton's Principia,* Oxford, 1965, p. 41.

43. 'Philosophy is written in that great book which ever lies open before our eyes – I mean the universe – but we cannot understand it if we do not first learn the language and grasp the symbols, in which it is written. This book is written in mathematical language, and the symbols are triangles, circles, and other geometrical figures, without whose help it is impossible to comprehend a single word of it; without which one wanders in vain through a dark labyrinth.' *Opere Complete di Galileo Galilei,* Florence, 1842ff, vol. 4, p. 171, cited by E. A. Burtt, *op. cit.,* p. 75.

44. See Burtt, *op. cit.,* pp. 76ff; and J. D. Bernal, *op. cit.,* vol. 2, p. 429f.

45. Cf. Einstein and Infeld, *op. cit.,* p. 92: 'Galileo formulated the problem of determining the velocity of light, but did not solve it. The

formulation of a problem is often more essential than its solution, which may be merely a matter of mathematical or experimental skill. To raise new questions, new possibilities, to regard old problems from a new angle, requires creative imagination and marks real advance in science.'

46. See Newton, *Opticks or A Treatise of the Reflections, Refractions, and Colours of Light,* 4th edit. 1730, Dover publication, New York, 1952, p. 404ff. Cf. F. S. C. Northrop, *The Logic of the Sciences and the Humanities,* New York, 1949, pp. 22ff.

47. Galileo Galilei, *Dialogue Concerning the two Chief World Systems – Ptolemaic and Copernican,* tr. by S. Drake, London, 1962. Galileo, however, retained Aristotle's phenomenalist and dualist epistemology, which was then modified and built into his System of the World by Newton.

48. See Burtt, *op. cit.,* ch. 6, pp. 162ff.

49. See Bacon's *Aphorisms,* 19, 22, 24, 26, 36, *Novum Organum, pars secunda, The Works of Francis Bacon,* collected and edited by J. Spedding, R. L. Ellis, and D. D. Heath, 1972, vol. 1.1, pp. 159ff. Cf. Newton, *Opticks,* p. 1: 'My design in this book is not to explain the properties of light by hypotheses, but to propose and prove them by reason and experiments.' Newton's much cited *hypotheses non fingo,* on the other hand, refers to his refusal to explain the mysterious cause of gravitation, and is not a rejection of the proper use of hypotheses, *Principia Mathematica,* edit. by F. Cajori, 1966 reprint, Berkeley and Los Angeles, vol. 2, p. 547, 'The General Scholium'.

50. J. Herival, *op. cit.,* p. 53; cf. from p. 42.

51. See Newton's communication to the Royal Society, *Philosophical Transactions of the Royal Society,* No. 80, Feb. 19, 1672, reprinted by H. S. Thayer in *Newton's Philosophy of Nature, Selections from His Writings,* New York & London, 1953, pp. 68ff; and Newton, *Opticks,* 4th edit., London, 1730, reprinted, London, 1931, with a Foreword by A. Einstein, and Introduction by E. T. Whittaker, pp. 339–375.

52. Burtt is surely right in saying, 'What Descartes had meant was that through a part of the brain a quite unextended substance came into effective relation with the realm of extension'. *Op. cit.,* p. 122f.

53. See Burtt, *op. cit.,* pp. 122ff, 180ff, 229ff. Cf. R. Boyle, *The Origin of Forms and Qualities,* 1666.

54. *Opticks,* pp. 134f, 370f.

55. *Philosophiae Naturalis Principia Mathematica,* tr. by Andrew Motte, 1729, revised and edited by Florian Cajori, Berkeley & Los Angeles, 1966 reprint, III, 'General Scholium', p. 544ff; *Opticks,* pp. 400ff; Preface to the second edition of the *Principia* by Roger Cotes, xxxiff.

56. *Principia,* p. vxiif; cf. *Opticks,* p. 131f, for this demonstration of other phenomena.

57. Cited in Sir David Brewster, *Memoirs of Sir Isaac Newton,* Edinburgh, 1850, vol. 1, p. 102.

58. *Principia,* pp. xviii, 546f; *Opticks,* p. 401f.

59. *Opticks*, p. 401: 'Such occult qualities put a stop to the improvement of natural philosophy, and therefore of late years have been rejected.' See also Cotes' preface, *Principia*, pp. xxviff.

60. *Principia*, pp. xxviiff; *Opticks*, p. 369f.

61. *Principia*, p. xviii; *Opticks*, p. 401f.

62. *Principia*, p. xxvii, italics added. Cf. here Leibniz's conception of the differential relation between God and the created universe, which once created necessarily is what it actually is. 'On the Ultimate Origin of Things', 1697 – *Leibniz Selections*, edit. by P. P. Wiener, New York, 1951, pp. 345ff.

63. See Newton's 'rules of reasoning in philosophy', at the beginning of Book III of the *Principia*, pp. 398ff.

64. *Principia*, p. xvii: 'Therefore geometry is founded in mechanical practice, and is nothing but that part of universal mechanics which accurately proposes and demonstrates the art of measuring.' This seems to anticipate Clerk Maxwell's notion of 'embodied mathematics' and the importance of mathematics in its bearing on 'physical relations', *Scientific Papers*, edit. by W. D. Niven, 1890, vol. 1, pp. 160, 187; *Treatise on Electricity and Magnetism*, 1873, preface; and Einstein's conception of geometry as a 'natural science' inseparable from physics and constituting its inner epistemological structure. *Sidelights on Relativity*. II. 'Geometry and Experience' – tr. by G. B. Jeffrey and W. Perrott, London, 1922; *Relativity, The Special and General Theory*, tr. by R. W. Lawson, New York, 1961, pp. 1ff.

65. *Opticks*, p. 369.

66. *Principia*, p. 192: 'In mathematics we are to investigate the quantities of forces with their proportions consequent upon any conditions supposed; then, when we enter upon physics we compare these proportions with the phenomena of nature, that we may know what conditions of those forces answer to the several kinds of attractive bodies. And this preparation being made, we argue more safely concerning the physical species, causes and proportions of the forces.' See also p. xviif, and *Opticks*, pp. 404–5.

67. A. Einstein, Foreword to the *Opticks* as reprinted in 1931, p. vii.

68. *Principia*, p. 550; and see the 4th rule of reasoning, p. 400; and further, the letter to Cotes, extracted by H. S. Thayer, *op. cit.*, p. 7.

69. *Principia*, p. 547, and *Opticks*, p. 369.

70. See Newton's letter to Oldenburg of 1672, cited in Thayer, *op. cit.*, p. 7f.

71. *Opticks*, p. 404f; see also *Principia*, xxf, and 398f.

72. *Opticks*, p. 369.

73. *Principia*, p. 547. Cf. p. 400: 'In experimental philosophy we are to look upon propositions inferred by general induction from phenomena as accurately or very nearly true, notwithstanding any contrary hypotheses that may be imagined, till such time as other phenomena occur, by which they may either be made more accurate, or liable to exceptions. This rule must follow, that the argument of induction may not be evaded by hypotheses.'

74. See Newton's letters to Cotes and Oldenburg cited by Thayer, *op. cit.*, pp. 5–8.

75. Thayer, *op. cit.*, pp. 82–89, and see Thayer's own notes and further references, pp. 192ff. Cf. further *Opticks*, p. 244: ' . . . And in this respect the science of colours becomes a speculation as truly mathematical as any other part of opticks.'

76. *Opticks*, pp. 339ff.

77. *Opticks*, p. 131f.

78. 'Hypotheses ought to be applied only in the explanation of the properties of things, and not made use of in *determining* them; except in so far as they may furnish experiments.' Cited from a letter of Newton to Oldenburg, Thayer, *op. cit.*, p. 5f. See also Newton's *Opera Omnia*, edit. by Samuel Horsley, London, 1779 *et seq.*, vol. iv, pp. 314ff.

79. *Principia*, p. 398f.

80. *Principia*, p. 399. The importance of the analogy of nature for inductive operations was early noted by John Locke, *An Essay Concerning Human Understanding*, 4.16.12, and George Berkeley, *Siris*, sect. 252, who called it 'a grammar for the understanding of nature'.

81. E. A. Burtt, *op. cit.*, p. 226.

82. *Principia*, xvii: 'I wish we could derive the rest of the phenomena of nature by the same kind of reasoning from mechanical principles . . . but I hope the principles here laid down will afford some light either to that or some truer method of philosophy.' Cf. also pp. 244, 302, 400; and Burtt, *op. cit.*, pp. 212f, 221f; and Jammer, *op. cit.*, pp. 94ff.

83. S. L. Jaki, *The Relevance of Physics*, 2nd edit., Chicago and London, 1970, p. 63.

84. *Principia*, p. 21.

85. *Principia*, pp. 11f, 29f, 36ff, 130ff, 249ff, 488ff. See also the notes of Cajori, pp. 653ff, and of Herival, *op. cit.*, pp. 17, 32.

86. See especially Newton's exposition of his method in *De quadratura curvarum*, 1704, and F. Cajori, *A History of the Conceptions of Limits and Fluxions in Great Britain*, Chicago and London, 1919, pp. 2–32.

87. Cf. A. Einstein, *The World as I See It*, tr. by Alan Harris, London, 1935, pp. 147–50.

88. *Opticks*, p. 401f.

89. Cf. Newton's preface to the first edition of the *Principia*: 'The solution of these problems is required from mechanics, and by geometry the use of them, *when so solved*, is shown.' P. xvii, italics added. For instances, see p. 488. Cf. also Cajori, p. 654f, and Bernal, *op. cit.*, p. 487f.

90. *Principia*, p. 13f.; and cf. Jammer, *op. cit.*, p. 95f.

91. J. D. Bernal, *op. cit.*, p. 488.

92. But cf. query 30 in the *Opticks*, p. 374f.

93. *Principia*, p. 8.

94. *Principia*, p. 6.

95. Cf. Jammer, *op. cit.*, pp. 99f, 103f.

96. *Principia*, p. 6f.
97. This is Einstein's way of interpreting Newton's thought in his Foreword to Max Jammer, *op. cit.*, p. xivf.
98. 'But because the parts of space cannot be seen, or distinguished from one another by our senses, therefore in their stead we use sensible measures of them. For from the positions and distances of things from any body considered as immovable, we define all places; and then with respect to such places, we estimate all motions, considering bodies as transferred from some of those places into others. And so, instead of absolute places and motions we use relative ones; and that without any inconvenience in common affairs.' *Principia*, p. 6.
99. 'Wherefore relative quantities are not the quantities themselves, whose names they bear (i.e. 'time' and 'space'), but those sensible measures of them (either accurate or inaccurate), which are commonly used instead of the measured quantities themselves.' *Principia*, p. 11.
100. 'As the order of the parts of time is immutable, so also is the order of the parts of space. Suppose those parts to be moved out of their places, and they will be moved (if the expression may be allowed) out of themselves. For times and places are, as it were, the places as well of themselves as of other things. All things are placed in time as to order of succession and in space as to order of situation. It is from their essence or nature that they are places, and that the primary places of things should be movable is absurd. These are therefore absolute places, and translations out of those are the only absolute motions.' *Principia*, p. 8.
101. See the definition iv, *Principia*, p. 2; and Einstein and Infeld, *op. cit.*, p. 10f.
102. Compare the definitions, *Principia*, pp. 1ff, with the analysis of the scholium, pp. 7ff; and see Jammer, *op. cit.*, p. 97.
103. *Principia*, pp. 7–9.
104. *Loc. cit.*
105. *Principia*, p. 12, also p. 8f. Cf. Burtt, *op. cit.*, pp. 249ff.
106. Cf. Einstein: 'We can see indeed from Newton's formulation of it that the concept of absolute space, which comprised that of absolute rest, made him feel uncomfortable; he realised that there seemed to be nothing in experience corresponding to this last concept.' *The World as I See It*, p. 135.
107. See again Einstein, *op. cit.*, pp. 134ff, 146ff.
108. See the first two rules of reasoning, *Principia*, p. 398; and the preface to the second edition, pp. xxff; and cf. Jaki, *op. cit.*, pp. 345ff.
109. Cf. A. N. Whitehead's discussion of this role of time and space in his essay 'The Anatomy of Some Scientific Ideas', *The Aims of Education and Other Essays*, New York, 1929, pp. 180ff.
110. A. Einstein, *op. cit.*, pp. 135ff, 150ff.
111. *Ibid.*, p. 133f.
112. From Einstein's Foreword to Max Jammer, *Concepts of Space*, p. xiv.

113. The minimum nature of this theoretic component (demanded by Newton's first and second rules of reasoning: 'We are to admit no more causes of natural things than such as are both true and sufficient to explain their appearances', and, 'Therefore to the same natural effects we must, as far as possible, assign the same causes', *Principia*, p. 398) was clearly one of the primary reasons why Newton declined to make hypotheses, since the more they are employed the wider the gap between the theoretic and empirical components of scientific structure. Cf. here A. N. Whitehead, *op. cit.*, p. 218.

114. *Principia*, p. 547.

115. *Principia*, pp. 543ff.

116. *Principia*, p. 544f: 'It is the dominion of a spiritual being which constitutes a God; a true, supreme, or imaginary dominion makes a true, supreme, or imaginary God. And from his true dominion it follows that the true God is a living, intelligent, and powerful Being; and, from his other perfections, that he is supreme, or most perfect. He is eternal and infinite, omnipotent and omniscient; that is, his duration reaches from eternity to eternity; his presence from infinity to infinity; he governs all things and knows all things that are or can be done. He is not eternity and infinity, but eternal and infinite; he is not duration or space, but he endures and is present. He endures for ever, and is everywhere present; and, by existing always and everywhere, he constitutes duration and space.' Cf. Jammer, *op. cit.*, p. 108ff.

117. *Opticks*, pp. 370, 403.

118. *Principia*, p. 544f; *Opticks*, p. 400f. Cf. also Cotes' preface, *Principia*, p. xxviif. Newton explicitly rejected the pantheistic idea that God is the soul of the world, *Principia*, p. 544; *Opticks*, p. 403.

119. *Principia*, pp. xxxif, 544, 546f; *Opticks*, p. 369.

120. *Principia*, p. xxxii.

121. *Principia*, pp. xxvii, xxxif, 545f; *Opticks*, p. 403; Letters to Richard Bentley, Thayer, *op. cit.*, pp. 47ff, 53, 57f; cf. 65fff.

122. *Principia*, p. xxvi, xxxif, 544ff.

123. *Principia*, p. xxxii: 'Without all doubt this world, so diversified with that variety of forms and motions we find in it, could arise from nothing but the perfectly free will of God directing and presiding over all. From this fountain it is that those laws which we call laws of nature flowed, in which there appear many traces indeed of the most wise contrivance, but not the least shadow of necessity.'

124. *Principia*, p. 545. The italics are Newton's. Cf. also the passage cited by Sir David Brewster, in which Newton spoke of God as 'containing in himself all things as their principle and *place*'! *Op. cit.*, 11, p. 154.

125. Thus Einstein, *The World as I See It*, p. 152.

126. See the notes of Cajori to the General Scholium, *op. cit.*, p. 670.

127. *Principia*, p. 545. The following sentence, however, in Newton's text seems to make this ambiguous: 'It is allowed by all that the Supreme

God exists necessarily, and by the same necessity exists *always* and *everywhere'*, for *always* and *everywhere* are used univocally of God and time and space.

128. This was Einstein's way of expressing it, Jammer, *op. cit.*, p. xv.

129. *Principia*, pp. 7ff, 20, 419. See also the passages cited by Brewster, *op. cit.*, 11, pp. 154, 349.

130. *Principia*, pp. xxviiff; *Opticks*, pp. 369ff.

131. *Opticks*, p. 370. In fact, every true step in natural philosophy brings us *nearer* to a knowledge of the first cause, even though no step brings us immediately to knowledge of God, *ibid;* cf. p. 405.

132. *Principia*, pp. xxvii, 544, 546f; *Opticks*, pp. 369f, 400ff.

133. *Principia*, p. 546.

134. *Principia*, p. xxvi; *Opticks*, p. 402.

135. The point Newton felt so intensely is that which A. N. Whitehead has expressed well in *The Function of Reason*, 1929: 'The universe, as construed solely in terms of efficient causation of purely physical interconnections, presents sheer, insoluble contradiction.' 1969, edit., p. 25. 'A satisfactory cosmology must explain the interweaving of efficient and final causation.' p. 28.

136. *Opticks*, p. 402. Cf. the discussion by Stanley L. Jaki, *op. cit.*, p. 429f.

137. Letter to Bentley, Thayer, *op. cit.*, p. 48f. See also the second letter to Bentley, p. 52f; and *Opticks*, p. 352f.

138. The third letter to Bentley, Thayer, *op. cit.*, p. 55f; and *Principia*, pp. 543f, 546f.

139. *Opticks*, p. 403.

140. Pierre Simon de Laplace, *Méchanique céleste*, 1799, xv, p. 324. This remark was made in response to Napoleon: *Je n'ai pas besoin de cet hypothèse.*

141. See F. Cajori, *op. cit.*, p. 678, who refers here to Weierstrass and Poincaré. Today, however, mention must be made of the relevance of the Gödelian theorem, in its demand for open structures in all logico-deductive systems of a sufficient richness, and thus also in mechanical systems. See J. R. Lucas, 'Mind, Machines and Gödel', *Philosophy*, vol. 36, 1961, pp. 112ff; and S. L. Jaki, *The Relevance of Physics*, pp. 52ff, 141ff; and *Brain, Mind and Computers*, New York, 1969.

142. *Opticks*, p. 369f.

143. Cf. my discussion of this question in *Divine and Contingent Order*, 1981.

144. Brewster, *op. cit.*, 11, p. 154.

145. G. Berkeley, *Of the Principles of Human Knowledge*, I. 117; *Complete Works*, edit. by A. C. Fraser, 1901, vol. 1, p. 323. See also vol. I, pp. 190, 319ff, 519ff; II. pp. 15f; III. pp. 231ff, 253ff.

146. *A Collection of Papers which passed between the late learned Mr Leibniz and Dr Clarke*, London, 1717. See the reproduction of the main passages in P. P. Wiener, *Leibniz Selections*, New York, 1951, pp. 216ff. For accounts of Leibniz's concept of space, see B. Russell, *The Philosophy*

of Leibniz, Cambridge, 1900, pp. 118ff; and Max Jammer, *op. cit.*, pp. 112ff.

147. That is, as Leibniz claimed, in the direction of Spinoza's thought, *op. cit.*, p. 220.

148. Thus there results the so-called 'Galilean principle of relativity' – see Einstein and Infeld, *op. cit.*, pp. 5ff, 158.

149. F. S. C. Northrop, *The Meeting of East and West, An Inquiry Concerning World Understanding*, New York & London, 1964, pp. 74ff, 282ff. Northrop's discussion is particularly illuminating for the relation between Newton's ideas and those of John Locke.

150. In other words, Locke examined and justified the place of 'sensible measures' presupposed in Newton's mathematical time and space, from which his inductive operations started, and to which they returned in deductive experimental verification.

151. John Locke, *An Essay Concerning the Human Understanding*, 5th edit., 1706, 11.1.2.

152. *Ibid.*, 11.1.24; 11.4f.

153. *Ibid.*, 1.2.1f; 11.1.2, 22ff.

154. 'The Epistle to the Reader', and 11.21.73.

155. This was the view advocated by Thomas Hobbes, *Treatise of Human Nature*, 1650, 11.4.

156. *Ibid.*, 11.23.1ff.

157. *Ibid.*, 11.21.73.

158. *Ibid.*, 11.8.7ff.

159. *Ibid.*, 1.2.15; 11.1.2ff.

160. *Ibid.*, 11.1.23–25; 2.2f; 8.7ff, 16ff; 26.1ff; 31.1ff; cf. IV.11.1f.

161. *Ibid.*, 11.23.1ff, 15ff; 27.1–26; IV.4.1ff.

162. See especially 11.27.23–26.

163. Regarded in this way, the fourth book of Locke's *Essay Concerning Human Understanding*, in which he discussed knowledge as the perception of the agreement or disagreement of ideas, is more consistent with the new theory of ideas expounded in book two, than is usually accepted.

164. George Berkeley, *Commonplace Book, Berkeley's Complete Words*, edit. by A. C. Fraser, 1901, vol. 1, pp. 29f, 33f, 63f; *Of Principles of Human Knowledge*, I.8–81, 133, vol. I, pp. 276ff, 298, 333; *Three Dialogues between Hylas and Philonous*, vol. I, pp. 408ff.

165. David Hume, *A Treatise of Human Nature*, edit. by L. A. Selby-Bigge, 1967 edit., I. iv, sect. 2, 5, 6, especially pp. 252ff; cf. also pp. 634ff.

166. *Op. cit.*, I. iii.i4, pp. 155ff; *Enquiry Concerning Human Understanding*, edit. by L. A. Selby-Bigge, 1902, sect. 4–8, pp. 25ff, 40ff, 60fff.

167. *Treatise*, I.iii.8, p. 103. The place that Hume gave to *imagination* by which we are able to pass beyond our impressions suggests a transcending of his empiricism, and helped him to explain the manner 'in which we reason beyond our immediate impressions, and conclude that such particular causes have such particular effects'. I.iii.14, p. 155. Cf. also I.iv.7, p. 267f. Hume could also speak in this

connection of a 'determination of the mind', I.iii.14, p. 167, which appears rather like an anticipation of Kant's way of thinking.

168. If the interlocutor Philo in Hume's *Dialogues Concerning Natural Religion* represents Hume's own deepest judgment, as seems likely, then Philo's argument in Part 9 would confirm the fact that Hume accepted the reality of causal necessity in nature even though it could not be established on strictly empirical grounds.

169. Cf. Hume's admitted dilemma in regard to the problem of the self or personal identity, in the appendix to the *Treatise*, p. 636. See also Norman Kemp Smith, *The Philosophy of David Hume*, 1941, chs. xxi and xxii for a critical appreciation of Hume's doctrine of natural belief.

For a more positive assessment of Hume's contribution, see F. S. C. Northrop, *The Meeting of East and West*, p. 301.

170. Cf. F. S. C. Northrop, *op. cit.*, pp. 193ff, 301f.

171. *Critique of Pure Reason*, tr. by N. Kemp Smith, Edinburgh, 1929, B XIII, XIV, A 125, B 163, A 645, B 673.

172. *CPR*, A 127.

173. *CPR*, A 126. Cf. Kant's discussion in *Prolegomena to any Future Metaphysics*, edit. by P. Carus, Chicago, 1902, of the question 'How is the science of nature possible?', pp. 50ff, and especially pp. 79ff.

174. *CPR*, A 651–B 679; cf. A 542–B 570.

175. *CPR*, A 647–B 675. 'Reason does not beg here but commands.' A 653–B 681.

176. *CPR*, B 139.

177. *CPR*, B 138.

178. *CPR*, B 137: 'An object is that in the concept of which the manifold of a given intuition is united.' Cf. also *Prolegomena*, pp. 42ff.

179. Gerd Buchdahl, *Metaphysics and the Philosophy of Science*, 1969, p. 640. For a defence of Kant's view of the object in a more realist sense, see F. Brentano, *The True and the Evident*, London, 1966, pp. 9ff.

180. *CPR*, A 538–B 566.

181. *CPR*, A 249, B 306–309, A 257, A 289. Cf. also *Prolegomena*, pp. 77, 111f.

182. *CPR*, A 566–B 594. This also follows from Kant's rejection of intellectual intuition, *CPR*, B 307, A 286.

183. *CPR*, B 307–309, A 286, B 343, A 287, B 344.

184. *CPR*, B 310–312, A 286–289, B 343–347. 'The concept of the noumenon is, therefore, not the concept of an object, but is a problem unavoidably bound up with the limitation of sensibility.' B 344. Cf. the way Kant expresses this in *Prolegomena*, p. 72f: 'They serve as it were only to decipher appearances, that we may be able to read them as experience . . . Beyond this they are arbitrary combinations, without objective reality, and we can neither cognise their possibility *a priori*, nor verify their reference to objects, let alone make it intelligible by an example.'

185. *CPR*, A 289; and cf. A 565–567 or B 593–595.

186. *CPR*, A 546–B 574.
187. *CPR*, B 300.
188. This is what happened in Kant's treatment of 'the practical reason'. See *The Groundwork of the Metaphysic of Morals*, reproduced as 'Fundamental Principles . . .' in T. K. Abbott, *Kant's Theory of Ethics*, 3rd edit., London, 1883, pp. 78ff; and *The Critique of the Practical Reason, ibid.*, pp. 131ff, 200, 231ff. Cf. the note by H. J. Paton, *The Moral Law*, p. 145, n. 120:' To comprehend is to make intelligible *a priori.*'
189. *CPR*, B 130–140. It is consistent with this that Kant's notion of truth should shift from the truth of being to cognitive truth, 'conformity with the laws of understanding', B 350, A 294. Cf. also *Prolegomena*, pp. 45, 103, 152.
190. *CPR*, B 138. Cf. *Prolegomena*, pp. 36ff.
191. *CPR*, B X–XII, A 221, B 271, A 240, B 300, A 713–14 & B 741–55, A 734–B 762; cf. *Prolegomena*, pp. 35ff, 146.
192. G. Buchdahl, *op. cit.*, p. 555. Cf. also pp. 572, 626ff.
193. Cf. the valuable discussion of Kant's notion of 'construction' by Jaako Hintikka, 'Kant on the Mathematical Method', *The Monist*, vol. 51, 3, 1967, pp. 352–375, in which he takes his cue from *CPR*, A 713–B 741, and argues that for Kant 'construction is tantamount to the transition from a general concept to an intuition which represents the concept, provided that this is done without recourse to experience'. But does he not construe Kant's 'construction' in terms of 'setting-out', rather than 'setting-out' in terms of 'construction' – i.e. read Kant too closely in line with Euclid, Aristotle, Descartes and Newton, at the expense of playing down the force of the 'Copernican revolution' (at least until he comes to pp. 372–3)? His desire to push Kant into a more operational mode of thought is certainly in line with post-Kantian developments.
194. *CPR*, Preface to the second edition B XIII.
195. This is forgotten by those who, as we noted earlier, mistakenly want to father technological or instrumentalist science upon Bacon. Science is power, Bacon held, but only in so far as the inquirer approaches nature humbly as a servant or a child. On the other hand, he showed that 'our steps must be guided by a clue, and the whole way from the very first perception of the senses must be laid out upon a sure plan'. *Instauratio magna, prooem.* Cf. *Theological Science*, p. 71.
196. *CPR*, B XIII.
197. *Loc. cit.*
198. See Israel Scheffler, *Science and Subjectivity*, Indianapolis, New York and Kansas City, 1967, p. 13, who speaks of this as the *paradox of categorisation:* 'If my categories of thought determine what I observe, then what I observe provides no independent control over my thought. On the other hand, if my categories of thought do not determine what I observe, then what I observe must be uncategor-

ised, that is to say, formless and nondescript – hence again incapable of providing any test of my thought.' See also p. 39f.

199. F. S. C. Northrop, *The Meeting of East and West*, p. 198.

200. *Groundwork*, Abbott, *op. cit.*, p. 72f.

201. *Ibid.*, p. 65.

202. 'Hence the distinction between the laws of the natural system to which the will is subject, and of a natural system which is subject to will (as far as its relation to its free actions is concerned) rests on this, that in the former the objects must be the causes of the ideas which determine the will; whereas in the latter the will is the cause of the objects; so that its causality has its determining principle solely in the pure faculty of reason, which may therefore be called a "pure practical reason".' *Critical Examination of the Practical Reason, op. cit.*, p. 134.

203. *Crit. of Pract. R.*, pp. 90ff, 101, 133f, 136f, 144ff.

204. *Crit. of Pract. R.*, pp. 90f, 131ff, 139f, 230; cf. also *Critique of Judgment*, edit. by J. H. Bernard, 1892, London, p. 403. This implies, of course, that the notions of immortality, freedom and God are no more than postulates, regulative ideas or limiting concepts, for they necessarily lack the intuition of being. *Crit. of Pract. R.*, pp. 218ff, 229ff; *Crit. of Judg.*, p. 402f: 'For determining our ideas of the supersensible we have no material whatsoever, and we must derive this latter from things in the world of sense, which is absolutely inadequate for such an object.' Cf. The British Academy lecture by W. H. Walsh on 'Kant's Moral Theology', *Proceedings of the British Academy*, vol. xlix, 1963, p. 282f.

205. *Crit. of Pract. R.*, pp. 88f, 105, 112f, 129ff, 136ff, 144. This is much the same notion of 'objective' as Kant advanced in *CPR*. Cf. also *Prolegomena*, p. 56: 'Objective validity and universality for everybody are equivalent terms.'

206. *Crit. of Pract. R.*, pp. 148ff, 157f, 232ff.

207. *CPR*, A 632–642 & B 661–670.

208. *Groundwork*, pp. 65–84.

209. *Groundwork*, p. 45; cf. p. 75; *Prolegomena*, p. 113f. Cf. H. B. Acton, *Kant's Moral Philosophy*, London, 1970, pp. 7f, 41f.

210. *Groundwork*, pp. 20ff, 44ff, 60ff, 75ff.

211. *Crit. of Pract. R.*, pp. 140f, 216ff.

212. This is particularly evident in the theology that stemmed from Albrecht Ritschl, with its stress upon value-judgments *(Werturteile)* which in accordance with the Kantian emphasis upon *practical use* are understood as 'help-conceptions' *(Hilfsvorstellungen)*. That is, in the absence of theoretic and objective knowledge of God, we rely on practical reasons for belief, so that theological concepts are to be construed, not in terms of their ontological reference, but in terms of their moral use. Cf. Kant's term, *fürwahrhalten*, W. H. Walsh, *op. cit.*, p. 283.

213. This took place rapidly as soon as 'Occam's razor' was brought in to sheer away the noumenon as a useless empirical postulate – thus in different ways, R. Avenarius, H. Helmholz, E. Mach, and H. Vaihinger.

214. Again this is evident in Ritschl's complete detachment of knowledge of God from knowledge of the world, his rejection of ontology, and therefore his severing of the connection between theology and metaphysics and theology and science. It is, then, to the sharp division between the religious and the scientific, reposing upon the Kantian distinction between the practical and the theoretic, that we must trace the strange denigration of scientific theology. Contrast James Denney: 'The separation of the religious and the scientific means in the end the separation of the religious and the true; and this means that religion dies among true men.' *Studies in Theology,* London, 1894, p. 15.

215. H. B. Acton, *Kant's Moral Philosophy,* pp. 35ff.

216. F. S. C. Northrop, *The Meeting of East and West,* p. 201; cf. also p. 214ff.

217. Bertrand Russell, *My Philosophical Development,* London, 1959, p. 16.

218. M. Planck, *Wissenschaftliche Selbstbiographie,* Leipzig, 1948, cited from Ilse Rosenthal-Schneider, 'Presuppositions and Anticipations in Einstein's Physics', P. A. Schilpp, *Albert Einstein: Philosopher-Scientist,* New York, 1949, p. 136f. Max Planck's indebtedness to Kant is very clear in his influential work, *Where is Science Going?* London, 1933, to which Einstein wrote an appreciative foreword.

CHAPTER II

*The Integration of Form in Natural and in Theological Science**

IN RECENT years a distinct shift has been taking place in the philosophy of science, which is now becoming very noticeable. Not so long ago when one asked a natural scientist to give an account of his scientific method, it often became evident that he had not reflected very deeply about it, and just as often he tended to put forward a theory of science which did not seem to accord very well with the empirico-theoretical steps he had taken in making his discoveries,[1] but in which he fell back upon earlier positivist ideas derived through his own theoretical upbringing, not least the uncritical assumption that all things in the last analysis are capable of logico-causal explanation in purely physico-chemical terms. This sort of thing has certainly been reflected in many of the professional philosophers of science whose names are so familiar to us, especially those who have produced textbooks on scientific method for students.[2] The situation is rather different today, for in the rapidly advancing knowledge of science, not only of physics but particularly of biology and the neural sciences, the whole concept of

*Presented to the Jubilee Symposium of the Académie Internationale de Philosophie des Sciences, at Drongen-Gent, Belgium, September 11, 1972

science itself is in process of change. This is very apparent, for example, in the recent work of Sir John C. Eccles, *Facing Reality*, sub-titled *Philosophical Adventures of a Brain Scientist*,[3] in which he has been forced by the very nature of his subject-matter, the interaction of brain and conscious mind, to reflect deeply upon what he has been doing, and forced as he proceeded to come to terms with the reconstruction of science itself demanded by 'the emergence of properties which are of a different kind from anything that has been as yet related to matter with its properties as defined in physics and chemistry'.[4] What Eccles has in mind throughout is the impasse created by what Schrödinger called the 'exclusion principle',[5] the impossible and tragic distortion of our efforts to give an account of the world when we leave out 'the primary reality' of our *conscious experience*; but he also has in mind the effect upon science itself of taking the experiencing subject fully into account. While this way of thinking involves at least 'two kinds of reality'[6] – namely the primary reality of our conscious experience and the secondary reality of all the world revealed by perceptual experience – it necessarily rejects any disjunction between them, for it develops a concept of the universe as structured in various levels of reality which does not permit the reduction of one level to determination solely in terms of another level.[7] And so Eccles writes: 'It can be predicted that, when developments of science have been brought about by its rebuilding, science itself will have been completely transformed, so the present dogmatism of reductionism has no relevance or meaning. The revolution of science that must come about in order to account for the existence of matter in a world of conscious experience will result in an understanding so far transcending our present inadequate concepts that our present science, even its most sophisticated aspects, will appear as primitive and naive.'[8]

Behind these old views now being superceded lies the dualist bifurcation of nature which has resulted not only in the extremes of objectivist positivism and subjectivist idealism, materialist verificationism and existentialist detachment from externality, but therein an approach to science which is unable even to formulate properly the basic problems that now challenge us. This means that the real issues at stake can be clarified only along with a profound revision of the first principles of science. In order to get into clear focus what is involved, it may be helpful to glance at the two conceptions of science which have prevailed hitherto in western culture, which we shall speak of as Greek (including mediaeval) science and modern science.

Greek science aimed at determinate, indubitable knowledge in which we penetrate through the appearances of things to their underlying realities and thus ground understanding of them upon their essential natures. Science of this kind is concerned with the necessary, the universal, the unchanging, and the essential, in contrast to the contingent, the particular, the fleeting, and the accidental. It thus envisages a deep split in the cosmos between a realm of being and a realm of phenomena, or between the intelligible and the sensible, and correspondingly a cleavage between knowledge and opinion, contemplation *(theoria)* and practice; but at the same time it develops cognitive instruments by means of which we may abstract from the world of sensible phenomena the rational forms of the unchanging world of essential reality in which they fleetingly participate or which they embody or somehow reflect, and in terms of which we reach universal, necessary and true, that is scientific, knowledge. Greek science was thus thoroughly *essentialist* in character: it rested upon ultimate and unchanging foundations. As a classical example of this kind of science we may refer to Aristotle's *Posterior Analytics*.

Modern science, on the other hand, is directed to the realm of observable phenomena, to what is contingent, which it regards as accessible to empirical and intelligible inquiry, without reference to any 'metaphysical' realm of essential reality, and therefore without recourse to so-called 'occult causes'. It is concerned with space and time, with the concrete and the particular as well as the general, with bodies in motion and all the manifestation of nature, develops mathematical instruments with which to analyse and quantify their interconnections, and so seeks to 'explain' their causal sequences in terms of rational coordinations or equations. At the same time it tries to reach high-level concepts of the greatest generality through which to coordinate the universe of multiform phenomenality in terms of simple, universal, differential law. Science of this kind makes no claim to explain the ultimate nature of causes, but is content to offer an account of phenomena only in respect of their external mechanical connections apart from any sub-structure, thus completely ignoring, or methodologically bracketing off from its purview, not only the realm of mind or consciousness but also any concept of being or substance as refractory to its analytical method. It works, therefore, with theories or mental constructs of an exploratory or provisional kind which cannot be identified with ontic structures in nature and need not be, even partially, descriptive of the real world. Rather are they convenient functional arrangements of observational concepts, which are operationally defined and experimentally controlled, but which as such are strictly neither true nor false. In the nature of the case, the structures of the world which this science discovers reduce in the last analysis to the economical sets of relations or equations it has developed in its account of phenomenal sequences and their particulate nature, and they are regarded as objective in the sense that they are necessarily the same for all men and independent of the observer.[9] Thus modern science also envisages a deep split in the universe, not only between the phenomenal and the noumenal, subject and object, but between structure and substance, form and being, and correspondingly a split between operational theories together with their highly sophisticated formalisations, on the one hand, and the heterogeneous universe of empirical reality, on the other hand, which it conjoins only in an inorganic pragmatic way as it seeks through its theoretical tools to reduce the world to orderly understanding and to harness it for the use of man. Modern science is thus essentially *instrumentalist,* for here the true being or underlying reality of essentialist science is resolved, for all practical purposes, simply into the most economical coordination of scientific relations or facts. As a classical example of this kind of science we may refer to *The Science of Mechanics* by Ernst Mach.[10]

Admittedly, this contrast between the Greek and modern conceptions of science is somewhat overdrawn, for there are overlapping features. Greek science was not without its hypothetical and experimental elements, and it certainly made important discoveries about the contingent universe, for example in astronomy, optics and even mechanics, while its mediaeval form was deeply affected by the basic concept, introduced through the Christian theologians of Alexandria, of the inherent intelligibility of contingent and created reality. Moreover, in the Epicurean and Aristotelian idea that there is nothing in mind which was not first in the senses, Greek and mediaeval sciences carried within it the seeds of modern positivism. Modern science, on the other hand, in its very foundations, laid by Galileo and Newton, was evidently concerned to develop theories which aim at describing the real world, and which attempt, through theoretic linkage with structures inherent in nature to account for the appearances of things.[11] Thus even though it developed into observationist and positivist science, a profound element of essentialism remained in the distinction between primary and secondary qualities which clearly went back to Greek roots. Beneath everything else, it is of course the deep-going dualism found in both which brackets them together, yet it is just there that they were bound to diverge, for it was inevitable that relatively greater stress should be laid on one or other side of the split. In Greek science, where the stress is upon unchanging foundations of knowledge, there takes place a reduction of contingent phenomena upwards (a sort of *Aufhebung*) into the necessary and essential natures of things. In modern science, however, when the stress is laid upon the empirical world of contingency and change, there takes place a reduction downwards in a physicalist direction from phenomena to atomic particles, for the theoretic structures it develops are essentially pragmatic and instrumentalist in nature. It is owing to the intrinsic nature of this dualism that modern science, until recent times at any rate, has tended to exhibit so widely the typically positivist conjunction of conventionalism and materialism. This is very evident in the thought of Ernst Mach, although with his critique of Newtonian notions of space and time, deep changes are clearly on the way. Nevertheless, the hang-over of conventionalism and positivism, not least in those philosophers of science influenced by 'the Vienna Circle' stemming from Mach, in spite of the epoch-making changes in science that have taken place this century, indicates that it is an inveterate and pervasive dualism which not only presents the deepest problem in the historic conceptions of science, but still constitutes the difficult recalcitrant element in the advance of modern science and philosophy to working out the implications of the revolution now going on in the foundations of science.

It is significant to note that modern science, as I have been describing it (largely in terms of analytical mechanics), was already being undermined in the nineteenth century along several lines. First, Faraday's discovery of the electromagnetic field and Maxwell's successful account of it in partial differential equations began to break down the belief that all phenomena can be explained mechanically, that is, in terms of forces acting between material particles. Thus as Einstein and Infeld have said: 'The formulation of these equations is the most important event in physics since Newton's time, not only because of their wealth of content, but also because they form a pattern for a new type of law . . . Maxwell's equations are laws representing the *structure* of the field.'[12] The realisation that a continuous field, thus defined with physical properties and a precise structure, is something real, undermined the classical concept of matter and was the starting-point for the new field-physics.[13] Then, mathematicians, from Gauss's overthrow of the supposed *a priori* nature of three-dimensional Euclidean space to the elaboration of four-dimensional geometries of space and time by Lobachewski, Riemann, and others, opened up the way for

Minkowski's discovery of space-time and for the concept of the *metrical field* in which geometrical structures are found to be intrinsic to the spatio-temporal continuum, which quickly connected up with the new concept of objective structure in field-physics.[14] And further, the advances of biology brought insistently to the fore heterogeneous features in living organisms which cannot be quantified, and which resist mathematical formalisations that can compound only like with like. This is a finding which still holds good in spite of the enormous advances of biochemistry and molecular biology in physico-chemical analysis, and which requires some concept of *multivariable organic order* or *open field-structure* – something that is not without wider relevance in the whole range of science, as has become evident today in the emergence of system-theory.[15] The cumulative effect of these developments in the nineteenth and early twentieth century was to call in question the split between structure and substance, form and matter, and to provide evidence for the grounding of scientific knowledge in the objective structures and transformations of the real world, even though knowledge could only take hypothetical and provisional form.[16]

It was of course only with quantum theory and relativity theory that the gigantic revolution in science really began to set in, for these developments demanded, not simply a modification of the classical laws of motion as formulated by Newton, but a rethinking of the way in which the first principles of science are reached and established, together with a logical reconstruction of the theoretic basis of science itself, from which its hypothetico–deductive operations may be carried out. Both of these theories made it clear that 'there is no logical bridge between the phenomena and their theoretical principles', thus overthrowing the idea of the eighteenth and nineteenth century physicists that the fundamental concepts and postulates of physics 'could be deduced from experience by "abstraction" – that is to say by logical means',[17] but at the same time they showed that there is a real, and not just a symbolic, conventional, or pragmatic, relation in the coordination between scientific concepts and experience, most evident in the congruence or parallelism between mathematical equations and the operations of nature. These enormous scientific advances, then, imply and rest upon a foundation in which the theoretical and empirical components are coordinated in a different way from that conceived in the foundations of classical modern science.

There is certainly a relative difference in this respect between relativity theory and quantum theory, at least in its statistical form, for the spatial functions in the equations of the latter describe the physical realities of nature only indirectly through the probabilities of their occurrence or change in time,[18] and do not represent the field-laws of their material and dynamic structure.[19] Quantum theory thus still retains something of the dualism inherent in the earlier conceptions of science. Nevertheless, both relativity theory and quantum theory involve operations and coordinations that are incompatible with the principles of Newtonian mechanics. However, the break with classical physics which they involved was achieved in such a way that the new forms of law to which they gave rise merge into classical laws (i.e. field-laws into mechanical laws) under certain limiting conditions. Thus, as Einstein has pointed out, with the introduction of his quantum-hypothesis Planck 'dethroned classical physics as applied to the case where sufficiently small masses are moved at sufficiently low speeds and high rates of acceleration, so that today the laws of motion propounded by Galileo and Newton can only be allowed validity as limited laws'.[20] But now another important fact emerges. Since the basic theories of classical physics are not like *ad hoc* hypotheses that are kicked away once they have done their work in enabling science to advance to a higher level (for example, the service of 'ether' to the 'physical properties' of space),[21] but are actually regained in rigorously reconstructed forms from that higher level, there is introduced into science a many-layered or multilevelled structure parallel to the hierarchy of levels discovered at the same time in nature (including man himself). And this, as has already been noted, is a principal feature in the transformation of the sciences now going on, one to which we must give further consideration in due course.

In the removal of these difficulties and contradictions that arose between field-physics and classical physics, attention had to be given to the dualism inherent in the fundamental concepts of modern science, for it was clearly there that the root of the trouble lay, but this meant that attention had to be given to the general structure of science over against the structure of the universe as a whole, as an entire intelligible system. That was the immense task to which Einstein addressed himself: a thorough remodelling of our understanding of the universe, together with a clarification and rectification of the axiomatic basis of science[22] – and such is the scope and significance of his achievement in relativity theory. The troublesome dualism was traced back to Newton's double distinction between absolute and relative time and absolute and relative space,[23] in which time and space were made to play a double role;

the part of a carrier or frame for things that happen in physics, and that of being an 'inertial system'.[24] Absolute time and space juxtaposed were regarded as the infinite container of all material bodies without being themselves dependent on them or affected by them in any way. That is to say, they formed an immutable, homogeneous inertial system, causally conditioning all bodies and their motions in the universe and constituting them into a comprehensive mechanical system; and as such they served as the absolute mathematical framework by reference to which all the phenomena of nature in relative time and space are to be analysed and ordered in our understanding. It was that interconnection of dualism and the particulate, mechanical view of nature that fell foul of the new concepts forced upon science by the discovery of the electromagnetic field. And so, in two stages, represented by his special and general theories of relativity, Einstein applied the concept of the metrical field (as extended by Lorentz[25]) to embrace all phenomena, replacing the old framework of absolute space and time by the space-time continuum as the objective but imperceptible structure for the ordering and understanding of all events.[26] In his general theory he rejected the idea of space-time as a continuum devoid of matter and energy that acts itself without being acted upon, but developed a four-dimensional space-time continuum, with a reciprocal action between it and the constituent matter and energy of the universe, together with an inner connection between mass and energy.[27] This involved such a different geometrical structure from that required by the separation of space and time and their independence of all material content, that all the laws of nature had to be adapted accordingly. While this did not resolve away entirely the duality of matter and space, the material point and the continuous field,[28] it did effectively eliminate the dualism inherent in Newtonian physics, replacing its rigid absolutes in the foundation of science with a more profoundly objective but dynamic relatedness inherent in the structure of the universe, invariant for any and every observer. The immense unification this achieved in our ideas of the universe and the corresponding coordination of the theoretical and empirical components in the structure of science, are particularly evident in the fusion of geometry and physics, not to speak of mechanics and gravitation.[29]

The radical change this makes in our approach to things (well beyond the bounds of physics) can readily be brought out if we start with relativity and space-time, and then consider the difference that is made through the separation of space and time which has become so natural for us: with space constituting a three-dimensional continuum and time being treated as an independent continuum.[30] Two empirical facts and their consequences have here to be taken into account. (i) Light moves with such a high velocity that our senses cannot cope with it in relation to the relatively very low velocities in our ordinary experience. We are unable to visualise, therefore, a non-Euclidean four-dimensional continuum, and space-time inevitably becomes refracted through our crude observation into space and time, each with its separate structure different from that of space-time.[31] Thus the structure of separate space is three-dimensional, open to our 'flat' perception, homogeneous and rigid, (unaffected by matter and energy), and therefore spatially divisible, whereas the structure of space-time is four-dimensional, non-observable, heterogeneous and fluid or 'curved' (affected by matter and energy), a continuous whole. (ii) Although the velocity of light remains invariant, i.e. having the same standard value irrespective of the motion of the source or the observer, nevertheless it is limited or finite, and in that sense also relative. The invariance of light in space-time thus means that although space-time is a continuous dynamic field of contingent events, far from being merely a convenient tool of thought, it is an objective, structured framework inseparable from the intrinsic relatedness of the universe; and as such it is to be contrasted with the detached infinite magnitudes of absolute space and time posited by Newtonian science to regulate and coordinate the complex of appearances bound up with the sensible magnitudes of relative space and time, and so to constitute the necessary, unchangeable scaffolding of the common objective world.

From the point of view of space-time, then, the double split between space and time, and between the absolute and the relative, corresponds to the dualism between primary and secondary qualities, those which belong to the public world which holds for all men, and those which are private and vary with each observer[32] – that is, it corresponds to the destructive dichotomy of object and subject, being and form, substance and structure, that has infected all European science, philosophy and theology in one way or another. However, according to relativity theory, from a relation irrespective of the motion of the object or the observer, the primary qualities are just as relative as the secondary qualities (e.g. apparent shape and colour are both equally indefinite until the condition of the observer is specified), but instead of being relegated to the category of the merely apparent or unreal, they are established as real on the level of our ordinary experience of low velocities and crude perceptions, where the classical separation of space and time obtains, through being accounted for from the higher level of the continuous functions of the space-time metrical field. Thus although separate space and time remain inalienable aspects of the real world as we experience it, the role assigned to primary qualities in Galilean and Newtonian physics of describing the objective continuum of the universe is now fulfilled by configurations in space-time (invariances and symmetries, and relations between vectors, semivectors and tensors) which transcend any coordinate-system and thus retain the same standard value regardless of the 'observer'. This implies that the consistency in the scientific coordin-ation of observational data which is required to obtain a real external world beyond our variable sense-impressions and private perspectives is seen to derive, not from any rational synthesis achieved at the level of our observational experiences under the limits and conditions of low velocities, but through explanatory correlation with concepts and relations drawn from a higher level of reality. In this way they gain in intelligibility, for apart from this cross-level connection with the metrical field the coordinations and configurations that derive from split space and time have the character of artificial idealisations (e.g. the absolute velocity of light, flat space, or even Euclidean geometry) which lack proper congruence with the actual state of affairs in nature – hence the inevitable tendency to conventionalism in all positivist science operating by abstraction from observations. Looked at in reverse, however, this means that unless the configurations developed by science in the spatio-temporal continuum can account for the appearances and their low-level synthesis in split space and time, in such a way that the laws of nature formulated at the higher level of the space-time metrical field reduce to the laws of classical physics at their first approximation, or as their limiting cases valid for low velocities,[32] the scientific results claimed at the higher level are devoid of application to existence and must be regarded as little more than sophisticated but ultimately meaningless mental con-structs. It belongs to the merit of relativity theory that at this crucial point it passes the supreme test in its achievement of the closest and most precise correlation of actual empirical content and fundamen-tal theoretic constructs. It is not surprising, therefore, that Einstein could claim science of this kind to be concerned with comprehend-ing 'existence and reality'.[33]

From the foregoing discussion it should be evident that science is now advancing beyond the eras of Greek–essentialist and modern-instrumentalist views of science in which the fundamental concepts were deeply affected by a dualist outlook upon the universe, into a *third era* in which a very different conception of science has been forced upon us through the incompatibility of the old dualistic structures of thought with a widening range of empirical facts. Unlike its predecessors, this new science starts from a unitary approach to the universe in the belief that it has 'a completely harmonious structure' and in the hope of 'grasping the real in all its depth',[34] and it operates with an integration of form which transcends the limits of analytical methods and their disintegrating effects. It has arisen together with the discovery of the space-time metrical field of fused matter and energy which constitutes a continuous whole of harmonious dynamic connections and transformations, and as such it entails radical changes not only in the first principles of science but in the nature of first principles and the way they are derived from intrinsic features of the universe. Changes that go as deep as that, however, are not easy to effect, for it is very difficult for human beings entangled in a determinate system of ideas to break free from it, but these changes are up against the causal absoluteness of space and time which ever since Newton has been the back-bone of modern science and the primary feature of its structure. It is not surprising, therefore, that the scientific revolution they demand, far from being a case of sudden conversion, appears to be involving a considerable transitional period in which reactionary ideas after more than half a century are still militant, as the continuing strength of reductionism bears witness.[35] On the other hand, the ecological chaos which has clearly arisen through an instrumentalist misuse of nature, reflecting the detached objectivism of positivist science, may well help to complete the transition to the new science of the third era, more quickly.

Since this new conception of science is geared to the entire universe as an integrated intelligible system, the fundamental changes which it introduces into our thought inevitably point far beyond themselves and the province of reality in which they were first envisaged. It will be important for us, therefore, to review these changes, at least in respect of their primary implications, in order to interpret their revolutionary significance and to discern their wider relevance.

1. Here we have a *different conception of reality* from that which has generally obtained in modern science since Galileo and Newton.[36]

In classical physics the real world was identified with the causally necessary and the quantifiable, the world of 'real, mathematical time and space', as Newton called it, in contrast to the apparent and often quite illusory world of our sense-experiences, from which nevertheless knowledge of it is extracted. This distinction, between the real and the apparent corresponds, as we have seen, to that between primary and secondary qualities. Two chief conceptions of reality are thus found in European thought: one which stems from Greek-essentialist science, the world of true being or enduring substance, sharply differentiated from the transient world of phenomena; and one which stems from modern-instrumentalist science, the world of mechanically connected phenomena, which scientifically reduces to the simplest common structure of relations which we derive by abstraction and synthesis from the variable private worlds of observers. In the nature of the case, this tends to bifurcate again into the twin conceptions of the materialist and the conventionalist approaches, but both of them operate with a thoroughly pragmatic notion of reality, and reject the essentialist notion of being or substance underlying appearances, as an empirically empty 'noumenon' or merely a 'metaphysical reality' irrelevant to science.

For the new science, however, these notions of 'reality' wither away, as soon as the dichotomies (between the apparent and the real, subject and object, form and being, etc.) that lie at their root are eliminated, together with the artificial correctives they forced upon science but which are now seen to be incompatible with the actual world of empirical fact. Here the real world is that which forces itself upon our inquiries in the imperious light of its own intrinsic order, as one in which intelligible structure and material content exist in mutual interaction and interdetermination. This is a world in which relations between bodies are just as real as the bodies themselves, for it is in their interrelations that things are found to be what and as and when they are. Thus, as relativity theory has brought to light, space and time are not only fused with one another but fused with the matter and energy of the universe in such a way as to constitute an unresolvable four-dimensional continuum with rationally and physically objective properties. Far from being amorphous, therefore, nature is disclosed to be permeated by the invisible structure of the metrical field which is the source of our forms of thought about it. Even though our minds may first have to 'construct' forms before they can penetrate into the inherent structures of the universe, the rational forms of space-time are not imported into it by our minds but are discovered to belong to it independently of them. The real world confronts us, then, as a continuous integrated manifold, in which structure and substance, form and being, are inseparably conjoined in the immanent relatedness of the universe. This is not 'substance', however, in the old instrumentalist and anti-metaphysical sense, the unknowable and empirically useless substance or substructure that vanishes under the process of abstraction from phenomena, but precisely that which seizes and upholds thought and binds it objectively to concrete reality: it is the epistemic constant without which there could be no thought and with which our thought conflicts when it is false.[37] Nor is this 'being' in the old essentialist sense, some detached essence transcending phenomena, but that which is what it is and which cannot be other than it is, and therefore what it must be in our knowing of it if we are to know something in accordance with its nature: it is the epistemic invariant without which there could be no truth or falsity, and which we are obliged to know according to what it is in itself in its own inner relations. Since the real world exhibits itself to scientific inquiry in this profound unity of form and being, or structure and substance, it not only gives evidence of its existence as an intelligible system independent of our perceiving and conceiving of it,[38] but thereby discriminates itself perpetually from our scientific constructs about it, and remains in its independence the final judge of their truth or falsity. All this implies a powerful restoration of *ontology,* not only for the philosopher or the theologian, but also for the scientist, who precisely as scientist finds that it is 'existence and reality' that he wishes to comprehend.[39]

Closely connected with this new conception of reality there arises a deeper conception of *objectivity:* an objectivity of depth corresponding to the dimension in depth in which the real world forces itself upon our understanding. This involves the overthrow of the twin conceptions of objectivity which have prevailed in the objectivist and conventionalist approaches of modern science, which we shall call 'observationalist objectivity' and 'methodological objectivity'. Observationalist objectivity is that of naive empiricism, according to which our thought is held to be controlled by observations or observational facts which have a condition independent of the basic rational factors that arise in our scientific constructions, and which operates with a concept of the universe as inherently independent of intelligible form or intrinsically amorphous. Such a universe of course would not be accessible to scientific inquiry, let alone any form of intelligent observation. Whatever the demerits of Kant's notion of the synthetic *a priori* it at least had the merit of recognising that empirical and theoretic factors operate together in all our knowledge of the phenomenal world. The unity of form and being, however, or of structure and matter, which has compelled the emergence of relativity theory in science determined to be utterly faithful to real states of affairs in the universe, implies not only that empirical and theoretical factors are inseparably interwoven from the very start but that rational as well as physical properties are equally and inseparably grounded in the conditions of the space-time universe independent of our perceiving and conceiving of it. Hence true human thought is objectively controlled by an intelligible state of affairs in the real world independent of us, but precisely because it is intelligible not apart from our intelligent apprehension and interpretation, the objective control operates through constant ontological and evidential reference of our concepts and theories to that intelligible state of affairs in the real world, a reference which we may not rationally evade.[40]

Methodological objectivity arose in modern science first out of the phenomenalist dualism posited by Galileo and Newton in the foundations of science. As we have seen, the real external world was identified with a common, public world that transcended all private perspectives, knowledge of which was reached through a synthesis constructed out of the many variable sense-experiences of private observers. This distinction between real and apparent, however, could only be upheld by a distinction between absolute and relative, in which absolute space and time, regarded as constituting a homogeneous inertial system, were erected as the rigid support and scaffolding for all scientific concepts and operations. In these circumstances, objectivity became equated with the causal absoluteness of space and time. But all this took a conventionalist turn when Kant extended the Galilean and Newtonian dualism into a sharp dichotomy between the phenomenal and the noumenal, so that the combination of the theoretical and empirical components in knowledge was traced back to a synthetic *a priori* activity on the part of the human mind, detached from any grounding in alleged relations inherent in things themselves. With space and time now construed in terms of *a priori* forms of synthesis and perception outside the range of experience, and thus deprived of their physical and objective properties in the Newtonian system, a conventionalist rather than a materialist conception of objectivity set in. That is to say, the real world was resolved into the mental construct which we devise in order to reach a structured coordination of our sense-experiences which will be common for all men. Objectivity now reduces to a pragmatic necessity, corresponding to the pragmatic notion of reality discussed above: it is a methodological instrument to cope with observational relativism in the absence of any control from the side of the universe through structures inherent in it and independent of ourselves. Such a notion of objectivity, however, together with its prescriptive framework of *a priori* synthetic forms of space and time detached from experience, inevitably collapses when the dualism that gave rise to it succumbs to the realisation that space and time, far from being independent in the sense of Newton or of Kant, are fused together with one another and with empirical content in the intrinsic interrelations of the universe, and as such are integral to the objective structure of indivisible space-time.

Thus both observational objectivity and methodological objectivity fall away and are superceded in face of the new conception of the real world. The causal absoluteness of space and time erected by modern science is now seen to be essentially an artificial device designed to cope with the relativity of appearance, but that kind of corrective is no longer relevant. Instead, there emerges a new and profounder conception of objectivity grounded in the invariant relatedness inherent in the universe, in which form and being, structure and matter, coinhere in a very different kind of synthesis, that of space-time, in which many fields of relations and forces cohere together through the natural correlation of their different levels in an indefinite range of depth, or height, in such a way that ordinary experience and even so-called appearances figure as real on their own level in correlation with other levels of reality, and are thus treated as relative aspects of the totality of existence. The kind of objectivity envisaged here is not flat, which can be wholly determined in terms of observations or conventions, but one that reaches out into dimensions of orderly reality far beyond our understanding and which we are aware of apprehending only at comparatively elementary levels.[41]

There are of course important aspects of objectivity taken up in the traditional notions which must certainly be retained, such as impartiality and universal agreement. What is truly objective must be independent of the subjectivity of the observer, uncoloured by individual feelings and opinions, that which has been submitted to the critical tests and checks of independent standards and is detached from all unwarranted preconceptions and presuppositions, and therefore what is truly objective must belong to a common world which holds for all men in accordance with universally acknowledged principles and rules. Necessary as all this is, however, it does not constitute sufficient condition for objectivity, for objectivity, as we now understand it in the light of relativity theory, must be grounded in invariant structures inherent in the space-time universe irrespective of any and every observer. In the nature of the case, objectivity is something that cannot finally be captured by our theoretic constructions no matter how faithfully they may bear upon those invariances through their referential and ontological relations.

2. Along with this new conception of reality there comes about a *change in the way we derive our concepts,* or at least in the way we think we derive them.

All science since its inception has been concerned with the connection between the theoretical and the empirical factors in knowledge, ancient science with their antithesis, and modern science with their coordination. It is distinctive of modern science that it has laid the emphasis upon direct contact with experience, and given full place to empirical factors in respect of both the content and the control of knowledge, but this has tended to mislead people into thinking that scientific theories are *directly derived* from experiences by the logical means of abstraction and deduction. Thus Newton's claim that he did not invent hypotheses but deduced them from appearances or phenomena[42] (which is not easy to square with the actual way in which he came up with his basic concepts) has been used regularly to support this view until recent times. But, as Einstein has pointed out, 'A clear recognition of the erroneousness of this notion really only came with the general theory of relativity, which showed that one could take account of a wider range of empirical facts, and that too in a more satisfactory and complete manner, on a foundation quite different from the Newtonian than was possible with it'.[43] That is to say, as soon as we operate with the concept of the four-dimensional space-time continuum in which the metrical structure is not independent of but determined by matter and energy, we cannot engage in operations in which we separate structure from material content, without destroying the fundamental concept of the metrical field, replacing it with an abstract structure which is logically and not ontologically derived. But it was precisely because that kind of abstract structure (e.g. the geometry of relations between rigid bodies which are independent of time, or Newton's system of the world axiomatised in terms of that geometry) was found to be incongruent with the actual structure of the universe that it had to be set aside or reconstructed as a first approximation with only limited validity.

It is thus on the actual ground of scientific evidence that a change is demanded in our approach to the relation between concepts and experience. We do not derive theoretical principles by abstracting them from observations, for that would not be grasping the real in all its depth, in the indissoluble unity of structure and matter in motion, but would mean the abstraction of forms from their empirical content and thus a serious distortion in our knowledge of the real world. Nor do we derive them by a chain of logico-inductive processes starting from direct observations or so-called sense-data, for that would involve carving up the continuous field into atomic particulars instead of treating it as 'an independent, not further reducible fundamental concept',[44] and also an illegitimate substitution of nominalist particulars for atomic particulars denoted by them.[45] Behind that kind of thought lies both the analytical procedure which results from split space and time and a nominalist empiricism.

There is, and must be, of course, a real harmony between our concepts and experience, and they must be capable of being elaborated in a logically coherent manner in order to serve as the basis for deductive reasoning, otherwise we would never get beyond our immediate observations and no explicatory science would be possible at all. But it is easier to speak of this harmony negatively than positively, for since we are not concerned with a logical but a trans-logical or an extra-logical relation between concepts and experience, it is impossible to say precisely how concepts are correlated with experience, or to devise a clear-cut systematic method for that derivation.[46] This is increasingly evident the further we penetrate beyond immediate and crude observation into the inherently non-observable structure of the space-time framework of the universe. Clearly, however, it is the empirical and ontological reference of our concepts that must be the controlling factor in helping us to find the right path, for all knowledge of reality begins with experience and ends in experience, even though it may involve arduous intellectual activity throughout. On the other hand, the fact that space-time, which embraces all our human experiences, in its fusion of structure with matter and energy, is itself an *experienced imperceptible,* an intangible magnitude, must be allowed to prevent us from restricting the nature and range of experience to the crude and limiting conceptions of it which we tend to acquire when operating within split space and time. The discovery that space-time plays such a regulative role not only in the structure of the universe but in our ordinary experience, serves to disclose that knowledge at all levels arises on grounds that are not always or completely identifiable, and that there is much in the activities of our minds in their correlation to the intelligibility of the world around us that transcends our ability to track it down. This is why wonder must be accorded an important place in scientific inquiry, for it keeps our minds open to an indefinite range of possibility, not least when something novel in our experience conflicts with forms of thought that are already stereotyped in our minds.[47]

Somehow, or other, then, we must probe into the depth of being in order to grasp it in its own inherent forms and patterns, without being caught in the treachery of abstraction and reduction to what we already claim to know, and thus learn from nature itself a knowledge of the relevant first principles through attending to the continuous organisation of variables in relation to the whole indivisible field.[48] We do not start, then, with discrete particulars, spatial instances or temporal instants, and aggregate them into wholes through empirical generalisations, for the differentiations within the field are what they are only through the irreducible field-structures of the whole system. We have to keep attending to all that the field embraces in its profound relationships until the relevant principles have revealed themselves to us. Here we have to do with an informal and inarticulate operation of the mind, upon which Michael Polanyi has thrown a great deal of light, while showing it to be an essential if unaccountable element in science.[49] He speaks of this as *the logic of tacit inference,* in which we come to know more than we can tell but which has such a bearing upon the real world that it carries within it an anticipatory awareness of a coherence in nature upon which we rely as a clue in the development of explicit knowledge. It is in this way that our natural perception operates through 'subliminal clues' rooted in the involuntary, internal operations of the body (such as spontaneous muscular movements) which we cannot experience in themselves, but in virtue of which we engage in a process of learning without awareness.[50] What holds good for the structure of ordinary perception holds good also for the structure of *scientific intuition,* in which we find ourselves engaging in discovery without awareness, which is after all but another form of learning from nature. It is in this informal way, then, with steps which we cannot specify, that we come upon the basic clues which form the initial premises for our explicit scientific operations.[51]

This fully accords with Einstein's insistence that the connection of concepts with experience is 'purely intuitive, not itself of a logical nature'; thus there is 'no logical path' to the laws of nature – 'only intuition resting on sympathetic understanding of experience, can reach them'.[52] On the other hand, while *experience suggests* the appropriate concepts and remains the sole criterion of their physical utility, they require creative and constructive activity on the part of the human mind, as in mathematical concepts, for their discovery.[53]

This is why Einstein can speak of these basic concepts and fundamental principles as 'free inventions' of the human intellect,
although 'they cannot be justified by the nature of that intellect or
in any other fashion *a priori*'.[54] 'The concepts which arise in our
thought and in our linguistic expressions are all – when viewed
logically – the free creations of thought which cannot inductively
be gained from sense-experiences.'[55] That is to say, *from the point of
view of logic,* they are 'freely chosen conventions', since they are
neither logically derived nor logically controlled, but are fundamental and irreducible.[56] The 'freeness' of these concepts and
principles, however, is restricted from the side of nature. 'The
liberty of choice is of a special kind; it is not in any way similar to
the liberty of a writer of fiction. Rather it is similar to that of a man
engaged in solving a well designed word puzzle. He may, it is true,
propose any word as a solution; but, there is only *one* word which
really solves the puzzle in all its forms.'[57] Elsewhere Einstein offers
another instructive analogy for this kind of empirical fit between
concepts and experiences. 'For even if it should appear that the
universe of ideas cannot be deduced from experience by logical
means, but is, in a sense, a creation of the human mind, without
which no science is possible, nevertheless this universe of ideas is
just as little independent of the nature of our experiences as clothes
are of the form of the human body.'[58] This fact, that our concepts
and their proper interconnections are intuitively related to and
controlled by nature or the real world, implies an astonishing
harmony or correlation between its inherent comprehensibility and
the structure of our human comprehending; the fact that the world
of our sense experiences is comprehensible to us, said Einstein, is a
miracle.[59]

It is because of this correlation, then, between pure thought and
the intrinsic intelligibility of the universe, that we are able, not only
to reach basic concepts by worming them out of nature, but are able
to establish 'mental connections' between them by means of which
we can orient ourselves in the labyrinth of sense-impressions,
discover the setting of real objects in the real world, and detect the
presence of law and order in the world – which is precisely the task
of science.[60] That is to say, we attempt to produce a theoretic and
logically coherent structure, built up from intuitively derived basic
concepts, so that through it, we may seek to bring to light the
inherent and coherent structure of nature. No matter how successful such a *theory* (in the original sense of *theoria*) may be in
mediating insight into the latent organisation or systematic connectivity of any field, it would still remain valid that there is *no logical*

bridge between the structure of that theory and the objective structure of the real world. Hence, just as it was not through any logical
nexus that the basic concepts (out of which the theory was built)
were derived from experiences, so likewise there is at the conclusion no logical nexus by means of which it can be demonstrated or
verified: the all-important connection at the end must be just as
empirical and intuitive as it was at the start.[61] Thus, the meaning,
the success and the validity of a scientific theory depend on its
ontological import, i.e. its *power of objective reference* to point to and
reveal the hidden structure in the world to which it is correlated,
and which determines its cognitive or heuristic value. It is this
'extra-logical problem', according to Einstein, which is the essential
problem and which the scientist will only be able to solve *intuitively.* That is to say, the connection of theory with experience is
something that can only be experienced.[62] This does not rule out of
course the necessary deductive operations by means of which we
test a theory's coherence and draw out its implications, but in the
last resort it is the establishment of a referential or ontological
connection between deductions from a theory and a set of empirical
facts that is the crucial test. No direct comparison between scientific
concepts or statements and empirical facts is involved, for that
would be illegitimate,[63] but what is involved is an *analogical reference*
in which an indirect comparison is in place, between 'empirical
facts' imported by the theory and an actual set of empirical facts.
That is surely the significance which Newton gave to what he
called 'the analogy of nature', which the positivist and the rationalist traditions in science have so often forgotten.[64]

3. A change takes place in *the relation of science to ordinary human
experience and knowledge*: from what we have already seen it will
be apparent that the new science maintains close links with the
natural structure of perception and thought and develops them.

Modern classical science by its methods of extensive abstraction,
logical analysis and synthesis, achieves something so detached from
the concrete conditions of actual observers and their motions, that it
has difficulty in accounting for them except as appearances or
relative aspects of apparent space and time and motion, which it
seeks to bring under control by clamping down upon them a
system of mechanistic concepts and connections. That is more and
more the way in which human life is related to science in the
technological society, in which the distinctively human finds itself
mutilated and suppressed, in spite of the magnificent way in which
the resources of nature are harnessed and used for its end, for man
himself is being exploited along with nature through the sheer

momentum of the technological machine he has created.[65] The particular point in all this that interests us immediately is that in the procedures of classical modern science there takes place an analytical disjunction of pre-existing connections together with an abstraction from inner organisation in any field under investigation, which leads to the disintegration of natural form and its replacing with unnatural form arising from the employment of an artificial isomorphic framework of thought: absolute space and time. In spite of the careful concentration upon phenomena, even the latent interrelation of appearances becomes disrupted as soon as any phenomenological detachment or bracketing off takes place, so that some way of fitting the appearances together into a coherent whole is needed – the result is a mechanical organisation of phenomena merely in terms of their external and quantifiable relations, such as that exhibited in the classical model of the clash of billiard balls.

Now of course a necessary movement of scientific thought is involved here, which Ernst Mach spoke of as economy or simplicity,[66] the need to operate with a minimum of concepts and relations, readily accepted by Einstein.[67] This arises out of our human requirement to 'reproduce' facts and their interrelations in thought. This we do by means of symbolic or abstract representations which we combine and manipulate in language and mathematics, but in which only a minimum of basic terms or cyphers may be employed if they are to be handled easily and with an economy of mental effort. Thus there occurs a replacing of actual experiences by forms prescinded from experience, and a replacing of real physical connections by the semi-mechanical operations of logical and mathematical relations. In this way *formal precision* is achieved at the expense of *real precision,* i.e. with the sacrifice of natural connections and inner organisation. In the nature of the case, the more conventionalist the structures of science become, through the supplanting of real entities and connections with mental artifices and convenient arrangements, the more it will be incompatible with concrete states of affairs in empirical reality, or to express it the other way round, the more limited will be the areas and aspects of the real world with which scientific method can cope – hence, for example, the difficulty that the kind of organisation found in the electromagnetic field presented to classical mechanics. It was in fact, as we have seen, the problems which modern science created for itself in this way that occasioned the rise of relativity theory. But these problems are no less acute in face of the kind of complex organisation embodied by living beings, with which we have to do in our daily experience, but which resists the methods of abstraction, analysis and synthesis.

The fundamental difficulty with abstractive science is that it withdraws or disengages our thought from the *inner form* embedded in the field under investigation, and thus omits an essential part of its *empirical* content, precisely that part which is already fused with form or structure. That is why it fails to come up with the appropriate conceptual form or theoretical component in know-ledge through which it may be grasped. Natural form, the kind of form which inheres in the nature of what we seek to apprehend, may be grasped only through a constructive and interpretative operation of the mind in which we freely produce a form of thought correlated with the form immanent in the nature of things through an ontological and referential relation to it. Logically speaking, as we have seen, this is what Einstein has called a 'free invention' or a 'free creation' of thought for it cannot be inferred or inductively gained from sense-experiences, but it is far from being merely a fiction or a convention, since it arises in us intuitively as we allow our minds to fall under the compulsion of a state of affairs in empirical reality. Thus we apprehend the world of our experi-ence with the help of concepts which are not logically connected with experience but which are not *a priori* either; and since we cannot make sense of experience without them the conceptual elements are so closely combined with experimental elements in our knowledge that it is not easy to distinguish them.

Now this holds good not only for scientific activity, but also, and first of all, for our pre-scientific perception and the primitive concepts of everyday life, in which we regularly make use of elements which are not extracted from experiences but which are free creations that we cannot do without. As an example of this, Einstein points to *the series of integers* which is obviously an inven-tion of the mind for the simplification and ordering of certain sensory experiences, but 'there is no way in which this concept could be made to grow, as it were, directly out of sense experi-ence'.[68] He goes on to point out, against Bertrand Russell, that if concepts which are not empirically derived are to be consistently excluded as 'metaphysical', then that would absolutely exclude thinking of any kind as 'metaphysical'.[69] All this makes it quite clear, then, that science does not operate with a structure different from that of ordinary perception and thought, but is in fact an extension of our ordinary way of knowing, or 'a refinement of everyday thinking'.[70] This is nowhere more evident than in the way relativity theory disposes of the lofty support and scaffolding artificially erected by classical physics in the concepts of absolute space and time, and brings down the fundamental framework of scientific thought from the clouds to ground it in the definite relatedness that permeates the actual universe.[71]

The new framework supplied by space-time is certainly invisible as far as our commonplace observations are concerned, yet it can be used by science to account for our ordinary, day to day experiences by providing on its own rigorous level an account of the theoretico-empirical structure of knowledge which is discerned to be not basically different from but a refinement and development of pre-scientific knowledge. Indeed the invisible structure of space-time, which regulates the behaviour of all that it embraces in the universe, links up with the unsuspected relations and imperceptible reactions within ourselves to the world around us, and constitutes together with them the ultimate ground of man's inarticulate grasp of the world out of which emerge the basic clues which we use in ordinary experience as well as in scientific experience – that is the objective ground for what Polanyi has called the tacit dimension which underlies and underpins all human and scientific knowledge. Moreover, the new science is also able, as we have seen, to explain the development of classical physics in the latter's account of the phenomena that arise from the separateness of space and time, in such a way that the new synthesis grounded on space-time reduces the Newtonian synthesis within the bounds of its restricted accuracy, and indeed legitimates it within its limited foundations. In so doing, however, it traces the abstract, impersonal objectivism of the classical account, which creates such a gulf between it and ordinary human experience, to the dualism between primary and secondary qualities, and object and subject, with which it operates, and to the artificial correctives it has to introduce to check unwarranted subjectivism.

More positively, by grounding scientific knowledge in the existing patterns and inner organisations that are naturally latent in the world, thus connecting up the structure of scientific knowledge at its various levels with that of our natural experience and thought, the new synthesis extends an unbroken, graduated bridge between the various sciences, not least from the mathematical sciences through the biological sciences to the human sciences. In this way there are opened up wider, deeper heterogeneous aspects of reality for scientific investigations which are ruled out by older methods as alleged violations of natural law, but which now yield their more complex organisations to orderly interpretations in terms of open field-structures and fluid field-laws. Thus a considerable change comes about in our understanding of science in its relation to distinctively human experience, at the lower end on the plane of crude observation and at the higher end on the plane of experienced imperceptibles and intangibles, so that the harmony or unity of nature detected by the new science behind our variable experience is not flat but constituted in depth or height (whichever we may prefer), in level after level of coordinated fields of organisation, hierarchically ordered but openly oriented in an ever widening perspective of a consistent intelligibility which soon transcends the limits of human understanding and reaches far beyond.

Perhaps the most startling feature of the new science in all this is the recognition that must be accorded to the place *man himself* occupies in scientific knowledge: rational man cannot be separated from the consistent structure of the universe in which he exists and of which he is a constituent element. Since the continuous field of space-time is not independent or absolute, but both affects and is affected by the behaviour of all matter and energy in the universe, man himself cannot be excluded from the syndrome of action and reaction in nature, either as rational agent investigating the universe or as an essential participant in its rational and objective structure. This surely means that it is in and through the interaction between man and the universe that the deepest nature of the universe, which would otherwise remain latent, assumes a form in which it may be disclosed and expressed. In spite of its immanent intelligibility independent of our perceiving and conceiving of it, the world of nature is not automatically self-disclosing. In accordance with its nature, especially as it comes to light through general relativity theory, it acts and reacts upon us in determining our knowing of it and it yields to our action and reaction toward it in disclosing itself to our inquiries: it requires to be questioned in order to be known, while we human beings are what we are in our rationality not apart from reciprocal action between us and the world around us. The fact that rational man and the universe in the space-time track of its development and unfolding are relative to each other, implies that that relativity must be construed as belonging to the profound relatedness immanent in nature and not simply as something that arises in the human mind.

All this inevitably raises in a deeper way the question as to the relation between human knowing and the object known. That a real correlation between the two is implied, may be traced back to the unity of structure and matter, or form and being, which is forced upon us particularly through general relativity, for that unity demands from us a corresponding way of knowing in which knowing and being, instead of being split wide apart as in traditional modern science and philosophy, are reconciled and conjoined.[72] Here we have to do, then, with rather more than the astonishing fact that the universe is accessible to our rational inquiry, so compellingly evident in the coordination that can be achieved between its inherent comprehensibility and our rational formalisations. What confronts us is an inner correlation between the structure of human knowledge and the structure of the world known by man, for while the universe unfolds its structure in coordination with the scientific inquiries of man, man himself develops along with the disclosure of the structured universe around him. In Michael Polanyi's language,[73] there is 'a correspondence between the structure of comprehension and the structure of the comprehensive entity which is its object', or 'a structural kinship between subject and object'. Evidence for this is adduced in the stratified structure of science parallel to the stratification of levels of reality which we find in the universe, together with a similar parallelism which we find in ourselves, in the structural kinship exhibited between the behaviour of our bodily activity in the acquiring of skills and in the behaviour of our mind in learning.[74]

It is important to note that the kind of correlation that this involves does not import any subjectivism but resists it;[75] nor does it link up with the built-in static subjectivity that derives from the fixed categories posited by Kant outside the range and modification of experience. It is a correlation in which the rational subject is openly oriented towards the object, and which therefore excludes all ego-centred activity. It is indeed only the rational subject who can engage in genuinely objective operations, for he alone can distinguish what he knows from his knowing of it while allowing his knowing to be determined by the nature of the object. The intrinsic unity of form and being in the object of his knowledge means that it is only conscious mind that can cope with it adequately, for it is only through mental penetration into the form inherent in the object together with intelligent interpretation of it that the human knower can bring its inherent intelligibility to rational expression, but since that intelligibility is inherent in being, his knowing of it must rest on the compulsive ground of that being and not upon himself. Thus far from opening the gates to the intrusion of distorting subjective factors into knowledge, the kind of correlation envisaged here commits the knowing subject to a situation in which he is inescapably bound to what he discerns to be the case and is obliged to refrain from imposing anything, least of all himself, upon the object of his knowledge. On the other hand, as the advance of science in the third era makes increasingly clear we do distort the world we seek to know quite seriously through abstractive procedures in which we retire our conscious mind from it, and thereby withdraw our thought from grasping it in its natural form and innate organisation, for then we cut off from the universal reality of experience what Sir John Eccles has called 'the primary reality', and at the same time omit the all-important ingredient in the subject-matter.[76] While the results of that kind of activity may hold good within the narrow brackets in which it is conceived and elaborated, nevertheless they entail a methodological mutilation of nature which the new science is no longer ready to tolerate.

This brings us back to the point at which we began, where we found Eccles claiming that the classical methods and laws of science face an impasse in neural science, for they are unable to cope properly with the main issue: the interaction between conscious mind and brain; and therefore speaking of the revolution in science that must come about if we are to account adequately for the full reality of our experience in accordance with the complex nature of what confronts us in it. As we have seen, however, that revolution has long since begun, although the profound changes it necessitates in our understanding of nature and science, have not yet been worked out fully or with sufficient courage. We have tried to probe into that profound transition in thought, and to trace out some of its chief implications especially for the integration of human thought among the sciences. Before we proceed further, however, in developing what we have learned and in attempting to apply it in areas of theological and human science, it may be well to summarise the discussion so far of the changes introduced into science especially by relativity theory.

The general effect of these changes has been to delimit the range and utility of the analytical methods of classical physics which created the atomistic or particulate view of nature that has dominated all modern science, to challenge its neglect of the immanent patterns of dynamic connectivity or the routes of continuous passage between points and instants already found in the universe, and to call in question the kind of system or organisation it built out of the constituent particulars into which it had dissected nature, i.e. the mechanistic conception of the universe. The discovery of the importance of the metrical field, together with the unity of form and being or the mutual interaction of structure and matter in motion which it embodies, has changed our concept of the real world, and calls for corresponding changes in our understanding of scientific concepts and theories in their correlation to human experience. This overthrow of the dualism embedded in the basic structures of modern science has shifted the emphasis from analysis to integration, and opened up the way for profounder conceptions of system and organisation, so that justice may be done to the multivariable, many-layered character of the universe. Thus, if the abstractive methods of modern science, with their exclusion of the rational subject and conscious mind from the domain of nature, led to the disintegration of natural form, the integrative methods of the new science, with their inclusion of man as rational subject and conscious mind, lead to the recovery of natural form and a grasp of the real in greater depth. The former led to the atomic reduction of nature into component particles without adequate attention to the all-important fields of force which structured them together and thus necessitated the erection of an artificial framework for the imposition of order upon nature, but the latter, in spite of all the apparent fragmentation that increasing specialisation brings, lay hold of the dynamic field-structures in which nature is already integrated and so carry our thought forward to a new conception of the stratified universe with an all-embracing synthesis which promises to be profounder than any hitherto achieved.

We have examined the primary changes introduced into our thought through the transition of physical science from an analytical to an integrative approach to things, and reviewed some of their revolutionary implications which point far beyond the areas of investigation where they were first conceived. Now as we turn to think particularly of *theolgical science,* we must bear constantly in mind one basic overall characteristic of the new science, that it is committed to look at things and investigate them according to their distinctive natures and to comprehend them in the light of the structures that are naturally embedded in them or in which they are naturally embedded, for that should prevent us from simply transferring the concepts attained in physics, for example, to the new fields of inquiry.[77] We have already found that this principle applied within physics itself led to the discovery of the significance of the continuous field which made it possible to consider problems of greater complexity than ever before, and that in the course of discovery science became much less delimited and rigid, and more flexible and subtle, reflecting the heterogeneity of the actual universe. It is owing, then, to that essential variability arising out of fidelity to the nature of things, that science acquires a wider range of applicability, as wide in fact as human experience itself.

By thinking everywhere strictly in accordance with the nature of things in their different field-structures, the new science is able to attain this variability without having to sacrifice real precision or proper clarity. Precision is now reached, not by prescinding from the nature of things in the old abstractive way, but by letting thought be moulded as faithfully as possible by the nature of things as it becomes progressively revealed under our inquiries, and therefore in such a continuously *a posteriori* way that it remains everywhere open to whatever may yet be revealed from the side of things being investigated. At the same time, this also allows for the utmost clarity possible within the bounds of the subject-matter, but the kind of artificial clarity that is induced by abstract formalisations or economical symbolisation at the cost of the all-important ontological import of concepts and statements is eschewed in the interest of a profounder objectivity, i.e. one grounded in the actual nature of things and their inherent intelligibility which can never be completely reduced to our conceptual explications. What is determinative for both precision and clarity is a mode of disciplined thinking in accordance with the nature of things and controlled by the consistent structure of their intrinsic order, even though it outruns the limits of our human powers of comprehension and expression. In spite of what may appear to be the case on the linguistic and formal-logical surface, everything becomes finally imprecise and obscure where that kind of ontological depth and therefore the ultimate mystery of being and its comprehensibility are cut away. This is particularly important to remember whenever science turns to the higher level of organised being, e.g. living organisms and rational beings, where the subject-matter in accordance with its nature is more resistant than ever to reductionist simplification.

We begin with the fact that the empirical realities we seek to apprehend in any field are already interfused with relations and patterns so that the theoretical and empirical components of our knowledge arise together, indissolubly conjoined in our knowing from the very start.[78] This applies both to ordinary knowledge and to scientific knowledge, and indeed scientific knowledge is reached only by way of extending and refining the kind of cognition that already informs our everyday experience. Two points must now be stressed.

(a) The theoretical components of knowledge are not derived by abstractions from observations, but arise in our minds under the impress of objective relations in the field we are investigating. That is to say, they go back to non-observable, imageless relations inherent in the nature of things, and are grasped through intellective penetration into them, which Einstein called extra-logical intuitive apprehension, and Polanyi called participation and tacit non-formal inference. They are of course empty and scientifically meaningless apart from their evidential and ontological reference to empirical states of affairs and therefore when disjoined from the empirical components of knowledge. But likewise these empirical components of knowledge are not what they are when abstracted from the imageless relations inherent in things and thus disjoined from the theoretical components of knowledge, and so become scientifically useless. Moreover, since empirical states of affairs are not grasped, and empirical components in knowledge are not defined, except through the theoretical components, the latter play a basic role in scientific knowledge: they are regulative as well as heuristic in their functioning. It must also be added that while empirical components in knowledge inevitably vary in respect of the observer and his experience, the non-observable theoretical components remain the same or are invariant from person to person, a fact which gives them an even stronger position as regulative principles in knowledge.

(b) A distinction must be drawn between the empirical and theoretical components in knowledge and the observable and non-observable elements in the objects of knowledge, although knowledge depends entirely upon correlation of the former with the latter. Both observable and non-observable elements, perceptible realities and imageless relations, are found to be fused together in the continuous metrical field of space-time where the imperceptible and intangible structure of space-time and all matter and energy in the universe are in continuous interaction in such a way that they reciprocally affect one another. This reveals that even the empirical elements in the objects of knowledge reach beyond the domain of the perceptible and tangible into that of the imperceptible and intangible: they are non-observable imageless entities and relations in the real world. That is the area of crucial significance for our knowledge, for it means that the empirical and the theoretical are fused together not simply as components in our knowledge, but as grounded in empirical and structural elements in the intelligible state of affairs independent of our knowledge. That is an essential aspect of the nature of things to which we must be faithful in all rigorously scientific thought, 'the experienced imperceptible', and therefore must learn to make room in our science for empirical relations with imperceptible, immaterial reality in accordance with its nature.

All this forces upon science a revision of its conception of what it means by *theory*. Instead of the old instrumentalist and conventionalist notions of theory as a methodological device composed of 'scientific fictions' which need not have any direct bearing upon intrinsic order in nature, theory is now understood as a cognitive construct of empirico-theoretical components through which we penetrate non-logically into the inner organisation or natural form of things in order to let it become disclosed to us, and then in the light of that which becomes disclosed from time to time we refine the theory that it may become a more transparent medium for scientific insight into the objective order in things, in virtue of which they are what they are independent of our knowing of them as well as in our knowledge of them. A refined theory of this kind, in spite of its essential revisability, is much more than a tentative hypothesis, for it becomes built into the basic axiomatic structure of science. It plays a regulative as well as a heuristic role in knowledge, i.e. not a prescriptive role but a descriptive one in which we allow real states of affairs in nature to prescribe how we are to think of them. That is why in the last analysis we have no control over the shape of a theory or the course which it will follow, any more than we can control what a lens will reveal of the matter to which it is applied. Thus in the last resort it is reality itself which is the final judge of the truth or falsity of our concepts and statements about it.

All this applies with no less force to theological science, especially when we bear in mind that here too we must think only in accordance with the nature of the object, the living God, and in accordance with the specific nature of the field in question, God's interaction with the whole continuous field of space-time, and not just with the interaction within space-time between metrical field and material content. Here more than anywhere else we have to do with imageless relations and invisible structures as primary on the objective side of knowledge and therefore as supremely regulative. And here much more than anywhere in natural science we have to do, not with a static ontology such as that yielded by essentialist science, but with a dynamic ontology, yet far transcending that which emerges out of general relativity theory. Here we have to do with the Creator of all being and the Source of all form who is continuously present to his creation through his Spirit and maintains it throughout all its dynamic transformations in relation to himself as the transcendent ground and ultimate end of its immanent and contingent intelligibility. If in the case of natural science, the control in all our heuristic operations finally rests with the compelling structure of nature itself, so that we easily speak of our discoveries metaphorically in terms of nature disclosing itself or revealing itself, here the metaphor naturally falls away, for we learn nothing of God but what comes from his active self-disclosure, and no inquiry takes place without a Word from God which starts it off. It is not surprising, then, that in strict accordance with the nature of its object theological science replaces the category of discovery with that of revelation.

What all this implies for theology becomes startlingly apparent when we look at it in the light of the phenomenalist and observationalist investigation of the historical Jesus in modern times. That begins with a phenomenological bracketing off of the evangelical material from any realm of things in themselves and their internal relations, for consideration as a collection of phenomena or appearances relative to observers, i.e. quite independent of any compelling structure beyond themselves. Then the methods of observationalist and analytical science are applied to those appearances so that they become abstracted from the frame of their natural connectivity in the evangelical witness and inevitably become fragmented like the phenomenal particulars of observationalist natural science. The natural coherence in which the evangelical material has come down to us is explained away as an imposition upon the original appearances through the use of screen images thrown up out of the consciousness and worship of the early Church. Nevertheless, something is needed to take its place, and so artificial and unnatural frameworks are produced by scholars, one after the other, for this purpose. At first, the framework used is borrowed from natural science, the closed continuum of cause and effect used in the construction of the nineteenth century mechanistic universe. Accordingly, everything in the traditional life of Jesus which could not be causally connected up or explained in that sort of way is excised from the basic collection of phenomena. Then when this scientific method is found to eliminate virtually everything from the tradition, scholars search round for some other kind of framework in which some at least of the appearances can be saved by being fitted into a coherent pattern. All this is still within the phenomenalist game of piecing together what has already been doomed to fragmentation by its initial assumptions and analytical methods, so that all artificially contrived frameworks inevitably collapse one after the other. That would seem to be the constant dénouement of the observationalist quest for the historical Jesus.

Looked at from the perspective of the new science, however, it seems obvious that the New Testament presentation of Jesus can be construed in terms of observationalist and analytical science even less than the electromagnetic field. The lessons we have learned from the failure of classical mechanics at this point, in the rejection of dualist structures of thought and the recovery of the unity of structure and substance or form and being, have their application here. Several things may thus be said to the modern quest for the historical Jesus. Phenomenal events can be discerned to form a pattern only when treated as empirical correlates of a higher level of reality. Hence the phenomenological detachment of the phenomenal level for consideration by itself can never succeed. Because structure and substance, form and being, are already fused together in the real world, the only adequate theoretical structures or conceptual forms with which we may operate are those ontologically derived from the actual field which we are investigating. Hence the use of artificial theoretical structures abstracted from their natural context, thus entailing a divorce of structure and substance, or form and being, inevitably break down in face of empirical reality. What is required of us, therefore, is an integrative approach to the whole field in question, in which primacy is given to its own innate organisation and structure, and in which we operate simultaneously on both levels and learn to think of them conjunctively. That is actually the way we think in our everyday experience of common-sense objects such as tables and chairs, in which we operate with imageless relations and forms which are not sensed nor derived from appearances, although without them the appearances of things would disintegrate in chaotic confusion, but which are grasped through intellective intuition under the impress of structural features in the real world. That is why, as we have seen, science as a rigorous extension and refinement of our ordinary ways of knowing operates from the very start with the closest correlation of the theoretical and empirical elements and components, the perceptible and the imperceptible, the tangible and the intangible, coinhering at every point.

It is not otherwise in theology where imageless relations and invisible structures interfuse our basic experience and are primary on the objective side of our knowledge and therefore supremely regulative for our understanding. But here we are up against the dynamic forms of God's self-revelation to us requiring on our part participation in its communicated pattern and inner organisation, which gives the coordination of the empirical and theoretical elements in the immediate field of apprehended reality a coherent force, and the empirico-theoretical structure in our knowledge an ontological depth, not found elsewhere. That is why we find that in strictly scientific activity neither an approach to Jesus Christ starting from his humanity on the phenomenal level alone, nor an approach to his deity through speculative insight detached from the empirical context, is in place. We must approach Jesus Christ simultaneously on both the empirical and the theoretical levels in the space-time field in which he and we encounter each other. From the very start of our theological interpretation, therefore, we must learn to think conjunctively of him as God and man in the one indivisible fact of Jesus Christ. It is only as we treat the historical events in Jesus' life as empirical correlates of divine acts in an inter-level synthesis, that we can do justice to their intrinsic organisation and their inner form even as empirical and historical realities, that is, without the mutilation and artificial manipulation of the observationalist and phenomenalist approach.

What we have just been describing, of course, applies to the secondary level of specifically scientific activity in theology, but it presupposes the all-important level of intuitive intellective contact with divine reality which is the creative source of our basic convictions and primary concepts and relations. It is through religious experience, in the context of tradition in the continuity of the life of the Church where learning through others, meditation upon the message of the Holy Scriptures, prayer and worship regularly take place, that these basic convictions and primary concepts take their rise. As in every other area of human knowledge this is the level on which we participate in the natural organisation created in the empirical field under the compelling structure of objective reality, and thereby gain our initial insight into the fundamental pattern of things and acquire the first significant clues which prompt and direct further inquiry at a deeper level. It is then at this level (which of course we never leave behind) that we engage in what Polanyi calls *tacit knowing*,[79] in which we come to know more than we can actually tell at the time, but in which we may begin to pass from implicit to explicit awareness through the process which he describes as *indwelling*.[80] This is the activity in which we let our minds dwell within some context of experience, using the framework which it supplies to help us gain access to deeper and fuller meaning. It is significant that Polanyi should use here the language found in the Fourth Gospel, where Jesus speaks of the mutual indwelling between himself and his disciples, their dwelling in his Word and his dwelling in them through the Spirit, enabling them to enter into more intimate knowledge of his mind as the revelation of the Father, and so be led forward into the truth. It is in this way that there take shape in our minds the primary concepts which are directly and intuitively connected with the basic complex of Christian experience, and which we need for scientific theological activity.[81] Although as they take shape in our minds they may not be very pure through being mixed up with foreign elements already lodged in our consciousness, unless they embody at least a partly true conception of the nature of things, Polanyi points out, they cannot serve to guide further inquiry. It is however the emergence of a problem calling for a clarification of our pre-scientific conception of the nature of things that becomes the occasion for our thought to pass on to the secondary level of specific scientific activity.[82] A problem arises with the partial discernment of a pattern lying behind things which we anticipate will bring deeper order into our experiences if they can be evidentially connected up with it. When that connection is made and results in a more consistent ordering and illuminating of our experiences we are convinced that we have attained a deeper grasp upon reality.

Specific scientific activity in theology is not different from that kind of thought-activity that permeates our everyday experience and knowledge, but it does represent a rigorous refinement of it. If we let the Gospel and that to which it bears witness represent again the field of empirical reality into which we inquire, we proceed, under the guidance of what we deem to be a significant clue, to select several of the basic concepts imposed upon our minds as we dwell in this field and become intimate with it. Then we organise them into a preliminary 'model' or 'cognitive instrument', through which we try to penetrate into the heart of the field in order to trace something of its innate organising connections, which we can bring to bear upon the rest of the material. If the concepts we select do not fulfil our hopes, we try again with what promises to be the most hopeful, until we find some that will enable us to get inside the field in such a way as to discern its inner cohesion and organisation. We extend this, by organising the main relations and connections we find, and with them probe more deeply into the structure of the field, making some use of hypothetico-deductive argumentation in order if possible to make explicit the inner logic of the subject-matter. This does not mean that there is only one set of concepts, only one determinate model which can be used, the right one, for this purpose. Other concepts can and should be used in the same way, and if they all lead to the same basic result, then we are convinced not only that we are in touch with reality but have succeeded in grasping it in real depth. Thus, to take an analogy from natural science, several different sets of concepts can be used to reach some natural law, so that we end up by having different theoretical representations of it, all equally possible and valid, but the very fact that we can do this and arrive at the same result, is as powerful a demonstration of the truth of that result as one could have.[83] It is something similar that has happened all through the history of Christian theology in which scientific activity has come up again and again with something like the doctrine of the *hypostatic union*: it keeps on forcing itself upon our minds and we are convinced that here we have penetrated deeply into the inner logic of the evangelical material. Moreover, when we carry our thought a stage further, we find that we penetrate into a higher level of unity and simplicity which gives coherent order to the whole stratified structure of our theological concepts. This is the doctrine of the Holy Trinity which is forced upon our understanding as the fundamental grammar of theological thought, but in such a way that our apprehension of God is evidently grounded, in some measure at least, upon relations internal to his own eternal Being. The doctrine of the Trinity as such certainly represents an apprehension of God on our part which falls far short of what he is, for precisely in knowing God in this way we know him to be infinitely greater than we can conceive, but it also represents what in view of God's self-revelation as Father, Son and Holy Spirit, we are compelled to think and say of him, convinced that basically these thoughts and statements have validity beyond their immediate evidential grounds and indeed beyond the range of any possible human experience in this world. Here we have the theological counterpart to the uncircumscribed objectivity that we find in natural science when we are forced to formulate laws that are claimed to hold good beyond their observed range.

This stratified structure of our thought which has arisen out of our probing into the inner organisation of the evangelical subject-matter would be no more than a pyramid of speculative constructs, if it did not throw any light upon that subject-matter and could not be evidentially and epistemically correlated with it in such a way that the witness of the evangelists is opened up in its power of ontological reference, so that our experience becomes considerably deepened. But that is what does happen. Thus the doctrines of the Trinity and of the hypostatic union together enable us to enter into the inner cohesion of the evangelical narratives so deeply that we discern the connected pattern in the realities to which they refer as we could not do before. Here we do not need to resort to the expedients employed by observationalist and phenomenalist analysis in which organising frames of thought deriving from preconceptions outside the actual field of investigation are used to reduce it to order, and in which all too often 'data' that do not fit into the pattern thus imposed are cut away. This understanding of the hypostatic union of divine and human natures in Christ and of the triunity of God, while not logically deduced from experience, does not break down in the face of actual experience like the artificial frameworks noted above, but on the contrary is able to ground it and account for it in a scientifically satisfactory way. And what is more, it is able to account for the interpretation of the historical Jesus and the course which that interpretation must take within the dualist delimitations within which it is conceived and inevitably breaks down.

We return to the point implied throughout this discussion of scientific procedure that theology operates with a way of thinking in which theoretical and empirical components are inseparably conjoined in our knowledge from start to finish, but in which the non–observable imageless relations inherent in the field of God's interaction with the world, through Christ and in the Spirit, play a regulative role. They are certainly empty and scientifically useless apart from connection with experience or when disjoined from their referential content, but since empirical states of affairs are not grasped or defined without them, they occupy a primary place in the objective, invariant side of our knowledge. They constitute the invisible, imperceptible structure which is known only in accordance with its invisible, imperceptible nature, through intuitive insight in direct contact with divine realities, i.e. through the intellectual or spiritual eye. This takes place, however, only within the continuous context of the space-time universe, where the invisible, imperceptible structure of space-time is regulative and invariant for all the contingent events within the universe, and therefore it is unthinkable that the apprehension of the invisible structure with which we are concerned in theology should take place apart from, although it must be distinguished from, the imageless perception of the structure of space-time. That is to say, the invisible structure that becomes revealed to us through God's interaction with us, through Christ and in the Spirit, itself interacts with the invisible structure of space-time, in a way not unlike that in which the latter interacts with the imperceptible movements within our bodies which play such an important but subsidiary part in the tacit knowing or intuitive apprehension of forms and patterns that is so basic to ordinary and scientific knowledge alike.

This connection between the different invisible structures of theological and natural science in man's apprehension of God and the universe, brings us forcibly back to reconsider and assess the place of man himself and his conscious mind in science, whether theological or natural science. Earlier we were faced with the fact that the withdrawal of the conscious mind of the knowing subject from the domain of nature, so characteristic of modern instrument-alist science, broke down when faced with the interaction of mind and brain disclosed in neural science. Then we saw that the damag-ing dualism that lay behind the exclusion of mind from what is known was overcome through relativity theory and the reconstruc-tion of the basis and methodology of science which it entailed, owing to the discerned integration of structure and matter or form and being in nature, which seemed to call for a reconciliation of knowing and being in the depths of man's knowledge of the universe. Thus all-embracing ground was provided for the fact that, since the universe discloses itself in its intrinsic forms not automatically but only through human interaction with it, man's developing knowledge of the universe belongs to the dynamic structure of the universe. Or, to express it differently, since man is an essential constituent of the universe, his knowing of its intrinsic form falls within its inner dynamic unity of form and being. Far from implying an essentially egocentric approach to the universe, this serves to open up knowledge of the universe for us in its uncircumscribed objective structure, for it is only rational agents who are capable of objective operations in which what is known is not confused with knowing it. As Paul Tillich used to say, objectiv-ity in the ontological structure of knowledge requires both cogni-tive union and cognitive distance or separation.[84]

Now in view of the inseparable connection between the theoretical and empirical factors in knowledge and in the realities known, we must say of man that he is that constituent element in the universe and its pervasive intelligibility in whom and through whom the invisible and visible structures are found to coalesce in such a way that the latent intelligibility of the universe is brought to conceptualisation and expression. Man is thus to be regarded in natural science as well as in theological science as the creature who exists on the boundary of the invisible and the visible, the intangible and the tangible, the unlimited and limited. This both determines the distinctive structure of his human being and constitutes man as that being through whom the universe of being reveals and unfolds its distinctive forms. From this perspective, therefore, science may be defined as the extending and refining of our apprehension of the consistent structure of reality to which we belong and within which we live. This is a possible enterprise because the structure of reality all round us is one in which we share ourselves or, to put it the other way round, because the structure within ourselves is part of the structure of the universe at large. It is because this is so that an egocentric or anthropocentric approach must be ruled out, for the structure in which we share in life and thought is one that reaches out indefinitely beyond ourselves, and is as such essentially an open structure. It is precisely because the structure of our existence is part of the indefinite range of structure in the universe and so indefinitely open to what is beyond it that it is what it is in that correlation to what is beyond, that we cannot let the limits of our specific human structure be the limits of the structure beyond us, as if we could prescribe what it is like beforehand or anticipate it *a priori*. But this openness, as we have already had occasion to see, applies to the universe itself since the structures everywhere manifest in it are open-ended, making the structure of the universe in its entirety a stratification of structural levels each open upward to the other indefinitely. This clearly implies that the universe as an entire intelligible system is unable to offer out of itself a sufficient reason for this state of affairs, and that as an entire system it is consistent in its stratified structures only if it is finally incomplete or unbounded. If a sufficient reason is to be found (and sufficient reason there must be for such an intelligible system, otherwise it would disintegrate in meaninglessness), it must come from beyond the universe altogether. If, on the other hand, the universe were as an entire system quite circumscribed and bounded within itself, it would be essentially a closed system which would affect all the structures within it for they would finally be closed and not open-ended. But that would drag us back again into the self-contained mechanistic universe, from which science has at last broken free, not only through relativity and quantum theory, but, as is evident here, also through the vast implications of the Gödelian theorems.

The all-important place which man occupies in science can be expressed by saying that he constitutes 'the boundary conditions'[85] in the structure of the space-time universe where it is open beyond itself, and where the mystery of its meaning becomes constantly disclosed. On the one hand, he is the creature who, through the structure of his own being so participates in the structure of created reality all round him that through the coordination of the theoretical and empirical components in his knowledge the inherent intelligibility of the universe is brought to expression, while he himself develops as rational man in correlation with that intelligibility. On the other hand, he is the creature who through God's interaction with him within the space-time structure of the universe, constitutes the point on the boundary between the inconceivable and the conceivable, heaven and earth (to use theological terms), at which the universe is kept open to its transcendent ground which is the source of its meaning, while man himself reaches his destiny in communion with the living God. Looked at in this way, it may well be said that religious experience and theological understanding can and should play a fundamental role in the development of science in helping it both to overcome the materialist obsession with perceptible, tangible magnitudes and to break free from the paradigmatic preoccupation of western culture with observational images, but also more positively in cultivating in human society the ability to apprehend imperceptible, intangible magnitudes, upon which science more and more relies as it penetrates more and more deeply into the non-observable structures regulating the universe and our understanding of it. Only as man's mind is constantly lifted up in wonder and worship toward God the Creator of the space-time universe so that his thought is ultimately anchored in factors that transcend the universe altogether, will he be able to think in detachment from the refractory effects of split space and time and the reductionist observationalism and materialism that seem regularly to result from the old homogeneous geometrical structures of space independent of time.

This understanding of man as the being who exists on the boundary of the visible and invisible, of earth and heaven, clearly constitutes the place where natural science and theological science not only overlap but may contribute to each other. Modern science has now stormed back through the barrier between the visible and the invisible, and embraced the invisible within the realm of what is objectively cognisable. So long as science operated with the old dualisms, the realm of the visible and material, together with what could be abstracted from it, alone was regarded as the realm of the factual and the real, so that the invisible was denigrated as essentially non-cognitive, beyond the realm of the real. But now there has come about in the advance of science a right about face, for it is precisely the realm of the inherently invisible structure of space-time that is primary and regulative on the objective side of knowledge. Yet the more rigorously our understanding of this state of affairs is developed, the more it is found that far from being self-explanatory and self-sufficient the universe is characterised by boundary conditions that are and must be left open and indeterminate by its own internal relations.[86] Like a man-made machine it exists and functions only through relation to factors that are extraneous or transcendent to it. Thus in an astonishing way, science has returned to the point so strongly made by Newton that the mechanical connections operating within the universe, in terms of which we explain for example the motions of the heavens, cannot be extrapolated to account for the origin of its order – for that a different kind of 'cause' is required, the agency of will. That is to say, Newton insisted that the universe cannot be conceived to be a mechanical system complete and consistent in itself, for its immanent order is not completely explainable within that system, but the universe may be conceived as a consistent mechanism, he held, if it is related to the counsel of a voluntary and intelligent Agent beyond it, the living God who rules over all.[87] What has been permanently destroyed in Newton's thought, of course, is the dualist frame within which all this was conceived, the inertial system of absolute time and space which causally conditions all things within the universe reducing them to a rigid mechanical system, and the regulative role which is also attributed to God *within* the mechanical connections of the universe (in view of its alleged 'irregularities'). Thus Newton came very near to operating with a mythological synthesis between God and the universe, which is as impossible for theology as for mechanics. But while all this is now gone, the basic fact adduced by Newton remains, that the universe is finally an open system dependent, in ways that are not determinable from within itself, upon factors that are transcendent to it. This does not mean that we may identify the invisible open structure of space-time with the transcendent order of God's creative and providential activity, or merely relate them asymptotically to one another, for that also would be some form of mythological synthesis. But it does mean that the contingent nature of the universe can be taken with the fullest seriousness only if we realise its utter dependence on determinant factors utterly beyond it, and that the interaction of God with the universe can be taken with full seriousness only if we think of him as the transcendent ground of the creation and as the transcendent integrating factor that lends depth to all our human experience including natural science. In ordinary practice this means that it is religion which is the integrating factor in human life and culture in so far as through divine worship man learns to discern the invisible realities and to rely upon them as the 'constants' of human knowledge, whether of God or of nature. So far as the Christian faith is concerned, however, the central point of reference which gives depth and perspective to our place in the universe, must be the *Incarnation*, where God's interaction with the universe takes the form, not just of another creaturely mediation, but a real communication of *himself* to us in our own space-time existence. This means, in terms of our discussion above, that the invisible structure of God's interaction with creaturely existence intersects the invisible structure of space-time with cosmic and eschatological implications in the redeeming and renewing of all things, in all of which it is Jesus Christ who constitutes the 'boundary condition', as it were, of the created universe where its ultimate meaning is to be discerned through and beyond the contingent intelligibilities of space-time in the transcendent intelligibility of God the Father Almighty, Maker of heaven and earth and of all things visible and invisible.

NOTES

1. There is of course a proper distinction between how a scientist actually comes to find out something and how he subsequently writes it up and presents it, termed by Reichenbach the 'context of discovery' and the 'context of justification' (*Experience and Prediction*, Chicago, 1938, p. 6f), but it is another matter through rational reconstruction to clamp down prescriptively a hypothetico-deductive theory of scientific discovery and verification upon unformalisable heuristic operations.
2. I have in mind particularly Hempel, Nagel and Feigl.
3. London, 1970, Heidelberg Science Library, vol. 13.
4. p. 59.
5. That is, the exclusion of the subject of cognizance from the domain of nature that we endeavour to understand. E. Schrödinger, *Mind and Matter*, London, 1958, pp. 38ff, 43, 66.
6. The reference here is to E. Wigner, 'Two kinds of reality', *The Monist*, **48**, 248, 1964; and to another article, 'Are we machines?', *Proc. Am. Phil. Soc.*, **113**, 95, 1969, in which he argued that in order to deal with the phenomenon of life the laws of physics will have to be changed, not only reinterpreted.
7. At these points, Eccles is indebted particularly to Michael Polanyi, *The Tacit Dimension*, New York, 1966, etc.
8. *Facing Reality*, p. 61.
9. See A. d'Abro, *The Evolution of Scientific Thought from Newton to Einstein*, second edition, New York, 1950, p. 367ff.
10. The second English edition, Chicago and London, 1902.

11. Cf. Karl Popper, *Conjectures and Refutations,* 3rd edition, London, 1969, p. 100ff.
12. A. Einstein and L. Infeld, *The Evolution of Physics from Early Concepts to Relativity and Quanta,* London and New York, 1938, p. 143, p. 142ff, 150ff.
13. *Ibid.,* pp. 142ff, 150ff.
14. Einstein remarked that without Minkowski's contribution 'the general theory of relativity . . . would perhaps have got no farther that its long clothes'. *Relativity, The Special and General Theory,* 1961 edition, New York, p. 57. For Minkowski's famous paper on space-time see *The Principle of Relativity. A Collection of Original Memoirs on The Special and General Theory of Relativity* by H. A. Lorentz, A. Einstein, H. Minkowski and H. Weyl, with notes by A. Sommerfeld, New York and London, 1952, pp. 73–91.
15. Cf. the works of Ludwig von Bertalanffy, *Modern Theories of Development. An Introduction to Theoretical Biology.* Oxford, 1933; *General System Theory,* New York, 1968.
16. This latter point is clearly made by Popper, *op. cit.,* p. 116.
17. A. Einstein, *The World As I See It,* pp. 125ff, 135f.
18. This is to be understood in terms of what Popper has called 'objective probability', *op. cit.,* p. 227.
19. The need to extend quantum theory into this deeper dimension where it attempts a description of physical reality in its inner structure, irrespective of the observer, is the main theme of the fascinating correspondence between Einstein and Born, London, 1971, entitled *The Born-Einstein Letters,* with commentaries by Max Born.
20. A. Einstein, *The World As I See It,* London, 1935, p. 129.
21. A. Einstein and L. Infeld, *op. cit.,* p. 164ff, 172ff.
22. A. Einstein, *The World As I See It,* p. 132ff.
23. Isaac Newton, *Principia Mathematica.* (edit. by Cajori), Los Angeles and London, 1934, pp. 6ff.
24. Cf. A. Einstein, *Relativity, The Special and General Theory.* 1961 edition, New York, p. 143f.
25. See his essays reproduced in *The Principle of Relativity,* pp. 1–34.
26. A. Einstein, *The Meaning of Relativity,* 5th edition, 1954, Princeton reprint, 1970, p. 55ff. Cf. here the exposition by H. Weyl, *The Principle of Relativity,* p. 201ff.
27. 'Mass is energy and energy has mass.' Einstein and Infeld, *op. cit.,* p. 244.
28. Of course the concept of the material point, or mass-point, is now recast through deducing it by means of transformation rules from the continuous functional relations of the metrical field.
29. See especially *Sidelights on Relativity.* II. 'Geometry and Experience', London, 1922.
30. Cf. the discussion of A. d'Abro, *op. cit.,* p. 444ff., which I have found very enlightening; and A. Einstein, *Relativity, The Special and General Theory,* p. 56.

31. Classical physics operates, of course, also with a four-dimensional continuum, comprising three spatial coordinates and one time coordinate, but they are not fused into an unresolvable continuous structure. Hence, as Einstein remarks, 'on the basis of classical mechanics this four-dimensional continuum breaks up objectively into the one-dimensional time and into three-dimensional spatial sections.' *Relativity, The Special and General Theory*, 1961, edition, New York, p. 149.

32. *The World As I See It*, page 140; cf. also pp. 136, 138.

33. 'No fairer destiny could be allotted to any physical theory, than that it should of itself point out the way to the introduction of a more comprehensive theory, in which it lives on as a limiting case.' A. Einstein, *Relativity, The Special and General Theory*, p. 77. Cf. *The Principle of Relativity*, p. 157ff.

34. The expressions are Einstein's, *The World As I See It*, pp. 138, 141.

35. Cf. T. S. Kuhn, *The Structure of Scientific Revolutions*, Chicago and London, 1962, p. 121, 148ff., where he shows that while a scientific revolution may involve a sudden 'gestalt switch', and cannot be forced, communication across the revolutionary divide is another thing.

36. Cf. Einstein's remarks on this in respect of Clerk Maxwell, *The World As I See It*, p. 159–160.

37. Cf. the discussion of substance by D. M. Mackinnon, *"Substance" in Christology – a Cross-Bench View'*, in Sykes and Clayton, *Christ, Faith and History*, London, 1972, with which I find myself in very full agreement.

38. Cf. A. Einstein, *The World As I See It*, p. 156, and his autobiographical notes in P. A. Schilpp. *Albert Einstein: Philosopher-Scientist*, New York, 4th edition, 1957, pp. 81, 684.

39. Einstein, *The World As I See It*, p. 140 and 173ff.; cf. also Northrop, in Schilpp, *op. cit.*, p. 407, and Wenzyl. p. 606.

40. See the acute analysis and discussion of this question by Israel Scheffler, *Science and Subjectivity*, Indianapolis, New York and Kansas City, 1967, pp. 13ff., 39ff., 62ff., 116ff.

41. See the account given by Polanyi, *Personal Knowledge*, London, 1958, pp. 3–17, 37, 43, 64f., 103f., 116f., etc.

42. Isaac Newton, *Principia Mathematica*, (edit. by Cajori) Los Angeles and London, 1934, p. 547.

43. A. Einstein, *The World As I See It*, p. 135f.

44. A. Einstein, *The Meaning of Relativity*, p. 140.

45. Cf. Israel Scheffler, *Science and Subjectivity*, p. 114 where he directs this criticism against the views of Neurath and Schlick.

46. A. Einstein, *The World As I See It*, pp. 128, 133ff., 173ff.; *Out of My Later Years*, New York, 1950, p. 60f.

47. Cf. Einstein, 'Autobiographical Notes', P. A. Schilpp, *op. cit.*, p. 9.

48. Cf. Einstein, *The World As I See It*, p. 128: 'Here there is no method capable of being learnt and systematically applied that leads to the

goal. The scientist has to *worm these general principles out of nature* by perceiving certain general features, which permit of precise formulation, in large complexes of empirical facts . . . He has to persist in his helpless attitude towards the separate results of empirical research, until principles which he can make the basis of deductive reasoning *have revealed themselves to him.*' (italics mine).

49. See especially the more recent works, *The Tacit Dimension*, London, 1966, Ch. I; and *Knowing and Being*, London, 1969, part 3.
50. *The Tacit Dimension*, pp. 8ff.; *Knowing and Being*, pp. 142ff., 161ff.
51. *The Tacit Dimension*, p. 15f.; *Knowing and Being*, p. 118.
52. P. A. Schilpp, *op. cit.*, pp. 13, 620, 680; *The World As I See It*, p. 125; *Out Of My Later Years*, pp. 61ff.
53. *The World As I See It*, p. 136.
54. *The World As I See It*, p. 134.
55. From Einstein's contribution to the P. A. Schilpp volume on *The Philosophy of Bertrand Russell*, New York, 1944, p. 287.
56. Cf. P. A. Schilpp, *op. cit.*, p. 13f.; *The World As I See It*, p. 134f.
57. From the paper on 'Physics and Reality', *Out Of My Later Years*, p. 63.
58. *The Meaning of Relativity*, p. 2. Cf. also *Out Of My Later Years*, p. 63: 'The relation is not analogous to that of soup to beef but rather of wardrobe number to overcoat.' This sounds more conventionalist!
59. *Out Of My Later Years*, pp. 60f., 95; *The World As I See It*, p. 126. Cf. also Stanley L. Jaki, *The Relevance of Physics*, Chicago, 1966, pp. 345ff.
60. *Out Of My Later Years*, pp. 60ff., 95ff.; *The World As I See It*, pp. 131ff., 156ff.
61. Cf. M. Polanyi, *Knowing and Being*, p. 108.
62. A. Einstein, *The World As I See It*, pp. 173–174, and see also p. 126.
63. This point is made with great force by Israel Scheffler, *op. cit.*, pp. 106ff., 114ff., 122f.
64. I. Newton, *Principia Mathematica*, (edit. by Cajori) p. 398; cf. also p. 192.
65. Consult for the following the analysis offered by Erich Kahler in *The Disintegration of Form in the Arts*, New York, 1967, in which the cross-connections between difficulties in art and science are very enlighteningly set out. Cf. 3ff., 22f., 27ff., 42f., etc.
66. E. Mach, *The Science of Mechanics*, pp. 481ff.
67. A. Einstein, *Out Of My Later Years*, 62f., 95f.; *The World As I See It*, pp. 134ff., 140f., 152; Schilpp, *op. cit.*, pp. 23, 29, 33, etc.
68. A. Einstein, 'Remarks on Bertrand Russell's Theory of Knowledge', in P. A. Schilpp, *The Philosophy of Bertrand Russell*, Chicago, 1944, p. 287.
69. p. 289.
70. *Out Of My Later Years*, pp. 59f., 95; *The World As I See It*, p. 173.
71. Cf. A. Einstein, *The Meaning of Relativity*, p. 2.
72. See the introduction by Ruth Nanda Anschen to F. S. C. Northrop, *Man, Nature and God*, New York, 1962, p. XIIff.

73. M. Polanyi, *The Tacit Dimension,* pp. 30ff.
74. M. Polanyi, *Knowing and Being,* especially 151ff., and 211ff.
75. Polanyi's stress upon personal commitment and personal knowledge has been seriously misunderstood in this respect.
76. See above, p. 2, and J. C. Eccles, *op. cit.,* p. 60ff.
77. This is part of the great significance of Stanley L. Jaki's work, *The Relevance of Physics,* in which he discusses the limits of the legitimate application of scientific methods and thus also the irrelevance of physics for other areas of knowledge.
78. This point is powerfully demonstrated in several of his books by F. S. C. Northrop. See especially, *The Logic of the Sciences and the Humanities,* (1947), Cleveland and New York, Meridian, 1959, chs. IV–VII, and *Man, Nature and God,* New York, 1962, especially the Introduction and ch. 4. The expression 'imageless' relations' used below is his.
79. M. Polanyi, *Knowing and Being,* pp. 142ff., 151ff., 161ff., etc.
80. *Knowing and Being,* pp. 134ff., 148ff., 160ff., 220f.
81. Cf. here Einstein's account of the relations of the various levels in our scientific operations, in the essay on 'Physics and Reality', *Out Of My Later Years,* pp. 58ff.
82. M. Polanyi, *Knowing and Being,* p. 130f.; also F. S. C. Northrop, *The Logic of the Sciences and the Humanities,* ch. II, pp. 19ff.
83. See the discussion of Richard Feynmann, *The Character of Physical Law,* Cambridge, Massachusetts, and London, 1965, pp. 50ff., 84ff., 168.
84. Paul Tillich, *Systematic Theology,* vol. I, pp. 105ff.
85. I have taken this expression from Michael Polanyi, *The Tacit Dimension,* pp. 40, 42, 45, 88; *Knowing and Being,* pp. 154ff., 175ff., 217ff., 226ff., 23ff. The expression seems to derive originally from Einstein – see *The Meaning of Relativity,* 5th edition, p. 164f.
86. No one has done more to elucidate thought here than Polanyi; see *Personal Knowledge,* pp. 328ff.; *The Tacit Dimension,* pp. 38ff.; *Knowing and Being,* pp. 175ff., 216ff., 229ff., etc.
87. *Principia Mathematica,* (edit. by Cajori), pp. XXVII, XXXIff., 544ff.; *Opticks,* pp. 369f. 400ff., etc.

CHAPTER III

The Place of Michael Polanyi in the
Modern Philosophy of Science*

IN THIS essay an attempt is made to plot the significance of
Michael Polanyi for modern philosophy of science by reference
to the thought of Einstein, Popper, Bohr and Gödel. Our concern
with Michael Polanyi's philosophy is not simply with what he
himself taught, but with what we, learning from him, may do in
carrying further the kind of scientific inquiry which he has taught
so many of us. Hence, it may be a help to relate the thought of
Michael Polanyi to some other giants in his own time, and in that
way to throw his significance into some relief.

This is not to suggest that Polanyi takes his starting point from
any of these, or that his thought is to be construed in terms of
theirs, for he has his own distinctive starting point and a highly
original contribution to make to the epistemology of scientific
activity. This is a contribution, however, which fits in with lines of
advance that derive particularly from Einstein, Bohr and Gödel,
meets them at least at one of the points where they converge, and
carries the advance farther in the most sensitive area, the nature and
process of scientific discovery. We shall be especially concerned
with the way in which Polanyi's discovery about discovery relates

*Presented to a Seminar on the thought of Michael Polanyi at the session of The
American Academy of Religion, Chicago, November, 1975.

to what Einstein called 'the free creations of thought which cannot inductively be gained from sense-experiences'[1] but which arise in our minds under the impact of the inherent intelligibility (*Verständlichkeit*) of the universe, and with the kind of wordless thinking that goes on when the scientist is caught up in wonder and in the indefinable acts of intuitive apprehension upon which his creative structures rest.[2]

Let us look, then, at Michael Polanyi's own starting point, or rather at those starting points in his thought from which I wish to develop this account of his philosophy of science.

First, let us go back to Polanyi's early reflections on the distinction between *pure science* and *applied science,* that is, between science freely pursued for its own sake and science pursued for some other socially or politically conditioned end, the first finding its home on academic soil, and the second in the factories and other quarters closely attached to practical life.[3] This is not meant to imply a denigration of applied science over against pure science, but to point out that they operate with different kinds of knowledge and indeed with different conceptual frameworks determined by rather different ends, and so to prevent a substitution of applied science in the form of technology for pure science, since that would damage the very basis on which scientific inquiry is pursued.[4] Science, to be science, operates with something irreducibly given, over which we have no control, 'a transcendent reality', as Polanyi calls it, reaching out beyond us in an indeterminate range of intelligibility but which through its intimations of hidden dimensions of meaning and order beckons us on in unceasing inquiry.[5] Here we have the root of Polanyi's profound faith in the objective intelligibility of the universe, to the knowledge of which we are inescapably committed as rational beings.[6]

Secondly let us go back to some of Polanyi's reflections arising out of his early scientific activity in medicine and chemistry. Two things may be singled out: *(a)* the inseparable connexion between the empirical and the theoretical, evident, for example, in the use of a medical instrument or probe in a surgical operation or in the process of a discovery;[7] and *(b)* the distinctive kind of order to be discerned in living organisms or in crystalline formations.[8] This is not the kind of order which arises under external constraint but one that arises spontaneously in the mutual adjustment of elements in the growth and formation of plants and animals, or in the structural arrangements that result from particles freely obeying the internal forces acting between them. Here we have a delicate and complex type of order in which something goes on which we are unable to reproduce by human artifice, although we may be able to provide the external conditions under which that order spontaneously arises. This kind of order has an interior power of organisation which in the nature of the case resists explanation, and cannot be made fully explicit, by analytical methods, yet it is a similar kind of order or process of integration in which we ourselves participate when learning and on which we count when teaching others.[9]

Thirdly, and this is not the least important, we turn to Michael Polanyi's reflections on the organisation of science within the State, as well as on the challenge of Marxist theory to the function of science in a free society, for it was in the course of those reflections that he came to devote himself to the theoretical and social problems in the philosophy of science, and indeed to 'the symbiosis between thought and society'.[10] Polanyi's concern here is with the social coefficient of pure science in the pursuit of the truth for the truth's sake, the bearing of the progress of scientific activity upon society, tradition, authority, and thus with the social message of science and the fact that science can develop, has developed, and continues to develop adequately only within the structures of human society.[11] Behind that lies the problem of 'the premises of science' or 'the fiduciary presuppositions of science',[12] the fact that our discovery and the acceptance of scientific knowledge are a commitment to certain beliefs which we hold, but which others refuse, and that, since there is 'a structural kinship' between what we know and our knowing of it,[13] there is a dynamic interconnection between the advance of pure science and the continuation of a free society. Scientific activity in society requires the same kind of free spontaneous ordering in its own organisation and in that of society as we find operating independently of us in nature.[14]

All these three starting points, as I have called them, the conviction as to the transcendent element in pure science to which we are rationally committed, the liberation from a positivist imposition of a hard causal order upon all human thought through the recognition of another kind of order having its own interior power of organisation, and the profound interrelation between that kind of order and the foundations of academic and scientific freedom, imply each other in a profound correspondence between the indeterminate open structures of the universe and the indeterminate open structures of scientific discovery. Together they carry a coherent philosophy of social science in relation to pure science which yields the notion of an 'open society' and the kind of creative freedom in socio-economic and legal structures with which we are also familiar in the writings of F. A. von Hayek and Karl Popper, both of whom seem to owe more to Polanyi than at first appears.[15] Just as the new concept of science which Polanyi advocates destroys positivism, so the social message of this new science destroys the kind of closed totalitarian society, as in Marxist States, which is the correlate to positivism. 'The general foundations of coherence and freedom in society may be regarded as secure to the extent to which men uphold their belief in the reality of truth, justice, charity and tolerance, and accept dedication to the service of these realities; while society may be expected to disintegrate and fall into servitude when men deny, explain away, or simply disregard these realities and transcendent obligations. The totalitarian State arises logically from the denial of reality to this realm of transcendent ideas. When the spiritual foundations of all freely dedicated human activities – the cultivation of science and scholarship, of the vindication of justice, of the profession of religion, of the pursuit of free art and free political discussion – when the transcendent grounds of all these free activities are summarily denied, then the State becomes, of necessity, inheritor to all ultimate devotion of men.'[16] That is not the side of Polanyi's thought, however, on which we are to concentrate here, so much as the free dynamic structure of scientific inquiry into the ordered reality of the world around us which, through its indefinite range or scope of objective intelligibility, always takes us by surprise.

We may now proceed to throw certain aspects of Polanyi's thought into relief by attempting to relate them to corresponding aspects in the thought of Einstein, Popper, Bohr and Gödel.

I

The Einsteinian revolution lies behind all Polanyi's thought, the rejection of Newtonian dualism and the dethronement of the mechanistic universe, and a new unitary outlook on nature dominated by the matter–energy equation.[17] In this understanding of the universe, in which space and time are held to inhere in the on-going processes of nature, scientific knowledge operates with the intrinsic unity of form and being, of structure and matter. All this involves a profound change in the fundamental principles of knowledge, which is of cardinal importance.[18] Two basic points may be noted.

(a) The rejection of the conventionalist and positivist notions of science, and of scientific theory, advanced by Ernst Mach for whom the structures of thought with which the scientist operates are to be construed in terms of convenient functional arrangements of observational concepts, without any claim on relation to being and which as such are strictly neither true nor false. It was, of course, out of Mach's philosophy of science that the so-called Vienna Circle developed, and the critical linguistic philosophy of analysis to which, in various forms, it gave rise.[19]

(b) The rejection of the Kantian notion of the synthetic *a priori*, through which knowledge of the phenomenal world is reduced to order without any penetration into the structure of things in themselves or in their internal relations. That follows with the departure from the phenomenalist approach to knowledge that goes back, in modern times, to Galileo (e.g. the distinction between primary and secondary qualities), and from the dualism which in somewhat different ways is inherent in the thought of Descartes and Newton. In its place there is put a profound conviction that the world is inherently comprehensible independently of our knowing of it, while our knowing of it is to be construed as an activity of the mind, guided by an intuitive contact with reality, in penetrating into the intrinsic coherences and objective structures in the fields of our inquiry. Moreover, the fusion of physical and intelligible elements in nature independent of us means that our knowing of nature involves from the very start processes in which the empirical and the theoretical are inseparable.

From this perspective two characteristics of Einstein's science stand out:

(a) Basic to everything is an intuitive apprehension of nature in its intrinsic relations – and by intuitive apprehension is meant rational but non-logical, non-inferential knowledge. Scientific hypotheses are not deduced from observations, as Newton claimed, for scientific concepts are not logically derived from experience. Scientific knowledge advances through *freely invented concepts*, i.e. not fictions, not freely invented conventions, but concepts that creatively arise in our minds under the compulsion of the objective structures of nature. From the point of view of logic, however, they may be regarded as freely chosen conventions, since they are not logically derived or logically compelled. That is why Einstein called them 'free creations', yet their freeness is restricted from the side of nature and controlled by the real world; as such they are inseparable from empirical experiences and subject to empirical testing. Thus while basic scientific ideas and relations are intuitively reached they are objectively determined and controlled.[20]

(b) Once we have reached these basic relations or ideas, we connect them up by theorems which enable us to deduce other ideas and relations, in an attempt to produce a theoretic and logically coherent structure through which we may seek to bring to light the

inherent and coherent structure of nature. Sometimes indeed Einstein could say (in a way which was shared by Eddington and Milne) that it ought to be possible from a few basic ideas to deduce the main system of scientific knowledge, yet it still remained valid for him that there is *no logical bridge* between the structure of scientific theories and the objective structure of the real world.[21]

This brings us to the fundamental question: How are our ideas related to experience? According to Einstein nothing can be said about the manner in which concepts are to be made and connected, and how we are to coordinate them to experience, although it is admittedly that relation that determines the cognitive value of systems of concepts.[22] He was content to fall back on what Leibniz called a 'pre-established harmony' between our ideas and the real world.[23]

It is at this point that we see the distinctiveness of Polanyi's thought. He was not content to remain there, but insisted on thinking out further the heuristic process in which we reach knowledge of the real world which we cannot infer from what we already know, and has succeeded in carrying further the coordination between our ideas and experience, which Einstein did not consider possible. Polanyi claims – and this is central to his basic position – that *we know more than we can tell,* for in addition to our 'focal awareness' and the explicit knowledge to which it gives rise, we always operate with a 'subsidiary awareness' and an implicit knowledge on which we rely in all our explicit operations. This is evident not only in the act of judgment on which we rely in operating a system of rules, for no system of rules, as Kant has shown, can prescribe the procedure by which the rules themselves are applied.[24] It is evident in the basic activity of knowing as in the recognition of a problem or the intuition of a latent coherence without which the mind's contact with reality would be blind and fruitless. This is what Polanyi has called 'the tacit dimension' both in the activity of scientific discovery through an unaccountable intuitive apprehension of a structure in reality, and in the development of knowledge through a process of integration in which largely unspecifiable clues are organised in response to the intimation of a true coherence in nature.[25] Since it is 'intuition' of this kind that is 'the tacit coefficient' of a scientific theory, by which it bears on experience, since an explicit statement can bear on reality only by virtue of the tacit coefficient associated with it, this seems to call for a significant modification in what we understand by knowledge, for knowledge cannot then be defined merely in terms of what is explicit, and also in what we understand by reality, for correspondingly, reality cannot be defined in terms of what is only correlated with explicit concepts and statements.[26] If that is the case – and it is increasingly being granted on both sides of the Atlantic that this is the case – then Polanyi's discovery about the structure of tacit knowledge is a contribution to modern philosophy of science of quite fundamental importance.[27]

It is not my purpose at the moment to discuss tacit knowing so much as to clarify certain aspects of it in Polanyi's account where there may be ambiguity or misunderstanding on the part of some of his interpreters and critics.

If we know more than we can tell, then in some sense we know before we know – how is that to be construed? That was the problem taken up by Plato in the *Meno* as to the possibility of inquiry and learning: Is it a learning of what we know or of what we do not know?[28] Polanyi expresses the problem in this way: 'Either you know what you are looking for, and then there is no problem; or you do not know what you are looking for, and then you are not looking for anything and cannot expect to find any-thing.'[29] Plato's solution to the problem was given in his doctrine of reminiscence or recollection, to the effect that learning is being reminded of something, a recalling of some truth which we have lost. While Plato's doctrine of reminiscence, especially in its Orphic form, is not acceptable, Polanyi does accept the fact that Plato has demonstrated that if all knowledge is explicit, then we cannot know a problem or look for its solution. Learning involves some kind of tacit knowledge in the intimation of something hidden, which we may yet discover. Polanyi's own solution of the problem lies in what he calls 'a tacit foreknowledge of yet undiscovered things'.[30] This has nothing to do with innate ideas or innate knowledge, but is a kind of vision which reaches out beyond what we explicitly know, enabling us to judge what things not yet understood are capable of being understood, and to guide our conjecture with reasonable probability in choosing a good problem and in choosing hunches that might solve the problem.[31] But does Polanyi mean by *foreknowledge*, some kind of preconception, some *a priori* know-ledge, or even what the existentialists call 'pre-comprehension' (*Vorverständnis*)?

What Polanyi proposes here is not any kind of preconceptuality, but something more like foresight, an intimation which a scientist derives from an intuitive grasp of a reality which he is unable to specify, and which constitutes the clue from which he takes his start, and by developing which he guides his probing inquiry into the structure of that reality. It is essentially an *intuitive insight,* the insight of a mind informed by intuitive contact with reality, an inductive insight with a semantic or ontological reference which is objectively correlated to an aspect of nature seeking realisation, as it were, in the mind of the inquirer.[32] What Polanyi intends by 'foreknowledge', then, is what the Greeks called *prolepsis,* a proleptic conception, an anticipatory glimpse, a tenuous and subtle outreach of the understanding with a forward thrust in cognition of something quite new. In the on-going process of inquiry it is an incipient knowing, in which the intimation of the coherence of hitherto not comprehended particulars, an intuitive grasp of things that goes far beyond what we can formalise in order to comprehend them meaningfully, is at work: and therefore Polanyi can speak of it as a prior tacit knowing leading to explicit knowing; it is not a foreknowledge that arises outside of or apart from the actual field under investigation, but under its impact upon us and its control over our minds.[33] It is an implicit apprehension that takes shape in our understanding under the imprint of the internal structure of that into which we inquire, and develops within the structural kinship that arises between our knowing and what we know as we make ourselves dwell in it and gain access to its meaning. Tacit knowing of this kind, in which our thoughts are deeper than we know, Polanyi claims, is the all-important, yet informal and unaccountable, element in scientific activity through which a line of inquiry is inspired and progressively integrated. Far from being, therefore, an *a priori* conception, or preconception, the foreknowledge with which scientific inquiry operates is an intuitive anticipation of a hitherto unknown pattern, or a novel order in things, which arises compellingly in our minds under the surprising disclosure and intrinsic claim of the subject-matter. It is an authentically heuristic act in which the understanding leaps across a *logical gap* in the attainment of a new conception, and then guided by an intuitive surmise evoked by that conception probes through deepening coherences to lay bare the structure of the reality being investigated.[34]

It was, of course, Einstein who destroyed the idea that scientific discovery is a logical process, in showing, as we have already seen, that there is no logical bridge between scientific ideas and experience – the clear recognition of that fact coming only with the general theory of relativity.[35] Thus, he paved the way for a radically new approach to induction. It is experience, he insisted, which *suggests* the appropriate concepts – they certainly cannot be deduced from it.[36] The task of establishing the principles which are to serve the scientist as the starting-point for his deductions is of an entirely different nature. 'Here there is no method capable of being learnt and systematically applied that leads to the goal: The scientist has to worm these general principles out of nature by perceiving certain general features, which permit of precise formulation, in large complexes of empirical facts . . . He has to persist in his helpless attitude towards the separate results of empirical research, until principles he can make the basis of deductive reasoning have revealed themselves to him.'[37] Thus the basic problem in scientific discovery, the relation between concepts and experience, is the *ontological reference* of scientific concepts and theories – but that is what Einstein called an 'extra-logical problem' which scientists will be able to solve only intuitively.[38]

II

Following upon Einstein, Popper has also taken issue with the belief in inductive logic (what he calls 'the myth of induction') for if there were such a thing as a purely logical principle of induction, there would be no problem of induction at all.[39] He also follows Einstein in attacking the idea that scientific theories are derived by way of deductions or generalisations from particular observations, as if we could start with observations alone, without any theoretical ingredient even of an incipient nature. As Einstein once expressed it, 'whether you can observe a thing or not depends on the theory which you use. It is the theory which decides what can be observed'.[40] There are no observations that are not already interpreted or informed by theoretical elements. Scientific theories, however, are invented through the creative imagination and are put forward as *conjectures* (which have no logical basis in observed facts) to account for problems, and are critically and systematically tested by asking for evidence that counts against them.[41] In this way incorrect or deficient conjectures are set aside by negative evidence and have to be replaced. This also applies to our treatment of fresh observations and experiments deriving from theories as we devise confrontations between them and these theories. Thus even though scientific theories and generalisations are not conclusively verifiable, although they may be demonstrated to have 'objective probability', the process of hypothetico-deductive testing of conjectures and theories opens up the way for sounder and maturer theories serving the growth of knowledge and its accumulation of positive content.[42] Popper claims to have solved the problem of induction, which he dates back to 1927, but there is little of essential importance regarding scientific method which is not already found in the thought of Einstein.[43] Moreover, as Harré has pointed out, 'the joint method of confirmation and falsification has been a common place of scientific method at least since the sixteenth century', while even then it was already held with particular force that 'experimental evidence *alone* is not enough either to confirm or to refute a theory or hypothesis, and that other rational procedures of decision must be looked for'.[44] Compared to Polanyi, however, Popper does not appear to give sufficient attention to the ontological reference of scientific concepts or therefore to the *heuristic act itself* – although that is perhaps understandable since Popper, unlike Polanyi, is not also an empirical scientist. Granted that we must not confuse how a theory arises with the scientific status of the theory once it has been put forward, Popper's way of distinguishing between logical processes and psychological processes leads him to pay insufficient attention to the all-important *epistemic process* in scientific discovery, for while he rightly rejects the view in which induction is construed as a logical process, he seems to take up a position in which little room is left for a rational or intellectual process in the heuristic act beyond 'highly informative guesses'.[45]

This is precisely the point, however, at which Polanyi seems to have advanced beyond Einstein in bringing to light the tacit power of the mind in discerning *Gestalten,* in the heuristic leap from parts to a whole, comprehending patterns of coherence, and in the informal (non-logical) but rational process of integration evident in verification as well as in discovery. Intuition, conjecture and the creative power of the imagination in problem-solving and in the formation of scientific hypotheses all have their place here, as in the thought of Einstein, but Polanyi probes into the epistemic structure of the heuristic act, the intellectual process of discovery, and spells it out as far as he finds it possible, without allowing it to disintegrate in, and be replaced by, an analytic and discursive movement of thought operating only with explicit, formal connections.[46] This is not by any means to depreciate the importance of analysis in which 'one proceeds from a recognition of a whole towards an identification of its particulars', which is complementary to the other movement 'from the recognition of a group of presumed particulars towards the grasping of their relation in the whole'.[47] It is indeed, Polanyi claims, through an alternation of analysis and integration that we are led to an ever deeper understanding of a comprehensive entity, but the resolution of everything into explicit, formal and specifiable relations would finally impede discovery, for the coherent existence of the whole would elude us – in any case even analysis properly undertaken depends upon an underlying and effective integration. This is where what Polanyi calls 'foreknow-ledge' or 'scientific intuition' plays such an essential role in the integrating of clues and particulars in a comprehensive whole. Thus 'the process of inductive discovery is in fact an oscillation between movements of analysis and integration in which, on balance, integration predominates'.[48] If this is the case, then it is evident that if analysis is to be effective and revealing it must remain *incomplete*; it destroys its own contribution to the discovery of meaning if everything is made completely explicit and all connections are formalised.[49] Thus Polanyi's contribution to our understanding of the process of discovery in science is to show that 'tacit knowing is the fundamental power of the mind, which creates explicit knowing, lends meaning to it and controls its uses'.[50] Behind all that people call 'hunches', 'guesses', 'intuitions', 'surmises', 'conjectures', it is an implicit integrative activity of the mind that is at work in the epistemic process of scientific discovery, on which we rely in discerning their ontological reference or in judging their bearing on reality, and therefore in distinguishing *right* hunches, guesses, etc. from those that are merely random. That is no less an intellectual activity even if in the nature of the case it cannot be logicalised and no rules can account for its operation.[51]

Polanyi thinks out the intellectual process in discovery on the model of 'the logic of perceptual integration'.[52] A stock example he uses is that of knowing or recognising a physiognomy by integrating our awareness of its particulars without being able to identify them. All visual perception operates in this way, for how we see the object on which we focus our attention depends largely on marginal clues which we may not notice at all, as well as subliminal clues in our bodily processes which we cannot detect or experience in themselves. He distinguishes here between two kinds of awareness, which he calls *focal* and *subsidiary*.[53] They operate conjointly in such a way that we are subsidiarily aware of marginal elements with a functional bearing on the object we know focally. This functional relation is a product of an integration carried out tacitly by our sense of coherence linking the subsidiary elements to the focal centre in such a way that our apprehension of the clues is transformed into an apprehension of the objective reality to which they point. Polanyi explains that further by reference to the way in which we use a pair of stereoscopic pictures. If we look at them separately we may notice a slight difference between them, but when we view them conjointly in a stereoscope we see something new, a single picture having a marked three-dimensional depth. This sight is the joint meaning of the two pictures. 'Applying this to perception, we can say that we are aware of the clues which guide our vision in the subsidiary manner in which we are aware of the two constituent pictures in a stereoscopic sight. The clues are integrated to the sight of the perceived object which is their meaning.'[54]

It is on that model, then, that Polanyi probes into 'the logic of discovery', for the structure of scientific intuition, he claims, is the same as that of perception.[55] Here, of course, when we move from ordinary perception which takes place effortlessly to the level of scientific activity, 'perception' needs to be highly trained if we are to discern the significant shapes and patterns that indicate a coherence in nature and progressively develop our grasp of it in order to attain a true conception of the nature of things we are investigating. All through this process, active scientific inquiry relies tacitly upon indefinable, integrative powers of thought through which the clues of which we are subsidiarily aware are brought to bear upon the object of our focal attention in such a way as to enable us to apprehend it as a comprehensive entity in its own coherent features and intrinsic structure, that is, in a dimension of objective depth. The clues with which we operate, however, and the intuitive apprehension of reality we gain through them, arise under the impact of that reality and its intrinsic structure upon our minds, so that what is distinctive here in the conjoint functioning of subsidiary and focal awareness is the way in which empirical and theoretical, or ontological and formal, elements are fused inseparably together, like the two pictures in one 'solid' indivisible stereo-image.[56] This becomes even clearer, when we turn to another of Polanyi's analogies, the light thrown upon visual perception through experiments with inverting spectacles, which makes one see things upside-down, or inverted between right and left, as the case may be. Here it has been shown that in overcoming the initial disorientation into which a person is thrown, it is not his visual image but his conceptual image that has to be changed, but that reveals how the visual and the conceptual images operate insepar-ably together in our orientation to the objective structure of the world around us.[57] It is this fusion of the rational and ontological elements in nature, and of the empirical and theoretical elements in our apprehension of it, that Polanyi took pains to establish in the opening chapter of his Gifford Lectures of 1951–2, by showing that twentieth-century physics, and Einstein's discovery of relativity in particular, demonstrate the power of science to make contact with reality in nature by recognising what is rational in nature.[58] It is because nature is inherently rational that reason cannot be separated from experience, or mathematical knowledge from empirical knowledge, but this is also the ground for the tacit dimension which underlies all our knowledge (that our thoughts are much deeper than we know) since in so far as it makes contact with reality it is linked to an objective structure with a depth and range of rationality that reaches far beyond our understanding as well as our formalisations.[59] It is out of that ontological reference that there arises the kind of foreknowledge which guides scientists to discovery.[60]

Since form and being are fused together in nature, they must be grasped together in our apprehension of nature. That is why the epistemic process in scientific discovery is essentially an *integrative activity*, rather than an analytical or an abstractive activity, for that would have the effect of tearing apart the theoretical from the empirical which would open up a fatal gap between the explicit and the tacit in which the all-important clues pointing to coherences in nature would vanish with the disintegration of the matrix in which they are born – just as we efface the clues from a solid stereo-image when we remove the stereo-pictures from the viewer and look at them separately with both eyes.[61] When that happens, no inferential or logical process can fuse the two separate pictures into a single spatial image. Hence, Polanyi argues, the fusion of the clues to the image on which they bear is *not a deduction, but an integration*. That holds good also of scientific activity, even in the case of the highest mathematical sciences, where the pursuit of discovery is essentially a tacit operation, 'with integration replacing deduction'.[62] Deduction could only operate through a prescinding of the formal elements from being and a logical connecting of them together apart from their ontological import, but that would eliminate the semantic function and thus impede the discovery of the unknown. Thus it is understandable that Polanyi should take such a strong stand against the predominance of a positivist and analytical philosophy of science on the one hand, and against an unbalanced reliance on explicit deductivism on the other hand, in the progress of scientific inquiry and verification, for, not only does explicit procedure fail to account for the creative, integrative operations in the epistemic process, but when made primary it attacks the dynamic nature of knowing and inquiry which are rooted in the tacit dimension.[63] Polanyi insists, therefore, that the non-formalisable or informal ingredient in knowing is not left behind by explicit logico-deductive or hypothetico-deductive processes, necessary as they are in developing consistent and coherent structures of thought. The explicit argumentation we develop and have to develop in scientific theories constitutes the link between the input and the output which is based on the processes of tacit knowing. The explicit argument is external to the input and output and is coordinated with it in a meta-theoretical, or perhaps a meta-scientific, way.[64]

In integration, then, it is not the discursive reason but the intuitive reason that is predominant, not only at the start but at any stage of a scientific inquiry. 'The scientist's intuitive powers consist firstly in the faculty of surmising with a fair degree of probability the presence of a hidden coherence in nature. It is this faculty that espies a problem, the pursuit of which the scientist may accept as his task. The inquiry goes ahead, then, guided by a series of surmises, which also have a reasonable chance of being right. Thus a discovery is reached – or may be reached – which solves the problem. Poincaré emphasises that illumination does not come without the previous work of the imagination.[65] This applies also to what I call intuition. A problem fit for inquiry comes to the scientist in response to his roaming vision of yet undiscovered possibilities. Having chosen a problem, he thrusts his imagination forward in search of clues and the material he thus digs up – whether by speculation or by experiment – is integrated by intuition into new surmises, and so the inquiry goes on to the end.'[66] That is to say, the intuitive judgments of the scientist become progressively more concrete, more fully grounded in focally observed evidence.[67]

However, that must not be allowed to obscure 'the essential kinship of heuristics and verification'.[68] This claim is one of the distinctive characteristics of Polanyi's philosophy of science: 'any critical verification of a scientific statement requires the same powers for recognising rationality in nature as does the process of scientific discovery'.[69] Foreknowledge, as we saw, is indispensable at the very start of scientific discovery, but all discovery is but a step towards the verification of that foreknowledge, and a scientific theory is held to be justified when the anticipatory insight which inspired the inquiry and guided its progress is accepted.[70] That means that deductive testing of scientific theories can have only an indirect and a limited bearing on their verification, for as there is no logical connection between our ideas and experience in discovery, so there is no logical connection between them in proof. Just as no rules can account for the way in which we reach new conceptions, so there are no firm rules for their verification or for the refutation of the proposed solution of a problem. Strict scientific procedure in accordance with formal rules has an important part to play in establishing the validity of an argument, but again and again, as Polanyi points out, scientific inquiry actually proceeds and triumphs by contradicting formal rules.[71]

Polanyi's steady emphasis upon *integrative knowledge,* together with a recognition of the limits of logico-deductive processes in scientific activity, clearly differentiates his position from the 'refutationalist' theory of scientific method advanced by Popper, although they clearly have a great deal in common, as in their common opposition to critical empiricism, their agreement that the deductive method of testing cannot establish or justify scientific statements, and therefore the need for scientists to take decisions in which they combine, as it were, the functions of judge and jury, in giving their verdict for one theory in preference to others, and their acknowledgement of the way in which scientific theories have to pass the test of acceptability within the advancing framework of scientific principles and knowledge. For Polanyi, however, the idea that the scientist actually *seeks* the refutation of his surmises or conjectures is both contrary to experience and logically inconceivable. 'The surmises of a working scientist are *born of the imagination seeking discovery*. Such an effort *risks* defeat but never *seeks it*; it is in fact his craving for success that makes the scientist take the risk of failure. There is no other way. Courts of law employ two separate lawyers to argue opposite pleas, because it is only by a passionate commitment to a particular view that the imagination can discover the evidence that supports it.'[72] Thus, as we have seen, there is an alternation of analysis and integration in the progress of scientific activity to an ever deeper understanding of the object or field of inquiry, but both in the discovery and in the confirmation of new knowledge the emphasis falls upon integration through which discovery and verification are interiorly and structurally related. That is evidently not the case in the theory of scientific method which divides the process of discovery sharply into the choice of a hypothesis and the testing of the chosen hypothesis, the first being deemed to be inexplicable by any rational procedure, and the second being considered to be a strict procedure which is the scientist's essential task. On the one hand, this fails to take into account the ontological reference of the epistemic process in which the nature of what we know has a distinct bearing on how we know; and on the other hand, the claim that hypotheses are strictly tested by confronting their implications with experience, itself implies that if any of the implications of a hypothesis conflicts with experience, such an hypothesis must be abandoned, but that even if it is accepted on the ground of having been confirmed in its predictions, it will always remain on trial and be instantly abandoned if any empirical evidence turns up that contradicts any of its claims.[73] In putting this theory of Popper's to the test, Polanyi comes up with many actual instances in the history of confirmed scientific achievements which contradict its claims.[74] He adduces examples to show that important scientific discoveries can be made and established without any subsequent tests, and that there have been great theoretical discoveries which had no testable experimental content. He points out how the theory of evolution, which interprets in a novel way a vast range of experience, was accepted by science and firmly held for many years, although its assumptions contradicted the laws of nature known at the time, and that it continues to be held by science, as other important theories are, although it has never been testable by predictions by which it could be empirically refuted.[75] All this would be more than sufficient to falsify a strict theory of refutationalism on its own terms, but with Polanyi this is not allowed to discredit such a theory so much as to modify it, on the ground that any exception to a rule, as it has been formulated, may not involve its definitive refutation but the promise of a deeper meaning and verification at a deeper level. That is to say, it may have the effect of deepening the problem and of calling for a deeper grasp of the structures of reality under investigation.[76] This is the way in which falsifiability contributes to the strength of on-going verifying processes.

Polanyi himself, however, as we have seen, prefers to take a more positive approach, closely in line with the actual way in which we think and act and learn in our daily life, and one grounded on the organic substructure of perceptual knowledge.[77] Science is, he claims, a great extension of perception in which we discern and integrate aspects and shapes of reality in the light of, and under the impact of, their latent coherences, in ways that are not precisely definable.[78] This scientific extension of perception is of course a severely disciplined activity, subject to rigorous critical testing and strictly controlled conditions throughout.[79] It is one in which we readily subject ourselves and our ideas to radical questioning both from the side of the subject-matter of our inquiry and from the universal community of scientific investigators and verifiers, if only in order to set aside all self-deception and corrupting intrusions and distractions, so that research may be carried out strictly in accordance with the nature of the field of inquiry and its intrinsic claims upon us. But it is still true that in spite of all these explicit processes of critical testing and rigorous control, essential as they are, scientific inquiry is found to have an organic substructure of knowledge, and to operate under the guidance of an intuitive grasp of objective unity underlying empirical diversity, similar to that which obtains in perceptual knowledge, in which we operate at every stage with indefinable powers of thought and with shapes and correlations in nature which cannot be precisely defined. That is indeed why there are problems and why there is science at all, but also why strictly speaking all natural sciences are inexact and why the results of science are not capable of strict proof.[80] 'They could all be conceivably false, but we accept them as true because we consider doubts that may be raised against them as unreasonable.'[81] In scientific as in perceptual knowledge there are imponderable elements to which no formal procedure, no system of rules, can apply, so that the scientist constantly finds himself having to make a responsible judgment without the aid of explicit criteria in picking out regularities that are likely to prove significant or in deciding what weight to attach to a particular set of evidence in confirmation or refutation of some proposition. In Polanyi's words: 'There are no strict rules for discovering things that hang together in nature, nor even for telling whether we should accept or reject an apparent coherence as a natural fact. There is always a residue of personal judgment involved in deciding whether to accept any particular piece of evidence, be it as proof of a true regularity, or, on the contrary, as a refutation of an apparent regularity. This is how I saw and accepted the fact that, strictly speaking, all empirical science is inexact. And as I came to realise that all integration is, like perception, based largely on tacit elements, of which we have only a vague knowledge, I applied this also to science, and declared that science was grounded on an act of personal judgment, and called this knowledge, therefore, a *personal knowledge.*'[82] What Polanyi means by personal knowledge we shall discuss later, but it should be pointed out here that the responsible decisions of the scientist are made under the judgment of the hidden reality he seeks to uncover, which exists independently of his knowing of it and is as such the external pole of his personal judgment. Thus to say that science is grounded on an act of personal judgment, means that in his quest for reality the scientist takes a responsible act in relating evidence to an aspect of external reality which he acknowledges to be objectively imposed upon him. Personal knowledge, as Polanyi intends it therefore, is no more and no less than the personal coefficient in the scientist's act of knowing as, guided by a sense of obligation to the truth, he submits himself to the compelling claims of reality upon him. Thus in the last resort it is reality itself which must be allowed to be the judge of the truth or falsity of his concepts or statements about it.[83] This implies of course not only a rejection of positivism but an attack on scientific rationalism, or scientism, and carries with it a unitary view of human rationality, of knowing as an activity that involves the whole man in correlation with the wholeness of things in the world around him.

III

Before carrying this discussion further, let us come at it from another line of thought. And here I wish to relate the thought of Michael Polanyi to that of Niels Bohr, by considering the different ways in which (evidently drawing from Gestalt psychology) they appealed to the analogy of using a stick as an instrument, for example, when someone attempts to orient himself in a dark room by feeling with a stick.[84] Bohr's interest in this lies in what he calls 'the reciprocal character of the perception of touch' for it helps us to grasp 'the reciprocal character of the results of measurements' in quantum theory. 'When the stick is held loosely, it appears to the sense of touch to be an object. When, however, it is held firmly, we lose the sensation that it is a foreign body, and the impression of touch becomes immediately localised at the point where the stick is touching the body under investigation.'[85] The two different ways of regarding the stick, as an object or as an instrument are mutually exclusive, and yet in the actual operation a 'reciprocal' relation comes into play. Here, then, in the structure of tactual perception we have something similar to what we find in atomic physics when we employ measuring instruments in an attempt to determine the behaviour of atomic objects, for there we find relations both of mutual exclusiveness and of reciprocity within one experience, i.e. what Bohr termed 'complementarity'. There is more to it than at first meets the eye, however, for, as Bohr understands it, here we come upon a fundamental feature in the problem of knowledge, namely, 'the fact that a complete elucidation of one and the same object may require diverse points of view which defy a unique description. Indeed, strictly speaking, the conscious analysis of any concept stands in a relation of exclusion to its immediate application'.[86] Expressed slightly differently: 'The nature of our consciousness brings about a complementary relationship, in all domains of knowledge, between the analysis of a concept and its immediate application.'[87] Stated thus there is an obvious similarity to Polanyi's thought: the mutual exclusiveness of two different ways of regarding the same thing, as in looking at it and looking from it;[88] 'two complementary efforts aimed at the elucidation of a comprehensive entity', analysis and integration;[89] and of course the master idea that while tacit knowledge is opposed to explicit knowledge they are not to be sharply divided but linked together through a functional relation in the activity of learning or inquiring, for explicit operations of the mind achieve their end by relying tacitly on what we know implicitly and cannot fully specify. In the nature of the case a completely explicit knowledge is an impossibility, since it cannot be detached from the personal judgment of the perceiver or knower or do without his indefinable mental powers in integrative activity.

Perhaps the closest point at which Polanyi approaches to the complementarity concept of Bohr is to be found in his analysis of the peculiar quality of a painting in which we find a fusion of content with an incompatible frame, which he speaks of as 'flat depth'.[90] 'This union', he says, 'is not a fusion of *complementary parts* to a whole, but a fusion of *contradictory features*. The flatness of a canvas is combined with a perspectival depth, which is the very opposite of flatness.'[91] For such an 'integration of incompatibles' Polanyi points to anaglyphs which combine two stereoscopic images with different colours which, when viewed through a corresponding pair of coloured glasses, present a fully three-dimensional image – but when viewed separately, the stereoscopic pictures, which are taken about four inches apart, actually differ at every point. A three-dimensional appearance is produced by fusing two conflicting flatnesses.[92] In a painting, however, an artificial integration takes place which produces an image essentially different from nature, something that may be said to be 'transnatural'. It is this quality, he points out, that modern art has exploited so startlingly by combining images, statements or actions within an incompatible artificial framework – but as such, it is not intended to tell us anything that can be true or false, or to convey any factual communication.[93] In the nature of the case, then, such an integration of incompatibles does not provide the kind of model which will be helpful in scientific knowledge, and yet it is in this notion that Polanyi approaches most closely to Bohr's stress upon the all-important element of 'mutual exclusiveness' in complementarity.

The dissimilarity between Bohr's thought and that of Polanyi is evident in the use he makes of the analogy from tactual perception, and, correspondingly, of the relationship of complementarity, in dealing with the epistemological problem, forced out into the open by the discovery of the quantum of action, as to the limits of an objective description of nature.[94] The problem may be put differently: how to correlate quantum theory on the one hand with classical phsyics, and its demand for an objective description of nature irrespective of the observer, and on the other hand with relativity theory which has revealed the subjective character of all the concepts of classical physics and still maintains the scientific demand to describe nature, in its internal relations and structures. What seems to be required, then, is a coordination with our observational experience, in which space and time are split because our senses can cope only with small velocities, but within which we are faced with the failure of our forms of observation because of the impossibility of a strict separation of phenomena from means of observation, *and* a coordination with attempts to penetrate behind the reference system of the observing subject in a direct description of objective reality under the unitary control of the space-time metrical field (as disclosed through Einstein's revision of classical physics in relativity theory), which is essentially non-observable because our senses cannot keep track with the velocity of light. Hence, as Bohr has shown, so far as the quantum of action is concerned, 'any attempt at ordering in space-time leads to a break in the causal chain, since such an attempt is bound up with an essential exchange of momentum and energy between the individuals and the measuring rods and clocks used for observation; and just this exchange cannot be taken into account if the measuring instruments are to fulfil their purpose.'[95] The crucial point here, Bohr maintains, is 'the impossibility of any sharp separation between the behaviour of atomic objects and the interaction with the measuring instruments which serve to define the conditions under which phenomena appear'.[96] Since we are faced with the choice of measuring either the position or the momentum of the atomic particle, we have to use measurements which demand mutually exclusive experimental arrangements, but in order to give an adequate description of nature *all experimental arrangements* have to be taken into account. The principle of complementarity was devised to do just that.[97] It enables science to offer an account of nature that does not artificially exclude the conditions under which it is observed, but at the same time to control the unavoidable reference to the observing subject and his instruments of observation (composed like himself of large numbers of atoms) by including them within strictly specified and defined conditions of observation, thereby avoiding the unwarranted intrusion of subjective elements and making possible an objective description of experience through operations that are intelligible and verifiable by all observers. As Bohr himself regarded it, complementarity is not just a device enabling us to express essential but exclusive aspects of phenomena in a coherent manner, nor merely a way of solving the problem how consistently to incorporate the quantum of action, which transcends the scope of classical physical explanation, into the conceptual framework of physics, but *a new kind of logical relationship* that belongs to the fundamental structure of knowledge.[98] That is why he finds parallels to complementarity in the analysis and synthesis of experience in other fields of knowledge, as (apart from the instances noted earlier) in visual perception in which it is impossible to distinguish between phenomena themselves and their conscious perception,[99] or in psychological experience in the mutually exclusive relationship which will always exist between the practical use of a word and attempts at its strict definition,[100] or in the field of psycho-physical parallelism where we have to reckon with the unpredictable modification of physical experience produced by an attempt at an objective tracing of the accompanying process in the central nervous system,[101] not to speak of the realm of biology to which Bohr devoted rather more thought.[102]

Be that as it may, what does this mean for the objective description of nature? Broadly speaking, it implies that for objective description and harmonious comprehension it is necessary in almost every field to pay attention to the circumstances under which evidence is obtained,[103] but from the perspective of quantum physics rather more is involved, a limitation in the objective description of nature owing to the fact that any observation necessitates an interference with the course of phenomena. 'Indeed the *finite interaction between object and measuring agencies* conditioned by the very existence of the quantum of action entails – because of the impossibility of controlling the reaction of the object upon the measuring instruments, if these are to serve their purpose – the necessity of a final renunciation of the classical ideal of causality and a radical revision of our attitude toward the problem of physical reality.'[104] The limitation, which nature imposes upon us in this way, finds its expression in quantum mechanics through its employment of a statistical form of causality in its account of quantal behaviour. This is nothing short of a radical change in our whole view of the role and meaning of science, and so Bohr claims that 'in our description of nature the purpose is not to disclose the real essence of the phenomena but only to track down, as far as it is possible, relations between the manifold aspects of our experience'.[105] Later on, in view of the criticism of Einstein, Bohr appears to have modified his views about the limits of objectivity when he spoke of 'disturbance of phenomena by observation' or 'creation of physical attributes to atomic objects by measurements'[106] for that language had given Einstein the impression that 'there is no reality independent of the probable subject'.[107] Nevertheless the word *phenomenon* is here applied exclusively to 'the observations obtained under specified circumstances, including an account of the whole experimental arrangement',[108] so that strictly speaking we are not offered an account of atomic realities in themselves or their object-ive interconnections so much as in their appearance to us, within the conditions of our scientific observation of them which is statistically defined.[109] Einstein remained critical, for he could only regard such a statistical approach in quantum mechanics as 'an incomplete and indirect description of reality',[110] whereas what was scientifically required, as he saw it, was a penetration into the inner relations of quantum realities and a description of their dynamic structure in terms of field-laws. In spite of this difference with Einstein, however, Bohr interpreted his work as concerned with the intrinsic stability and wholeness of atomic processes and with a harmony of content and form securing and enlarging the scope of objective description.[111]

We return now to Niels Bohr's epistemological model of the man feeling his way round a dark room with a stick, and recall the point he made: the stick functions as an effective instrument of investigation when it is held firmly but when it is held loosely it appears to the sense of touch as itself an object of our experience. Correspondingly, in scientific operations the measuring instru-ments must be coordinated closely with the observing agents if they are to fulfil their purpose, but here where we must consider the interaction between the measuring instruments and the object under investigation attention must be directed also to the instru-ments themselves. Thus the coordination of the measuring instru-ments with the observing subject must be brought within the whole experimental arrangement, and all that must be taken into account if we are to offer a faithful and objective description of the results of our investigation in accordance with the conditions under which they were reached. That is what the principle of complemen-tarity is designed to do, to widen the conceptual framework to take in the measuring agencies while providing at the same time a means of eliminating subjective elements. Thus because it takes in the relationship of mutual exclusiveness the notion of complementarity does not mean that the scientist loses his position as a detached observer but that his interaction with what he observes (through the measuring instruments) is included among the conditions for the logical comprehension of experience and its objective descrip-tion.[112] All this has the effect, however, of limiting the knowledge and description of the phenomena within the conditions under which they appear. Conversely, 'the notion of complementarity serves to symbolise the fundamental limitation, met with in atomic physics, of the objective existence of phenomena independent of the means of observation.'[113] Here there is undoubtedly an ambiguity in Bohr's thought, for while on the one hand he defines 'phenomena' by reference to the conditions under which they appear, on the other hand he speaks of the existence of 'phenomena' independent of the means of observation. That is not an ambiguity which Bohr finally resolved, and perhaps could not within the brackets of his epistemological assumptions.[114]

It should now be clear that Bohr's epistemological model, the use of a stick in exploring a dark room, is designed to show that the interaction between the observer and what he observes makes it necessary to define reference to the observing agency among the conditions under which the exploration of the objective world takes place. Thus the personal coefficient of knowledge is allowed to constitute, with a relation of complementarity, a factor not only in the describing of experience but in the experience described. According to Polanyi's theory of knowledge, however, all this would amount only to what he calls the *functional structure* and the *phenomenal structure* to knowledge.[115] Of course his concern with this epistemological model ('the use of a stick to explore a cavern, or the way a blind man feels his way by tapping with a stick')[116] is to distinguish two important aspects of knowledge, the focal and the subsidiary, the explicit and the implicit, or the specifiable and the non-specifiable, and to show how we tacitly rely on the subsidiary, the implicit or the non-specifiable in order to engage in focal, explicit or specifiable operations, as for example when we tacitly rely on one set of statements in formulating definitions of another set. We use tools, machines, medical probes, optical instruments, etc. in the same way, for their meaning lies in their purpose. They are not tools, machines, etc. when observed as objects in themselves, but only when viewed subsidiarily by focus-ing attention on their purpose.[117] That is what Polanyi calls the 'functional relation' between the two terms of tacit knowing: 'we know the first term only by relying on our awareness of it for attending to the second'.[118] We have already had occasion to note the point he makes (and which he shares with Niels Bohr) about the relation of mutual exclusiveness that arises between them when we look at them separately, for when we adopt one way of looking at something we destroy at the same moment some alternative way of seeing them. But what happens, he asks, when we rely on our awareness of one for attending to the second or rather to the

achievement of their joint purpose? Do we not cause a transformation in the *appearance* of both, and in the conducting of an experiment, 'does not the *appearance* of the experimental setting undergo
some change'?[119] He answers that there is a subtle change – for we
are aware of that *from* which we are attending *to* another thing, in
the *appearance* of that thing. For example a perceived object acquires
constant size, colour, shape; observations incorporated in a theory
are reduced to mere instances of it; the parts of a whole merge their
isolated appearance into the appearance of the whole. The whole
has a different look than the aggregate of its parts. This is what
Polanyi calls the *phenomenal* aspect or accompaniment of tacit
knowing, or the phenomenal structure of tacit knowing, which tells
us that we have a real coherent entity before us.[120] This is remarkably similar to the feature of knowledge which Bohr sought to
define through the principle of the relationship of complementarity.
But it is precisely at this point that we discern a subtle difference
between the thought of Polanyi and the thought of Bohr, in respect
of what happens when we combine the *functional* and the *phenomenal* aspects of knowledge, according to Polanyi's interpretation
of the epistemological model, with its distinction between the
implicit and the explicit operations of the mind. But here we must
let Polanyi speak for himself.

'Anyone using a probe for the first time will feel its impact
against his fingers and palm. But as we learn to use a probe, or to
use a stick for feeling our way, our awareness of its impact on our
hand is transformed into a sense of its point touching the objects we
are exploring. This is how the interpretative effort transposes
meaningless feelings into meaningful ones, and places these at some
distance from the original feeling. We become aware of the feelings
in our hands in terms of their meaning located at the tip of the
probe or stick to which they are attending. This is so also when we
use a tool. We are attending to the meaning of its impact on our
hands in terms of its effect on the things to which we are applying
it. We may call this the *semantic aspect* of tacit knowing. All meaning
tends to be displaced *away from ourselves* . . .'[121] This is what
Polanyi speaks of as the *from-to* relation in which all knowledge
consists.[122] An obvious instance of this is a mark that is used as a
sign – when looked at as an object it is merely a mark without
significance, but it does have significance when we look *from* or
through it to what it is intended to signify or indicate.[123] In this
respect Polanyi has a good deal to say of the *transparency* of
language, for words rightly used in coherent sentences are not
opaque cyphers but intelligible signs through which we are directed

to some meaning or some reality from which the words themselves properly have the meaning they carry.[124]

Every apparatus, however, physical or conceptual, should function in this way in the activity of inquiring and knowing, that is, not only measuring instruments but scientific theories themselves, for it is by means of them and through them that we discover and apprehend what we do. When in this manner, therefore, we combine the functional and the phenomenal aspects of knowledge, attending from or through them to something to which they are subsidiarily integrated in our knowing, we find our tacit knowing taking on a *vectorial* character in virtue of which we are directed toward a new meaning.[125] Here a group of hitherto apparently unconnected particulars fall into a coherent pattern which signifies an intelligible entity or some identifiable objective reality. That is what makes the difference between a mere noise and a tune, as for example when a group of sounds is discerned to have a significant order, such as a song which indicates the presence of a thrush or a nightingale as the case may be.[126] At this point the semantic aspect of knowledge leads to the *ontological aspect* of knowledge in which, as we have seen, our acts of inquiring and apprehending are directed to and fall under the intrinsic claims of a reality endowed with a rational structure or order which is independent of our knowing of it and has a power of manifesting itself in yet unthought of ways in the future.[127] It is important to note that the ontological and semantic aspects of knowledge operate together, for the meaning of things and of the terms designating them is discovered at the same time: the ontological reference would not be achieved without the information content in the semantic aspect, but the semantic aspect would be empty or meaningless if it did not bear on some aspect of reality independent of it. That is why the meaning of our statements, either in ordinary experience or in scientific inquiry, does not bear on conceptions but *through* conceptions *on* objective realities independent of them.[128] To permit of any relation of abstraction between the ontological and semantic aspects of a theory would result in a serious deprivation of information content and a loss of meaning for it would break up the *from-to* relation, replacing integration with disintegration, so that the essential clues would lose their vectorial quality. It is the integrative relation between the semantic and ontological aspects of knowledge arising in the activity of scientific inquiry that is all-important – this is why Polanyi lays such emphasis on the movement of thought *away from ourselves,* in which we tacitly rely on implicit knowing to engage in explicit scientific operations.[129]

This movement, away from ourselves, can be performed only by a rational agent: it is a distinctively personal act, for only persons are capable of that kind of transcendental reference to what is ontologically independent of them, and only persons are capable of distinguishing what they know from their own knowing of it, and of engaging in sustained self-critical operations in the interest of objectivity and consistency. Since we cannot give any account of what we know cut off from our knowing of it, we must give an account of our knowledge in a way that is consistent with this situation.[130] This is why the human (personal and social) coefficient of scientific knowledge must not only be frankly acknowledged but be explicitly endorsed, in terms of man's rational capacity to relate himself to realities objective to himself and to form consistent and appropriate conceptions of them. Expressed otherwise, this means that any critical, scientific account of some object or field under investigation must include a consistent account of how knowledge of it has been reached and formulated, so that it may be differentiated clearly in its own reality both from our experience of it and from the processes and theories through which it has become known to us. In such operations, however, we rely finally on acts of personal judgment to do what cannot be done by the 'impersonal' methods advocated by the empiricists and positivists. While we must certainly organise our knowledge of any field or object in articulate logical forms, so that it can stand up on its own, as it were, such an impersonal formalisation no matter how coherent in itself cannot do anything, mean anything or communicate understanding of itself. It requires from start to finish reflecting and semantic activity on the part of the scientist himself to relate it correctly to the subject-matter to which it refers and which it is designed to elucidate. But such an act of intelligence can be performed only by a personal agent. Carried out properly, with disciplined self-criticism, in a movement away from the knower to what he seeks to know, this is an act of personal participation in scientific knowledge which far from invalidating it enables the scientist to control and establish it properly on its own evidential grounds. Of course he devises and develops a critical apparatus as the instrument for this purpose and allows it to fulfil its own independent function in helping him, to distinguish what he knows from his own predilections and subjectivities, but nevertheless he himself must operate it, and operate it not arbitrarily but correctly, both in acquiring knowledge and in pursuing it, as we shall see, with what Polanyi calls 'universal intent', if it is to achieve the scientific end intended.[131]

To return once again to the epistemological model of the use of a stick as a tool or a probe, Polanyi contends that when we learn to use the stick effectively in this way we do not attend to the feeling of it in our hand but to what we feel at the far end of the stick when it touches an external object and to what we learn about it through that contact. The stick functions as a sort of extension to our bodies, on which we subsidiarily rely in all focal acts of perception and knowledge, but it also functions as a pointer to what is beyond ourselves. Thus the use of a tool or a probe in exploring the world around us reinforces the fundamental movement of knowing in which we attend away from ourselves to what we know, for it helps us to discriminate more precisely what we know from ourselves while tacitly relying on the role we ourselves play in the process of inquiry.[132] From this perspective the measuring instruments in scientific operations should be interpreted not so much as getting in the way of the movement from the observing subject to the object but as the means through which the scientist makes active and objective contact with the real world in its inherent and orderly inter-connections, and therefore in such a way as to distinguish it from himself and his subjective impressions.[133] Here the 'effect' of the subject on the object is rather the reverse of what is claimed by some quantum theorists who work with the assumption that the observing subject belongs in part to the content of what is observed.[134] This is a controlled interaction with the external world in which, instead of allowing the structure of his own subjectivity and the limits of his own concepts to be imposed upon reality, by the fundamental movement of his thought the scientist allows the reality he investigates in its own internal structures to impose itself upon his apprehension, so that in his contact with it he is committed to a boundless objectivity beyond himself together with an unceasing obligation to let himself and all his preconceptions be called radically into question in face of it. Since the intrinsic structure of reality is consistent and universal, and is independent of our knowing of it, scientific commitment to the investigation of the real world through submission to its compelling claims on our minds, carries with it what Polanyi calls *universal intent*.[135]

This means, on the one hand, that the scientist conducts his inquiries in acknowledgement of the universal jurisdiction of reality over him so that his contact with reality necessarily legislates for him how he must think and speak about it, but, on the other hand, it means that the conceptions he forms and the statements he formulates under the authority of reality he must affirm with a claim for universal recognition from all others who also have to acknowledge the jurisdiction of the same reality over them. Nevertheless, precisely because they are formed and formulated under the authority of reality, those conceptions and statements themselves fall under its judgment and are relativised by it – they have no absolute or final status in themselves and must not be allowed to usurp the legislative authority of reality for themselves. That is why all dogmatism is excluded. That is why in the on-going activity of his inquiry the scientist must always attend from the theories he constructs to those aspects of reality that are disclosed through them, and then in the light of such disclosure revise and reconstruct those theories, for the boundless objectivity of reality is such that his theories are true only to the extent that they serve that objectivity in an ever-deepening reflection of it.[136] Therein also lies, in the deepest sense, the objectivity of a scientific theory.[137] Moreover since reality, owing to its boundless objectivity, has the capacity to manifest itself in an indefinite variety of ways far beyond what we can explicitly predict and therefore constantly to take us by surprise, scientific statements that bear upon it inevitably have an irreducible indeterminacy or openness in virtue of which they have a built-in thrust for adaptation and for on-going modification. Thus both the objectivity and the revisability of a scientific theory are due to its bearing upon reality and to the wholly indeterminate scope of its true implications derived from reality. That bearing of a scientific theory upon reality, however, is maintained only as it is constantly directed by the scientist away from itself to the intrinsic rationality and boundless objectivity of the real world which it is meant to indicate and serve. In the nature of the case, however, this is not a logical or impersonal movement of thought carried out merely through formal operations according to definite rules, but one that can be undertaken only by a rational agent in the exercise of critical appraisal and judgment as well as intuitive discernment and apprehension. Formal rules and impersonal instruments do, of course, play a considerable and indeed an utterly essential role in scientific activity, but they have to be directed and controlled by the scientist, as from an active personal centre of intentionality, if they are to fulfil their purpose.

This is the context in which Polanyi developed his notion of personal knowledge, which has nothing to do with the inclusion of a personal, far less a subjective, factor in the content of knowledge, for the personal participation on the part of the scientist relates to the bearing of all his thought and statement upon objective reality, in so far as it is accessible to human understanding and description. It is a highly responsible activity undertaken in acknowledgement of the legislative authority of reality over his rational inquiries and in recognition that, because of its indeterminate depth and range of rationality, nature always transcends our attempts to formalise knowledge of it in determinate propositions. The discernment of a coherent pattern, the appraisal of order, the assessment of a probability, the choice between two conflicting theories both of which account equally well for the known facts, the judgment as to the weight to be attached to some evidence, the ability to see and to guess rightly the informal decisions that enter into the process of verification in relating observation to reality, and so on, are all personal, mental acts in which the scientist is constantly engaged throughout his inquiries, but they are made under the judgment of a hidden reality which he seeks to uncover, which is consistently and universally the same for all inquirers, and which is the ultimate judge of the truth or falsity of his conceptions and statements about it, and therefore far from being personally biased or prejudiced they reflect the strict impartiality of a rigorous and unrelenting scientific conscience.[138] It is precisely this kind of personal participation which prevents human knowledge from being merely subjective, by grounding it objectively beyond itself, for it belongs to the dynamic structure of knowledge that its fundamental act of understanding is directed *from* the knower *to* the object he seeks to know. While this is true of all knowledge in ordinary experience and daily life, it is the mark of distinctively scientific knowledge that this movement of thought is carried out with the greatest rigour, so that knowledge may be determined as precisely as possible in accordance with the nature and the structure of the comprehensive entity which is its object. Polanyi links this with what he calls the *intellectual passions*, in which the craving for understanding, commitment to the truth for the truth's sake, the rational appeal of consistency and excellence, elegance and beauty, the desire for integration, the discerning of new relationships, the impulsion of the mind for discovery and validation, the vision of reality as a whole, etc. all play their part in the drive to apprehend the real world out of itself and to distinguish it from our own fancies and subjectivities.[139] Regarded in this light, the personal coefficient of knowledge is the obligatory and controlled reflex of the intrinsic rationality and the unlimited objectivity of reality.

IV

There is at least one aspect of this that requires further discussion. This is the ingredient of an irreducible indeterminacy or openness

openness

in our conception and description of reality, corresponding to the indeterminate nature of its objectivity which, while accessible to our rational inquiry, reaches far beyond what we can overtake in our comprehension and formalisation, for it is that indeterminacy or openness which makes personal acts of judgment not only unavoidable but scientifically incumbent upon us.[140] This combination of objectivity and indeterminacy, however, means that we have to operate in scientific activity with a *controlled openness,* an openness which we are obliged to maintain in our conceptions and statements in faithfulness to the 'transcendent' nature of reality, yet one which is controlled by the latter's intrinsic structure or rationality in terms of which alone it is knowable.[141] This is a control that *bilateral reciproca:* must be envisaged as taking place *conjunctively on two levels*: a higher level through ontological reference to the consistent structure of reality, and on a lower level through reliance on the structure of tacit knowledge, i.e. when we rely on what is implicitly known for explicit operations. It is through the integrative activity on the lower level that we are provided with our principal clue to the reality of what we are investigating, the intuitive grasp of a significant coherence, but through its semantic structure it is open

it becomes disclosed to control from the higher level where it is deployed by explicit operations to serve our deepening penetration into the actual structure of reality as *it becomes disclosed* to us, or 'emerges', through our inquiries.[142] This is what Polanyi called *the principle of marginal control,* or *dual control,* in accordance with which the operations on the lower level are controlled through 'boundary conditions' where they are left indeterminate or open to the *higher level,* although the higher level relies on the operations of the lower level, without infringing them, for the fulfilment of its own operations.[143] That is to say, human knowledge functions conjunctively on different levels at the same time, constituting a stratified structure in which the all-important factor is the open but controlled semantic relation between the different levels. It is a stratified structure of a broadly similar kind that Polanyi finds in the universe, and it is indeed to this that the stratified structure in our scientific knowledge of it corresponds, for the structure of our comprehension is similar to the structure of what we comprehend.[144]

In order to throw this aspect of Michael Polanyi's thought into sharper relief, and to clarify what is meant by a multi-levelled structure in knowledge, it will be helpful to relate his thought to that of Kurt Gödel in his epoch-making essay of 1931, 'On formally undecidable propositions of *Principia Mathematica* and related systems'.[145] Behind this lay attempts by mathematicians, notably

Hilbert, to reduce a deductive system (e.g. Euclidean geometry) to a rigid system of axioms and to establish its consistency completely within itself, without reference to the assumed consistency of another system.[146] That meant the emptying of all propositions within the system of all content so that they could be treated merely as formal symbols without ontological reference, to be ordered and connected together in accordance with a precise set of rules. Such a formalisation of a system was held to be complete when every true proposition expressible within the system was formally deducible from its axioms in this way. This implies that the truth of a proposition within the system is relative to the system, but in that case we are faced with the problem of having to decide what is an acceptable axiomatic system. The all-important criteria for making such a decision are: *consistency,* meeting the requirement of the law of non-contradiction, and *completeness,* meeting the requirement of the law of excluded middle.[147] A system is consistent if no proposition can be both proved *and* disproved within it, and complete if every proposition formalised in terms of the system can be proved *or* disproved within it.[148] What is needed then, is a procedure enabling us to decide whether or not any proposition formalised in terms of the system can be proved within it, but such a procedure could not be incorporated within the formal system itself (for we cannot make statements about propositions in a formal system within the formalisation of that system), and hence we need another 'system', or 'meta-system', incorporating the precisely defined rules necessary for controlling the formalising operations in our primary system. Although this meta-system, relative to the primary system, is not itself formalised (since it is not empty of content or assertions), that does not detract from its effectiveness in controlling the formalisation of the primary system in the interest of consistency and completeness.[149] It was thus that Hilbert devised 'meta-mathematics' in which statements about the configurations and arrangements in a mathematical system were sharply distinguished from them. In this way he hoped to preserve the formal purity of mathematical relations within the axiomatic system so that deductive operations could be carried out with the greatest logical rigour from a fixed or finite set of independent axioms: this would have the effect both of cutting away the element of indeterminacy resulting from an indefinite number of axioms, and of achieving a closed consistency within the system. That would constitute an 'absolute' proof, establishing the consistency of an axiomatic system without assuming the consistency of another set of axioms.[150]

The classical embodiment of such a formalisation claiming to exhibit an 'absolute' proof of its consistency was provided by A. N. Whitehead and B. Russell in *Principia Mathematica*.[151] In that work they sought to transcribe pure mathematics into a completely formalised system of logical notions and relations, and at the same time, through a comprehensive system of logico-symbolic notation, to make tacitly accepted rules of inference and operational theorems entirely explicit. This had the effect of making the problem of the consistency of an axiomatised arithmetical system equivalent to the problem of the consistency of formal logic itself by establishing the consistency of the logical axioms of their deductive system. Moreover, those axioms were held to be 'complete' on the ground that every true statement that can be expressed in the system is formally deducible from them. Thus the formalisation of a deductive system elaborated in *Principia Mathematica* was meant to be complete as well as consistent. It was so extensive, Gödel points out, that all methods of proof then used in mathematics were formalised in them, i.e. reduced to a few axioms and rules of inference. 'It may therefore be surmised that these axioms and rules of inference are also sufficient to decide *all* mathematical questions which can in any way at all be expressed formally in the systems concerned.'[152]

Gödel's paper showed definitely that it is not the case that all methods of proof used in mathematics have been formalised in *Principia Mathematica* and related systems, and that in them 'there are in fact relatively simple problems in the theory of ordinary whole numbers which cannot be decided from the axioms'.[153] That is to say, he demonstrated that in any formalised system of sufficient richness there are, and must be, certain propositions which are not 'decidable' (capable of proof or disproof) within the given system, and therefore that it cannot be decided within the system whether the axioms of the system are consistent or mutually contradictory. He also showed that if we take any set of arithmetical axioms (and any augmentation of such a set by axioms), provided that they are consistent, it will be found that there are true arithmetical propositions that cannot be derived from it – hence there is no formalised system of more than a minimum complexity which is not incomplete *in principle*. Thus Gödel proved that it is not possible to solve the Hilbertian decision problem in an 'absolute' manner: the consistency of arithmetic cannot be demonstrated by inferential operations completely within the systematic formalisation of arithmetic.

What are we to say, then, of a meta-mathematical proof of

consistency? This would also have to be rejected, if it was one in which the meta-mathematical argumentation was included as an operation within the formal deductions of the arithmetical calculus, for that would be only another way of trying to demonstrate consistency within the initial system.[154] However, that does not mean that a meta-mathematical proof of consistency is impossible. On the contrary, it is possible if the system is incomplete, for, as Gödel showed, there are undecidable propositions in formal systems of mathematics which yet turn out to be decidable by meta-mathematical considerations relative to a more comprehensive system.[155] Expressed otherwise, there are mathematical propositions which cannot be decided in a formal system, if it is consistent, by deduction from a given set of axioms, but which can be established by informal inferential procedure from a meta-mathematical level. What Gödel did was to devise a coordinate way of representing meta-mathematical statements about a formalised arithmetical calculus by means of arithmetical formulae within the calculus in such a way that, while these formulae cannot be demonstrated within it, they can be established relative to a wider or richer system, and therefore in such a way that the inferential procedure in establishing them cannot itself be assimilated to the 'mechanical rules' within the calculus. This confronts us, therefore, with a proposition which asserts its own unprovability.[156] Here we have the famous Gödelian statement which is true if it cannot be demonstrated, i.e. one which while demonstrably undecidable within a formalised system says of itself that it is undecidable within the system, but which emerges as true. When it is asserted as such (i.e. as both true and formally undecidable) within the system, this statement represents an additional axiom, independent of the others, so that it becomes evident that the axioms of arithmetic are incomplete, provided that they are consistent (for if they were not consistent, both 'consistency' and 'inconsistency' could be 'proved' within the same framework). This would still be the case if we were to add to those axioms, for then another (and another . . .) such a true but formally undecidable statement could be constructed within it, which reveals that any such formal (and sufficiently comprehensive) system is necessarily or essentially incomplete.[157] Thus Gödel demonstrated the inherent limitation of the axiomatic method: it is impossible to elaborate a consistent and complete system in which all arithmetical truths are logically derived from a determinate set of axioms. The consistency of such a formal system, if it is consistent, cannot be demonstrated as a proof within it. If arithmetic is consistent, it is incomplete.[158]

This clearly implies that in the last analysis we operate in a formalised system with basic concepts or axioms which cannot be completely defined, so that, in other words, we cannot know what the axioms ultimately mean. Operationally, of course, we cope with this problem in controlling the uncertainty that arises by reasoning from a wider system of axioms, for even though we cannot prove the consistency of a formalised system, if it is consistent, within its own framework, we can prove it by meta-theoretical considerations. Since such a meta-theoretical proof is relative to a meta-system, in the nature of the case the same questions as to consistency and completeness would have to be raised with respect to it as were raised with respect to the initial system, so that the meta-system itself, if treated in the same way, would be relative to a meta-meta-system, and so on. Normally, of course, in scientific activity we operate only on three levels, the level of the statements we use in describing some set of structural relations in nature, the level in which we formalise our statements into a rigorous logico-deductive system, and a meta-level comprising our meta-theoretical reasoning or decision procedure. All this means, however, that consistent but incomplete formal systems, which require to be completed beyond themselves in coordination with more complex systems, far from being shut off from reality by being enclosed within themselves, like a self-sufficient empty tautological system, are necessarily characterised by a profound element of indeterminacy or openness making them semantically significant and empirically relevant. While it is certainly the case that these formal systems, which open upwards into even more abstract and comprehensive systems, become further and further removed from empirical reality as they are drained of their content, nevertheless the fact that all this leaves the basic axioms in the initial system ultimately undefined means that they are not deprived of their power to generate new theorems, or therefore of their heuristic possibilities in coping with new situations. It is because we place no antecedent limits on 'fluid axioms', for example, that we can operate effectively with them in penetrating into the intrinsic structure of some field of reality, from which we might be shut off from the very start by the limits of a determinate set of axioms. Yet the startling fact, in this respect, about Gödel's unprovability and incompleteness theorems is that they were proved through a method which took in the arithmetic of natural numbers in such a way as to show that the truth of arithmetical notions and relations cannot be established solely by operations within the framework of a formal system, apart altogether from reference to empirical existence (which would have to be the case if they had no 'existence' of their own). Thus they showed that number is not just a rationalisation but is what it is through coordination to external reality, and showed at the same time that the structure of relations that obtains in an incomplete formal system (comprising arithmetic) may hold good in another, very different realm or system of things, much as the projections on a map hold good in a distinctive way for the physical configurations of the land that is mapped. Thus Gödel's theorems are revealed to have semantic and practical value, for, in so far as they show consistent formal systems to have extra-logical or ontological reference, they may facilitate inquiry into the structures of empirical reality outside of us or beyond us. Since that referential activity is not amenable to logical formalisation, a formal system may be said to function only in virtue of unformalisable ingredients within it and by relying on an informal procedure of decision and control which through those ingredients bears upon the formal system as a whole. Otherwise the formal system as a whole would be devoid of semantic value: it would say nothing at all. The meaning of a formal system, however, becomes evident within the semantic focus constituted by a hierarchy of formal systems coordinated through those factors in each system which are decidable and made meaningful only from within its meta-system.[159] Yet if that semantic focus is to fulfil its objective, it must be served by the explicit operations of the formal system as the critical apparatus or effective instrument giving power to its informal denotative function. Thus the formal requires to be interpreted through reliance upon the informal if it is to have any empirical relevance, and the informal requires the explicit reasoning of the formal if it is to be successful in fulfilling its ontological reference in matching what it denotes with the reality on which it bears.

There can be little doubt that, although they have rather different starting points, Polanyi and Gödel have much in common, at least so far as their treatment of formalisation and its limits is concerned. This becomes particularly evident, on the one hand, when the implications of the Gödelian theorems are developed, as they have been by Church, Kleene, Tarski and others, and are seen to apply beyond the deductive systems of mathematics to syntactical and even mechanical systems, and to involve in the structure of different sciences a coordination of physical, logical and meta-logical levels; and, on the other hand, when the implications of Polanyi's distinction between the formal and the informal, the tacit and the explicit, the articulate and the inarticulate, are worked out and applied beyond the structure of knowledge to machines and organisms, and are shown to involve beyond logical levels distinct levels of reality testifying to the stratified structure of the universe.[160] Of special significance *vis-à-vis* Gödel's position is Polanyi's view of the way in which various parallel formalisms are informally combined in the functions of learning and knowing. While different logical levels are controlled by distinctive operational principles, they are coordinated within a hierarchic structure in such a way that the operations on the lower level leave undetermined or open certain boundary conditions which are controlled by operations on the higher level. The higher level on its part relies for its own operations on the principles governing the lower, but these operations are not explicable or specifiable in terms of the principles of the lower level.[161] Polanyi has much to say about the great value that comes from formalisation through symbolic representation and manipulation of our mental operations according to precise rules, for, while that does not of itself supply us with new knowledge, it represents an enormous enhancement of our intellectual powers in making it possible for us to formulate clearly complex sentences which would be incomprehensible in ordinary language and to perform feats of deductive argument which could not be conceivably attempted otherwise.[162] But he is equally emphatic on the point that formalisation must remain incomplete, if the open or indeterminate relation that obtains between the levels of formalisation giving them their semantic efficacy is to be maintained. Complete formalisation would be self-defeating for it would cut off formalisation from the fundamental acts of discovering and knowing which by their nature are essentially informal, yet the purpose of formalisation is precisely to enhance those non-formalisable operations.[163] It is all-important, therefore, to respect the limits of formalisation, evident in what Polanyi calls its 'uncovenanted functions', for it is just there that its fruitfulness lies.[164] This is most evident in the advance to really new knowledge in which we have to cross 'a logical gap' between a problem and its solution, or between one formalised framework and another, or from one logical level to another.[165]

In developing these ideas Polanyi makes some use of the Gödelian theorems, especially when he is concerned with the power and the limits of logical and inferential operations, for the Gödelian theorems have the effect of giving firm shape and justification to the multi-levelled structure of knowing which Polanyi finds so essential.[166] This is not to say that he derived these ideas from Gödel, for he has clearly come upon them through a very different approach and along quite independent lines of investigation, but the appeal to the Gödelian theorems is brought in to reinforce what he has to say about the process of discovery, about the all-important element of indeterminacy in our basic concepts and in their formal and consistent organisation, and about the need for stable open systems in our knowledge of the universe which, in Einstein's and Polanyi's philosophy of science alike, is characterised by an indefinite range or depth of objectivity and intelligibility.[167] As one would expect, however, there are significant differences in the way in which Polanyi handles these ideas, even when he draws explicitly upon support from Gödel. These differences rest upon the conviction that a symbolic formalism is itself the embodiment of our antecedent unformalised powers, and is to be regarded as an instrument skilfully contrived by our 'inarticulate selves' for the purpose of relying on it as our external guide.[168] As such formalisation reduces informal elements in our prior experience but only *partially* replaces them by a formal operation, for in the advance toward discovery and knowledge the mind operates, as we have seen, through an alternation of analysis and synthesis, or computation and intuition, and in that process it is the informal act of the human intelligence which remains at the centre controlling the formal operations toward the end for which they are devised.[169] This holds true even for mathematics where tacit or informal powers of integration and denotation are operative, both in the construction of a mathematical theory and in the functioning of it as it is made to bear upon the experience which it is meant to help us comprehend and articulate.[170] That is to say, a formalisation operates when we do not just hand over our thinking to its impersonal operation, for it inevitably gathers a momentum of its own in which it easily and irrelevantly far outruns the matter in hand, but when we control and guide it toward a discerned end, and that means that we must not only have some coherent outline of things in advance but be able to grasp the sequence of the formalisation as a whole so that we can hold it within a certain conceptual focus.[171] In other words, a formalism functions only within a framework of tacit knowing and personal judgment in which, while relying upon informal and spontaneous integrative operations at a basic level close to experience, we attend away from the theoretic formalisation of our concepts at another level, to the realities upon which they bear. A standard instance of this, already noted, is the simple one of definitions, in which we tacitly rely upon our knowledge of one set of terms based on some intuitive conception of the nature of things in order to formalise the meaning of another set of terms.

This corresponds to the meta-mathematical or meta-theoretical operations we have discussed above, but the distinctive point in Polanyi's treatment of them is rooted in his conviction that it is personal participation on the part of the thinker or scientist which spans the logical levels and therefore that it is the structure of personal knowledge which not only prevents the levels from separating from one another but conjoins their operations in such a way that they have semantic significance and are scientifically fruitful.[172] Corresponding to Polanyi's insistence that it is impossible to formalise the process of empirical inference or scientific discovery is his insistence that it is futile to attempt to depersonalise the process of deductive inference. Just as there are no mechanical means to discover what we do not know, so there are no merely mechanical ways of formalising what we come to know. Even the most completely formalised logical operations must include an unformalised tacit coefficient.[173]

A helpful guide to Polanyi's thought, once again, is his model of the use of a tool in active exploration and discovery, for it indicates clearly the fundamentally empirico-theoretical cast of his mind which will not allow him to dissociate thinking from doing in the coordinate functioning of mind and body.[174] 'Our body', he says, 'is always in use as the basic instrument of our intellectual and practical control over our surroundings.'[175] Hence we use tools by assimilating them to our bodies so that they can be extensions of our hands and extensions of our senses, and thus as instruments of our minds, in the subtle interconnection between subliminal clues in our bodily processes and an intuitive, proleptic grasp of a coherent pattern which we develop and allow to guide our explicit operations in penetrating into the internal structure of things.[176] As such tools are probes and pointers which do not have their meaning in themselves but in what they serve to disclose and indicate beyond themselves, and in the semantic and heuristic use to which they are put in that process. As we have already seen, this is the way in which Polanyi regards our whole articulate equipment as human beings, as constituting a tool-box for deploying our inarticulate faculties.[177] In this case symbolic representations and formalisms are to be interpreted and handled essentially as conceptual instruments fulfilling a subsidiary role in the active process of scientific inquiry, in which we continually put our questions to the subject-matter in hand and revise and deepen our understanding of the subject-matter in terms of that questioning. There is here a two-way or alternating movement in which we tacitly rely on informal integrative operations as we engage in explicit formalisation and tacitly rely on explicit formalisms as we engage in the informal activity of heuristic advance and verification.[178]

It is entirely consistent with this position that Polanyi should attack the empiricist and positivist separation of reason and experience, or of mathematical knowledge and empirical knowledge, and should appeal for justification of his own view to the striking evidence of the indissoluble unity of geometry and physics in modern field-physics as disclosed through relativity theory, for this implies not only a conception of the logical antecedents to science as internal to science but an understanding of nature as intrinsically of such a character that it is accessible to rational inquiry and description only in empirico-theoretical terms, i.e. only in sets of concepts and statements which at basic points comprise ontological reference.[179] That is why the formalisation of an empirical science constitutes a semantic system with interconnected logical levels: an empirical or object level, a level of theoretical formalisation, and a level of interpretation and application in terms of experience. If a formalism were complete and certain in itself it would have no reference to reality, for it would be separated from the other logical levels, but in so far as it actually refers to reality it is inter-connected with the others in an open system and suffers to that extent from a measure of 'uncertainty' or 'indeterminacy', which makes the informal participation of the knowing agent through acts of personal judgment and decision an all-important and necessary factor for significant and successful scientific inquiry.[180] Since this is the case, since here we have not only knowledge of things but our reflections on our knowledge of things, together with a decision procedure, the three-storied structure of logical levels is necessarily interlocked with the structure of personal knowledge in the ongoing *activity* of *empirical* inquiry.[181]

To return to our attempt to relate the thought of Michael Polanyi to that of Kurt Gödel, it must be said that while there is no difference in principle between them – for Polanyi accepts entirely the validity of the Gödelian theorems – the difference that does hold between them is due to the fact that Polanyi is a practising scientist whose chief interest in theoretical formalisations is in their heuristic value. What he has in view always is their empirical fertility in helping to disclose aspects or levels of reality which are what they are independent of our knowing of them but which become accessible to us in their own interior relations through an inquiry employing *a flexible axiomatic method* directed by heuristic vision, in which there takes place a constant adaptation of the structure of our knowing to the structure of what we seek to know.[182] A rigid

A closed, axiomatic system does not deal w/what is new

how we know

fact

axiomatic method, an axiomatic system operating with fixed axioms, copes only with what can be logically derived from what we already know and cannot cope with what is utterly new. Certainly the recognition of what is new requires as a base of operations a conceptual framework to help us distinguish it from what we already know, but what is new can be identified properly and grasped only as we are able to break free from an antecedent framework and if we are able to assimilate what we are able to grasp of it out of itself through a reconstruction of that framework. Such is the heuristic function to which a scientist hopes to put his formalisation, but a transformation of the formal framework on which we rely in scientific reasoning, an adaptation of it in the very act of applying it to something new, so that it will enable us to strengthen our grasp of it, is a feat of an educated and disciplined intelligence of considerable intuitive power: yet that is precisely what happens in the moments of great creative advance in science. To operate like that, however, by combining a revisable formalism with semantic openness, is precisely how our natural powers of perception cope with new situations in ordinary experience, so that Polanyi seems justified in claiming not only that our explicit formalisations embody antecedent informal acts of integration, but that the Gödelian process of innovation, through the combination of the formal and informal, the theoretical and meta-theoretical levels, is an extension of our ordinary and basic learning processes in which we enlarge our powers of apprehension to take in and give shape to new conceptions.[183]

It is therefore in terms of what Polanyi calls 'stable open systems' (revisable frameworks combined with semantic functions)[184] that he can go on to apply his teaching to living organisms and the rise of man with the aid of a highly illuminating analogy from machine-like operations explained in the same way as multi-levelled systems, operating and developing in accordance with 'the principle of marginal control' – that is, in such a way that while each level operates according to its own distinctive principles, it has a set of conditions left indeterminate by its own operational principles through which it is subject to control by the organisational principles of a higher level, although the latter do not derive from, and are not explicable in terms of, the operational principles of the lower level. It is in this sort of way that a machine functions as a comprehensive entity. Here we have a higher level functioning according to its own operational principles (with which we have to do in engineering), but that relies on another set of laws governing its constituent parts in themselves (with which we have to do in physics and chemistry) on the lower level; while the lower level is left undetermined by the laws of physics and chemistry at certain boundary conditions laying it open to control from the higher level, the engineering operations on the higher level are not explicable in terms of physics and chemistry. A complete physical and chemical analysis of a machine could only treat it as a material object, and could tell us nothing about it as a machine, how it functions and for what purpose; for that we need an additional science, engineering, combining with physics and chemistry. Only then will we be able to understand its organised structure, nature and purpose as a comprehensive entity. It is only by considering a system as a whole, and by attending to the end beyond it which it serves, for the attainment of which it is adapted, that we can really understand it; that is to say, just as the level of engineering operations controls the lower level through its boundary conditions, so the level of engineering operations is likewise controlled from a higher level through its own boundary conditions, for engineering operations are meaningless in themselves. Thus the way that logical levels are coordinated in a science, corresponds to the way in which nature itself is hierarchically structured in levels of reality, in which each level is open upwards to control from a higher and wider system in nature, but in which the higher and wider levels are not reducible to or specifiable in terms of the lower.[185] By carrying out comparisons of this kind, on different levels of reality, between the operations of inanimate, animate and mental systems, Polanyi is able to show that even inanimate systems (machines) and animate systems (impersonal organisms), in their own distinctive ways, function by a trans-level combination of formal and informal factors, much as in the mental field where formal logical operations and informal tacit comprehensions function together but where complete logical formalisation to the exclusion of informal tacit acts of knowing would be self-defeating and futile. But it would be equally futile and indeed meaningless to reduce one level of reality to another by formalising the higher exclusively in terms of the lower, for example, in the reduction of the level of organic life to that of physics and chemistry, or in the reduction of mind to the level of a machine or a neural model.[186] On the other hand, the construction of a machine in which we artificially impose shapes upon inanimate matter without infringing the laws of nature and thus use boundary conditions left undetermined by the laws of nature in an inanimate system to control it from operations on a higher level, helps us to see how in nature itself different levels of reality may function and develop through coordination with one another. It is indeed in line with these ideas, in which he rejects all reductionism, that Polanyi contributes a remarkable ingredient to the modern understanding of evolution, in showing how a higher level can emerge into existence through a process not manifest in the lower level or explainable in terms of it alone, yet without infringing the laws that govern operations at the lower level.[187] However, the application of Polanyi's scientific and meta-scientific thought in these directions is not something that we are able to pursue further here.

V

Michael Polanyi's Gifford Lectures of 1951–2, published as *Personal Knowledge*, were significantly sub-titled 'Towards a Post-Critical Philosophy'. What he meant by that may now be more fully appreciated in the light of the foregoing account of his philosophy of science. By 'the critical movement' he refers to the extensive deployment of symbolic representation and rigorous formalisation in knowledge which was perhaps the most fruitful effort ever sustained by the human mind, giving it in the field of scientific activity the enormous enhancement of man's mental powers which the invention of symbolism and the employment of a linguistic framework in ordinary knowledge gave him over the inarticulate learning of animals. That critical movement of thought was immensely successful because it relied throughout inarticulately upon a fundamental outlook on the general nature of things and a set of beliefs as to the inherent orderliness of the universe, which it inherited from classical Christianity and its reconstruction of Greek philosophy, and which as such constituted the ultimate presuppositions of the modern scientific enterprise and the latent premises underpinning the operation of its critical method. These presuppositions and premises are known subsidiarily only in and through the actual practice of science as maintained in the scientific tradition and are sustained within its framework as a set of beliefs internal to science to which science is committed. But while they are therefore open to a measure of epistemological analysis and are subject to continuous revision in the advance of science, they are not themselves capable of systematic analysis or complete formalisation, since by their very nature they constitute the necessary informal conditions for formal operations. We may recall here once again the paradigm case of definitions in which we formally define one set of terms and concepts by relying on an informal (undefined) knowledge of another set of terms and concepts which on their part become more fully known from an analysis of their application in the process of defining the first set of terms and concepts.[188]

Polanyi's charge against the critical movement of thought, however, is that it has over-reached itself by trying to carry out the complete formalisation of all its terms and concepts in such a way as to cut them off from the informal base upon which they rely, and by reducing fundamental beliefs to the status of subjectivities to discredit them as having no bearing upon the framework of science and therefore as deserving to be eliminated from it along with everything else which cannot be logically defined within the brackets of its formal systems. That conflicts sharply with Polanyi's own inquiry into the nature and justification of scientific knowledge, for the logical analysis of science, he claims, decisively reveals its own limitations, the necessary incompleteness of its formalisations, and its reliance throughout upon formally unprovable beliefs. And what is more, such analysis reveals that no intelligence, however critical or original, can operate outside what he calls 'a fiduciary framework'. 'While our acceptance of this framework is the condition for having any knowledge, this matrix can claim no self-evidence . . . Our mind lives in action, and any attempt to specify its presuppositions produces a set of axioms which cannot tell us why we should accept them.'[189] It is Polanyi's charge, then, that in modern positivism and scientism (which is what comes about with excessive analysis and formalisation according to specifiable rules) the critical mind has repudiated one of its two cognitive faculties, believing, and tried completely to rely on the other, formal reasoning, and thereby has depersonalised the processes of deductive inference and scientific theorising. In his own theory of knowledge, however, Polanyi has tried to restore the balance of our cognitive powers, that is, to restore the fundamental role of tacit knowing which jointly comprehends the informal and the formal levels of scientific activity, and thereby to offer a philosophy of science which will give an account of both scientific discovery and verification which corresponds with the actual practice of the scientist.[190] In so doing he can draw massive support from the thought of Einstein, Bohr and Gödel, but finds himself rather sharply opposed to the false objectivism and critical formalism which have come to characterise the philosophy of linguistic analysis. It was to such a post-critical philosophy of science that Polanyi devoted his Gifford Lectures, (but that applies also to all his works, especially since the publication of *Science, Faith and Society,* in 1946), and sought throughout to promote 'the stability of scientific beliefs' by showing that they necessarily inhere as premises in the essential framework of science.

Since Polanyi's concept of science as personal knowledge has met with considerable misunderstanding, not so much on the part of actual scientists as on the part of empiricist philosophers, it may be helpful in the concluding part of this discussion to offer several correctives.

1. Polanyi's rejection of the objectivist definition of truth and falsity in impersonal terms is not a retreat into a subjective conception of truth but the very opposite, for it is concerned to relate truth to the act of the self in claiming to recognise an objective reality or in the achievement of contact with reality, and thus to distinguish what is properly personal in the act, namely, submission to requirements acknowledged by the self as independent of itself, from what is merely or improperly subjective.[191] In speaking about something the human subject exercises an act of personal judgment in reflecting on his utterance and its bearing on the objective reality in question, to which as a rational person he is obliged to assent within the general framework of his commitment to reality – otherwise, of course, he lies and falsifies his relation to reality. In making a truthful statement, then, the speaker commits himself to a belief in what he has asserted, so that his assertion implies an appraisal of his own act in respect of its truth or falsity.[192] In other words, in speaking the truth we are concerned not only with the truth itself, in the sense of what is actually the case, but with a truthful relation to the truth, including an acceptance of our statement as true.[193] In this event the establishment of truth takes place in a context of commitment to reality which governs the link between the person speaking and the objective pole to which his statement refers. A double link is involved here, between the statement and the speaker, and between the statement and the reality to which it refers: both poles of that link have to be maintained, and maintained truthfully, in the assertion of a true statement.[194]

One pole of that link, however, the relation of the statement to the person asserting it, is precisely what objectivism suppresses by formalising it, that is, by treating truthful relation to the truth as equivalent to factual truth and therefore as capable of being included with it in the same formal calculus. Polanyi explains this in the following way. If we let p stand for a factual statement, 'p is true' expresses a speaker's identification of himself with the content of the factual statement, his endorsement of it as true. But 'p is true' cannot be said to be true or false in the same sense as the factual statement p can be. Actually the statement 'p is true' disguises an act of commitment in the form of a sentence, which misleads the objectivist who by formalising the relation of the statement to the

speaker expressing it casts it into the form of another factual statement. That in turn calls for another assertion that it is true that '"*p*
is true" is true', but since that is something that can be done
indefinitively it involves futile regress and logical paradox. That
does not arise, however, if we realise that there are two kinds of
statement here, a statement of commitment or belief which is
essentially informal, and a statement of fact which is formalisable.
In any assertion of a true statement both must be held together
without being confused with one another, for the act of belief or
endorsement of a statement of fact, necessary as it is to the assertion
of the statement as true, does not enter into its factual content.[195]
We may be truly or falsely, rightly or wrongly, related to the truth,
but that does not affect the truth in the sense of what actually is the
case. Even if everyone were to believe something different to be
true, there is only one truth; but that truth cannot be known or
expressed except by assenting to it in such a way that we both
distinguish it from ourselves and acknowledge it as having legislative authority over us and requiring of us an affirmation of it with
universal intent.[196] This is, as Polanyi admits, close to Tarski's
concept of truth indicated in the statement: '"snow is white" is true
if and only if snow is white', but in order to avoid ambiguity
Polanyi prefers to recast the statement in the form: 'I shall say that
"snow is white" is true if and only if I *believe* that snow is white.'[197]
He wishes to make the function of the personal coefficient in
objective commitment and reference unambiguously clear in order
to distinguish the assertion of truth as of a different order from the
statement asserted to be true and to maintain the semantic relation
between them, so that the factual content of the statement asserted
to be true may be recognised as true independently of what is
asserted. While formalisation has a legitimate purpose in reducing
the personal coefficient, the complete elimination of it would
eliminate its semantic focus and induce meaninglessness. Hence the
ideal of an impersonally detached truth needs to be reinterpreted, to
allow for the inherently personal character of the act by which the
truth is recognised, declared or reached, for without it the all-
important ontological reference of statements to objective reality
would be obscured and might even be formalised away
altogether.[198]

A proper place, of course, must be given to 'logical truth' or
'formal truth', as well as to factual truth, that is, to the formal
validity which propositions have when they are rigorously sys-
tematised in an inferential sequence according to specific 'rules of
truth'. Unlike factual truth, 'truth' of this kind is empty for it has no

semantic but only syntactic reference, except in so far as the system
within which it is found has some ontological reference as a whole:
and that is, as we have seen, what the Gödelian theorems establish
for incomplete or not completely formalisable systems. The statements of a formal system are held to be true, therefore, that is
consistent with one another, only if they are not completely formalised to constitute a closed system complete in itself. This is the
point that Polanyi makes when he claims that 'even the most
completely formalised logical operations include an unformalised
tacit coefficient', and that it is ultimately upon such informal factors
that a formal system depends for its meaning and truth – but truth
here has to do with the bearing of our formulated conceptions upon
objective reality.[199] This is why Polanyi calls for a rejection of the
objectivist notion of truth: complete depersonalisation leaves no
room for the informal acts of commitment to ontological reality
upon which the assertion of factual truth depends, or for the fact
that such a commitment necessarily implies certain basic beliefs
concerning the nature of reality with a claim to their universal
validity, since it is only in the light of those beliefs that he interprets
empirical facts and observations.[200]

It should now be evident that Polanyi's concept of truth is
entirely consistent with his sustained arguments for the inarticulate
along with the articulate intelligence or for implicit along with
explicit knowing, and therefore consistent with his restoration of
the cognitive balance between the informal operation of belief and
the formal operation of the critical reason in all scientific activity.
Regarded in this way, truth is the external pole of belief and belief,
far from being a subjective state of mind or therefore a merely
personal or private concern, is the submission of the mind to
objective reality in recognition of its universal and normative
authority, while reality is thus the external anchoring of our
commitment in making factual assertions. Yet such belief is but the
fiduciary component in the personal coefficient of knowledge
which is not itself included in our explicit statements about external
reality.[201] Thus by taking the personal coefficient into account in
our conception of truth we both distinguish it from our own
subjectivities and acknowledge it to be ontologically independent
of us and universally valid.

2. Polanyi's rehabilitation of the personal coefficient in scientific
knowledge does not imply a rejection of objectivity but of a
mutilated concept of objectivity which he speaks of as *objectivism,*
i.e. the severely restricted concept of 'objectivity' thrown up by the
positivist outlook which limits knowledge to the results of explicit

inferences and therefore leaves no room for basic beliefs or acts of the 'understanding' in its determination to achieve a proper scientific 'detachment'.[202] A real measure of detachment must naturally be maintained in the interest of strict impartiality, in distinguishing the object of our knowledge from our own subjective fancies and predilections and in a methodological disengagement from other points of view which for the time being are inadmissible. On the other hand, complete detachment in the rigorous sense which is the aim of positivists or empiricists 'can only be achieved in a state of complete imbecility well below the normal animal's level'.[203] The problem of objectivism, however, as Polanyi analyses it, is rather more serious: it falsifies our conception of truth, 'by exalting what we can know and prove, while covering up with ambiguous utterances all we know and *cannot* prove, even though the latter knowledge underlies, and must ultimately set its seal to, all that we *can* prove'.[204] At the same time it operates implicitly with a set of anti-metaphysical beliefs of its own in terms of which it damages science by detaching it from the framework of commitment to reality and thereby falsifying its conception of reality.[205] This is very evident in the way it represents scientific theory as 'a mere economical description of facts, or as embodying a conventional policy for drawing empirical inferences; or as a working hypothesis, suited to man's practical convenience – interpretations that all deliberately overlook the rational core of science'.[206] Here secondary features, such as 'simplicity', 'economy', 'symmetry', practicality, fruitfulness, or some formal model in terms of probabilities or constant conjunctions, important though they are, are set up as pseudo-substitutes for truth; that is to say, a pseudo-objectivity takes over which sets aside as irrelevant any claim that scientific theory bears upon being, for it no longer operates with a conception of truth as the achievement of contact with reality and is no longer guided by criteria of rationality internal to reality.[207] However, such a mutilated or distorted conception of objectivity, i.e. 'objectivism', is shattered by the discovery of a rationality inherent in nature independent of our formulations, for then personal, intelligent transactions on the part of the knowing agent by way of recognition, understanding, integration, commitment, belief, appraisal, etc. are involved in the ontological reference of scientific theories to reality, and far from being a weakness or an imperfection they are necessary ingredients in genuinely objective operations.[208]

The first thing Polanyi notes, in discussing genuine objectivity, is the unavoidable element of anthropocentricity in scientific operations. 'For, as human beings, we must inevitably see the universe from a centre lying within ourselves and speak about it in terms of human language shaped by the exigencies of human intercourse. Any attempt rigorously to eliminate our human perspective from our picture of the world must lead to absurdity.'[209] Properly understood, the Copernican revolution, in the exchange of a terrestrial for an imaginary solar standpoint, only abandoned the cruder anthropocentrism of our senses for a more ambitious anthropocentrism of our reason. When we claim greater objectivity for the Copernican theory, however, it is because through that theory as something other than ourselves we claim to have made contact with reality beyond our observational experience and to have discovered a rationality inherent in nature which commands our respect and lays a compelling claim upon our minds. Here the personal and human coefficient in our knowledge remains, evident above all in the intellectual satisfaction we derive from such a theory, but it plays an essential role in the criteria of objectivity, for by its very structure it is correlated to the intrinsic rationality of reality in such a way that we are intellectually committed to its claims and are obliged to affirm them in a responsible act claiming universal validity.[210] Within the framework of commitment to reality, it is this function of the personal ingredient in knowledge in submitting to the requirements of what is independent of itself, and in affirming them with universal intent, that saves personal knowledge from being merely subjective, for thereby it fulfils an active role.[211] 'Subjective knowing is classed as passive; only knowing that bears on reality is active, personal and rightly to be called objective.'[212]

However, objectivity, as Polanyi understands it, has to do not only with the bearing of our knowing upon reality but also, and preeminently, with its bearing upon the indefinite depth of rationality inherent in reality, in virtue of which reality has an inexhaustible capacity to reveal itself in unexpected ways in the future. It is indeed precisely in terms of that characteristic that Polanyi defines *reality*, that is, in terms of its independence and power to manifest itself in unthought of ways, and in corresponding terms that he defines *objective truth* in science, that is, in terms of the apprehension of real patterns inherent in nature, independent of our knowing of them, the implications of which extend indefinitely beyond the experience which they were originally meant to control.[213] 'In this wholly indeterminate scope of its true implications lies the deepest sense in which objectivity is attributed to a scientific theory.'[214] That is why the scientist is committed, as we have seen, to maintain open

conceptions and open structures of thought, which, just because
they are open to the disclosure of reality in its intrinsic order and
structure, are constantly revisable in the light of such a disclosure.
As such this revisability or ontological openness to reality is an
essential ingredient in the objectivity of a scientific theory, but that
inevitably throws the maintenance and fulfilment of objectivity
back upon the personal responsibility of the scientist himself: he
and he only is capable, as an active centre of rationality, of establishing the bearing of his knowing upon reality in this way. It should be
noted in passing that since this is what Polanyi calls 'personal
knowledge', it is rather different from what usually goes under that
name. 'Personal knowledge in science is not made but discovered,
and as such it claims to establish contact with reality beyond the
clues on which it relies. It commits us, passionately and far beyond
our comprehension, to a vision of reality. Of this responsibility we
cannot divest ourselves by setting up objective criteria of verifiability or falsifiability, or testability, or what you will.'[215]

Within this general framework of commitment to external reality, all responsible personal knowing appraises what it knows by a
universal or objective standard which it posits for itself. 'Responsibility and truth are in fact but two aspects of such a commitment:
the act of judgment is its personal pole and the independent reality
on which it bears is its external pole.'[216] Thus the scientist is himself
the ultimate judge of what he accepts as true or rejects as false, but
this judgment implies a submission to standards of judgment
independent of him which he freely accepts as the criteria for his
own judgments. This is what Polanyi calls 'the paradox of self-set
standards'.[217] Far from doing as he pleases the scientist forces
himself to act as he believes he must act under the requirements of
reality and its intrinsic rationality. He is compelled to rely throughout his inquiries on his own personal judgment, but this is objectively grounded for it functions through assent to the claim and
jurisdiction of external reality over him, so that reality itself is
accepted by the scientist as the ultimate judge of the truth or falsity
of his conceptions and statements about it. His own ultimate
judgment is thus an echo of the ultimate judgment of reality. Hence
within the framework of commitment to reality upon which all
scientific knowledge depends, the personal and the objective instead
of being opposed to one another are mutually correlated.[218]

3. While Polanyi uses the findings of Gestalt psychology as
initial clues in developing his theory of personal knowledge, and
also draws some support from phenomenology where it has also
learned from Gestalt psychology, his real concern is neither with

psychology nor with phenomenology but with the *ontology* of knowledge. Gestalt psychology shows how we may perceive a whole such as a physiognomy through the spontaneous equilibrium of its particulars impressed on the retina or the brain;[219] but Polanyi takes that down to a much deeper level and recasts it in terms of the integrating of our awareness of its particulars in the shape of a comprehensive entity which is apprehended through tacit knowing as having *being* and *reality* in its own right. Moreover, he disagrees with the idea of the Gestalt psychologists that the regulative powers of living beings and their mental powers of comprehension are akin to each other, and holds that they both embody principles not found in inanimate nature, but he then goes on to relate all these to one another through an ontological structure comprising different levels of reality.[220] Phenomenology, on the other hand, shows that different aspects or levels of existence manifest distinctive patterns of their own which are interesting in themselves and can be studied in themselves. Thus it distinguishes between the feeling of our body as it participates in our acts of perception (i.e. what Merleau-Ponty calls knowledge of the body 'through its functional value')[221] and the view of the body as an object from outside, but Polanyi recasts this in terms of his distinction between two kinds of awareness, looking *from* and looking *at,* which, together with his replacing of the shallower notion of empathy with that of interiorisation or indwelling, enables him to overcome the Cartesian dualism between mind and body which lies behind phenomenology, and so to extend this procedure from the human to the natural sciences. Phenomenology also attempts to safeguard the content of unsophisticated experience against the effects of destructive analysis, by showing how higher, less tangible levels of experience can be saved by not interpreting them in terms of the more tangible things in which their existence is rooted; but owing to the dualist and phenomenalist ideas that lie behind this, phenomenology is unable to prevent the reduction of man's mental existence to mechanical structures, with the result that phenomenology, unable to secure even its own position, remains suspended over the abyss of reductionism.[222] Polanyi, however, breaks through phenomenalism to a concept of science as the penetration into the nature of things in their own interior relations, and develops a theory of ontological stratification which, along with the logic of tacit knowing, does enable us, as phenomenology does not, to establish a continuous transition from the natural sciences to the study of the humanities.[223] Polanyi's quarrel with these psychological and phenomenological approaches to knowledge reduces in the end to their lack of a proper ontology, for unless the forms of thought which we develop about things are ontologically grounded in their reality, they are caught in an alienating dualism which can only strip them of meaning.[224]

In view of this it seems rather perverse that Polanyi's account of knowledge should be opposed, as it sometimes is, on the ground that it is psychological, not logical, in character. Polanyi's immediate reply to this charge is that the structure of scientific knowing, as he expounds it, is basically the same as that of perception in which we see an object in such a way as to assimilate it to past instances of the same kind. That is not by explicit but by implicit processes which he calls tacit. Moreover to perceive things rightly is part of the process of scientific inquiry and to hold perceptions to be right underlies the holding of scientific propositions to be true. 'If, in consequence we must accept the veridical powers of perception as the roots of empirical science, we cannot reasonably refuse to accept other tacit veridical processes having a similar structure.'[225] But that is what he has been urging all along since he first wrote '. . . that the capacity of scientists to guess the presence of shapes as tokens of reality, differs from the capacity of our ordinary perception only by the fact that it can integrate shapes presented to it in terms which the perception of ordinary people cannot readily handle'.[226]

The question at issue here is really that of *knowing* and *being*.[227] That is the question whether knowledge in the proper sense is objectively grounded on being or not, and whether the truth of a proposition lies in its bearing on reality. If this is the case, as Polanyi maintains, in face of the modern anti-metaphysical philosophies and philosophies of science, then the implications of true propositions are indeterminate, a conclusion which, as we have seen, Polanyi shares with Einstein and Gödel. But what is indeterminate cannot be spelt out without making it determinate. 'It can be known in its indeterminate condition only tacitly, by those tacit powers by which we know more than we can tell.'[228] If it is granted, therefore, that in all scientific (as in ordinary) knowledge we are concerned with a relation of *knowing* and *being,* the charge against Polanyi is bound to fail, for it is impossible in principle to spell out (at least completely) in explicit formal terms the relations between a knowing mind and the reality it knows: but of course the ontological reference of scientific theories, the claim that they have a bearing upon being, is precisely what the antimetaphysical philosophies will not grant.[229]

A scientist like Polanyi, however, cannot but take seriously the profound revolution in the foundations of knowledge resulting from relativity theory, especially as regards the ultimate inseparability of form and being, structure and matter, or geometry and physics, and the impossibility, reinforced by the Gödelian theorems, of detaching theoretical formalisations from their empirical or ontological import and making them complete in terms of what they are in themselves. While rejecting therefore, as scientifically unreasonable a demand for a theory of knowledge in completely explicit formal terms, it is natural that Polanyi should nevertheless seek a way of reconciling a reasonable demand for explanation in explicit formal terms with the fact that the relation between knowing and being cannot be completely formalised. That is what he does through *tacit knowledge,* i.e. a kind of knowledge we have of something only as we rely on it in attending to something else, or the kind of knowledge in which we rely upon what we implicitly know in order to engage in explicit operations. It is only by relying on a prior tacit knowing that we can formulate knowledge of an object, and it is within the dynamic structure of tacit knowing that explicit knowledge of an object in terms of its specifiable particulars and their relations is held together with knowledge of it as an integrated whole or a comprehensive entity. That is to say, it is in tacit knowing that we have to do with the *ontological reference* of knowledge, in virtue of which we establish empirical contact with reality in its intrinsic coherence and rationality, and therefore with that aspect of knowing in which its content is grounded evidentially and objectively, although informally, upon the structure of experience or reality.[230] As such, tacit knowing is the fundamental power of the mind which gives rise to discovery and makes it the true paradigm of all knowledge, and which creates explicit knowing, lending it meaning and controlling its uses. Certainly formalisation of tacit knowing, in so far as that is possible, immensely expands the powers of the mind by creating a machinery of precise thought and thereby opening up new paths to intuition, but only if the whole operation is undergirded and sustained from the beginning to the end by an epistemic relation between mind and being.[231] That is why, in Polanyi's view, epistemology and ontology necessarily imply and require one another, and why he reconstructs the received theory of knowledge in such a way as to overcome the objectivist detachment and impersonalism that result from the Cartesian and phenomenalist dichotomy between the mind of the knower and what he knows.[232]

The objectivist obsession with a knowledge limited to the results of explicit inferences requires a concept of science purified of references to consciousness or mind. This is particularly evident in behaviourism which reduces the mind of an individual to a bundle of particulars related to one another by a set of explicit inferences, but that, as Polanyi insists, is to replace the original subject matter 'with a grotesque simulacrum of it in which the mind itself is missing'.[233] A theory of knowledge based on tacit knowing does not require the reductive analysis and explanation of mind in terms of the laws of physics and chemistry on the operation of which it relies at a lower level of existence, as if the mind had no meaning or reality in its own right just because it cannot be known through a direct, focal awareness, for it does have meaning and is known to be real as we tacitly rely upon it in knowing other realities.[234] Thus a theory of knowledge based on tacit knowing requires both an 'ontology of mind' and an 'ontology of commitment', for two poles of being are involved, the being of the knowing mind and the being of what is known.[235] Hence, against the objectivist and positivist theory of knowledge which refuses to acknowledge the existence of comprehensive entities as distinct from their particulars, Polanyi argues, within the framework of epistemic commitment to reality, that the human mind is real and indeed more real than what we know through the mind on lower and more tangible levels of existence.[236]

The main argument here hinges upon two inter-related ideas: (1) the concept of reality as that which has the independence and power to reveal itself in an indefinite range of unexpected manifestations, which means that the mind possesses a deeper reality, for example, than a cobblestone, although the latter is admittedly more real in the sense of being more tangible;[237] and (2) the concept of ontological stratification in the universe comprising a sequence of rising levels, each higher one controlling the boundaries of the one below it and embodying thereby the joint meaning of the particulars situated on the lower level, which implies that 'all meaning lies in the higher levels of reality that are not reducible to the laws by which the ultimate particulars of the universe are controlled'.[238] Putting these two notions together, we find that they tell us that as we move up the hierarchy of levels of reality, from the more tangible to the more intangible, we penetrate to things that are *increasingly real and full of meaning*. Since what is most tangible, such as a stone, has least meaning, it is perverse to identify the tangible with the real. Rather we conclude that deepest reality is possessed by higher things that are least tangible.[239] In this sense profound reality is to be attributed to intelligence or mind, which is the superior principle governing living beings, but also to those intangible, imponderable things which transcend the human mind and beckon its deepening inquiry and understanding. 'Just as the sensory-motor levels of life leave themselves open to the control of intelligence, so the principle of intelligence leaves its powers open to the still higher principles of responsible choice. Human beings exercise responsibilities within a social setting and a framework of obligations which transcend the principle of intelligence.'[240] Thus when we put together 'the logic of tacit knowing' and 'the ontological principles of stratified entities' we find that they manifest a universe with an in-built principle of transcendence and a framework of knowing in which the human mind is left open at its own boundary conditions to the intimations and the indeterminate implications of reality transcending it altogether.[241]

This carries us back full circle to the beginning of our discussion, to Polanyi's early conviction that belief in such a transcendent reality, independent of our knowing of it and accessible to all men, is the ultimate determinant of the scientific enterprise, and that common dedication to that transcendent reality is the ground of our academic freedom. While the knowing of God, Polanyi remarks, is outside his argument, his conception of knowing opens the way to it: natural knowing expanding continuously into knowledge of the supernatural. 'Such, I believe, is the true transition from science to the humanities and also from our knowing the laws of nature to our knowing the person of God.'[242]

NOTES

1. From Einstein's contribution to P. A. Schilpp, *The Philosophy of Bertrand Russell, New York, 1944*, p. 287.
2. From Einstein's introductory remarks to P. A. Schilpp, *Albert Einstein: Philosopher-Scientist*, 4th edn, p. 9, New York.
3. Polanyi refers in this connexion to a discussion with Bukharin in 1935, *Science, Faith and Society* (1946), Phoenix edn, pp. 8ff. 1964; *The Logic of Liberty*, pp. 40ff. 76ff. 1951; *Personal Knowledge*, p. 238f., 1958; *Tacit Dimension*, p. 3f., 1967.
4. *Personal Knowledge*, pp. 174ff.; 320ff.
5. *Science, Faith and Society*, p. 81; *The Logic of Liberty*, pp. 40ff.
6. See especially *Personal Knowledge*, pp. 5f., 15f., 37, 43, 64f., 104, 311; 'Objectivity' is not to be confused with 'objectivism', pp. 286, 323, 381.
7. *Personal Knowledge*, pp. 55ff., 88ff., 101ff., 174ff., etc.
8. *The Logic of Liberty*, pp. 115ff., 154ff.; *Personal Knowledge*, pp. 33–48.
9. See the lecture 'On Body and Mind', in *The New Scholasticism* **43**, 195, 1969. Many of the illustrations Polanyi uses in the course of these arguments are taken from medical practice and physical skills. *Science, Faith and Society*, p. 17.
11. See the chapters 'Planned Science', in *The Logic of Liberty*, pp. 86ff.; and 'The Republic of Science', and 'The Growth of Science in Society', in *Knowing and Being*, pp. 49ff. and 73ff.
12. *Science, Faith and Society*, pp. 10ff., and 85ff.; *The Logic of Liberty*, pp. vif and 30.
13. See *Knowing and Being*, pp. 126, 134, 153ff., 218ff., 225ff.; *Tacit Dimension*, pp. 33f., 1967.
14. *The Logic of Liberty*, pp. 111ff., 154ff.
15. It should be noted, however, that Polanyi rejects the notion of 'openness' which does not admit of commitment to a distinctive set of beliefs; but holds that the rejection of those beliefs and the kind of academic freedom that goes with them leads to a closed society. See *Science, Faith and Society*, Chap. III, pp. 63ff.
16. *The Logic of Liberty*, p. 47; cf. also p. 39.
17. *Personal Knowledge*, pp. 3–17; 'From Copernicus to Einstein,' *Encounter* **5**, 1, 1955; reprinted in *Scientific Thought and Social Reality* (Edited by F. Schwartz) pp. 98–115, 1974; see also pp. 52, 73, 81.
18. See 'The Integration of Form in Natural and in Theological Science', *Sci. Med. Man* **1.3**, pp. 143ff, 1972; Chapter II above, pp. 61–105.
19. The different relations of Polanyi and Popper to the Vienna Circle mark to this day the difference between the thought of these two, but in some respects they are much more alike than is sometimes realised.

20. A. Einstein, *The World as I See It*, 1935, pp. 125f., 134ff.; *Out of My Later Years*, pp. 61ff., 1950.
21. See A. Einstein, *Ideas and Opinions*, pp. 270ff., 282f., 1954. It is this interconnection between creative or heuristic apprehension and deductive operations that appears to have set the field for Popper's thought. It is in his handling of that interconnection that his sharp difference with the assumptions of the Vienna Circle becomes evident, but also his difference with Polanyi's thought, for the deductivist ingredient in Popper's account of scientific method makes it more 'rationalist' (that is analytically specific) than Polanyi's and fails to leave sufficient room for the 'creative' and the 'integrative' operations which are so distinctive in Polanyi's concept of scientific verification as well as of discovery.
22. A. Einstein, *The World as I See It*, pp. 125f., 133ff., 173; *Out of My Later Years*, p. 60f.
23. *The World as I See It*, p. 126.
24. *The Critique of Pure Reason*. A 133–136, cf. 141; see M. Polanyi, *Knowing and Being*, p. 105f.
25. See especially, *The Tacit Dimension*, Chap. 1; and *Knowing and Being*, Chap. 10.
26. See the 1963 preface to *Science, Faith and Society*, Phoenix Ed, p. 10.
27. Polanyi himself claims that 'tacit knowing is in fact the dominant principle of all knowledge, and that its rejection would, therefore, automatically involve the rejection of any knowledge whatever'. *The Study of Man*, 1959, p. 13.
28. Plato, *Meno*, 82e *et seq*; cf. also *Euthydemus*, 275d *et seq*.
29. Polanyi, *Science, Faith and Society*, p. 14; *The Tacit Dimension*, p. 22. Cf. the discussion of S. Kierkegaard, *Philosophical Fragments*, English translation by David Swenson, 1936, p. 5f.
30. *The Tacit Dimension*, p. 23.
31. *Science, Faith and Society*, p. 14.
32. *Science, Faith and Society*, pp. 33ff.; *The Tacit Dimension*, pp. 32ff.; *Knowing and Being*, pp. 130ff.
33. *Knowing and Being*, pp. 76f., 82, 118f., 143f., 201ff.
34. *Personal Knowledge*, pp. 123, 124ff., 142ff., 150ff., 189f., 381ff. Polanyi refers to the work of his friend George Polya on mathematical heuristics, *How to Solve It*, Princeton, 1945; *Mathematics and Plausible Reasoning*, 2 vols, London, 1954; *Mathematical Discovery*, New York, London, Sydney, 2 vols, 1965. See also the papers by Polanyi and Polya in *De la Méthode, Méthodologies Particulières et Méthodologie en Général*, edited by S. Dockx, *Archives de l'Institut International des Sciences Théoriques*, 1972, pp. 11ff., and 27ff.
35. *The World as I See It*, pp. 125f., 135f.
36. *Ibid.*, p. 136.
37. *Ibid.*, p. 138.
38. *Ibid.*, p. 174: 'Concepts have reference to sensible experiences, but they are never, in a logical sense, deducible from them. For this reason I

have never been able to understand the quest of the *a priori* in the Kantian sense. In any ontological question, the only possible procedure is to seek out those characteristics in the complex of sense experiences to which the concepts refer.' See also Max Born *The Born-Einstein Letters,* trans. by Irene Born, p. 7, 1971.

39. Cited by Polanyi in 'Genius in science', In *De la Méthode. Méthodologies Particulières et Méthodologie en Général* (Edited by S. Dockx). *Archives de l'Institut International des Sciences Théoriques,* p. 22. 1972.

40. Cited by Polanyi, in 'Genius in science', *De La Méthode,* p. 22, 1972.

41. It still needs to be pointed out that Popper's so-called 'falsification principle' is not a principle of verification but only a 'demarcation principle' enabling a clear distinction to be drawn between empirical and non-empirical or non-scientific concepts and theories.

42. See the chapter on 'Truth, Rationality, and the Growth of Knowledge' in *Conjectures and Refutations,* pp. 215ff., in which Popper shows that in the growth of knowledge we operate with theories of increasing content, and so with theories of decreasing probability.

43. K. Popper, *Objective Knowledge, An Evolutionary Approach,* p. 1, 1972; see also the letter of Einstein to Popper, published in *The Logic of Scientific Discovery,* pp. 457ff.; and *Conjectures and Refutations,* pp. 34f.

44. R. Harré. *The Philosophies of Science,* p. 51f., 1972.

45. This in spite of the title of his book 'The *Logic* of Scientific Discovery'. Cf. p. 32, where Popper refers to 'an irrational element' or 'a creative intuition', in Bergson's sense, and refers to Einstein's statement regarding *Einfühlung (The World as I See It,* p. 125) translated as 'Sympathetic understanding of experience', which is very close to what Polanyi calls 'participation' and 'indwelling' (cf. *Personal Knowledge,* p. 150). Polanyi's, or Einstein's, concept of intuition, however, is not that of Bergson or that of Popper, for it is an act of *apprehension.* For Popper's notion of conjectures=guesses, see *Conjectures and Refutations,* p. 114f.; *Objective Knowledge,* p. 9ff.

46. Cf. Reichenbach: 'But the critical attitude may make a man incapable of discovery; and, as long as he is successful, the creative physicist may very well prefer his creed to the logic of the analytic philosopher.' From *Readings in the Philosophy of Science,* edited by H. Feigl and M. Brodbeck, p. 197, 1953. Cited by F. Schwartz, with respect to Polanyi's *cognitive* method, in his preface to *Scientific Thought and Social Reality: Essays by Michael Polanyi,* p. 11, 1974.

47. *Knowing and Being,* p. 125.

48. *Ibid.,* p. 130.

49. *Ibid.,* p. 164.

50. *Ibid.,* p. 156.

51. *Science, Faith and Society,* p. 23f.; *The Study of Man,* p. 35.; *The Logic of Liberty,* p. 52. *Knowing and Being,* pp. 105ff., 117f., 138f., 143f., 166, 172f. It is a weakness of Popper's position that because of his neglect of the epistemic source of conjectures and theories (which he wrongly confuses with their psychological source), he has to fall

back on some kind of *formal decision* reached (irrespective of content or empirical import) in accordance with accepted rules of procedure to determine whether conjectures and theories are right and scientifically acceptable – *The Logic of Scientific Discovery*, pp. 81ff., 106ff.

52. *Knowing and Being*, pp. 114ff., 138ff. In an interesting passage Niels Bohr points out that this was the path taken by Einstein 'of adapting our modes of perception borrowed from the sensations to the gradually deepening knowledge of the laws of Nature'. *Atomic Theory and the Description of Nature*, p. 90, 1934.

53. Polanyi also uses the language of anatomy to speak of the clues subsidiarily known as the *proximal term* of tacit knowing, and of that which is focally known as the *distal term* of tacit knowing. *The Tacit Dimension*, p. 10f.; *Knowing and Being*, p. 140f., etc.

54. 'Science and Man', the Nuffield Lecture for 1970, *Proceedings of the Royal Society of Medicine*, Vol. 63. p. 974, 1970.

55. *Knowing and Being*, pp. 118, 139.

56. *Knowing and Being*, pp. 144, 211f.

57. *Ibid.*, pp. 144, 198f.

58. *Personal Knowledge*, pp. 3–17. The implications of Einstein's view of the inner relation between geometry and physics are here contrasted with the positivist and conventionalist notions stemming from Ernst Mach for which no ontological claim is advanced – see Einstein, *Ideas and Opinions*, pp. 232–246, 272f., 1954.

59. *Ibid.*, pp. 37, 43, 64f., 104, 116, 311, etc. Cf. also 'Genius in Science'. *op. cit.*, p. 15f.

60. *The Tacit Dimension*, p. 32f.

61. *Knowing and Being*, p. 213.

62. *Ibid.*, pp. 194, 212.

63. In fact, 'A *wholly* explicit knowledge is unthinkable', *Knowing and Being*, p. 144. Complete explicitation is what Polanyi calls frequently 'the Laplacean delusion' which has been revived recently in the claims of cybernetics to reduce all knowledge to explicit operations of the mind.

64. 'On Body and Mind', *op. cit.*, p. 201f.

65. See the discussion of Poincaré's notions of illumination and intuition in mathematical heuristics, in *Personal Knowledge*, pp. 118ff, 260f.; and in *Knowing and Being*, pp. 201ff. Polanyi's 'scientific intuition', while no less unspecifiable, is more objectively grounded than Poincaré's 'illumination' through the coordination of its integrative acts with a coherence latent in reality. See *Knowing and Being*, pp. 118ff., 179.

66. *Knowing and Being*, p. 201f.

67. *Ibid.*, p. 203.

68. *Ibid.*, p. 203.

69. *Personal Knowledge*, p. 13.

70. *Knowing and Being*, pp. 120, 130f.

71. *Ibid.*, pp. 107f., 138f.

72. *The Tacit Dimension*, pp. 78f., 98f. Cf. *Personal Knowledge*, p. 30: 'It is of the essence of the scientific method to select for verification hypotheses having a *high* chance of being true'; and the citation from G. Polya (*Mathematics and Plausible Reasoning*, Vol. 2, p. 76): 'When you have satisfied yourself that your theorem is true, you start proving it.' *Personal Knowledge*, p. 131.

73. 'Genius in Science', *op. cit.*, p. 17f.

74. *Ibid.*, pp. 18ff., 21ff.; *Science, Faith and Society*, pp. 90ff. See also the discussion of the Michelson-Morley experiment, in *Scientific Thought and Social Reality*, pp. 106–111; *Personal Knowledge*, pp. 9–13, and G. Holton, 'Einstein, Michelson and the "Crucial Experiment".' In *ISIS* **60**, 133, 1969; and *Thematic Origins of Scientific Thought – Kepler to Einstein*, 1973.

75. 'Genius in Science', *op. cit.*, p. 20. See further *Personal Knowledge*, pp. 20f., 47, 63f., 167, for the limits of 'falsifiability', and also *The Logic of Liberty*, pp. 16ff., for the limits of 'prediction'.

76. 'Genius in Science', *op. cit.*, p. 21f.

77. Cf. again the path taken by Einstein: 'The whole of science is nothing more than a refinement of everyday thinking'. 'Physics and Reality', in *Out of My Later Years*, p. 59.

78. 'Genius in Science', *op. cit.*, pp. 14f., 21.

79. 'The scientific method was devised precisely for the purpose of elucidating the nature of things under more carefully controlled conditions and by more rigorous criteria than are present in the situations created by practical problems.' *Personal Knowledge*, p. 183.

80. Cf. the essay by Polanyi in 1936, 'The Value of the Inexact', in *Philosophy of Science*, Vol. III, pp. 233ff. In a way this corresponds to the point Popper makes when he insists that 'there can be no ultimate statements in science', *The Logic of Scientific Discovery*, p. 47.

81. 'Genius in Science', *op cit.*, p. 11.

82. *Ibid.*, p. 21. Cf. here Popper's use of 'personal' to describe the evaluation and appraisal of competing theories, where the gap between him and Polanyi clearly narrows, *Objective Knowledge*, pp. 142ff.

83. See *Personal Knowledge*, pp. 63ff., 211f., or *The Tacit Dimension*, pp. 25, 76ff., 87, etc.

84. This way of comparing the approaches of Polanyi and Bohr has been suggested to me by Dr Christopher B. Kaiser, in 'Niels Bohr and Michael Polanyi: Some interesting parallels', *Convivium* (Michael Polanyi Newsletter), No. 9, Winter, 1979/80, pp. 13–23. Dr Kaiser has given an exhaustive analysis of Bohr's epistemology in a thesis for Edinburgh University, *The Logic of Complementarity in Science and Theology*, 1974.

85. Bohr, *Atomic Theory and the Description of Nature*, 1934, p. 99. See p. 18f. for Bohr's critical reservation regarding the use of the term 'reciprocal', and its replacing by 'complementary'.

86. *Atomic Theory*, p. 96.

87. *Atomic Theory*, p. 20.

88. *The Logic of Liberty*, pp. 20ff.; cf. *Scientific Thought and Social Reality*, p. 119.

89. The word 'complementary' here is Polanyi's, *Knowing and Being*, p. 125. While not used in precisely Bohr's way, it may reflect his thought nevertheless. Cf. also *The Logic of Liberty*, p. 20ff. But contrast the use cited below.

90. 'What is a Painting?' *The American Scholar* **39**, 655, 1970.

91. *Ibid.*, p. 662.

92. *Ibid.*, pp. 658, 662.

93. *Ibid.*, pp. 663ff., 667: 'The arts do not exhibit things that *could be* really there and yet *are not* there; they exhibit things of a kind that cannot exist, either in nature or among men.'

94. This is commonly expressed by saying that 'we cannot know both momentum and the position of the atomic object'.

95. *Atomic Theory*, p. 98.

96. 'Discussion with Einstein on Epistemological Problems in Atomic Physics', in P. A. Schilpp, *Albert Einstein: Philosopher-Scientist*, p. 210. This discussion is reprinted in *Atomic Physics and Human Knowledge*, 1958, pp. 32–66, where the reference in question is p. 39f.

97. The discussion with Einstein noted above gives the most complete and systematic exposition of this which Bohr offered. See the estimation of this by J. R. Nielsen, *Niels Bohr's Collected Works*, Vol. 1, p. XLI, 1972.

98. Cf. Nielsen, *op. cit.*, p. XLf.

99. Bohr, *Atomic Physics*, p. 27.

100. 'Discussion with Einstein', *op. cit.*, p. 224.

101. *Atomic Theory*, p. 24.

102. 'Discussion with Einstein', *op. cit.*, p. 236; *Atomic Physics*, especially Chaps 1, 2 and 5.

103. *Atomic Physics*, p. 2.

104. 'Discussion with Einstein', *op. cit.*, p. 232f.

105. *Atomic Theory*, p. 18; cf. *Atomic Physics*, pp. 7, 25.

106. *Atomic Physics*, p. 73; 'Discussion with Einstein', *op. cit.*, p. 237. Rosenfeld includes the measuring instruments in the 'observed object' thus making it 'the observed phenomenon'; 'The Strife about Complementarity', in *Science Progress*, no. 163, p. 395, 1953.

107. *The Born-Einstein Letters*, p. 209; cf. also p. 158f.

108. 'Discussion with Einstein', *op. cit.*, p. 238; cf. *Atomic Physics*, p. 73.

109. Unlike classical physics which describes objects in space and formulates the laws of their changes in time, in quantum physics there is no place for laws governing changes in time of individual particles, but only laws governing large aggregations of individuals and therefore only laws governing the change in time of the probabilities of their occurrence. See Einstein and Infeld, *The Evolution of Physics*, 1960 edition, pp. 284ff.

110. *The Born-Einstein Letters*, p. 173; Cf. *The World as I See It*, p. 161 and *The Evolution of Physics*, pp. 287ff.; *Ideas and Opinions*, p. 275f.

111. 'Discussion with Einstein', *op. cit.*, p. 235, 239f.; see also the chapter on 'Unity of Knowledge' (1954) in *Atomic Physics*, pp. 67ff. Yet even here 'objective description' is equated with 'unambiguous communication', p. 67.
112. *Atomic Physics*, pp. 69–76.
113. *Atomic Physics*, p. 7.
114. Although elements of phenomenalism remain in this theory of knowledge, it does represent a greater break-away from Kantian presuppositions than that of Heisenberg. For a critique of the epistemological implications of quantum theory see the important essay by Popper, 'Quantum Mechanics without "The Observer"', in *Quantum Theory and Reality*, (Edited by M. Bunge, 1967); and also the chapter 'Epistemology without a knowing subject', in *Objective Knowledge*, pp. 106ff.
115. *The Tacit Dimension*, p. 10ff.; *Knowing and Being*, p. 141.
116. *Ibid.*, p. 12; cf. also *Personal Knowledge*, p. 55f.; *Knowing and Being*, pp. 127f., 145, etc.
117. *The Study of Man*, 1959, p. 30f.
118. *The Tacit Dimension*, p. 10.
119. *Knowing and Being*, p. 141; *The Tacit Dimension*, p. 11.
120. *Knowing and Being*, p. 141; *The Tacit Dimension*, p. 11. Cf. the citation which Polanyi adduces from William Whewell (*Philosophy of Discovery*, 1860, p. 254): 'To hit upon a right conception is a difficult step; and when this step is made, the facts assume a different aspect from what they had before: that done, they are seen in a new point of view; and the catching of this point of view, is a special mental operation, requiring special endowments and habits of thought.' *Knowing and Being*, p. 140.
121. *The Tacit Dimension*, p. 12f.; *Knowing and Being*, pp. 182, 218.
122. *Knowing and Being*, pp. 141, 161, etc.
123. *The Logic of Liberty*, p. 21.
124. *Personal Knowledge*, pp. 57, 116; *Knowing and Being*, pp. 145, 153f., 161f., 182ff., 193ff.
125. *Knowing and Being*, pp. 141, 181ff.
126. *Personal Knowledge*, pp. 57, 79, 344; *Knowing and Being*, pp. 108f.
127. *The Tacit Dimension*, p. 32f.; *Knowing and Being*, pp. 141f. That is why a true scientific theory indicates much more than it can actually formalise in explanation of the circumstances that provoked it. 'To hold a natural law to be true is to believe that its presence may reveal itself in yet unknown and perhaps yet unthinkable consequences; it is to believe that natural laws are features of a reality which as such will continue to bear consequences inexhaustibly.' *Ibid.*, p. 138.
128. *Knowing and Being*, pp. 179f., 187ff.; 'Science and Man', *op. cit.*, pp. 970ff.
129. *Knowing and Being*, pp. 145ff., 151f., 184f., 212f., 218.
130. This is what Polanyi calls 'the criterion of consistency', *Personal Knowledge*, p. 142; cf. also pp. 79f., 252f. At this point we can see

once again how close Polanyi is to Bohr, in respect of his demand that an account of what we know must include an account of the conditions under which it is known, with reference to the agencies of observation.

131. *The Study of Man*, pp. 11–26.

132. *Knowing and Being*, pp. 127f., 145.

133. There is a passage, however, in *The Study of Man*, p. 13, where Polanyi more or less concedes this: 'I deny that any participation of the knower in the shaping of knowledge must invalidate knowledge, though I admit it impairs its objectivity.' Polanyi is speaking here of 'tacit knowing', and by 'objectivity' he refers to 'the public, objective character of explicit knowledge', p. 12f. On the ingredient of personal knowledge in quantum theory, see also *Personal Knowledge*, p. 36.

134. Cf. *Personal Knowledge*, p. 393, n. 1. In all experiments, of course, we impose restrictions on nature in order to observe its behaviour under these restrictions, but here we are operating at two levels, that of the restrictions within the experimental arrangement (defined in terms of Newtonian principles), and that of the actual connections in nature which we are seeking to explain (which in the quantum of action transcends the level of thought in Newtonian physics), and from which we generalise beyond the restrictions imposed by the experimental arrangement. Only if the two levels are confused or run together would we be forced to read the conditions under which we observe nature into the actual content of our knowledge; but if the two levels are maintained intact in controlled relation with one another, that ought not to take place, for, as Polanyi argues, a boundary condition is *extraneous* to the process it delimits. Cf. *Knowing and Being*, pp. 225ff. This bears some resemblance to the operation of what Bohr called the 'correspondence principle', 'Discussion with Einstein', *op. cit.*, pp. 204, 208.

135. *Personal Knowledge*, especially pp. 63ff., 308ff.; *Knowing and Being*, pp. 33, 133f.; *The Study of Man*, pp. 27, 36.

136. *Personal Knowledge*, pp. 15ff., 59ff., 299ff.; *The Tacit Dimension*, pp. 77ff., 87.

137. *Personal Knowledge*, pp. 5f., 37, 64f.

138. This is a principal theme throughout *Science, Faith and Society*, but cf. especially Chap. 2 on 'Authority and Conscience', pp. 42ff.; and *Personal Knowledge*, pp. 160–170; 299–316.

139. See the long discussion in *Personal Knowledge*, pp. 132–202.

140. *Personal Knowledge*, pp. 95, 113, 252; *Knowing and Being*, pp. 156, 191.

141. It is this 'controlled openness' or 'obligation to be free' that Polanyi discerns in the interrelation of science and society, *Science, Faith and Society*, pp. 65ff.

142. See Chap. 2 of *The Tacit Dimension*, entitled 'Emergence', pp. 29ff.; *Knowing and Being*, pp. 218, 236.

143. *Knowing and Being*, pp. 153ff., 216ff., 225ff.; *The Study of Man*, pp. 46ff., 93ff.; *Scientific Thought and Social Reality*, p. 134ff.

144. *The Tacit Dimension*, pp. 32ff.; *Knowing and Being*, p. 154f.
145. *Über formal unentscheidbare Sätze der Principia Mathematica und verwandter Systeme I*, in *Monatshefte für Mathematik und Physik*, no. 38, pp. 173–198. English trans. by B. Meltzer, with Introduction by R. B. Braithwaite, 1962. Gödel never wrote the second paper he had projected.
146. For this background to Gödel's paper see E. Nagel and J. R. Newman, *Gödel's Proof*, 1959. Classical deductive systems operated with a set of undefined concepts and axioms formulated in terms of them, so that complete formalisation represents an attempt to get rid of that indeterminate ingredient in the system.
147. These criteria imply, of course, that the axioms of the system must be mutually independent.
148. This is Tarski's way of putting it – cf. E. H. Hutten, *The Language of Modern Physics*, 1956, p. 33f.; *The Origins of Science*, 1962, p. 173f.
149. See Nagel and Newman, *op cit.*, pp. 26ff.
150. This is Tarski's way of putting it – cf. E. H. Hutten, *The Language of Modern Physics*, 1956, pp. 33f; *The Origins of Science*, 1962, pp. 173f.
151. The first edition in three volumes appeared in 1910–1913, the second edition in 1925.
152. K. Gödel, *On Formally Undecidable Propositions of Principia Mathematica and Related Systems*, English trans., p. 37f. See also Nagel and Newman, *op. cit.*, pp. 37ff., 45ff.
153. Gödel, *op. cit.*, p. 38. The other comprehensive system to which Gödel refers is the axiom system for set theory of Zermelo-Fraenkel, later extended by J. von Neumann, p. 37.
154. Cf. Nagel and Newman, *op. cit.*, pp. 57ff., 68ff., 85ff.
155. Gödel, *op. cit.*, pp. 41, 62.
156. Gödel notes that there is nothing circular about such a proposition, since it begins by asserting the unprovability of a wholly determinate formula, and only subsequently does it emerge that this formula is precisely that by which the proposition was itself expressed, p. 41. n. 15. See Braithwaite's introduction, pp. 14ff.
157. Gödel, *op. cit.*, pp. 62ff., Cf. Nagel and Newman, *op. cit.*, pp. 86f., 94f.
158. Gödel, *op. cit.*, p. 70f.
159. This implies a rejection of any disjunction between analytic and synthetic statements, as well as between syntactic and semantic statements, and falls closely into line with Einstein's rejection of any disjunction between theoretical and empirical concepts and relations.
160. Cf. here Einstein's conception of 'the stratification of the scientific system' involving primary, secondary and tertiary layers, 'Physics and Reality', 1, *Out of My Later Years*, pp. 62ff.
161. *Personal Knowledge*, pp. 343–346; *The Tacit Dimension*, pp. 34ff., 40ff., 45ff.; *The Study of Man*, pp. 46ff., 58f., 71ff., 82f., 93ff.
162. *Personal Knowledge*, especially in chapter 5 on 'Articulation', pp. 69ff., and in chapter 8 on 'The Logic of Affirmation', pp. 249ff.

163. *Personal Knowledge*, pp. 70, 82ff., 86ff., 114ff.
164. *Personal Knowledge*, pp. 87, 94.
165. *Personal Knowledge*, pp. 123ff., 143, 151, 189, etc.
166. *Personal Knowledge*, pp. 94, 118f., 190ff., 259ff., 273.
167. Polanyi points to an analogy between the Gödelian process of innovation and the grammar of discovery outlined by Poincaré, *Personal
Knowledge*, pp. 118f., 261.
168. *Personal Knowledge*, pp. 131.
169. *Personal Knowledge*, pp. 29, 115ff., 130f.
170. *Personal Knowledge*, pp. 124ff., 184ff.; *The Tacit Dimension*, p. 21.
171. *Personal Knowledge*, pp. 81ff., 85ff., 93f., 103ff., 117ff.
172. *Personal Knowledge*, pp. 29, 63ff., 70, 119, 130f.; *The Tacit Dimension*,
pp. 20ff.; *The Study of Man*, pp. 44f., 94f.
173. *Personal Knowledge*, pp. 275ff. This applies also to the operations of
digital computers as machines of logical inference, for the necessary
relatedness of machines to persons does essentially restrict their
independence, p. 261f.
174. 'I regard knowing as an active comprehension of the things known,
an action that requires skill.' *Personal Knowledge*, vii.
175. *The Study of Man*, p. 31; cf. 22f., 25f., 44f.
176. See *Personal Knowledge*, Chap. 4 on 'Skills', pp. 49–65; *Knowing and
Being*, pp. 114ff., 159ff.; *The Tacit Dimension*, pp. 12ff.
177. *Personal Knowledge*, pp. 70, 88, 257ff.
178. *Personal Knowledge*, pp. 117ff., 124ff., 160ff., 257ff.; *The Study of Man*,
pp. 22ff., 20f., 44f. To speak of symbolic formalisms as fulfilling a
subsidiary role, is not to detract from their importance or necessity,
as is evident in the fundamental place of hypothetico-deductive
operations in physics made clear by relativity theory.
179. *Personal Knowledge*, pp. 6, 8–15, 144f., 160–171; 184f.
180. *Personal Knowledge*, pp. 343ff.
181. *The Study of Man*, pp. 93ff.
182. *Personal Knowledge*, pp. 169f. 187ff., 191ff., 257ff., 282ff., 289ff.,
183. *Personal Knowledge*, pp. 103, 105, 118, 124ff., 189, 261, 317.
184. *Personal Knowledge*, pp. 384, 402.
185. See *Personal Knowledge*, Part Four, pp. 327ff.; *The Tacit Dimension*, ch.
2, on 'Emergence', pp. 29ff.; *The Study of Man*, pp. 47ff., 93ff.;
Scientific Thought and Social Reality, pp. 133ff.
186. See 'Transcendence and Self-transcendence', in *Soundings*, Vol. 53,
1970, pp. 88ff.
187. Cf. in this connection Polanyi's discussion of the DNA molecule, in
'Science and Man', *op. cit.*, pp. 970ff.; *Knowing and Being*, Chap. 14,
'Life's Irreducible Structure', pp. 225ff.; and *Personal Knowledge*, pp.
381ff.
188. *Science, Faith and Society*, pp. 10ff., 43ff., 85ff.; *Personal Knowledge*, pp.
160ff., 264ff., 286ff., 299ff.
189. *Personal Knowledge*, p. 266f. Polanyi cites here the *nisi credideritis, non
intelligitis* which St Augustine appropriated from the Old Testament
for a similar purpose *(De libero arbitrio, I.4)*.

190. *Personal Knowledge,* pp. 160ff., 255f., 292ff. See also *Scientific Thought and Social Reality,* pp. 118f

191. *Personal Knowledge,* pp. 104, 147, 300ff. Such a statement properly transcends the disjunction between subjective and objective.

192. *Personal Knowledge,* pp. 252ff., 304ff., 308ff., 312ff.

193. This is what Polanyi calls 'the rightness of its assertion', *Personal Knowledge,* pp. 320, 337, which reminds us of St Anselm's definition of truth with reference to *rectitudo, Opera Omnia* (Edited by F. S. Schmitt), Vol. 1, p. 178. 25–27, 1938. cf. 'The Ethical Implications of St Anselm's *De Veritate,* in *Theolog. Zeitschrift,* **24,** 309, 1968.

194. *Personal Knowledge,* pp. 299ff., 308ff. This applies, of course, *mutatis mutandis,* to acts of knowing as well as acts of speaking.

195. *Personal Knowledge,* pp. 253ff., 305ff., 314ff.

196. *Personal Knowledge,* 308ff., 314ff.

197. *Personal Knowledge,* pp. 255f.

198. *Personal Knowledge,* pp. 71, 254ff., 305.

199. *Personal Knowledge,* pp. 257ff.

200. *Personal Knowledge,* pp. 264ff., 303ff., 311f.; *Scientific Thought and Social Reality,* pp. 57ff., 72ff.

201. *Personal Knowledge,* pp. 254ff., 286, 303ff., 315f. Polanyi suggests writing the prefix '⊢' used by Frege as an assertion sign, to be read as 'I believe' or some equivalent expression of endorsement. Such a prefix would not function as a verb, but as a symbol denoting the modality of the sentence. *Personal Knowledge,* pp. 28f, 255f. Otherwise it would make the scientific statement to which it was prefixed the impersonal assertion of a person!

202. *Personal Knowledge,* pp. 15ff., 214, 286ff., 323f.; *Scientific Thought and Social Reality,* pp. 49f., 59f., 120f., 126f., 138ff.

203. *The Logic of Liberty,* p. 25; *Scientific Thought and Social Reality,* p. 60f.

204. *Personal Knowledge,* p. 286f.,; *Scientific Thought and Social Reality,* pp. 50ff.

205. *Personal Knowledge,* pp. 286ff. Polanyi refers here to Kant's notion of *a priori* categories or forms of experience, and his regulative principles, pp. 113, 160ff., 307, 354. As F. Schwartz, interpreting Polanyi's thought, expresses it, ' the scientist's motives are denied, in the name of objectivity, only to enter into his choice of work by the back door, from a scientific id'. From the Preface to *Scientific Thought and Social Reality,* p. 14.

206. *Personal Knowledge,* p. 16.

207. *Personal Knowledge,* pp. 147, 166ff., 308f.

208. *Personal Knowledge,* pp. viif., 15f., 63ff., 292ff., 312, 381.

209. *Personal Knowledge,* pp. 3; *Scientific Thought and Social Reality,* p. 98.

210. *Personal Knowledge,* pp. 5–16, 37, 64f., 300ff., 311f.; *Scientific Thought and Social Reality,* pp. 98–115.

211. *Personal Knowledge,* pp. viif, 17, 63ff., 299ff.

212. *Personal Knowledge,* p. 403.

213. *Personal Knowledge,* pp. 5f., 15f., 37, 43, 64f., 116, 311; *The Tacit Dimension,* p. 32; *Knowledge and Being,* pp. 133f., 141, etc.

214. *Personal Knowledge*, p. 5.
215. *Personal Knowledge*, p. 64. In speaking here of 'objective criteria', Polanyi clearly means 'objectivist criteria', as the context makes clear. His use of the term 'objective', however, is sometimes rather ambiguous.
216. *The Tacit Dimension*, p. 87.
217. *Personal Knowledge*, pp. 63f., 95ff., 100, 104, 174, 183f., 195, 203f., 303f., 308f., 315, 396.
218. *Science, Faith and Society*, pp. 15, 38; *Personal Knowledge*, vii, 104, 165, 300ff., 308ff., 314f.
219. Cf. *Scientific Thought and Social Reality*, p. 91: 'The kinship between the process of tool using and that of achieving or perceiving a whole has in fact already been so well established by Gestalt psychology that it may be taken for granted without further argument.' Cf. also p. 121.
220. *Personal Knowledge*, pp. vii, 55ff., 61, 79, 93, 97f., 338, 342: *The Tacit Dimension*, pp. 6f., 43, 46: cf. *The Study of Man*, p. 28f., 102.
221. M. Merleau-Ponty, *Phenomenology of Perception*, 1962, p. 149 – cited in *Knowing and Being*, p. 222.
222. *Knowing and Being*, pp. 147ff., 155ff., 160, 169f., 221ff., 236f.; *The Tacit Dimension*, p. 16f.
223. *Knowing and Being*, p. 160; cf. also pp. 40ff.
224. *Knowing and Being*, pp. 143ff., 155f., 221ff. The same applies also, in Polanyi's view, to the philosophy of analysis as expounded, for example, by G. Ryle, pp. 155, 169f., 222f.; *Personal Knowledge*, pp. 98f., 372f.
225. *Knowing and Being*, p. 173.
226. *Science, Faith and Society*, p. 24.
227. For this see Part Four of *Personal Knowledge*, entitled 'Knowing and Being', and the essay with that title, which is reprinted as ch. 9 of *Knowing and Being*, pp. 123ff.
228. *Knowing and Being*, p. 172.
229. Polanyi appears to make some concessions to his critics when he speaks of this ontological reference as 'a logical process of inference even though it is not explicit', and entitles an essay 'The Logic of Tacit Inference'. Taken strictly, this would not be consistent with the claim that in tacit knowing integration replaces deduction. But since his model is 'the logic of perceptual integration', the tacit process of inference must be regarded as ultimately informal and not formalisable. 'We may call this a *tacit process* of inference by contrast to an explicit process of inference as defined by logic today.' *Scientific Thought and Social Reality*, p. 142; see also *Knowing and Being*, pp. 138ff., 155, 173, 194, 212; *The Tacit Dimension*, pp. 34, 49. After all, formalised logical operations must include an unformalised tacit coefficient, *Personal Knowledge*, p. 257.
230. *The Tacit Dimension*, pp. 13f., 33: *Knowing and Being*, pp. 141. 149, 218.

231. Cf. *Knowing and Being*, p. 156.
232. The distinction which Polanyi's critics make between psychological and logical processes, without leaving room for an epistemic correlation between the knowing subject and its object, is clearly one that is still caught within that dichotomy.
233. *Scientific Thought and Social Reality*, p. 127.
234. *Knowing and Being*, pp. 149f., 155f.; cf. *Personal Knowledge*, p. 372.
235. *Personal Knowledge*, pp. 264, 327f.
236. *Scientific Thought and Social Reality*, pp. 119ff., 133ff. Polanyi also applies this argument for the existence of comprehensive entities comprising the meaning of their particulars to establish the reality of *universals*, not however as separated entities, but as grounded in the reality of what they denote, and therefore capable of manifesting themselves indefinitely in the future. He does not, however, draw an adequate distinction between the reality of 'universals', 'solid objects' and a 'person's mind', which he establishes by the same argument. See *Knowing and Being*, pp. 167f., 170f., 190f.; and *Personal Knowledge*, pp. 110ff.
237. *Knowing and Being*, pp. 133, 138, 141, 168, 172; *The Tacit Dimension*, p. 32f. Cf. *Science, Faith and Society*, p. 10: 'Real is that which is expected to reveal itself indeterminately in the future. Hence an explicit statement can bear on reality only by virtue of the tacit coefficient associated with it. This conception of reality and of the tacit knowing of reality underlies all my writings.'
238. *Scientific Thought and Social Reality*, pp. 136ff.; *Knowing and Being*, pp. 153ff., 168ff., 218ff., *Personal Knowledge*, p. 382.
239. *Scientific Thought and Social Reality*, pp. 137ff; *Knowing and Being*, pp. 168ff., 218ff.; 'Transcendence and Self-transcendence', in *Soundings*, Vol. 53, 1970, pp. 88–94.
240. 'Transcendence and Self-transcendence', *op. cit.*, p. 91.
241. *Scientific Thought and Social Reality*, pp. 126ff., 147ff.; cf. *Knowing and Being*, pp. 135ff., 168ff., 218ff., 237f.
242. *Scientific Thought and Social Reality*, p. 127f., also p. 129. Cf. further *Personal Knowledge*, pp. 195–202, 279–286, 321–324, 374–380, 402–405.

CHAPTER IV

The Open Universe and the Free Society*

THIS theme goes to the heart of Michael Polanyi's own intention in 1948, when he relinquished his chair in chemistry for a personal chair in social studies, yet without leaving the ground on which empirico-theoretical scientific knowledge of the universe was actually being advanced. Unlike most philosophers of science, particularly of social science, he was a scientist; and unlike most philosophers he realised that philosophising can be done adequately only on the ground of active knowing of the universe, if it is not to be trapped in a constant rediscussion of historic problems in philosophy which so often arose out of inadequate or erroneous knowledge of the real world around us. Michael Polanyi had thus to pursue a course which proved very lonely, for it was essentially pioneering, as it broke away from the tramlines of the self-styled 'professionals'; but it was also remarkably prophetic, for the work he has done in the theory of knowledge, on the basis of the profound switch in rigorous scientific outlook that dates back to the essays of Einstein in the years 1905–1907, has proved astonishingly predictive of what is now taking place in the very foundations of knowledge. I take this opportunity to salute the University of

*Lecture delivered at the University of Manchester, Nov. 11, 1978, at the inauguration of the *Michael Polanyi Seminar Room.*

Manchester for its wisdom in providing Michael Polanyi with the opportunity and freedom to pursue the deep epistemological implications of the scientific revolution in related areas of philosophical, social and human studies; and I salute the Philosophy Department of this University in marking their appreciation of Polanyi's great achievements, in dedicating a Seminar Room to his memory.

My purpose is not to expound Michael Polanyi's thought in any detail but rather to set out his view of the profound integration between the advance of scientific thought and the society which supports it, and to show how subsequent advance in scientific knowledge greatly reinforces and develops, and sometimes adjusts and corrects, the basic insights he elaborated.

At the bottom of all Polanyi's work is the conviction that the independence of thought and obligation to transcendent reality go inseparably together. The interrelation of freedom and order, or of order and freedom, is thus a persistent theme in his patient elucidation of science, philosophy and society. Order without freedom is a destruction of order, and freedom without order is a destruction of freedom. This insight, as I interpret Michael Polanyi, is deeply rooted in his integrated understanding of science deriving from his basic training as a physician, e.g. in his functional approach to order in seeking to understand how chemical and organismic relations cohere in what he called a 'biological mechanism', and his grasp of the indivisible unity between empirical and theoretical factors both in what we know and in our knowing of things. This was not simply a return to the old idea that the whole is greater than the parts, but a bid to understand things in the light of their natural cohesion, which is inevitably disrupted by analytical methods and procedures, that is, in terms of 'reasons' as well as 'causes'. Nature must be understood in the light of its intrinsic creative coherences and patterns, and correspondingly scientific discovery takes place through a creative integration in human thought correlated to the emergent orderliness in nature and not imposed upon nature artificially from some extraneous stance.

This does entail, of course, as is the case with general relativity, a profound recovery of ontology and objectivity, together with a dynamic reconstruction of physical knowledge. It also involves a critical estimate of merely analytical science and of its limited low-level validity, together with a rejection of determinism and objectivism which result from an unwarranted generalisation of the Newtonian or particulate abstraction of causal connections from fields of force. This is why Polanyi was so concerned to uncover and eliminate unwarranted assumptions – in fact, perverse beliefs –

going back to people like Laplace, Kant and Mach, and thus to liberate the philosophy of science from the destructive tendencies of positivism, and philosophical and social studies from being trapped in obsolete dogmatic fixations.

On the positive side, Polanyi's recovery of natural cohesion or integration carried him further and further into a wide-ranging rethinking of human knowledge in which the old damaging dualisms deriving from Galileo and Newton, Descartes and Kant, are transcended, and subject–object relations are put upon a deeper, firmer basis. I do not wish to pursue that at the moment, beyond pointing out that it led Polanyi to develop a single, continuously varying conception of knowing in which the gap that has opened up, through abstractive procedures, between natural and human sciences is overcome. It led him to grapple with the distinctive character of natural connections and the way in which they are found to be coordinated in the universe independent of us. This gave rise to the realisation that the structure of scientific knowledge is analogous to the structure of the universe itself, so evident in the way coordination of different logical levels in the hierarchical structure of scientific knowledge reflects and corresponds to the stratification of levels of reality in the universe itself. This is a point at which the thought of Einstein and Polanyi come together and complement one another, not least where they make the claim (powerfully reinforced by the Gödelian theorems) that these levels are open upward but are not reducible downward, so that the more our knowledge of the universe advances the more we are convinced we are in touch with an objective rationality which transcends our actual experience and outruns our powers of grasping and representing it. This means that all our scientific structures that really bear upon the universe are ultimately indeterminate or open. Moreover, it is inevitable, Polanyi pointed out, that whenever we envisage the universe as an ascending hierarchy of meaning *as a whole*, 'our natural knowing expands continuously into knowledge of the supernatural'[1]. That is to say, within this integrated understanding of the universe and its ascending levels of intelligibility, it is impossible rationally to avoid the ultimate question as to the relation of the universe to God as its transcendent ground.

This carries us well beyond our immediate subject for this lecture, but there are two ingredients essential to Polanyi's epistemic outlook upon the universe, that I propose to single out for reflection: (1) Polanyi's conception of *reality* defined in terms of the objective power of the universe to keep on disclosing itself to us in still hidden truths; and (2) his conception of human community as the social counterpart to such a universe, embodying in its development a creative life resting upon belief in the reality of emergent meaning and truth, and manifesting therefore, unsuspected possibilities. Let me expand this a little.

Through examining the way in which actual scientific discoveries come about in the process of empirico-theoretical inquiry, Polanyi reached the conviction that comprehension is similar in structure to what is comprehended. He found there to be involved not only a deep inner connection between scientific knowing and the universe, but between scientific knowing and society as well. There is a deep structural kinship in the kind of order manifested in nature, science and society. Hence, admittedly, Polanyi shares a fundamental concept with the Marxists, namely a 'symbiosis between thought and society'[2], but the difference between them is actually immense, in their radically different understanding of reality and science.

Marxism is a socio-political counterpart to a positivist and materialist notion of science, rooted in an obsolete Newtonian determinism, and operating with a logical bridge between concepts and experience. Hence a Marxist correlation of science to social existence can force upon it, by logico-causal necessity, a community structure correlated with the isomorphic character of the universe conceived as a mechanistic system. Marxism attempts to overcome the dualism in Newtonian thought, not by transferring the inertial system of time and space from the mind of God to the mind of man as with Kant, but by grounding time and space in objective material processes deterministically conceived. In doing so, it seeks to achieve a unitary basis between physical and social existence for all man's working beliefs and convictions. Thus in Soviet Russia, a massive attempt was made to produce a logically coherent and integrated society which is causally and logically connected with the structures of the physical universe as they are defined in positivist science. That is why pure science (science for its own sake or science for the sake of the truth alone) had to disappear into technology and why the technological society had to reign ideologically supreme over all human thought and existence. But the king-pin in this whole structure is knocked away when it is found that there is no logical bridge between concepts and experience, as Einstein made so decisively clear, and therein opened up the whole structure of science to the vast unbounded intelligibility (Verständlichkeit) of the universe.

This is the point where Polanyi's thought came in. In wrestling with the problem of pure science in face of the Marxist rejection of it, he became convinced that no pure or genuine science is possible except on the ground of the acknowledgement of a truth independent of ourselves which we are unable to manipulate for our own ideological ends, or on the ground of a recognition of natural law as a real feature of nature which, as such, exists beyond our control. Pure science involves the unfettered freedom of inquiry and thought, but it is a freedom that is possible only on the ground of unconditional obligation to 'the reality of truth'–i.e. to a 'transcendent reality' over which we have no control. This set Polanyi the task of thinking out the relation between freedom and control, or what he came to call 'spontaneous order' in society as well as nature. The question had to arise from the side of pure science: What kind of society emerges as the correlate of pure science, and the unbounded, intrinsic intelligibility of the universe to which it is dedicated? To the *open universe* disclosed by the advance of pure science, there ought to arise something like the *free society*. But what is really meant by 'freedom'? The traditional concept of freedom, at least as it seems to have been applied in our socio-political institutions, reveals an internal contradiction by virtue of which freedom constantly betrays itself.

Polanyi's way of tackling the problem, characteristically arose out of his own empirico-theoretic scientific activity in chemistry and crystallography. There were, he found, two basic kinds of order: (1) order which arises through limitations imposed on the freedom of components, of molecules or cells; and (2) order that arises as full scope is given to their mutual interactions. Both kinds of order have their appropriate place or occasion, and they may combine in the way mutually exclusive functions combine, each fitting into the gap left by the other. The deeper he probed into the natural cohesions and configurations, into the morphological structures embedded in the real world, the more he found *spontaneous order* operating within a relatively determinate framework restricted but not determined by it. This is the kind of order we find in crystalline formations which spontaneously arise within a certain set of conditions, but it is a polycentric kind of order that cannot be induced or imposed. That kind of order is achieved through a natural equilibration of matter and energy. But in living organisms we also find a kind of spontaneous order which Polanyi speaks of as the function of living mechanisms: this is an order that arises on the ground of physico-chemical relations, but is not finally determined by them or explicable in terms of them, for it arises at the boundary conditions left open by physico-chemical relations and develops structural or functional principles of its own.

All this implies the rejection of the determinist basis of Newtonian mechanics, evident still in the natural selection theory of evolution, and involves the idea of a stratified structure of the universe which we noted earlier, in which different levels are held to be coordinated with one another in such a way that a higher kind of organisation spontaneously arises, which rests on a lower level of organisation without being wholly controlled or determined by it. The lower level of organisation must rather be seen as the limiting case of the higher and freer and more widely-ranging organisation. This is the kind of organisation, then, where freedom and order, spontaneity and structure, are found operating together – where freedom without order ceases to be freedom and order without freedom ceases to be order.

That is precisely the kind of order, Polanyi shows, that is to be found operating in our basic acts of perception: in the spontaneous way in which our minds integrate clues and thereby enable us to grasp reality in its latent dynamic structures, which we inevitably lose or destroy when we analyse them into the constituent particulars of which they are composed. It is in this way that our epistemic activity takes place, in fundamental acts of cognition, in which spontaneous intuitive acts are involved within a framework of traditional beliefs, or under the constraint of a set of rules or of institutions. But it is in this way also, that Polanyi understands our most rigorous scientific and mathematical operations to take place – e.g. in the interrelation between the formalisable and the non-formalisable, the mathematical and non-mathematical, factors. It was along this line that Polanyi developed his understanding of scientific discovery, as neither a logical nor a psychological act, but as essentially an epistemic act at grips with intrinsic yet unexpected patterns of reality. It is in this light also, that Polanyi offered an account of the structure of science itself, including scientific institutions and scientific communities, in the course of which he became the champion of academic freedom in face of attempts that gathered strength after the second World War to impose State control upon scientific research. It was the clash between those who advocated a centrally planned order and those who advocated spontaneous order in academic and scientific institutions, that sparked off Polanyi's determination to devote the latter part of his life to clarifying the foundations of freedom in science and society on the ground of his scientific insights into the nature of reality.

As it was indicated earlier, Polanyi held that both kinds of order, planned and spontaneous, may well combine, yet in such a way that each is correlated with the other at the boundary conditions where they are left indeterminate to one another. Nevertheless the constant emergence on level after level of new spontaneous forms of organisation, each richer in order and less restricted than that on the lower level on which it rests, makes it clear that in the natural conditions of the universe the spontaneous development of order has and must have the primacy within the structure of dual control that operates at each level of organisation. It is in this way that Polanyi expounds the kind of order that obtains in a free society, one in which spontaneity and social organisation combine, but combine in such a way that the social constraints yield higher orders of freedom. This is the kind of order that is found developing in the free yet orderly activity of academic and scientific institutions. Much the same applies to the pursuits of arts and crafts, and to the professions such as law and religion. All these areas of free interaction operate within a tradition, disciplining them but also making room for innovations in the sorts of mutual adjustments and criticisms individuals make *vis-à-vis* one another's activities.[3] Order is achieved in human society by allowing people to interact with one another on their own initiative, subject only to laws which uniformly apply to all of them. This kind of order, on Polanyi's scientific analogies, he speaks of as 'polycentric' and 'spontaneous'. But decentralised order of this kind arising from mutual adjustment cannot be brought about deliberately through a corporate body, nor can it be imposed prescriptively from a central planning authority. It belongs to the very core of this combination of spontaneous and social order through mutual interactions, checks and adjustments, i.e. by mutual authority, that time or temporal connection enters into it as an essential inner coefficient, for the aggregate of individual initiatives can lead to the establishment of spontaneous order only if each takes into account in its action what the others have done before in the same context. Here, for example, Polanyi pointed to what Adam Smith called 'the invisible hand' in the spontaneous ordering of marketing systems, or to the development and operation of common law through sequences of adjustments between succeeding judges guided by a parallel reaction between the judges and the general public.

There is no need to go further into this, but it ought to be remarked that this approach, by no means implies a *laisser-faire* concept of freedom – the freedom of mere self-assertion – for that, on Polanyi's showing, would involve a notion of freedom fraught by internal contradiction which leads into its very opposite in the destruction of freedom. All-important here, are Polanyi's conception of the nature of reality, which, far from being necessitarian or determinist, is characterised by internal freedom or spontaneity by virtue of which it constantly takes us by surprise; and the way in which Polanyi holds different levels to operate in cross-level coordination with one another: the higher level resting on laws obtaining at the lower level, yet not finally determined by it but rather controlling the boundaries of the level below it through a richer and wider organisation which it is made to serve.

Doubtless there are aspects of Polanyi's account of spontaneous order which require correction and adjustment, as indeed happens in all areas of scientific and rational knowledge. But Polanyi is undeniably right in the broad thesis that a Marxist or indeed a Fascist type of State is the social correlate to a determinist and mechanist conception of the universe; and that the totalitarian State arises logically from the denial of reality to the realm of transcendent intangible reality over which we have no control, but to which we are bound in rational obligation, and that when the transcendent grounds of free activities are summarily rejected, the State of necessity becomes the inheritor to all the ultimate devotion of man.[4] But he is also surely right in the claim that the epistemological and social implications of the profound revolution in knowledge that dates from the first decade of this century, when adequately worked out and appreciated – as we are far from doing yet – will yield or ought to yield as its counterpart a free society, in which spontaneity and order combine to produce results which we cannot prescribe or anticipate.

How far is Polanyi's own scientifically based account of spontaneous order within the framework of reality justified by subsequent scientific developments? It is in answer to that question that we come to the main intention of this address. I wish to argue that both of Polanyi's main contentions as to the nature of reality, and as to the emergence of spontaneous order, now receive even greater support from the on-going revolution in scientific knowledge, in astrophysics and thermodynamics.

1. THE CONTINGENT, NON-NECESSITARIAN, NATURE OF
(PHYSICAL) REALITY – EVEN OF ITS INHERENT
INTELLIGIBILITY

Basic to this question is the problem of how to cope with time and motion in the actual subject-matter of science. This problem was raised in different ways by Newton and Leibniz, but classical physics and mechanics operating from a point of absolute rest, end up with a static description of the physical world, leading eventually within that frame of thought to the later problem of position and momentum in quantum theory, which would seem to indicate that in spite of relativity theory quantum mechanics, at least in its Copenhagen/Göttingen form, is only half-liberated from the Newtonian dualist framework of particle and field. The difficulty evidently goes back to the fact that in classical physics time, regarded as an empty receptacle, is treated only as an unchanging geometric parameter externally associated with motion – it was not allowed to enter integrally into the substance of scientific subject-matter. We have a similar problem in classical and modern logic where time is externally bracketed off from the relations of ideas and statements: formal and symbolic logic lack even a conceptual counterpart to four-dimensional geometry. So far as scientific description of the universe is concerned, the problem is perhaps best seen in the fact that classical mechanics is concerned not with time as such, but with acceleration of motion, for it is acceleration that can be represented in precise mathematical terms. Expressed in another way, it is idealised mathematisation that eliminates actual motion and thus time, and so yields a necessitarian or determinist view of reality. Granted that the application of the differential calculus to the universe of bodies in motion was intended to account for its dynamic nature, actually what it did do was to break down the trajectory of time into digital timeless points, whose succession is governed by necessitarian mathematical law. This was reinforced by Newton's translation of the differential character of the universe in terms of the axiomatic structure of Euclidean geometry, which has to do with the relations between rigid bodies irrespective of time. What we require is a profound switch from kinematic to kinetic thinking, and an appropriate conceptual instrument to effect this change and the description of the physical world in genuinely kinetic terms.

Today, however, science is concerned with space-time in which time, as well as space, is regarded as a function of on-going processes in continuous and indivisible fields of force. We still have the problem of the duality of the particle and the field, although that is evidently now being overcome, for example in particle theory in which most of the so-called particles are recognised not to be discrete particles so much as energy-knots in fields of force and where the relations between particles are ontologically essential to the structure of the fields and the particles themselves – that is, to use a theological term, where we are forced to think in onto-relations. The hang-over from the past is still with us, even for example, in the immensely significant and scientifically fertile Schrödinger equation dealing with the complex function of position and time in wave mechanics, which still operates with a form of differential equations – which of course does not invalidate it but limits it, even in the time-dependent form it is given, in our grasp and expression of the actual flow and movement of time. As Einstein once said, 'The De Broglie-Schrödinger wave fields were not to be interpreted as a mathematical description of how an event actually takes place in time and space, though, of course, they have reference to such an event. Rather they are a mathematical description of what we can actually know about the system. They serve only to make statistical statements and predictions of the results of all measurements which we can carry out upon the system.'[5]

On the other hand, microphysical science has revealed that atoms and molecules and nuclei all reveal a history – that is to say, time enters into what they now actually are. Evidently, as V. F. Weisskopf has pointed out (in his recent presidential lecture to the American Academy of Science) that does not apply to protons, or nucleons and electrons which have no intrinsic properties revealing what happened to them in the past. Time or history is clearly embedded in self-reproducing structures from the smallest to the largest organisms, for their evolution is written into what they now are and are still in process of becoming. All this has to say that the history of matter enters into our scientific understanding of it.

This introduction of the element of time or history into the physics of nature has been greatly reinforced through the discovery in 1965 by Penzias and Wilson of the 2.7°K cosmic background radiation resulting from the incredibly immense explosion with which the expansion of our universe was initiated, but deriving from a period some million years afterwards when the universe was still in a state of near thermal equilibrium, between radiation and matter.[7] The scientific and epistemological implications of this are very far reaching. It means that in its progressive expansion, the universe is never characterised by perfect thermal equilibrium, and that in this expansion time is allowed for many interactions leading to quite new features. (The significance of this we shall see shortly when we turn to consider recent changes in thermodynamics.) This expansion of the universe also implies that the universe is finite in time as well as space, and that the whole expansion of the universe must be regarded as a vast singular event – in fact, a unique historical event characterised by irreversibility or the arrow of time. This has the effect of smashing the old dualist disjunction between accidental truths of history and necessary truths of reason, and calling into complete question the idea that science is ultimately concerned with timeless and necessary truth, for now it is evident that all scientific truths are as contingent as the universe itself.

Now, of course, all modern empirical science has relied upon the fact that the universe is contingent. It is because it is contingent and not necessary (it might well have been other than it is; it might not have been at all), that we can gain knowledge of the universe only by asking empirical questions of it – that is, through experimental operations. But the problem – and this is one of Polanyi's major insights which he shared with Einstein – is that when we start to formulate our knowledge of this and produce our generalisations we almost inevitably lapse back into necessitarian modes of thought, confounding in the generalisation of a theory its comprehensiveness with what is universally and timelessly true, and converting temporal relation back into logico-necessary relation. Reality, as Polanyi has shown, is very different, even in the kind of rationality or intelligibility which it exhibits: it is such that even when we make our discoveries, nature surprises us and reveals patterns which we could not have anticipated from what we already claim to know. Nature is characterised by an unbounded range of freedom, an indeterminate depth of intelligibility, by virtue of which it has an unlimited capacity for disclosing itself in ever new ways and revealing ever new truths. It is in the context of this understanding of reality that all our academic and scientific operations have to be carried out, and all our human activities, social as well as artistic and intellectual, ought to be directed and organised.

In the general frame-work of classical physics there appears to be still a considerable obstacle to this view of reality and its contingent order – the laws of thermodynamics, which in their classical form tend to be the last hole of refuge for the positivists and determinists. But now even here we have a fundamental upturn in our ideas.

2. THE EXTENSION AND APPLICATION OF THERMODYNAMICS TO OPEN OR NON-EQUILIBRIUM SYSTEMS

The empirical fact with which we have to deal with here is that when we move away from states of equilibration that give rise to the stability and permanence with which we are concerned in classical physics, we find not only, as the laws of thermodynamics predict, random fluctuations and disorder, but quite unexpected and surprising features: the spontaneous rise of new kinds of order.

Classical thermodynamics, which was long limited to the study of equilibrium states of physico-chemical systems in their interaction with one another, is concerned with entropy or the degree of disorder in such equilibrium or closed systems. Thus the second law of thermodynamics deals with the irreversible increase in the measure of disorder or disorganisation in such systems or structures. That would seem to imply that the further back we go in evolution or the expansion of the universe, we would expect to find less entropy and more homogeneity and order. However, it is an empirical fact that the evolution of the universe in its orderly developments, and above all in the rise of biological structures, manifests increasing measures of organisation and order. How are we to hold these apparent incompatibles together? Some kind of integration carrying our understanding beyond that state of affairs has long been demanded. Now, through the work of Ilya Prigogine of Brussels and others we have been shown that non-equilibrium can be a source of order, and we have been given an extension and application of the second law of thermodynamics beyond its classical or traditional frame of reference to take in non-equilibrium or open systems, in such a way as to account for the order which spontaneously arises out of apparently random fluctuations far from a state of equilibrium.[8] Here closed systems obeying the classical laws of entropy on one level are coordinated with open systems at a higher level characterised by a minimum of entropy (the least dissipation of energy) and are to this end controlled by them at their boundary conditions to yield stable open systems.[9] When crystalline formations take place, the crystal constitutes an equilibrium structure: it continues to exist independently of any exchange of matter or energy with the world around it, what Prigogine calls a 'non-dissipative structure'. A non-equilibrium structure, on the other hand, continues only if it is constantly fed by supplies of energy and matter in exchanges with the world around it, and as such is known as a 'dissipative structure'. This is, of course, the kind of organisation we have in evolution, but we could only give an account of that, as Polanyi so often reminded us, by a deterministic account of natural selection which failed to give adequate appreciation to the processes of mutation and adaptation in the rise of ever higher levels of order in the universe.[10] Now, however, a much more satisfactory account of this can be given as it is disclosed that non-equilibrium may become a source of order, irreversible processes leading to new dynamic states of matter called 'dissipative structures'. Here, Prigogine argues, thermodynamic law, the law of entropy, operates in opposite ways when near a state of equilibrium and far from a state of equilibrium and thus is capable of accounting for the spontaneous order that arises through fluctuations. (So far as evolutionary theory is concerned, the old idea of survival of the fittest is replaced by 'optimal stability' creative of new order, i.e. order of a new and increasing organisational complexity through fluctuations.) This kind of order could not be anticipated or inferred, for it is an irreversible process that is not amenable to deductive or logical operations. What Prigogine has done is to develop a transformation theory, involving non-unitary equations of motion which enable us to move from one type of description to another, from a thermodynamic to a dynamic description of it, in which *time*, needed for many interactions, is given its integral place within the orderly structures that spontaneously arise. Here we have a new type of time-dependent functional order coordinating space-time behaviour to dynamic processes within the system, but it rests nevertheless on the validity of connections holding at the lower level which are subject to thermodynamic laws in the classical formulation – including thermodynamic irreversibility and the rejection by the second and third law of any *perpetuum mobile*.[11] (Incidentally, this seems to represent another nail in the coffin of a 'steady-state' or 'oscillating' theory of the universe.)

Undoubtedly the hierarchical coordination of levels of order involved in this approach throws a very helpful light on evolution in the expanding universe: higher and higher levels of organisation and order spontaneously emerge which rest on the basis of physico-chemical relations at a lower level obeying classical thermodynamic law, while at the same time those levels of organisation are shown to be indeterminate, to use Polanyi's expression, in that they are left open and are controlled by the higher level at their boundary conditions. Here, then, where we least expected it, precisely in thermodynamics, scientific account can be given of how in the expansion of the universe new forms of coherence and order of a richer and more open-structured kind continuously and spontaneously emerge. This applies, of course, to the highest form of life, man himself, for within the perspective of natural science, he is to be regarded as the product of such spontaneous self-organising order. But in this event it applies no less to personal and social structures of life which man develops: they are to be understood in the light of the same principle that governs the coordination of open-structured connections at a higher level with the more restricted structures at a lower level. Indeed, in accordance with this principle, as Polanyi used to point out, man must be regarded as one whose level of rational existence and behaviour is to be understood only if it is coordinated with a higher level beyond him – that is, with the transcendent level of God's interaction with man in the space-time track of the universe.

Be that as it may, what I have been concerned to show, in this brief and all too inadequate account of the extension and reformulation of thermodynamics, and its application to open systems to account for the emergence of new, unexpected, unpredictable forms of spontaneous order, is that we are given strong support for the earlier account of Polanyi, who must be said in a very remarkable way to have anticipated the discoveries which were recently acclaimed with the award of the Nobel Prize. A passing reference[12] to Prigogine's early thought shows how quick he was to appreciate the development that was to follow from the slender clue given at that time (1945), but there is little doubt that the structure of Polanyi's own creative developments carried within it points toward the fuller development of the thermodynamic programme. What lay behind that was his persistent conviction as to the contingent yet profoundly intelligible character of reality replete with inexhaustible possibilities of order. As a scientist and as a human person of great sensitivity he opened his mind to those possibilities and allowed them to draw him away from stereotyped theories and formalisations into a more open and dynamic theory of knowledge appropriate to such a universe. The fact that he anticipated in his own epistemological way the fresh discoveries we have been discussing, must prompt us to deeper examination of Michael Polanyi's own pioneering thought both in the foundations of scientific knowledge of the open universe, and in the extension and application of the kind of spontaneous order it manifests to human existence and social order in the free society.

NOTES

1. *Scientific Thought and Social Reality*, Vol. VIII/N. 4, Monograph 32 (Edited by F. Schwartz), p. 12, International Universities Press, New York, 1974.
2. 'Background and Prospect', the 1963 preface to *Science, Faith and Society*, p. 17, Phoenix Books, Univ. Chicago Press, Chicago.
3. *Meaning*, p. 198, Univ. Chicago Press, Chicago 1975.
4. *The Logic of Liberty*, Routledge & Kegan Paul, London, p. 47, 1951.
5. 'The Fundaments of Theoretical Physics', *Out of My Later Years*, p. 104, The Philosophical Library, New York, 1950.
6. V. S. Weisskopf, *The Frontiers and Limits of Science 1975, Am. Scient.* **65,** 1977.
7. Sir Bernard Lovell, *In the Center of Immensities*, p. 97f, Harper & Row, New York, 1978.
8. See I. Prigogine and A. Babloyantz, 'Thermodynamics of Evolution', *Physics Today*, no. 11, pp. 23–28; no. 12, pp. 38–44, 1972; P. Glandsdorff and I. Prigogine, *Thermodynamics of Structure, Stability and Fluctuations*, New York, 1971; I. Prigogine and G. Nicolis, *Self-Organisation in Non-Equilibrium Systems*, New York, 1977, etc. See further: I. Prigogine, *From Being to Becoming, Time and Complexity in the Physical Sciences*, W. F. Freeman, San Francisco, 1980.
9. Cf. *Personal Knowledge*, pp. 382, Routledge & Kegan Paul, London, 1958.
10. Cf. *Meaning*, p. 162f.
11. See I. Prigogine, 'Time, Structure and Fluctuations', *Science* **201,** 777–785, 1978; and 'The Metamorphosis of Science: Culture and Science Today', *Abba Salama* **IX,** 155–183, 1978.
12. *Personal Knowledge*, p. 384.

CHAPTER V

Ultimate Beliefs and the Scientific Revolution*

L ET ME begin with a startling statement from David Hume:
'Reason is, and ought only to be, the slave of the passions, and
can never pretend to any other office than to serve and obey them.'[1]
When I first read that, I was rather appalled, but then I came to
understand that Hume was referring to the basic way in which even
as rational beings we react to the world about us, in which feeling
and imagination play a more important role than logic. This is the
insight that gave rise to Hume's doctrine of *belief* as well as his
doctrine of sympathy.[2] In his attempts at analysis of our judgments
and his examination of our sense-perceptions Hume found a *natural
belief* already entrenched there in a quite distinctive form, a belief
which actually enters into our sensory experience and is essential to
it.

We cannot enter now into a full account of all this but I would
like to refer to two points about belief, as Hume envisaged it: (1)
this belief is so deep-seated and essential that it is impervious to
critical dissection and analytical explanation; (2) our really crucial
decisions do not rest upon the 'reason' or the reflective judgment,

* The Maxwell Cummings Lecture, University of McGill, Montreal, March 16,
1978.

so much as upon 'feeling', i.e. 'causally determined propensions or beliefs'.

Here we have singled out an elemental attitude of mind as in itself something of primary importance in human knowledge, *ultimate belief,* as I have called it. This is so ultimate that Hume frankly acknowledged that persuasive power lies with it and not with our explicit reasoning or with our philosophical argumentation. This means that the conclusions of our abstract thinking do not really arise from the logical basis on which they seem to repose, important as that is. They come from something deeper, a certain habit or set of mind which arises in us compulsorily from the ground of our experience in the world which gives the arguments we advance their real force. That is to say, science and belief are not to be treated as opposed to one another but rather as belonging to one another and as operating together in the acquisition of knowledge.

That is the theme for our discussion here: the ultimate place of fundamental belief in scientific knowledge and argument, which is of particularly crucial importance in a period of scientific revolution and change.

I began with a reference to Hume because he is widely held to be the father of positivist scepticism and empiricism in their denial that we can know more than tangible, sensible facts, and the relations we deduce from them. But, as we have seen, for Hume himself, belief which is not rationally explicable or derivable occupies a place of primary force. As a Christian theologian and philosopher of science, I myself have serious reservations about Hume's 'natural belief', reservations which derive from a healthy Christian scepticism of his naturalism, to which I shall return later. But I do accept Hume's pinpointing of the significance of belief in the regulative basis of scientific knowledge.

Hume held that in all 'demonstrative sciences', where we have to do with the relations of ideas, reason and logic reign supreme, but that this is not the case when we move beyond the range of those sciences to questions of matters of fact and existence; there not reason and logic but feeling and belief are in supreme control. Since that is the case, complete scepticism, in which all belief is discounted, is impossible, for scepticism cannot function without the natural beliefs which control the relation of the reason to matters of fact and existence. 'Thus the sceptic still continues to reason and believe, even tho' he asserts, that he cannot defend reason by reason.'[3] That is to say, our rational arguments operate with beliefs that are not themselves rationally or logically demonstrable. As Hume understood it, it was particularly important to establish the status of two forms of natural belief, belief in continuing and independent existence, and belief in causal dependence, for without them no physical science, let alone objective, rational behaviour, would be possible. Hume himself contrasted belief and knowledge, much as John Locke had done before him, but he did see that belief has an essential role to play in the establishment of knowledge in spite of its non-logical character.

In our own day, however, it has become more and more apparent as the foundations of knowledge have been exposed, not least in connection with active scientific discovery, that belief and knowledge cannot be contrasted in the way advocated by Locke and Hume, for belief plays an essential if informal part in the basic operations of knowing as well as in formal, symbolic operations through which the body of our knowledge is established in a consistent form. But today we have also come to realise more clearly that true beliefs of this kind are not open to logical proof or disproof. This is a position that has been powerfully advocated by Michael Polanyi in a number of works, with respect to the ultimate presuppositions or beliefs which constitute the premises of science,[4] and not least in his Aberdeen Gifford Lectures of 1951-2, in which he claimed that 'all our ultimate beliefs are irrefutable and unprovable'.[5] We shall have occasion to return to him later, but meantime let me refer to a complementary argument put forward by J. W. N. Watkins, in clarification and development of Popper's line of thought, in respect of scientific statements in their relation to falsifiability and verifiability.[6] This may be expressed diagramatically as follows:

	Verifiable	*Unverifiable*
falsifiable	circumscribed existence-statements	(A) general laws (e.g. for all x, if x=g, then x is an f)
unfalsifiable	uncircumscribed existence-statements	(B) regulative principles (e.g. every event has a cause, i.e. every event has some cause)

(B) statements not themselves empirical (e.g. there is order in the universe) cannot be *shown* to be true or false, but are the presuppositions of

(A) statements that are open to refutation/confirmation.

That is to say, the controlling statements with which we operate in science are both unfalsifiable and unverifiable. They are statements which express what we have called *ultimate beliefs,* beliefs without which there would be no science at all, beliefs which play a normative role in the gaining and developing of all scientific knowledge. Yet these ultimate beliefs are by their very nature irrefutable and unprovable. They are irrefutable and unprovable on two grounds: (1) because they have to be assumed in any attempt at rational proof or disproof; and (2) because they involve a relation of thought to being which cannot be put into logical or demonstrable form. Ultimate beliefs, then, are to be understood as expressing the fundamental commitment of the mind to reality, which rational knowledge presupposes and on which the reason relies in any authentic thrust toward the truth. Far from being irrational or non-rational, these ultimate beliefs have to do with the ontological reference of the reason to the nature and structure of things, which all explicit forms of reasoning are intended to serve, and without which they are blind and impotent. It is indeed not finally through formal reasoning that knowledge and understanding are advanced, but through the responsible commitment to reality in which our minds fall under its intelligible nature and power, and thereby gain the normative insights or ultimate beliefs which prompt and guide our inquiries, which enable us to interpret our experiences and observations, and which direct the reasoning operations of our inquiries to their true ends.

Since this is the case, it is irrational to contrast faith and reason, for faith is the very mode of rationality adopted by the reason in its fidelity to what it seeks to understand, and as such faith constitutes the most basic form of knowledge upon which all subsequent rational inquiry proceeds.[7] There could be no rational inquiry, no reflective thought without prior, informal knowledge directly grounded in experience and formed through the adaptation of our minds faithfully to the nature of things, in the course of which our basic beliefs spontaneously arise. These beliefs, of course, must have to do with what is real, and therefore they need to be put to the test in order to be distinguished from what is merely subjective or illusory. Without objectively oriented beliefs of this kind at a deep level of our consciousness, knowledge could not develop, nor could rational reflection which presupposes it and depends on it.

That knowledge does arise in this way, on the ground of faith, has always been the claim of the Judaeo-Christian tradition. This was often explained in Patristic theology with reference to the words of the Old Testament prophet, 'If you will not believe, you will not understand' where 'understand' was reckoned to have the same meaning as 'be established'.[8] At its root faith is the resting of our mind upon objective reality ('that which really is', 'the nature and truth of things'), and scientific theological knowledge is not basically different, since what it does is to draw out faith in its rational connection with the reality on which it reposes, which has the feed-back effect of clarifying the initial act of faith in its direct bearing upon reality. But this applies, as the early Christian fathers saw, no less to natural science than to theological science.[9]

In view of all this it is not surprising that scientists who have done so much to advance the frontiers of knowledge have insisted on the indispensable need for faith or belief as a prescientific but fundamental act of acknowledgement of some significant aspect of the nature of things, or an epistemic awareness of the mind more deeply grounded than any set of scientific evidence, without which scientific inquiry would not be possible. Again and again they have made great discoveries and advanced theories beyond what was warranted by the evidence under the compulsion of a faith in the sheer intelligibility of nature and in a new vision of its intrinsic order. Einstein's statements to this effect are well known. 'Belief in an external world, independent of the perceiving subject, is the basis of all natural science.'[10] 'Without the belief that it is possible to grasp reality with our theoretical constructions, without the belief in the inner harmony of the world, there could be no science. This belief is and always will remain the fundamental motive for all scientific creation.'[11] Heisenberg, to refer to another, insisted that belief is the mainspring of all Western science, and in his scientific autobiography, kept on speaking of faith in 'the central order', which he identified with God, as the driving impulse in his own scientific activity.[12]

No one has written more trenchantly about the need for faith than Michael Polanyi. 'Any account of science which does not explicitly describe it as something we believe in is essentially incomplete and a false pretence. It amounts to a claim that science is essentially different from and superior to all human beliefs that are not scientific statements – and this is untrue. To show the falsity of this pretension, it should suffice to recall that originality is the mainspring of scientific discovery. Originality in science is the gift of a lonely belief in a line of experiments or of speculations which at the time no one else considered to be profitable. Good scientists spend all their time betting their lives, bit by bit, on one personal belief after another.'[13] Again: 'Science or scholarship can never be more than an affirmation of the things we believe in. These beliefs will by their very nature, be of a normative character – that is to say, claiming universal validity – and they must be responsible beliefs, held in due consideration of the evidence and of the fallibility of all beliefs; but eventually they are ultimate commitments, issued under our personal judgment. To all further scruples we must at some point finally reply: For I believe so.'[14]

Citations of this kind could easily be multiplied,[15] for the great scientists realise that behind and permeating all scientific activity, reaching from end to end of their inquiries, there is an elemental, intuitive, unshakable faith in the significant nature of things in the universe, faith in the intelligibility of the universe, faith in its pervasive and unitary character, faith in its regularity and stability and constancy and simplicity; but faith also in the possibility of grasping the real world with our concepts, together with the faith that the intelligibility of the real world holds good when it transcends our conceptions and formulations, faith in the truth over which we have no control, but in the service of which our human rationality stands or falls. Thus faith in the reason itself and faith in the intelligible structure of the universe, for which we can offer no logical demonstration, are locked inseparably together, under the inescapable obligation which reality itself lays upon our minds.

The ultimate beliefs which arise in our minds in this way constitute what Michael Polanyi called a 'fiduciary framework', outside of which no intelligence, however critical, operates, but on which it relies for all its explicit rational operations.[16] This framework of beliefs comprises the set of controlling convictions to which the scientific conscience, face to face with the intrinsic intelligibilities of the universe, finds itself committed in a relation of ultimate obligation, and on the ground of which the scientific reason finds itself coming to decisions which it has to affirm with universal intent. It is thus within the fiduciary framework and the commitment situation it involves that the very conception of universal validity arises and applies.[17]

In order to clarify the rational status of these ultimate beliefs, it may be helpful to differentiate them from the regulative principles with which Kant sought to answer the question as to the conditions under which valid knowledge is possible, or the structures of the consciousness which Lonergan brings into play in his analysis of methodological processes. For Kant the 'forms of sensibility' and the 'categories of the understanding' with which the human mind organises all that it grasps as objects of its knowledge are formal *a priori* structures independent of experience (i.e. absolute) and thus inertially condition our knowledge without being modified by

empirical reality.[18] Fixed, unalterable concepts or categories of this
kind, conditioned by the nature of the understanding, import a
rigidity and built-in subjectivity in our knowledge which are
incompatible with the nature of the universe and its intrinsic
lawfulness as revealed by relativity theory, and were steadily
rejected by Einstein.[19] Lonergan's structures of the consciousness,
however, are not ultimately different from Kant's, for they have the
same kind of unalterability conditioned by the nature of the understanding. They are characterized by what he called an 'invariance'
inherent in the consciousness apart from the 'lower jaw' or 'the
cutting edge' (the two images he uses) of our empirical operations
in knowing.[20] There is here little corresponding to Einstein's notion
of an invariant relatedness in the real world independent of our
consciousness in perceiving or conceiving of it.

The ultimate beliefs of which Polanyi speaks, on the other hand,
are objectively grounded in, and ontologically derived from, the
intelligibility of the real world so independent of our understanding
that it reaches out in an objective depth far beyond what we can
bring within the range of any masterful comprehending on our
part. Beliefs of this kind, calling us to personal commitment, differ
from the natural beliefs of David Hume, which he spoke of as
causally induced determinations of the mind, and not as free acts
resting on grounds or reasons.[21] According to Polanyi, 'Every
belief is both a free gift and the payment of a tribute exacted from
us. It is held on the personal responsibility of the believer, yet in the
clear assumption that he cannot do otherwise.'[22] In other words,
belief is at once a free and an obligatory act, an act which we cannot
rationally resist: it is thrust upon us from the given.

What Polanyi means may be made clear by reference to two
earlier thinkers, Clement of Alexandria and Duns Scotus. Clement,
under Stoic influence, spoke of faith as a 'willing assent' of the mind
to reality, an act in which the truth of things seizes hold of us and
brings us to assent to it in accordance with its own self-evidence.[23]
Faith of this kind involves an immediate apprehension which
provides the anticipatory conception (or *prolepsis*) with which we
are in touch with reality, and without which we never learn
anything and have no ground for any scientific inquiry. But
through critical questioning and demonstrative argument this incipient faith is turned into an accurate faith – i.e. a conceptual assent
that corresponds precisely to the nature of the reality apprehended.
Thus, whether it is in the course of demonstrative reasoning or
through immediate apprehension, the faith that arises in us is a
voluntary act of assent, but it is nevertheless an assent called forth

from us by the compelling power of reality.[24] This was the understanding of faith as the ground of rational inquiry that found its
way into the epistemological furniture of Greek Patristic theology
in which the personal and the compulsive elements in Christian
faith are held inseparably together.

When applied to God, however, the concept of 'willing assent' or
'faith' involves not only a moment of the will on our part in
knowing God but a moment of the will on God's part in revealing
himself to us and summoning us to know him in accordance with
his nature as freely revealed. It is here that a later distinction by John
Duns Scotus is helpful, one that he drew between an 'involuntary'
and a 'voluntary' object.[25] An involuntary object is the kind of
natural object which, in our knowing of it, has to be known, but a
voluntary object, such as a human being or a rational agent, does
not have to be known by us when we know it, but is known only as
it willingly lets itself be known. Here a real moment of the will is
involved on both sides of the knowing relationship. But when we
know someone as he freely lets himself be known, as he reveals
himself to us, calling forth a corresponding moment of the will in
which we respond in knowing him, within that movement of
willing object and willing knower, there arises an element of
compulsion, for we know him truly only as we know him in
accordance with the demands of his nature as it is disclosed to us.
To know him truly is to know him in the way in which we are
obliged to know him, and not otherwise. That certainly applies to
our relationship with God, whom we cannot know against his will
but only as a 'voluntary object',[26] but when he presents himself as
the object of our knowing, our minds come under the compelling
claims of his reality and cannot rationally avert acknowledgement
of what he reveals.[27]

Given, then, the difference between God and the universe, which
we must respect, the difference between a 'voluntary' and an
'involuntary' object (which Scotus also spoke of as a difference
between a 'supernatural' and a 'natural' object), it is nevertheless the
case that in our knowledge of natural objects there is a combination
of personal and compulsive elements involved in fundamental
assent or belief. It is for this reason, Polanyi argues, that even in our
most rigorous and objective scientific operations we cannot escape
the personal pole of commitment and responsibility any more than
we can escape the demands of the scientific conscience. After all,
only a person, a rational agent, can engage in objective operations;
only a person is capable of distinguishing what he knows from his
knowing, and is capable of willing, responsible assent to what is

demanded of him by the intrinsic nature and structure of what he seeks to know, while acknowledging its reality independent of himself. That is why belief plays an inseparable and constant role in all scientific activity.[28]

We now come back to the point where we may take a deeper look at the function of ultimate beliefs in scientific activity. Because these beliefs are held under submission to an ultimate obligation imposed on us by the very nature of things, they are held with a claim to universal validity. Thus they have a *normative* character, which affects the entire scope and shape of our developing inquiry. More explicitly, ultimate beliefs exercise a *directive* function in the way we put our questions, interpret our observations and weigh the evidence. And it is upon the strength of their bearing upon all this that we make our decisions one way or the other; and it is the extent to which we allow these ultimate beliefs, in which we share, to have this role in our argumentations, that they have their really persuasive force.

Because these ultimate beliefs form the basic framework on which we rely in performing explicit operations in inquiry and reasoning, they fulfil their function in an informal way and constitute what Polanyi has called the *tacit dimension* or *coefficient* of rational knowledge.[29] Polanyi points to the paradigm case (first pointed out by Pascal) of definitions, in which we formally define one set of terms and concepts by relying on an informal knowledge of another set of terms and concepts which for this purpose remain themselves undefined.[30] They do, of course, acquire a mode or measure of definiteness as they are actually put to work in exercising a normative or directive function in the explicit, formal operations through which we establish knowledge; yet they cannot be defined in terms of those formal operations both because they are axiomatically assumed in them and because by their very nature as fundamental forms of recognition they cannot be further analysed. Because they function in this informal or tacit way, ultimate beliefs are not normally noticed. Indeed, one must say that the actual force of their role in regulating our scientific operations is in proportion to the way in which they belong to the axiomatic principles or assumptions of explicit formalising operations. The more absolute their place in our presuppositions, the less they are brought to our notice in the ordinary course of our science.

However, when the advance of knowledge reaches the point where really fundamental change is demanded of us, and profound epistemological decisions have to be made, then our ultimate beliefs are forced out into the open. That is to say, we reach the stage where we have to ask if the regulative principles with which we have been operating are really grounded in reality or not, whether our ultimate beliefs are really ultimate, or whether we have been operating with substitute-beliefs which have misled us. This is what happens when the normative principles with which we have been operating begin to show evidence of conflict with each other.

As I understand it, that is the kind of situation in which we now find ourselves in the scientific revolution of our times. This is a revolution which more than any other in the history of our scientific culture affects the very foundations of knowledge, so that it is not surprising that the question has been raised whether science ought to operate with any ultimate beliefs at all. Yet that question is raised not by those who have been responsible for the great advances in our science, such as Einstein, Planck, Bohr, Schrödinger, Heisenberg, Born, Eddington or the like, but by scientists in the positivist tradition committed to the position that scientific ideas are derived by deducing them from our observations, that is by logical inference, and that scientific theories are no more than convenient arrangements of our operational ideas to suit certain pragmatic ends. That is to say, positivism makes no claim that our scientific conceptions bear upon being, or the structures inherent in the universe independent of us; what it does at every point is to reduce the relations of our thoughts of the real world into relations of ideas with one another, and thus seeks to eliminate the very ground upon which our ultimate beliefs arise. Of course, it is understandable that when that objective ground is ignored or eliminated positivists should regard beliefs as nothing more than arbitrary personal manifestations which must be discarded if we are to achieve scientific detachment – i.e. what they mean by 'objectivity'. Far from achieving genuine detachment, however, positivism is actually attached to definite presuppositions which it will not allow to be questioned – that is to say, attached to unreasonable beliefs disengaged from any ground in the intrinsic intelligibility of the universe.[31]

This is the position that has been so radically undermined by the scientific revolution of our times, in which it has been disclosed to us that all science operates with basic beliefs, ultimate acts of recognition or acknowledgement, which are irrefutable and unprovable in the logical way demanded by the positivists and empiricists. Moreover, the advance of scientific knowledge has made it clear that to claim that you strictly refrain from believing anything that could be disproved is merely to cloak your own will to believe your beliefs behind a false pretence of self-critical severity.[32]

The positivist doubts everything for which he cannot give a logical explanation, except himself and his belief in himself; whereas the rigorous science of our day insists that it is above all the self, with its uncritical presuppositions, that must be put to the test, until it is left only with those ultimate presuppositions or beliefs without which there would be no science at all, or even any rational knowledge. One of the tragedies of positivism is that in discounting the fundamental role of belief in science it makes science essentially different from, and cynically superior to, all distinctively human beliefs, and every area of human knowledge and behaviour affecting our daily and basically human life. In other words, positivism drives deep wedges between its extensive abstractive operations and the very foundations of human life and culture – hence the deep splits in our civilisation which it has fostered. The exact opposite is the case with the new integrative scientific approach which takes its cue from the fundamental relations of the mind to the nature of the world around us, and seeks to refine and develop them, thus laying the foundation for a profound synthesis in human thought across the whole range of human knowing and living, not excluding the relation between natural and theological science.

Another and indeed a principal feature of positivism is its attempt to offer an exclusively causal account of everything in the universe, including man and human activity, even science itself. On thoroughgoing positivist principles science is made out to be an impersonal mechanism which, through the operation of necessary rules, will produce universally valid results. But here it shows itself to be internally self-contradictory, for it excludes from its account of science states of rational consciousness and acts of the mind on which it relies even to elaborate such a position. Behind this contradiction lies the absurd *belief* that the human mind can be replaced by artificial or machine intelligence, putting into mechanical operation the mathematically impossible idea that logico-deductive systems can be consistent and complete at the same time! What we are concerned with here, however, is that by concentrating exclusively on mechanical or logico-causal connections, positivism takes away all rational ground for men's convictions and actions, eliminating from scientific activity any operation involving responsible judgment and decision; it ignores the fact that science constantly puts us in a position in which, face to face with ultimate obligations laid upon us by the nature of reality, we have to make ultimate commitments. But this is the area where, as we have seen, our basic knowledge arises and where universal validity applies, the actual ground of our obligatory acts of recognition and of our ultimate beliefs. In other words, positivism by its very nature discounts the fundamental relationships between thought and being, or understanding and reality, which any science precisely as science must presuppose. Positivism thereby ensures its own demise, which is now increasingly evident, particularly in the realm of pure and hard science, and which has the effect of making even more prominent the all-important and unavoidable role of *ultimate beliefs* in all our scientific inquiry. Hence it is not surprising that a scientist of the calibre of Polanyi should insist on rigorously epistemological and scientific grounds that we must give up the false pretence that science can operate without belief; rather must we openly declare the beliefs we hold about the nature of things which guide the course of our scientific investigations, beliefs which in science we hold with a claim to universal validity, and thus restore the balance of our cognitive powers between faith and reason.[33]

This does not mean that we are simply to accept whatever people may claim to be ultimate beliefs, without due consideration of whether they are genuine or not – that is to say, without proper consideration of the evidential ground upon which our beliefs rest. Are they beliefs which we cannot help having if we are to remain rationally faithful to the nature of things in the universe to which we belong, beliefs such that, if we refuse to adopt then, we would, as it were, be cutting our own throats as responsible rational agents? Ultimate and finally unanalysable as they may be, we must submit our minds to them responsibly with due consideration of their intelligible ground and with a view to their role in obliging us, in all scientific understanding, interpretation and decision, to respect objectivity and truth.

A distinction should be drawn within our fundamental beliefs and their normative function in affecting our on-going scientific inquiries. This is a distinction between *ultimate beliefs,* for which we have no alternatives, and *penultimate beliefs,* for which we are faced with alternatives. The ultimate beliefs, which do not admit of any alternatives, nevertheless call for our affirmation and commitment, for any alternative to them would be unreasonable. They are ultimate beliefs which we cannot reasonably avoid; we can do no other than submit to them, for they repose upon the unalterable nature of things, while precisely as ultimate they admit of no higher court of appeal. Among ultimate beliefs of this kind we must put the existence or reality of the universe, and the order and intelligibility of the universe, together with the stability, constancy and simplicity of that rational order. Along with the affirmation of these ultimate beliefs must surely go dependent beliefs or corollaries, such as the belief that we can apprehend, at least in some measure, and bring to theoretical expression that rational order, or belief in the validity of mathematical or logical reasoning, which we have to presuppose from beginning to end in all mathematical and logical operations. That is to say, along with ultimate belief in the intrinsic rationality and lawfulness of the universe goes our belief in rational and scientific thought, although this belief, properly held, admits of the limitations of our science.

There are, however, other beliefs which carry normative authority in our basic outlook upon things and thus exercise a regulative function in our scientific activity. I have called these beliefs *penultimate,* because we can hold them only by rejecting alternatives which can, it is claimed, be 'reasonably' held. In respect of these controlling beliefs, the context of our affirmation or choice of them is of particularly acute importance, for decision is demanded of us as a result of a conflict in our operative beliefs which is not logically resolvable: we have to choose one way or the other, and the way we actually choose excludes the alternative. We cannot balance these alternatives, for belief at this penultimate level is demanded of us by our ultimate belief in the nature of things. We have to make our decision to accept or reject these operative beliefs on the ground of whether they are epistemically correlated to the nature and structure of reality independent of our perceiving and conceiving. In the great scientific transition in outlook in which we are now caught up, such deep conflicts in beliefs have arisen that clarification and change in our regulative beliefs are unavoidable.

A further point about these penultimate beliefs must be noted: the very possibility of alternatives, even in the regulative beliefs with which we operate in science, is itself grounded in the belief that the universe might have been other than it is, that it could well have been different, and it is not a necessary universe. That is to say, our belief in the contingency of the universe, and indeed in its contingent intelligibility, is the ground for the recognition that in respect of penultimate beliefs we may well have to agree to change. But it is this contingent character of the universe and its intelligible order which is also the determining ground for our conviction that in the search for regularities or significant patterns we cannot do without experiment: that is to say, if we are to detect and grasp the order inherent in the contingent processes of the universe, we have to devise appropriate ways of putting our questions to those processes which will allow them to disclose their rational structures, questions which are genuinely open to whatever may be disclosed and which do not determine the answers through hidden stipulations. Since this is a contingent universe, characterised throughout not by a necessary but by a contingent intelligibility, and therefore characterised throughout by a kind of spontaneous order which we cannot anticipate in any *a priori* way, or necessarily and logically deduce from our experience, the choosing of our regulative beliefs and the ongoing process of empirical inquiry cannot be separated from one another. If these beliefs are not, like Kantian or Lonerganian structures of the human consciousness, independent of what is called the external world, but are grounded in the nature and structure of reality, it is the objective, ontological reference of our regulative beliefs that makes them revisable, for their regulative character derives from the fact that they are grounded in an invariant relatedness inherent in the universe beyond themselves and that they are what they are precisely by serving that invariant relatedness in things.

Before looking at some of these penultimate beliefs and the regulative work they do in our science, let me pause to point out that the all-important concept of *contingent intelligibility,* upon which empirical science depends, and which requires us to consider reasonable alternatives to these beliefs, is of definitely Christian origin. The concept of contingent intelligibility is quite impossible alike for Greek or Oriental thought, but derives from Christian theology in its attempt to think out the relation between the incarnation and the creation. There is no need to go further into that here, but it should be pointed out that this is an indication of the profound interconnection between theological and natural science, and indeed between Christian belief and scientific advance in the very foundations of our knowledge which is one of the major elements that have been brought to the surface in the scientific revolution of our times.

Let us now consider *three* of the *regulative beliefs* which have played a determinative role in the development of Western science, and ask what becomes of them in the basic transition in the foundations of knowledge where we are called upon to make an ultimate choice one way or the other.

1.   BELIEF AS TO THE DUALIST OR NON-DUALIST CHARACTER OF THE UNIVERSE

By dualism here is meant the outlook that characterised ancient science, which took on durable form in the Ptolemaic cosmology, in its radical separation between terrestrial and celestial mechanics;

but by dualism reference must also be made to that form of it which developed through Galileo's distinction between geometry and appearance into the Newtonian system of the world with its radical dualism between absolute mathematical time and space and relative apparent time and space, which determined the structure of all modern science until the early decades of this century. The alternative regulative belief is in a non-dualist or unitary (but not a monist) outlook upon the universe. This was the outlook which entered our Western culture through the Judaeo-Christian tradition, and which gave rise to the concept of the unity of the created order, in rejection of Greek polytheism, polymorphism and pluralism. It was within the establishment of this unitary outlook that the Christian doctrines of creation, incarnation, redemption, resurrection and ultimate renewal of the creation, took their classical shape. But while these doctrines have remained in the Christian tradition, not without deepening reinterpretation and revision, Western culture, first in a Ptolemaic and then in a Newtonian form, became radically dualist, with a wide-ranging dichotomy between the spiritual and the material, the eternal and the temporal, the supernatural and the natural, as well as between the subjective and the objective, the formal and the ontological, and the theoretical and the empirical, with disastrous distortions of both poles of the dichotomy. Within the set of beliefs that became normative for that dualist outlook, Christian theology tended to become trapped, and tended to throw up again and again notions of a deistic detachment of God from the world he has created, reinforcing the Newtonian idea of time and space as an inertial system determining the frame of the universe as a vast mechanism of ineluctable cause and effect. As Christian thought allowed itself to be bound by that dualist framework, it yielded to ideas of God in which he is not allowed to interact with the universe, so that not only incarnation, but notions of prayer and providence suffered savagely, and then in a show of preserving these Christian doctrines, it mistakenly elaborated oblique reinterpretations of them in terms of poetic symbolism and myth.

How does such an approach look, in the context of the scientific revolution today, in which the dualist outlook on the universe, whether in its Ptolemaic or in its Newtonian form, has been overthrown, and a profoundly unitary outlook is in the process of establishing itself in which the formal and the ontological, the theoretical and the empirical, the structural and the dynamic, are held indivisibly together? Negatively, one can say that Christian theology is now liberated from the rigid framework clamped down upon it by the conception of the mechanistic universe. Positively, this means that Christian theology may now operate on its own proper ground, and develop out of its grasp of the intrinsically intelligible structure of God's interaction with the contingent universe, a fresh and more powerful understanding of creation, incarnation, redemption, resurrection and renewal. So far as modern theology is concerned, this has the effect of making utterly anachronistic pluralist as well as deist, spiritualist as well as mythical reinterpretations of the Judaeo-Christian faith. But it also means that modern science has made contact again with the basic concepts deriving from classical Christian theology which have been latent in its own advances, in such a way that an era of integrative thought spanning natural, human and theological science has begun, which is bound to transform the whole of the future for all science, natural as well as theological.

2. BELIEF AND DISBELIEF IN THE SINGULARITY AND UNIQUENESS OF THE CREATED UNIVERSE

Paradoxically, belief in the singularity or uniqueness of the universe has suffered a good deal since the Newtonian rejection of the Aristotelian/Ptolemaic dichotomy between terrestrial and celestial motion. On the one hand, the massive rise of empirical science reinforced belief in the non-necessary, contingent universe upon which it rested in order to be empirical; but on the other hand, the dichotomy between the mathematical and the apparent gave rise to a conception of science as the progressive rationalisation of all phenomena in the universe by reference to notions of the absolute and the infinite. Thus scientific results were accepted as valid in so far as the theory they enshrined could be generalised into what is universally and timelessly true. This outlook was steadily reinforced through the passion for mathematical idealisation of knowledge. The overall effect of this development, however, has been a lapse back into the Greek and mediaeval identification of the rational with the necessary, which could not but introduce deep internal contradiction into the heart of empirical science. Thus it is not surprising that serious conflict should arise in our regulating beliefs.

This is perhaps nowhere more apparent today than in the startling advances of astronomy and astrophysics, in the conflicting cosmological theories which have popularly gone under the name of the 'big bang' and 'steady state' (or 'continuous creation') theories. Between these two there is evidently a fundamental conflict in regulative belief rather than between the evidence or the logic each involves. Matters have recently come to a head, with the universally recognised discovery of the 2.7°K background microwave radiation, which can be traced back, on present calculations, to some million years after the initial immense explosion that began the expansion of the universe. Granted that the empirical evidence for what happened prior to the time from which these microwave signals have come to us is very meagre, and that we can only speculate as to the primeval 'black hole' and its explosion, the empirical as well as the theoretical evidence for the expansion of the universe as a vast irreversible singular event has irretrievably undermined any 'steady state' theory of its 'origin', while nevertheless showing that our universe has evolved from a pristine state that was remarkably isotropic and homogeneous.

The point that must engage our attention now is that here we have disclosed in the depth of our science a *unique event* of a staggering kind. It is this singularity that causes the trouble, for it arouses in so many people once again a latent horror of the unique event. It was rejection of the unique event that lay behind notions of the cyclic universe, or modern notions of the oscillating universe, or the concept of 'continuous creation' in the universe, as Stanley L. Jaki has shown so clearly,[34] for there seems to be a regulative belief in many people's minds which insists that everything must be relative and thus equivalent, and that the world goes on now as it always has in the past and always will go on in the future. When people still insist on holding this belief, although there is evidently no logical or scientific ground for doing so, it seems clear that they are clinging, with incredible obscurantism, to a belief that cannot be traced back to any ultimate ground in the nature of things in the universe. Here again it is the concept of sheer contingence that is at stake, and the notion of contingent intelligibility abhorred by the rationalists and empiricists.

Let us regard it in this way. Long ago Lessing drew a distinction between necessary truths of reason, with which we have to do in science, and accidental truths of history, with which we have to do in Christianity – e.g., the saving acts of God in Jesus Christ.[35] That distinction, between timeless necessary truth and temporal contingent truth, has for two centuries become an operative, regulating belief which has severely damaged our Western understanding of the historical Jesus Christ (not to mention our view of history), making people think that the real (scientifically acceptable) truth of Jesus lies not in himself or what he did but in the self-evident timeless truth which we may grasp if through the device of symbolic representation and interpretation we idealise 'the historical Jesus', and thus get rid of anything unique in what he did and said and was.[36] But here, out of the heart of pure science, we meet once again with the inescapable fact of the *unique event*, the immense singularity of the irreversibly expanding universe, which means that all scientific truth within the expanding universe is ineluctably contingent. The regulative belief behind so much of modern historical research is thus called completely into question on the very ground where it was thought to be established.

It is a well-known fact that hatred is often manifested against discoveries which threaten to undo some cherished belief – which happens from time to time just as bitterly in science as in religion. That is the sort of reception that is being given in some quarters today to the fact of the singularity or uniqueness of the universe. But the sharpness of the conflict reveals that what we are concerned with here is not a conflict between formal reasonings, or theoretical scientific constructions, but a conflict between radically opposing beliefs in which we are forced to choose one way or the other. It is a safe prediction that when our secularised culture has got over its bitter opposition to the unique event, as surely it will, the interrelations between a scientific and a Christian understanding of the universe will be put on a very different basis, one on which integrative relations will develop spontaneously and naturally.

3.   BELIEF IN THE PRIMACY OF THE VISIBLE AND TANGIBLE OVER THE INVISIBLE AND INTANGIBLE

This is a controlling belief that lies behind our modern secular materialist outlook, and is characteristic of the positivist approach which concentrates on observation. This outlook distrusts the realm of invisible and intangible things, questioning their very existence, and seeks for explanation solely in terms of observable relations, offering only a causal interpretation of human experience. Now this whole approach has suffered a severe set-back: *(a)* by the discovery that it is the space-time metrical field, which is inherently invisible and profoundly objective, that controls all observable objects in our experience; and *(b)* by the disclosure of the multi-levelled structure of the real world together with a corresponding multi-levelled structure in our scientific knowledge of it. Here science operates with a hierarchy of levels of meaning and explanation which are open upward but not reducible downward. For example, the organismic relations of living beings, while presupposing the laws of physics and chemistry, are not explainable in terms of them but are coordinated to them at the boundary conditions where they are open to the biological level above them and are to that extent under its control. Hence the higher up the scale of levels we move, the greater or the richer is the meaning we encounter. Thus we reach the realisation that 'All meaning lies in higher levels of reality that are not reducible to the laws by which the ultimate particulars of the universe are controlled . . . What is most tangible has the least meaning and it is perverse to identify the tangible with the real. For to regard a meaningless substratum as the ultimate reality of all things must lead to the conclusion that all things are meaningless. And we can avoid this conclusion only if we acknowledge instead that the deepest reality is possessed by higher things that are least tangible.'[37] That is to say, the materialist approach is now put into reverse. But once the old regulative belief lying behind observationalism is replaced by one which gives primacy to the invisible and intangible over the visible and the tangible, the whole scope and shape of scientific development and our 'modern' culture will begin to undergo transformation.

Nowhere, perhaps, is the effect of this scientific revolution becoming more evident than in Soviet Russia, where the sheer rigour of scientific thought in faithfulness to the objective structures of the universe, so necessary in the space-programme, for example, has forced scientists to revise their criticism of relativity and quantum theory, not to speak of the second law of thermodynamics, and where the consequent undermining of the positivist and necessitarian approach to understanding the universe involves also the undermining of the materialist and positivist programme for the ordering of society. Thus the open structures of the new science spell the end of totalitarian control, and demand as their social correlate a free and open-structured society where men's convictions and actions are controlled by transcendental reference to the truth over which we have no control and by the restoration of the invisible and intangible realities of the spirit in the regulative beliefs of society. If Marxism is the correlate of a positivist and materialist science, the end of that kind of science spells also the *dénouement* of Marxist notions of society. This is evidently what is actually now going on in Soviet Russia.[38]

In conclusion I would like to show the bearing of distinctively Christian belief upon the foundational changes that are coming out of the scientific revolution. This may be done by pointing to a different area of conflict or tension in belief, with respect to our ultimate belief in the intrinsic orderliness of the universe, and by asking the question 'What of *disorder* in the world and in our human experience? What of the destructive tendencies of which we are only too aware in modern life, in our social as well as in our ecological chaos?'

Unlike the natural beliefs of David Hume, which may be clarified not by any kind of rational justification but only by tracing them to their sources in the constitution of human nature and the empirical course of matter-of-fact occurrence, the ultimate belief in order, with which we are deeply concerned in Christianity, has its ground in the Love of God, for it is ultimately God's love which is the power of order in created existence. Here we have to do not only with belief in the order of the created universe as it becomes disclosed to us in our scientific inquiries, but with the kind of order that *ought* to be actualised in the universe for it is the law of God's Love *for* the universe. This is a concept of order which we have to think out not only by relating the incarnation of the Word of God to the creation, which gave rise to the notion of contingent intelligibility in the universe, but by relating the creation to the incarnation, and, therefore, the *actual order* which we find in the creation to the *redemptive order,* the new order which lies at the heart of the Gospel. The difference between a Humean understanding of order and the Christian understanding may be made clear by saying that the Humean is blatantly naturalistic, whereas the Christian takes seriously the presence of evil and of destructive elements in the universe. Christianity looks for a new order in which the damaged order, or the disorder in our world, will be healed through a creative reordering of existence in which it is restored to its ultimate ground in the creative love of God. In relating the creation to the incarnation in this way, Christian faith identifies the ultimate source of all rational order with the Love that God himself eternally is, and which has freely become incarnate in our world of space and time in Jesus Christ. Hence, far from allowing us to think of the saving acts of God in Jesus Christ as in any way an interruption of the order of creation, or some sort of violation of natural law,[39] this means that we must think of the incarnation, passion and resurrection of Christ and his miraculous acts of healing as the bringing of order into our disorder – as the way the ultimate Source of all rationality, God himself, brings that rationality to bear upon the disordered structures of our created existence, which is the way of his redeeming Love. Belief in this kind of order is normative in a much profounder sense than that which has been occupying our attention so far, for it is *creative as well as regulative* – not of course that our belief is creative in itself but that as belief it is correlated to the ultimate power of order, the Love of God creatively at work in our midst in and through Jesus Christ.

In order to see the relevance of this belief for the role of ultimate belief in scientific knowledge, let us apply the Christian doctrine of justification by faith to our acts of knowledge. In the moral realm justification by faith signifies that we are unable to justify ourselves before God, for we are incapable by our own moral acts of putting ourselves in the right with him; we can never bridge the gap between what we actually are and what we ought to be. Rather are we summoned to put our faith in the justifying acts of God in Jesus Christ, who out of his sheer love and grace freely forgives our sin and puts us in the right with himself. But this applies no less to our acts of knowledge when we are in error: we are unable to justify or verify our knowledge of God, for we cannot put ourselves in the right or truth with God. In faith, however, we rely ultimately on God himself to relate our thinking and knowing to the truth of his own Reality, and thus to make our human thinking and knowing of him terminate on God himself as their true ground beyond anything we can achieve of ourselves. Verification by faith thus entails an ultimate commitment to the objective reality of God, before which our own thinking and knowing of him is relativised.

Formally, it is the same sort of thing that takes place in our scientific operations, especially in view of the unity between form and being, or the indivisible relation between the theoretical and empirical components of our knowledge. We are unable by theoretic constructs of our own inventing to ground them upon reality, far less to capture reality within the net of our scientific operations. True theoretic constructs arise in our science only as we allow our minds to fall under the power of the intrinsic order of being or reality itself. Ultimate belief thus stands sentinel at the head of our scientific operations, because we can engage in genuinely heuristic acts and gain true knowledge of the universe only through ultimate commitment to its objective reality and intelligibility beyond our own mental operations. But ultimate belief also stands sentinel at the end of our scientific operations, for in the last resort it is reality itself that must be allowed to be the judge of the truth or falsity of our thoughts and statements about it. Hence science is ultimately cast upon the grace of reality for the justification or verification of its theories and results. That is to say, justification by faith alone applies no less in the realm of scientific knowledge than it does in the realm of theological knowledge, for in both we rely entirely upon the dynamic processes of order inherent in that which we seek to know, the contingent universe or God the Creator of the universe. We express that reliance by the affirmation of our *belief*. The great statements of the Christian faith in God, expressed for example in the Nicene Creed, are prefaced by a definite *Credo*. But even in natural science, as Polanyi has pointed out, we finally reply to all critical scruples, *For I believe so.*[40]

There are, naturally, significant differences between the kind of order in which we believe in theological knowledge and the kind of order in which we believe in natural knowledge, yet we believe that there is only one creative Source of order and rationality in the universe, God himself. The order that derives from him is always creative – creative of the contingent order in nature, and creative of order in our understanding of it. This is the creative order of the *Word* through which all things that come to be are made, and through which our thought and speech of God take form and shape as they are grounded in it. The kind of order which obtains in the outermost fringes of our universe, disclosed to us through light signals that radiate across many millions of years, we have to decipher and convert into words if we are to understand and communicate them, and through them build some knowledge of the expanding universe. But the kind of order with which we have to do in knowledge of God is order that has entered into the domain of our human structures of being and knowing when the Word was made flesh in Jesus Christ, full of grace and truth, and when through communion with that incarnate Word we have come to know the creative and redeeming love of God which we acknowledge to be the ultimate ground of all order in the universe. Hence we come back to the all-significant point reached by early Christian theology, when it laid the epistemic foundations for our Western science in thinking out, within the structures of space and time, the interrelations of the incarnation and the creation. It is more than ever upon that ground that theological and natural science come together.

NOTES

1. D. Hume, *A Treatise of Human Nature*, bk. II, sect. iii, L. A. Selby-Bigge edition, p. 413.
2. For a full discussion see N. Kemp Smith, *The Philosophy of David Hume*, 1941, chs. xxi and xxii.
3. D. Hume, *A Treatise of Human Nature*, bk. I, sect. iv, p. 187.
4. M. Polanyi, *Science, Faith and Society*, 1946, especially pp. 85ff (1964 edit.), etc.
5. M. Polanyi, *Personal Knowledge*, 1958, p. 271; cf. p. 299ff.
6. J. W. N. Watkins, 'Between Analytic and Empirical', *Philosophy*, 1957, pp. 112–131; 'Confirmable and Influential Metaphysics', *Mind*, 1958, pp. 344–365; and 'When are Statements Empirical?', *The British Journal for the Philosophy of Science*, 1960, pp. 287–308.
7. This is the point made by John Macmurray in his insistence that the rationality of thought does not lie in thought itself but depends on its reference to the external world as known in immediate experience. Hence he defines reason as the capacity to behave in terms of the nature of the object. See *Interpreting the Universe*, 1933, Ch. vi, and *Reason and Emotion*, 1935, ch. 1.
8. Isaiah 7.9, LXX. See Clement of Alexandria, *Stromateis* I.1; 2.2, 4; 4.21; Augustine, *De libero arbitrio* 1.4; *De Trinitate*, 15.2. Cf. also Anselm, *Proslogion*, Prologue and ch. 1, where he formulates the principle variously as *fides quaerens intellectum*, and *credo ut intelligam*.
9. See my discussion of Clement's scientific method, 'The Implications of Oikonomia for Knowledge and Speech of God in Early Christian Theology' in *Oikonomia. Heilsgeschichte als Thema der Theologie*, edit. by F. Christ, 1967, pp. 223–238.
10. A. Einstein, *The World as I See It*, 1934, p. 60 (also *Ideas and Opinions*, 1954, p. 266).
11. A. Einstein and L. Infeld, *The Evolution of Physics*, 1938, p. 312f.
12. W. Heisenberg, *Physics and Beyond*, 1971, pp. 11, 14, 84, 214, 216, 241, 247.
13. M. Polanyi, *Scientific Thought and Social Reality*, 1974, p. 51.
14. *Op. cit.*, p. 66.
15. See Stanley L. Jaki, *The Relevance of Physics*, 1966, pp. 345ff; and 'The Role of Faith in Physics', *Zygon*, 1967, 2.2, pp. 187–202.
16. Michael Polanyi, *Personal Knowledge*, 1958, p. 266, cf. pp. 264ff, 292f, 299ff.
17. Michael Polanyi, *The Logic of Liberty*, 1951, pp. 22ff; *Personal Knowledge*, 1958, pp. 64f, 300ff, 308ff, etc.; *Knowing and Being*, 1969, pp. 33f, 133f; *Scientific Thought and Social Reality*, pp. 57ff, 79ff; (with H. Prosch) *Meaning*, 1975, pp. 61ff, 195f.
18. Immanuel Kant, *Critique of Pure Reason* (edit. by N. Kemp Smith), pp. 66ff, 111ff.

19. A. Einstein, *The World as I See It*, 1935, p. 174; *Out of My Later Years*, 1950, p. 61; in P. A. Schilpp, *Albert Einstein: Philosopher-Scientist*, 1951, pp. 11f, 674, 680, etc. Cf. in the same volume, H. Reichenbach, pp. 307ff, and C. F. Lenzen, pp. 365ff.

20. B. Lonergan, *Collection*, 1967, p. 145f; *Insight* (1957), 1970 edit., pp. XXVff, 304, 335f, 346, 731f; *Method in Theology*, 1972, pp. XII, 12ff, etc. See P. Corcoran (editor), *Looking at Lonergan's Method*, 1975, p. 120f.

21. David Hume, *A Treatise of Human Nature*, I. iii. 7–9, pp. 94ff; I. iii. 14, pp. 155f; I. iv. 1–2, pp. 180ff. See N. Kemp Smith, *The Philosophy of David Hume*, chs. xvi–xvii, xxi–xxii.

22. M. Polanyi, *Scientific Thought and Social Reality*, p. 79.

23. Clement of Alexandria, *Stromateis*, II.8.4; II.12.54; II.54,5f; V.1.3; V.13.86.

24. For a full exposition of Clement's views, see 'The Implications of Oikonomia for Knowledge and Speech of God in Early Christian Theology', *op. cit.* See also S. R. C. Lilla, *Clement of Alexandria. A Study in Christian Platonism and Gnosticism*, 1971, pp. 118ff.

25. Duns Scotus, *Ordinatio*, prol.n. 64–65; I d.1 q.1–4; *Quodlibet*, q.13.14.

26. *Ordinatio*, prol. n. 64–65; I d.3 n. 56–57.

27. *Ordinatio*, I d. 1 n. 91–92; II d.6 q.2 n. 11; d. 42 q.4 n. 5, 10–12; *Reportata*, II d.42 q.4 n. 7, 13; *In Metaphysicam*, IX q.15 n.6; *Quodlibet*, q.16 n.6. See further 'Intuitive and Abstractive Knowledge from Duns Scotus to John Calvin', *De doctrina Joannis Duns Scoti, Acta Congressus Scotistici Internationalis*, 1966, vol. IV, 1968, pp. 291–305.

28. See especially the chapter on 'Commitment' in *Personal Knowledge*, pp. 299–324.

29. Michael Polanyi, *Personal Knowledge*, pp. 95ff, 187ff, 255ff, 264ff, 286ff, etc. See also *The Tacit Dimension, passim*.

30. *Personal Knowledge*, pp. 160ff, 264ff, 299ff; *Science, Faith and Society*, pp. 10ff, 43ff, 85ff.

31. Cf. Michael Polanyi, *Scientific Thought and Social Reality*, p. 57.

32. Michael Polanyi, *Personal Knowledge*, p. 271.

33. Michael Polanyi, *Personal Knowledge*, pp. 264–268, etc.; *Scientific Thought and Social Reality*, pp. 57ff, 73, 118ff.

34. See especially, S. L. Jaki, *Science and Creation*, 1974, *passim*, and *The Road of Science and the Ways of God*, Gifford Lectures 1974–76, 1978, pp. 262ff, etc.

35. G. E. Lessing, *Theological Writings*, ed. by H. Chadwick, 1965, p. 55.

36. 'The development of revealed truths into truths of reason is necessary at all costs.' G. E. Lessing, *The Education of the Human Race*, par. 76.

37. M. Polanyi, *Scientific Thought and Social Reality*, p. 137f.

38. See Sir John Lawrence, *A History of Russia*, 6th edit., 1978 (Meridian Press, New American Library), especially pp. 316–324, 331–335.

39. Thus David Hume, *An Inquiry concerning the Human Understanding*, X.I, 90.

40. M. Polanyi, *Scientific Thought and Social Reality*, p. 66; *Personal Knowledge*, pp. 253ff, 299ff.

CHAPTER VI

Christian Faith and Physical Science in the Thought of James Clerk Maxwell*

THE recent commemoration of the death of James
Clerk Maxwell in 1879, followed shortly afterwards by the
celebration of his birth in Edinburgh a hundred and fifty years
earlier in 1831, have directed public interest at one whom physicists
had come to rank with Newton and Einstein as one of the greatest
scientists of the modern age whose work has fundamentally transformed our understanding of the world and the way we live in it. It
is perhaps only in the light of Einstein's frank acknowledgment of
his own indebtedness to him that we have been able to assess the
real greatness and far-reaching import of Clerk Maxwell's
achievements, but this has had the effect of making us want to
know rather more of Clerk Maxwell himself and to gain a deeper
insight into the interrelation between his personal life and his
scientific work.[1] Like Michael Faraday with whom he had such a
deep affinity, Clerk Maxwell was a very devout and humble
Christian believer in the Reformed tradition. It is significant that in
his article on Michael Faraday for the *Encyclopaedia Britannica* Clerk
Maxwell made a point of referring to the other side of Faraday's
character which was 'reserved for his friends, his family and his

* Presented at a Symposium of the *Institut für Wissenschaftstheoretische Grundlagenfors-
chung,* Paderborn, January 3–6, 1982.

church', his public profession of faith and his opinion with respect to the relation between his science and his religion.[2] What Clerk Maxwell recounted of Faraday there was very self-revealing. In a lecture before the Royal Institution in 1854 on the subject of mental education, Faraday felt constrained to conclude on a more personal note about his faith in God and the future life. After claiming 'an absolute distinction between religious and ordinary belief, he declared: 'Yet even in earthly matters I believe that "the invisible things of Him from the creation of the world are clearly seen, being understood by the things that are made, even His eternal power and Godhead"; and I have never seen anything incompatible between those things of man which can be known by the spirit of man which is within him, and those higher things concerning his future which he cannot know, by that spirit'. Then Faraday added a note to the effect that 'These observations . . . are so immediately connected in their nature and origin with my own experimental life, considered either as cause or consequence, that I have thought the close of this volume may not be an unfit place for their reproduction'.[3]

Faraday was evidently aware of the fact that his Christian faith and his experimental science affected each other, but the interconnection was of a deeper kind than he could bring to clear expression. He could not set aside the fact that the basic features of nature which he struggled to bring to light had to do with the way they had been created by God, so that the compulsive probing of his scientific inquiries could not be detached from the insistent outreach of his faith toward the Creator who makes himself known to us through his revealed Word. It was owing to this devout commitment to God that he was overwhelmed by such a profound sense of the integrity and orderliness of nature which underpinned his experimental researches and gave him confidence in looking for the right theory in guiding research and accounting for its results. At the same time it is to the deep sincerity and humility of his Christian faith that there must be traced back his openness to self-criticism in the face of different points of view and his determination to put all theories to the test in an unprejudiced attempt to reach the truth. As William Berkson has said of Faraday, 'He felt that it was prideful to believe in his own theories above all others and so he thought Christian humility demanded a lack of bias'.[4] It is not astonishing, therefore, that the remarkable success that met Faraday's experimental research, especially the discovery of the induction of electric currents, which surprised and overwhelmed him as it brought to light quite fundamental features of the created universe, should have had the effect of reinforcing his Christian convictions and his disclaimer of any incompatibility between humble belief and the scientific spirit.

If throughout his career as an experimental and theoretical physicist Clerk Maxwell constantly appealed to the pioneering work of Michael Faraday and the persistence and humility in which he approached his problems, it is because he shared with Faraday the same fundamental conceptions and the same basic impulses that grew out of their type of commitment to God as he has revealed himself in Jesus Christ. Far from detracting from the independence of his mind or the rigour of his own scientific thought Clerk Maxwell's deeply grounded evangelical convictions, matched with a correspondingly Christian way of life, fostered his scientific inquiries and urged them to break new ground in an untrammelled and reverent investigation of nature's secrets. In view of what he called 'the unsearchable riches of creation', Clerk Maxwell had little use for mere empiricism or narrow scientific professionalism obsessed with measurements carried out in a physics laboratory. An approach of that kind which left no room for a theologically and philosophically empowered grasp of things in their natural wholeness and continuity was finally unable properly to assess analytical particulars or to come up with genuinely new ideas. Hence Clerk Maxwell took care in his 'Introductory Lecture on Experimental Physics' at Cambridge to stress the fact that science appears in a very different aspect when we find out how it bears upon our ordinary life and activity in the world. 'The habit of recognising principles amid the endless variety of their action can never degrade our sense of the sublimity of nature, or mar our enjoyment of its beauty. On the contrary, it tends to rescue our scientific ideas from that vague condition in which we too often leave them, buried among the other products of a lazy incredulity, and to raise them into their proper position among the doctrines in which our faith is so assured, that we are ready at all times to act on them.'[5] For Clerk Maxwell scientific understanding of the universe and faith in God were profoundly integrated.

Under the stained glass window erected to the memory of James Clerk Maxwell in Corsock Kirk in Kircudbrightshire the following inscription is to be read. 'This window is erected by admirers of a genius that discovered the kinship between electricity and light and was led through the mystery of nature to the fuller knowledge of God.' That reflects the verdict of his contemporaries and his successors who, in Britain at any rate, were to some extent aware of the bearing of Clerk Maxwell's science upon his faith, even though they may sometimes have smiled at it as an eccentricity. Few of them, however, were aware of the bearing of his Christian beliefs upon his physical science, for unlike him they had little concern for the metaphysical foundations of science, and were in no position to appreciate the profound change in the philosophical and theoretical structure of scientific knowledge which Clerk Maxwell's modes of thought initiated. Undoubtedly one of the features which makes Clerk Maxwell stand out for us among nineteenth century scientists was his unusual sensitivity for 'fundamental ideas' which he owed to the impact of realist Scottish theology and philosophy upon his formative years in Edinburgh, and his consuming conviction that the advance of science can only be arrested if scientists themselves succumb to a kind of 'mental inertia' (an expression he took over from Michael Faraday) before the struggle for epistemological clarity demanded by fresh revelations of nature. At these decisive points Clerk Maxwell could call upon religious and theological resources which never failed him.

There are still people who look askance at the suggestion that the faith of a Newton or a Clerk Maxwell may well have had an influence at basic points in the formation of their scientific theories, but the history of Western thought actually shows that the development of natural science cannot be divorced from basic ideas that derive from the Judaeo-Christian tradition. There is a deeper interaction between theology and science than is often realised. It will be evident alone from the long prevalence of Augustinian theology and metaphysics that a distinctive slant has been given to all Western culture, including its science, not least in respect of its dualist epistemological substructure. It should be made clear, however, that the development of Christian theology has had both beneficial and harmful effects upon the rise and progress of empirical and theoretical science. It was through Greek patristic theology, for example, that radicalised notions of contingence and contingent order were injected into the foundations of our understanding of the created universe, which eventually gave rise to empirical science in a form unknown and quite impossible in the outlook of ancient or oriental thought.[6] Mention should also be made of dynamic and relational views of space and time deriving from the same source which have now at last come to such prominence in modern physics and cosmology.[7] On the other hand, it was through the mediaeval doctrine of God as the unmoved Mover that a damaging mode of thought was injected into the very basis of Western science. Neoplatonic ideas combined with Aristotelian forms – not to mention significant ingredients from Muslim philosophy through Avicenna and Alfarabi – were grafted on to patristic concepts of the impassibility and immutability of God to yield the notion of an inertial relation between God and the universe which was then built into the fabric of modern science through Isaac Newton.[8] It was this concept of inertia which lay behind the development of the mechanistic universe from which we have been struggling to emancipate our science and culture.

This brings us back to the pioneering work of James Clerk Maxwell, for it was due to his fresh, ruggedly independent way of thinking, under the influence of his Christian faith, that a breach was made in the hard mechanistic structure of Newtonian science and the way was opened for the irrevocable change in our understanding of the universe that is now going on. What he achieved remains highly instructive for a grasp of the subtle interrelation between Christian faith and physical science.

In order to appreciate Clerk Maxwell's distinctive orientation, it may help us to recall what his biographers tell us about his early life at Greenlair in Kirkcudbrightshire. This was a beautiful family estate in the south-west of Scotland where the young Clerk Maxwell revelled in the glories of nature and was encouraged by his mother to 'look up through nature to nature's God'.[9] There he gained an intimate rapport with the riches of creation in all its physical and organic variety, while his experimental and inquiring bent of mind were given free and ample room for spontaneous development. He was already fascinated, we are told, by the behaviour and effects of light and the mysterious continuities that ran through the manifestations of nature, and determined to understand the secrets of natural process. Woven indivisibly into all this and overarching it all, however, was an ever-deepening evangelical faith in God imparted to him through his parents in which childlike simplicity and relentless inquiry without scepticism were combined.[10] That was a trait which he was to carry all through his scientific career, when he was to claim that he believed with the Westminster divines and their predecessors *ad infinitum* that 'Man's chief end is to glorify God and enjoy him for ever'.[11]

The principal point to be noted here, however, is his acquisition of a deep intuitive grasp of God in relation to the world he had created and ceaselessly sustains, and the relation of nature in all its harmony and intricacy to the kind of Creator he knew through Jesus Christ. In his years at Greenlair where his appreciation of nature and his worship of God naturally belonged together he developed a mode of thinking in which the practical and the theoretical were held inseparably together. As he was later to say, in the inaugural lecture at Cambridge to which we have already referred, to bridge the gulf between the abstract and the concrete in this way is not just a mere piece of knowledge, but to acquire 'the rudiment of a permanent endowment'.[12] It is in this way that our powers of thought are awakened by each fresh revelation of nature and new ideas are born. As Clerk Maxwell was to argue in a review of *The Elements of Natural Philosophy* by W. Thomson and P. G. Tait, in 1873, every science must have its 'fundamental ideas', or 'modes of thought by which the process of our minds is brought into complete harmony with the process of nature'.[13] We shall have occasion to take up this point again in regard to Clerk Maxwell's characteristic way of relating the mathematical to the physical in scientific inquiry and theory, but it is important at this point to see that this 'new *mathesis* by which new ideas may be developed' arose out of his early experience at Greenlair where he began to discover that under God the human mind and the world he had created were correlated in a fundamental way with one another. That was the source of his life-long determination to get at 'the natural truth' as distinguished from all 'artificial' ideas or systems of thought.

This way of thinking which had been formed at Greenlair as a natural growth in the inner structure and operation of his mind saw further development when Clerk Maxwell plunged midstream into his high school training at Edinburgh Academy, and then went on to study physics and metaphysics at Edinburgh University where his independent and distinctive outlook made him rather an oddity, but where the theological and epistemological climate served to fuse further together his 'natural realism' and his 'mystical tendency'.[14] The effect of this was given startling exhibition in several papers read to the Royal Society of Edinburgh in which 'physical thinking' and 'mathematical vision' were brought together in an unusually fertile way which governed all his scientific work ever afterwards. When Clerk Maxwell left Edinburgh after several years for more advanced study in mathematics at Cambridge, he began right away while still a student and later as a teaching fellow to inculcate modes of scientific inquiry in which physical and mathematical, empirical and theoretical factors were shown to inhere naturally in one another, so that it was in the light of the 'wholeness' they constituted that experimental and theoretical activity had to be carried out if fidelity to nature was to be maintained. When years later Clerk Maxwell was appointed the first Professor of Experimental Physics in Cambridge he set about building that way of thinking into Cambridge physics and mathematics, and thus gave Cambridge University its characteristic orientation in natural science, to which the whole scientific world has been indebted.[15]

Before we go on to ask how precisely Clerk Maxwell's Christian faith affected his scientific activity, it should be pointed out that Clerk Maxwell himself regarded theological convictions deriving from the Christian message to be 'as cogent, being more *clear, if* less distinct than scientific truths'.[16] He seems never to have had any doubts about the reality of God's self-revelation in Jesus Christ his incarnate Son or in the full sufficiency of atonement that flowed from the love of God the Author of salvation. While he insisted on bringing every belief and every theological statement to the severest test, the steady ground of his religious conviction was in the love of God which remains, even though all knowledge vanishes away. He sought to live a daily life directed and shaped by that love through what he frequently referred to as 'union with Christ'.[17] But it was impossible for Clerk Maxwell to segregate these convictions in the great verities of the Gospel from the rigorous questioning and clarifying operations of scientific inquiry or philosophical reflection. All his convictions and thoughts were of one piece. He considered it to be 'the chief *philosophical* value of physics that it gives the mind something distinct to lay hold of', which if we don't, nature at once tells us that we are wrong. Thus he thought of physics as opening up the road for 'all scientific truth, whether metaphysical, mental or social', and for 'the investigation of *the* question, "How does knowledge come?"' [18] This was not to claim that all knowledge must finally reduce to physics, and all sciences to 'material sciences', but rather that physics seeks to bring to light the laws of the physical creation and is thus concerned with establishing the general framework within which all human knowledge, including theology, is pursued and brought to careful formulation. However, Clerk Maxwell's claim went further than that, for since the universe created by God is essentially one, there are fundamental affinities between all its laws, and even analogies between the constitution of the human intellect and that of the external world, so that although physics does not and cannot mediate to us knowledge of other truths it may well supply us with real analogies which we may use to give new distinctness and precision to knowledge we reach on other ground, as in Christian theology.[19] For example, the teaching of Jesus that knowledge of the truth brings freedom (John 8.32), is found to apply in an appropriate way in the physical realm where our minds are given something distinct to lay hold of, and from which we may turn back to gain a more definite and precise grasp of the principle enunciated by Jesus in the

Gospel. Physics tells us that all we see, our own bodies included, are subject to laws which cannot alter, so that if we wish to do anything we must act according to those laws, or fail – that is why we study those laws in physics. Instead of being consciously, or wilfully, free, while really in subjection to unknown laws, we seek to act consciously by law and are then free from the interference of unrecognised laws. It is not otherwise in theology where obedience to the truth makes us free, or in church where lawfulness and liberty are mutually related.[20] Thus while theological convictions and truths have their own certainty and cogency which rest on more ultimate ground than that of scientifically established truths and laws (which have to do with 'the calculus of probabilities'), they may sometimes, nevertheless, be given a more graspable formulation through the use of real analogies discovered in nature. In that process, instead of being sheltered they are subjected to critical clarification in relation to truth everywhere in God's creation, which will have the double effect of showing whether they are objectively grounded in reality or not and of exhibiting their bearing upon other spheres of knowledge. Clerk Maxwell's refusal to accept any compartmentalising of Christian beliefs and scientific beliefs was entirely consistent with his complete freedom from any kind of 'mental dualism'.[21] Typical was his drafted reply to an invitation to join the Victoria Institute in 1875. 'I think men of science as well as other men need to learn from Christ, and I think Christians whose minds are scientific are bound to study science that their view of the glory of God may be as extensive as their being is capable of.'[22] It is from that perspective, then, that we must now try to set forth the ways in which Clerk Maxwell's Christian faith bore upon his physical science.

(1) Clerk Maxwell's Christian faith entrenched in the back of his mind exercised a *regulative role* in the choice and formation of his leading scientific concepts. It was not that he intruded theological ideas specifically or directly into his scientific theories, but that the basic cast of his mind, shaped through an intuitive apprehension of the relation of God to his creation, provided him with a 'fiducial point or standard of reference' for a discriminating judgment, for example, in respect of 'determinism' (which we shall come to shortly).[23] The Christian slant to his unified outlook had a double influence here. On the one hand, by directing him to an end external to himself, it liberated him from his own subjectivity, and gave him the real *objectivity* he needed for critical scientific activity. Since Christianity insists that nothing must be covered up, and no place must be left sacred or immune from scrutiny, it was Clerk

Maxwell's Christian commitment that led him to make it a rule 'to let nothing be wilfully left unexamined. Nothing is to be *holy ground* consecrated to stationary faith, whether positive or negative . . . Now I am convinced that no one but a Christian can actually purge his land of these holy spots.'[24] On the other hand, his Christian faith provided Clerk Maxwell with certain truths for which science itself could not account but which it could use as premises for its deductive operations.[25] Thus he became imbued with what he called 'root ideas' or 'fundamental conceptions' which guided him in the hard work of wedding thought with fact and grinding out 'appropriate ideas' (Whewell's expression), i.e. what Clerk Maxwell himself spoke of as scientific *modes of thought* or *physical truths* matched to the revelations of the processes inherent in nature.[26] It was then in steady appeal to the regulative force of fiducial points in this way that Clerk Maxwell constantly found himself judging whether scientific theories, his own and others, were finally 'workable' or 'tenable' or not, and being pointed in the direction of more adequate and realist ways of understanding and describing the phenomena of the physical world.

(2) Christian theology and realist philosophy combined to build into Clerk Maxwell's root ideas the principle of the contingent nature of the universe, which had a radical effect in his reassessment of the Newtonian outlook and the determinism and necessitarianism to which it gave rise. That nature is essentially contingent and not necessary in its inherent relations and that scientific truths themselves, therefore, are contingent and not necessary in character, had become one of the established tenets of Scottish realist philosophy and its account of 'natural philosophy' or physics, but that view owed not a little to the influence of Reformed theology in the Scottish Universities.[27] Governing Clerk Maxwell's own outlook was the doctrine, which he fully accepted, that the world had been created by God out of nothing. This implied for Clerk Maxwell that the atomic and molecular constituents of nature, 'the foundation stones of the material universe', have been *made* and were 'not eternal and self-existent'. Hence even though science may yet have much to tell us about the internal relations of atoms and molecules, we must understand them after the analogy of 'manufactured articles'.[28] Natural science, therefore, must reckon with the fact that there are 'singularities' or initial factors in its basic axioms for which it cannot give a scientific account, and also with the fact that as it brings these axioms to bear upon the knowledge of contingent events gained through observation and experiment, it must reckon with the inclusion in the formulation of these laws of

new elements that are to be traced back to a higher level. This means that there are limits beyond which scientific activity cannot penetrate, but which must be frankly acknowledged.[29] This was a point which Clerk Maxwell took care to spell out in his 1873 lecture to the British Association.

'Thus we have been led, along a strictly scientific path, very near the point at which Science must stop – not that Science is debarred from studying the internal mechanism of a molecule which she cannot take to pieces, any more than from investigating an organism which she cannot put together. But in tracing back the history of matter, Science is arrested when she assures herself, on the one hand, that the molecule has been made, and, on the other, that it has not been made by any of the processes we call natural.

'Science is incompetent to reason upon the creation of matter out of nothing. We have reached the utmost limits of our thinking faculties when we have admitted that because matter cannot be eternal and self-existent it must have been created. It is only when we contemplate, not matter in itself, but the form in which it actually exists, that our mind finds something on which to lay hold.

'That matter, as such, should have certain fundamental properties – that it should exist in space and be capable of motion – that its motion should be persistent, and so on – are truths which we may, for anything we know, be of the kind which metaphysicians call necessary. We may use our knowledge of such truths for purposes of deduction, but we have no data for speculation as to their origin.'[30]

(3) Clerk Maxwell was further convinced that contingent events have a distinctive order of their own which is not to be confused with necessity or determinism, even though we must employ the kind of necessary relations we have in mathematics to enable us to grasp and formulate the kind of laws governing contingent order. The contingent events and singularities we find in nature are not to be treated like random or chance events, for nature does not manifest itself to us as a *magazine* but as a *book* that is *regularly paged*. If nature is not a book but only a magazine, no one part could throw light on another.[31] But this is not the case. Contingent events and dynamic processes in nature manifest throughout their various fields continuous configurations, inter-dependence and real analogies, which shows that the universe is everywhere endowed with a rational order which, while contingent in nature, is nevertheless accessible to formulation in terms of physical law.[32] How are we to account for the coordination of necessary connections, or chains of physical causes, and contingent operations in laws of this kind?

In answer Clerk Maxwell appealed to a modified form of the concept of *final cause*. He pointed to the fact that while the operation of physical laws is evidently inflexible when once in action, it depends in its beginning on an act of divine volition, and is not therefore characterised by an absolute necessity. This we can see through an analogy from our own acts of will which initiate a series of events entailing necessary consequences.[33] So far as the investigation of science is concerned, however, when two chains of physical causes are ascertained to be 'contingently connected' for the same end, they give true evidence of design, but in that case 'the evidence of design must be transferred from the absolute fact to the existence of the chain'.[34] Thus the ultimate contingent ground of physical law in the free activity and mind of the Creator must be allowed to determine our understanding of the operation of physical law throughout the chains of physical causes. Hence Clerk Maxwell claimed: 'The doctrine of final causes, although productive of barrenness in its exclusive form, has certainly been a great help to inquirers into nature; and if we only maintain the existence of the analogy, and allow observation to determine its form, we cannot be led far from the truth.'[35]

Two significant points are being made here. First, Clerk Maxwell insists that causal connections have to be looked at on two different levels, a lower level where *subordinate centres of causation* operate, and a higher level where we have to do with the operation of a *central cause,* the first being treated as a limiting case of the second. In his investigation of causal chains and determination of their laws, which it is the business of the scientist to do, he has to focus 'the glass of theory and screw it up sometimes to one pitch of definition, and sometimes to another, so as to see down into the different depths', otherwise everything merges dimly together. Thus through a proper adjustment of 'the telescope of theory' he is enabled to see beyond the subordinate foci of physical acts and their immediate consequences, to the central focus or cause where he is concerned with the original act behind all subordinate causal connections.[36] Secondly, this central cause with reference to which secondary causes are to be understood is not treated by Clerk Maxwell as an inertial centre, like the unmoved Mover in the mediaeval concept of a final cause or the absolute framework of the Newtonian system, but after the analogy of a *moral* centre of activity.[37] For Clerk Maxwell himself, as we have already seen, this central cause or focus of reference was understood in the light of the dynamic nature of the living God revealed in the incarnation of his Son Jesus Christ. Thus it was a distinctly Christian understanding of God the Creator that exercised a regulative force in the foundations of Clerk Maxwell's conception of physical law. That is to say, his profound appreciation of divine creative activity at work in the processes of nature made him reject the classical concept of final cause which inevitably imposed an artificial uniformity or causal homogeneity upon natural phenomena and thus had the effect of rubbing out the all-essential contingent features through which nature reveals and interprets its own secrets to us.[38] Thus the scientist must take the utmost care in wedding thought to fact or theory to observation so that he does not impose abstract necessary patterns of thought prescriptively upon nature but allows the intrinsic relations of nature to determine for him the laws of his thought about its behaviour.[39] This anticipates the next aspect of Clerk Maxwell's science which we have to consider.

(4) This concerns the inter-dependence or mutual involution of empirical and theoretical factors in scientific knowledge of the universe, or more specifically with what Clerk Maxwell called 'physical concepts' or 'embodied mathematics'.[40] It also has to do with the fact underlying all this, that there is a mysterious analogy between 'the constitution of the intellect and that of the external world', and therefore with the laws which govern the two orders of thought and things.[41] This was the theme of several essays he read to 'The Apostles' Club' in Cambridge, from that of 1856 entitled 'Are there Real Analogies in Nature?' to that of 1873 entitled 'Does the progress of Physical Science tend to give any advantage to the opinion of Necessity (or Determinism) over that of the Contingency of Events and the Freedom of Will?', which he read to a company including the famous Anglican theologians, Lightfoot, Hort and Westcott.[42] In the latter he sought to relate the statistical and the dynamical ways of investigating nature, one which science employs in determining the uniform patterns manifested by groups of recurring events or aggregates of matter, and the other which it requires for an appropriate understanding of contingent events in which there are singularities that do not recur and of continuous fields of force. These were essays of a more philosophical nature, but in his strictly scientific papers and works, in which his mind was devoted to grasping real or physical relations in nature, the essence of the matter Clerk Maxwell held to concern the natural interpenetration of mathematical and physical features in the universe, which called for a correspondingly 'appropriate', 'primitive' or 'natural' method in terms of *physical* and *dynamical reasoning*.[43]

Before we proceed let us note that Clerk Maxwell considered that the scientist engaged in this difficult but delicate task of

combining the mathematical and the physical in his understanding
of created nature was reproducing, as it were, the pattern of God's
creative operation, or at least exhibiting 'the essential constituents
of the image of him who in the beginning created, not only the
heaven and the earth, but the materials of which heaven and earth
consist'.[44] 'Happy is the man', he wrote, 'who can recognise in the
work of to-day a connected portion of the work of life, and an
embodiment of the work of Eternity. The foundations of his
confidence are unchangeable, for he has been made a partaker of
Infinity. He strenuously works out his daily enterprises, because the
present is given him for a possession. Thus ought man to be an
impersonation of the divine process of nature, and to show forth
the union of the infinite with the finite, not slighting his temporal
existence, remembering that in it only is individual action possible,
nor yet shutting out from his view that which is eternal, knowing
that time is a mystery which man cannot endure to contemplate
until eternal Truth enlighten it.'[45] It was from deep within religious
convictions of this kind that Clerk Maxwell found himself unceas-
ingly compelled to be as faithful as possible to the inherent structure
and dynamic configuration of the world as it came from the
wisdom and power of the Creator, and was therefore determined to
pursue a way of scientific thinking which would not allow the
natural integration of things to break up in his handling of them.
Along with his natural bent of mind that was the secret behind his
insistent demand for *embodied mathematics*.

From his earliest days at Edinburgh Academy and Edinburgh
University, as Richard Olson has rightly pointed out,[46] Clerk
Maxwell was deeply interested in the embodiment of geometrical
patterns in the physical relations exhibited by nature in its static and
dynamic forms. Thus in the essay on real analogies in nature he
could instance the mathematical forms of crystals 'bursting in upon
us', and add: 'It is because we have blindly excluded the lessons of
these singular bodies from the domain of human knowledge that
we are still in doubt about the great doctrine that the only laws of
matter are those which our minds fabricate, and the only laws of
mind are fabricated for it by matter.'[47] Geometrical patterns are
found, however, not only in rigid structures like crystals but in the
dynamic relations and configurations found at all levels of being
and motion in the universe which science must seek to bring to
appropriate mathematical expression as far as that is possible.[48]
Thus in Clerk Maxwell's thought we have a clear rejection of the
post-Kantian dualist and positivist outlook which he found firmly
entrenched in the continental molecularist and determinist science

as exhibited, for example, by Laplace. He severely questioned the analytical, atomistic and rather artificial interpretation of nature in terms of abstract mathematical symbols, necessary as they were in their proper place, for it had the effect not only of dissecting nature but of distorting the real dynamical relations that are all-important in nature's actual behaviour and regular manifestations, and nowhere more than in the electromagnetic field.

It was typical of Clerk Maxwell, therefore, that he should determine to read no mathematics on the subject of electricity till he had first read through Faraday's *Experimental Researches in Electricity,* especially when he became aware of the difference there was supposed to be between Faraday's way of conceiving of phenomena and that of the mathematicians.[49] That is to say, to use an expression of Clerk Maxwell's friend, C. J. Monro, he refused to allow mathematical equations 'to lead him by the nose', for, to say the least, that would tend to trap him in 'the fallacy of insufficient interpretation'.[50] As Clerk Maxwell proceeded with the study of Faraday, however, he 'perceived that his method of conceiving the phenomena was also a mathematical one, though not exhibited in the conventional form of mathematical symbols'.[51] Faraday conceived of all space as a field of force and with lines of force traversing space in his mind's eye he saw a medium where the mathematicians saw only action at a distance, and so he sought the seat of electromagnetic phenomena in the real actions going on in the medium in which the lines of force belonging to bodies were in some sense part of them. Faraday concentrated on 'physical relation' and 'physical truth' and struggled through the constant interplay of experiment and theory to find a way of reasoning with 'physical hypotheses' which would be true to the actual states of affairs disclosed in experimental research.[52] Clerk Maxwell tells us that when he translated Faraday's ideas into mathematical form, he found that 'Faraday's method resembled those in which we begin with the whole and arrive at the parts of the analysis, while the ordinary mathematical methods were founded on the principle of beginning with the parts and building up the whole by synthesis'.[53] What was generally supposed to be 'the natural method' was far from being that, whereas Faraday's method was in fact more 'primitive' and more 'natural'. Convinced that there must be a mathematical method in which we proceed from the whole to the parts instead of from the parts to the whole, Clerk Maxwell produced his now famous 'partial differential equations' which he claimed to belong essentially to the method which he called that of Faraday.[54] This was a way of mathematical reasoning in unbroken correlation with the changing configuration in a field of force, that is 'physical reasoning as distinguished from calculation'.[55] 'My aim', he explained in another context, 'has been to present the mathematical ideas to the mind in an embodied form, as systems of lines or surfaces, and not as mere symbols, which can neither convey the same ideas nor readily adapt themselves to the phenomena to be explained.'[56]

Clerk Maxwell's scientific relationship with Michael Faraday thus proved to be immensely helpful.[57] Faraday's physical and yet implicitly mathematical way of thinking in wholistic groups of continuous relations greatly reinforced Clerk Maxwell's own deep convictions about 'embodied mathematics' and increased his dissatisfaction with merely analytical mathematics. Faraday also provided him with a significant foil for his own innovative work which combined a heuristic leap forward of the mind with a basic change in the nature of scientific knowledge. For Clerk Maxwell this meant that the truth of mathematical propositions, that is their integration with the intrinsic properties of matter and motion, or their 'physical truth', had to take primacy over their certainty, that is their formal validity in tautological symbolic systems which have no inherent bearing on the real world. Mathematical truths of this kind fully shared with the truths of nature a basically contingent character which can never be grasped in any final or necessary way. This imported a radical change in the axiomatic and epistemological substructure of physical science which was not really appreciated in the nineteenth centry. It was, however, a signal illustration of Clerk Maxwell's own notion of a *new mathesis*, to which we have already alluded, namely, a quite fresh way of deriving knowledge in which new ideas are gained and developed under the power of nature's own self-revelation and in harmony with its dynamic process, one in which the scientific mind operates at all levels with the mutual involution of empirical and theoretical elements.[58]

(5) We must now take up Clerk Maxwell's concept of the *field* for, together with his partial differential equations and integrations which apply throughout all space, it represents the most significant breakthrough in the advance of physical science between Newton and Einstein. Here once again we must trace his thought back to his early studies in Edinburgh, and to the root theological and philosophical ideas with which his mind became imbued, and not least the concept of *relational thinking* which he found, for example, in the teaching of Sir William Hamilton.[59] Evidence for this is apparent in Clerk Maxwell's 1856 essay on analogy where he showed that analogical resemblances and differences are embedded

in the structural patterns of nature throughout the universe. Analogies are sets of relations which bear upon each other and point beyond themselves and thus supply us with fundamental clues for heuristic inquiry beyond the limits of empirical and observational knowledge. Hence, he claimed, 'in a scientific point of view the *relation* is the most important thing to know'.[60] Clerk Maxwell insisted, however, that the relations he referred to were not just imaginary or putative but *real* relations, relations that belong to reality as much as things do, for the inter-relations of things are, in part at least, constitutive of what they are. Being-constituting relations of this kind we may well speak of as 'onto-relations'.

Here we have a distinctive element in Scottish and Reformed theology which dates back to Duns Scotus' development of the concept of the person as it emerged from the Trinitarian teaching of Richard of St Victor, and was passed on through Duns Scotus' *Commentaries on the Sentences of Peter Lombard* to John Major in Paris and then to John Calvin and back, not least through the *Syntagma Theologiae Christianae* of Amandus Polanus, to Scotland.[61] This was a theological mode of thinking which rejected the analytical, individualist notion of the person that was put forward by Boethius and Thomas Aquinas and was later reinforced and built into western social philosophy through the positivist individualism of John Locke and Auguste Comte who thought of persons as separated individuals connected through their external relations, rather like Newtonian particles.[62] In the Reformed theological tradition the notion of the person is held to be controlled by the person-constituting and person-intensifying activity of God in the Incarnation, such that union with Christ becomes the ground for inter-personal relations in the Church. Relations between persons have ontological force and are part of what persons are as persons – they are real, person-constituting relations. That was the theology underlying Clerk Maxwell's concept of union with Christ and of inter-personal relations in Christ, which it was not his nature to isolate in some compartmentalised way from his understanding of real, ontological relations in the physical universe.[63]

Clerk Maxwell also held, as we have already seen, that relations of this constitutive kind obtain as parts within a complex whole. They are not to be known through merely analytical operations but only through contemplation of the unifying whole and its interior relations.[64] Even the fact that we number things in a series implies a previous act of intelligence in which we pick things out of the *universe* – 'nature seems to have a certain horror of partition', he added. In other words, even the use of mathematical units in analysing a set of events implies a pre-analytical intuition of the whole.[65] It is under the guidance and control of such an intuition that we may grasp something of the internal relations of a dynamic coherence inherent in nature without distorting dismemberment of it.

It was with these fundamental convictions and constitutive beliefs that Clerk Maxwell studied Faraday's researches which had resulted in the discovery of electromagnetic induction and the magnetic rotation of light rays, and had led him to put forward the idea of 'moving lines of force' as a field of force having independent existence, in rather sharp contrast to the severely analytical approach of Newtonian science and its artifical notion of bodies acting instantaneously on each other at a distance and within empty uniform space and time. It is not surprising that Clerk Maxwell should have a deep affinity with this non-analytical wholistic approach and with the modes of thought which Faraday brought to it. Owing to the creative power of his own ideas, however, Clerk Maxwell was able to offer a quite distinctive mathematical interpretation of Faraday's physical hypotheses which went well beyond what contemporary science or mathematics had conceived, even beyond Willam Thomson's (Lord Kelvin's) appreciative development of Faraday's ideas, and rather startled Faraday himself.[66] Writing rather later in life of Faraday's scientific conceptions in relation to his own, Clerk Maxwell put his finger on the essence of the matter rather well. 'He never considers bodies as existing with nothing between them but their distance, acting on one another according to some function of that distance. He conceives of all space as a field of force, the lines of force being in general curved, and those due to any body extending from it on all sides. He even speaks of lines of force belonging to a body as in some sense part of itself, so that in its action on distant bodies it cannot be said to act where it is not. This, however, is not a dominant idea with Faraday. I think he would rather have said that the field of space is full of lines of force, whose arrangement depends on that of bodies in the field, and that the mechanical and electrical action on each body is determined by the lines which abut on it.'[67]

In these views Clerk Maxwell was presented with a rather fresh outlook upon the constitution of the universe as a vast field of matter and space governed by a basic unity of different forces, gravitational, electric, magnetic, chemical, etc., which were probably convertible into one another. This was a way of understanding nature which came rather close to the way in which Clerk Maxwell had himself come to appreciate dynamic and subtle connections manifested in created reality as it is continuously sustained by God. Of particular significance for Clerk Maxwell was the way in which Faraday conceived of material bodies or particles, moving lines of force, and fields as merging into one another, which pointed to the idea that in the last resort bodies are so interconnected in fields of force that they must be regarded as the converging points of force rather than as discrete bodies in motion in empty space and time. Moreover, since forces of this kind with real or physical existence do not interact on each other at a distance apart from time but only in neighbourly relations, changes in the configuration of fields need time to take place through the interaction of forces, which points to the idea that time as well as space must belong to the vast field of force which is the underlying reality of all phenomena in the universe.[68]

Faraday's interpretation of the dynamic behaviour of nature in terms of moving lines of force, as forces act upon contiguous forces progressively through the field, did not square with Newtonian laws, but he on his part failed to determine the laws governing fields of force. As Clerk Maxwell understood it, this notion of physical force interacting with force in a contiguous field, implying 'the maxim that might is right', demanded a mechanical explanation, even if it was not a causalist or determinist explanation in the Newtonian sense.[69] He tackled the problem in two distinct stages.

The first stage was marked by his paper *On Physical Lines of Force* which he wrote in 1856 although it was not published until five years later.[70] His problem was to account for the way in which electric and magnetic forces or particles act on one another through external but contiguous relations, and to find a mathematical form for its description. He saw that while integral equations are the appropriate mathematical expression for a theory of action between particles at a distance, differential equations must be used for a theory of action between contiguous parts of a medium. But in order to develop these equations he made use of a highly artificial and intricate mechanical model of magnetic vortices and electric currents, with 'idle wheels' interposed between contiguous vortices, with a view to giving his physico-mathematical vision something distinct to work with in struggling to grasp the mechanics of the interaction of forces rather than causes in the electromagnetic field. This strange mechanical model was merely an *ad hoc* heuristic device, but unsatisfactory as it was it enabled him to work out in the form of embodied mathematics a rigorous formalisation of the laws of the electromagnetic field, in the course of which he both derived the all-important partial differential equations and came up with his electromagnetic theory of light.[71] In the very event of these brilliant achievements, however, Clerk Maxwell insisted that he did not put forward his imaginary mechanical model as 'a mode of connexion existing in nature', but only as a provisional model to show that 'such a mode of connexion . . . is mechanically conceivable'.[72] That is to say, his paper *On Physical Lines of Force* was meant to provide a mechanical interpretation of electromagnetic phenomena in a form that would still harmonise with Newtonian mechanics. Nevertheless he was far from being happy with this approach, which perhaps explains why he held it back for several years. William Berkson has put the matter well. 'Maxwell invented and worked with a theory he thought to be basically untenable, but he produced results amongst the most fruitful in the history of science.'[73] The effect of Clerk Maxwell's equations was to establish in an indubitable way the independent reality of the field but it also had the effect of altering his concept of the field as a medium of contiguous forces and demanding its reconsideration.

This was the task he undertook in a second stage, with the publication of another work *A Dynamical Theory of the Electromagnetic Field* in 1865, which he had read before the Royal Society of London in December of the previous year.[74] In this paper he embodied his partial differential equations in a thoroughly *relational* interpretation of the electromagnetic field without recourse to Newtonian mechanics.[75] The way for that had been opened by his realisation that electromotive force is quite different from mechanical force, for it acts on electricity and not like mechanical force on the discrete bodies in which electricity resides, but now that realisation was much reinforced by the discovery of the identity in nature and speed between electromagnetic and light waves.[76] This pointed to the fact that nature is ultimately governed by continuous fields of energy, even though the energy is manifest in two forms with respect to position and motion, in the dynamics of fields and in the mechanics of bodies in interaction.[77] Clerk Maxwell's aim was not only to free his partial differential equations from the mechanical model but to derive them without recourse to mechanism.[78] This is precisely what he managed to do, in showing that these equations enabled him to derive the structural laws of electromagnetic radiation and electromagnetic fields at any point in space and for any instant of time.[79] As Einstein has expressed it: 'The formulation of these equations is the most important event in physics since Newton's time, not only because of their wealth of content, but also because they form a pattern for a new type of law . . . Maxwell's equations are laws representing the *structure* of the field . . . All space is the scene of these laws and not, as for mechanical laws, only points in which matter or charges are present.'[80] Thus in contrast to classical Newtonian science, the reconstruction of physical science brought about by Clerk Maxwell makes us conceive physical reality in terms of *continuous*, not just contiguous, fields of force throughout space and time.

Several comments about Clerk Maxwell's physical science may be worth making at this point.

(a) While Clerk Maxwell worked out a thoroughly *relational* account of the field in *A Dynamical Theory of the Electromagnetic Field*, he did not entirely discard his earlier mechanical account, but in accord with his view that there may be two ways of looking at things, brought both together in his major work *A Treatise on Electricity and Magnetism (1873)*, constantly adjusting the focus of theory to the different levels of mechanical and dynamical interpretation, yet in such a way that it became clear that a mechanical interpretation represents a rather artificial approach which does not get at the real connections in nature, and can only be regarded, therefore, as a limiting case of a relational and dynamical account, and thus as having the status of a working model which must not be taken for more than it really is.[81] The final effect of Clerk Maxwell's work, however, was that the continuous field appeared side by side with the material point as the representative of physical reality. This dualism, Einstein remarked, remained until his own day, disturbing as he found it for the orderly mind.[82]

(b) Clerk Maxwell's dynamical and relational theory of the field went beyond established observations and known experimental evidence, but the fact that the constant radiation of electromagnetic waves from a centre predicted by his equations was experimentally verified by Hertz showed that Clerk Maxwell's concept of the continuous field was consistent with reality.[83] This was a significant event, for Clerk Maxwell's dynamical approach was so foreign to the atomistic and molecularist determinism of continental physics particularly that it was not taken seriously. Even Lord Kelvin on reading Clerk Maxwell's *A Dynamical Theory of the Electromagnetic Field* charged him with falling away into mysticism when he departed from the mechanical model.[84] Through Hertz's discovery, however, as Max Planck pointed out, the greatest sensation was produced in the scientific world, for 'the speculations of Maxwell were translated into fact and a new epoch of experimental and theoretical physics was begun'.[85]

(c) Doubtless from a strictly scientific point of view, the decisive factor in Clerk Maxwell's switch from a mechanical to a relational interpretation of the electromagnetic field was his derivation of partial differential equations as the natural expression of continuous fields, but behind that lay the masterful conviction which would not let him go, that nature as the God and Father of Jesus Christ had created it, does not behave in a mechanical way. That is to say, in the ultimate analysis it was Clerk Maxwell's Christian faith which exercised a regulative role in his scientific judgment and choice of concept and theory at this supreme juncture in the advance of physical science. The question had to be raised, if the electromagnetic field is not susceptible of mechanical explanation, how about the biological field? We do not know very much about Clerk Maxwell's reaction to evolution, but what we do have shows that he was uneasy about the mechanistic features of Darwinian theory.[86] Of course in Clerk Maxwell's view all scientific theories no matter how rigorous fail to match the subtle and flexible modes of connection in created reality itself, but abstractive and mechanistic theories in particular he felt to be 'unworkable'.[87]

(6) The last matter we must discuss is the implication of Clerk Maxwell's theories, and especially of his electromagnetic theory of light in a continuous field, for concepts of space and time. It is signficant that there seems to be no evidence in Clerk Maxwell's papers and books for Newtonian container notions of space and time, while Kantian notions are resolutely brought into line with realist relations in the created universe.[88] Questions of time and space were raised in his Cambridge essay on real analogies in nature when he discussed the close relations between the laws of nature and the constitution of the human intellect, but he concluded, as we have seen, that we have to operate with objectively controlled concepts, even though they are formulated in accordance with the laws of the human mind. That is to say, Clerk Maxwell did not work with *absolute* notions of time and space, either in the Newtonian or Kantian sense of 'absolute' as unaffected by on-going empirical reality.[89]

This concept of 'objective truth' in scientific notions of time and space was deepened and reinforced in Clerk Maxwell's rejection of action at a distance notions and his commitment to the independent reality of the continuous field in which we have to reckon with the fact that light waves travel through space and take time to do so.[90] This implies that spatial and temporal relations are inherent features in the dynamic structure of the field that underlies all the phenomena of physical reality. That is an implication that was mathematically established by Clerk Maxwell's equations which describe the structure of the field at any point in space and for any instant of time. If these equations show us that rates of change in the configuration of fields involve time and space, they also show conversely that time and space are empirical features in the vast field of the universe. Moreover, in so far as Clerk Maxwell's partial differential equations establish the independent reality and intelligibility of the continuous field, they show that the temporal and spatial structures of the field do not depend on the activity of the human observer in conceiving or measuring changes in the field. This has the conjunct effect of liberating notions of time and space from the dominance of the massive subjectivity in the Kantian metaphysical idea that they are *a priori* forms of man's sensory perception unaffected by empirical objectivity, and therefore of opening up the notions of time and space for radical reconsideration.

As we have already noted, Clerk Maxwell was impressed with the physical relevance of W. R. Hamilton's equations of motion and used them to help him derive an embodied-mathematical account of moving lines of force,[91] but while he was aware of Riemannian four-dimensional geometry he does not seem to have discerned its implication for realist notions of space and time, let alone space-time, though he did apparently realise that a newer and deeper kind of continuity was being suggested.[92] Evidently Clerk Maxwell's thought was on the brink of the next revolution that was to be brought about by Einstein in 1905 with his essay on special relativity, but perhaps Clerk Maxwell's hesitation to reject the notion of ether, even though it did not seem to have much importance for him,[93] prevented him from seriously entertaining the idea that light waves might not need a medium through which to propagate themselves. However, enough has been said to show that Clerk Maxwell's dynamical theory of the electromagnetic field in which magnetism, electricity and light were unified in a single comprehensive theory, together with his partial differential equations, provided the basic material out of which, and in the light of the Lorentz transformations, Einstein claimed to have crystallised his theory of relativity which has transformed our notions of space and time.[94]

There is no evidence to show that Clerk Maxwell directly allowed his Christian beliefs in the creation and the incarnation to influence his understanding of space and time, in the way that those cardinal doctrines affected the mind of the early Greek fathers who first put forward the relational notions of space and time, with which we work in science as in theology today. We know from his biographer that Clerk Maxwell loved to study the fathers and older divines, whom he preferred to modern theologians,[95] which may indicate that he found their understanding of the created universe rather congenial. But it is certainly clear that the kind of physical science which he advocated is much more congenial to Christian theology than that which developed when absolute notions of space and time were arbitrarily clamped down upon the empirical world and had the effect of reducing understanding of it to a hard and closed mechanistic system. For Clerk Maxwell himself rigorous scientific inquiry and simple devout Christian faith were life-long partners, each in its own way contributing to the strength of the other. Hence it would not be unfitting to end this discussion of the bearing of Christian faith upon physical science with a prayer which Clerk Maxwell left among his papers.

'Almighty God, who hast created man in Thine own image, and made him a living soul that he might seek after Thee and have dominion over Thy creatures, teach us to study the works of Thy hands that we may subdue the earth to our use, and strengthen our reason for Thy service; and so to receive Thy blessed Word, that we may believe on Him whom Thou hast sent to give us knowledge of salvation and the remission of our sins. All which we ask in the name of the same Jesus Christ our Lord.'[96]

NOTES

1. See Ivan Tolstoy, *James Clerk Maxwell. A Biography*. Edinburgh, 1981.
2. *The Scientific Papers of James Clerk Maxwell*, edited by W. D. Niven, Cambridge, 1890, vol. 2, p. 792f.
3. The work to which Faraday referred was *Experimental Researches in Chemistry and Physics*. London, 1859.
4. William Berkson, *Fields of Force. The Development of a World View from Faraday to Einstein*. London, 1974, p. 56; cf. also p. 18.
5. *Scientific Papers*, vol. 2, p. 243.
6. See in this respect the works of S. L. Jaki, *Science and Creation. From eternal cycles to an oscillating universe*. Edinburgh, 1974; *The Road of Science and the Ways to God*. Edinburgh, 1978; *Cosmos and Creator*. Edinburgh, 1980.
7. Cf. my essay *Space, Time and Incarnation*. London, 1969.
8. See also my work, *Divine and Contingent Order*. Oxford, 1981, pp. 5ff, 40ff, etc.
9. Lewis Campbell and William Garnett, *The Life of James Clerk Maxwell, with a selection from his correspondence and occasional writings and a sketch of his contributions to science*. London, 1882, p. 32.
10. *Ibid.*, pp. 163–180, 188f, 414–433.
11. *Ibid.*, p. 158.
12. *Scientific Papers*, vol. 2, p. 248.
13. *Ibid.*, p. 325.
14. Campbell and Garnett, *op. cit.*, p. 108.
15. The Cavendish Laboratories in Cambridge which were designed by him, organised, and given their scientific purpose, are a tribute to Clerk Maxwell's permanent mark on the university. Cf. Lord Kelvin's tribute to Clerk Maxwell's influence, *ibid.*, p. 357. It was typical of Clerk Maxwell that he should have had carved on the doors of the Cavendish Laboratory the words: *Magna opera Domini exquisita in omnes voluntates ejus.*
16. From a letter to his friend Lewis Campbell on taking Priest's Orders in 1887, Campbell and Garnett, *op. cit.*, p. 294.
17. *Ibid.* p. 294, cf., pp. 170ff, 310ff, 328ff, 338f, 387, 414ff, 433.
18. *Ibid.*, (from a letter to R. B. Litchfield), p. 305.
19. *Ibid.*, pp. 235ff, 304f.
20. *Ibid.*, pp. 293f, 304f.
21. This was F. J. A. Hort's expression of Clerk Maxwell's unitary outlook, *ibid.*, p. 419.
22. *Ibid.*, p. 404f.
23. *Ibid.*, 435. Cf. the statement by Sir William Hamilton, Professor of Metaphysics in Edinburgh: 'If it is true that our *primary experience* be a faith, the reality of our knowledge turns on the veracity of our constitutive beliefs. As ultimate, the quality of these beliefs cannot be

inferred; their truth, however, is in the first instance to be presumed. As given and possessed, they must stand good until refuted; *neganti incumbit probatio*. It is not to be presumed, that Intelligence gratuitously annihilates itself – that the Author of nature creates only to deceive . . . But though the truth of our instinctive faiths must *in the first instance* be admitted, their falsehood may *subsequently* be established: this, however, only through themselves – only on the ground of their reciprocal contradiction.' *Discussions on Philosophy*. London, 2nd edit., 1853 – cited from Richard Olson, *Scottish Philosophy and British Physics 1750–1880*, Princeton, 1975, p. 142. Cf. also my essay on 'Ultimate Beliefs and the Scientific Revolution', *Cross Currents*, vol. xxx, no. 2, New York, 1980, pp. 129–149: now reprinted as Chapter 5 of this book.

24. From a letter to Lewis Campbell, Campbell and Garnett, *op. cit.*, p. 178f; cf. p. 177, and *Scientific Papers*, vol. 2, p. 482.
25. Campbell and Garnett, *op. cit.*, 359f.
26. *Ibid.*, 165, 215, 289, 326. Cf. further *Scientific Papers*, vol. 2, pp. 248, 258, 325; *A Treatise on Electricity and Magnetism* (1873), Dover edit., 1954, vol. 1, p. x, etc.
27. Cf. R. Olson, *op. cit.*, pp. 39, 43, 46, 60, 68f.
28. Campbell and Garnett, *op. cit.*, 359, 393f, 424; *Scientific Papers*, vol. 2, pp. 376f, from Clerk Maxwell's lecture on 'Molecules'; and pp. 482ff, from his article on 'Atom' for the *Encyclopaedia Britannica*, pp. 482ff.
29. *Scientific Papers*, vol. 2, pp. 376, 482; for the reference to 'singularities', see Campbell and Garnett, *op. cit.*, p. 442f.
30. *Scientific Papers*, vol. 2, pp. 375ff.
31. Campbell and Garnett, *op. cit.*, 243; *Scientific Papers*, vol. 2, p. 759.
32. In addition to the essay on real analogies in nature, Campbell and Garnett, *op. cit.*, pp. 235–244, see *On Faraday's Lines of Force*, *Scientific Papers*, vol. 1, pp. 156f; and Richard Olson, *op. cit.*, pp. 299ff.
33. Campbell and Garnett, *op. cit.*, p. 241f.
34. From the 1853 essay at Cambridge on 'What is the Nature of Evidence of Design?', Campbell and Garnett, *op. cit.*, p. 225f.
35. Campbell and Garnett, *op. cit.*, p. 243.
36. *Ibid.*, pp. 226, 237f. The argument here is taken from the analogy of moral activity. See also *Scientific Papers*, vol. 1, p. 208: 'It is a good thing to have two ways of looking at a subject, and to admit that there *are* two ways of looking at it.' And cf. *A Treatise on Electricity and Magnetism*, vol. 1, p. xf, (59–62) pp. 62–70; vol. 2, (502) p. 158f, (525) p. 175f.
37. Campbell and Garnett, *op. cit.*, pp. 226, 242.
38. *Ibid.*, p. 243f.
39. *Ibid.*, p. 244.
40. *Scientific Papers*, vol. 1, pp. 155ff, 187f; *A Treatise on Electricity and Magnetism*, vol. 1, p. ixf, (10) 9f; vol. 2, (528–29), 175ff. See R. Olson, *op. cit.*, pp. 299ff.

41. Campbell and Garnett, *op. cit.*, p. 238.
42. *Ibid.*, 235ff, 434ff, cf. 326.
43. *A Treatise on Electricity and Magnetism*, vol. 1 (10), p. 9; vol. 2, (528–29), pp. 176f; (550), p. 196ff, (567) p. 209f, (568), pp. 211ff, (604), p. 247.
44. *Scientific Papers*, vol. 2, p. 377.
45. Campbell and Garnett, *op. cit.*, p. 200.
46. R. Olson, *op. cit.*, p. 302.
47. Campbell and Garnett, *op. cit.*, p. 244.
48. *Scientific Papers*, vol. 1, pp. 1ff, 40ff, 30ff.
49. *A Treatise on Electricity and Magnetism*, vol. 1, p. viii.
50. Campbell and Garnett, *op. cit.*, p. 378. Cf. Clerk Maxwell's warning against 'partial explanation', *Scientific Papers*, vol. 1, pp. 155f.
51. *A Treatise on Electricity and Magnetism*, vol. 1, p. x.
52. *Ibid.*, vol. 1, p. x, (59) p. 62f, vol. 2, (528) p. 175: 'The method which Faraday employed in his researches consisted in a constant appeal to experiment as a means of testing the truth of his ideas, and a constant cultivation of ideas under the direct influence of experiment.' See further (540) p. 187f; *Scientific Papers*, vol. 1, p. 208.
53. *A Treatise on Electricity and Magnetism*, vol. 1, p. ix; vol. 2 (529) p. 176f.
54. *Ibid.*, vol. 1, p. x; vol. 2 (529) p. 177.
55. *Ibid.*, vol. 1 (10) p. 9; vol. 2, (567), p. 209f; *Scientific Papers*, vol. 1, p. 241; vol. 2, p. 309.
56. *Scientific Papers*, vol. 1, p. 187.
57. See Clerk Maxwell's essays on Faraday, *Scientific Papers*, vol. 2, pp. 355–360; pp. 786–793.
58. *Scientific Papers*, vol. 2, p. 325. It was for this reason that Clerk Maxwell developed such a liking for W. R. Hamilton's 'calculus of quaternions', for he saw the possibilities of their embodiment in empirical reality and thus of their heuristic promise in physical knowledge. See *Scientific Papers*, vol. 2, pp. 259f; *A Treatise on Electricity and Magnetism*, vol. 1, (10) p. 9; vol. 2, (553), pp. 199f, (561), p. 205, (618) pp. 257ff.
59. Cf. R. Olson, *op. cit.*, p. 290f. See Campbell and Garnett, *op. cit.*, p. 108f. A similar view was held by J. D. Forbes, Clerk Maxwell's physics teacher in Edinburgh, *ibid.*, p. 228.
60. Campbell and Garnett, *op. cit.*, p. 243. Cf. *An Elementary Treatise on Electricity*, edit. by W. Garnett, 1881, p. 51: 'The similarity which constitutes the analogy is not between the phenomena themselves, but between the relations of these phenomena.'
61. The *Syntagma* of Polanus was prescribed reading for Scottish theologians for some 2 centuries. Evidence of its knowledge is found even in David Hume's *Dialogues on Natural Religion*, in ideas he put into the mouth of the interlocutor *Philo*.
62. Cf. Campbell and Garnett, *op. cit.*, p. 205, 'Comte has good ideas about method, but no notion of what is meant by person.'
63. See *op. cit.*, pp. 294, 311, 387, etc.
64. *Ibid.*, pp. 165–8.

65. Basically the same point was made by Einstein in his critique of the phenomenalist particularism of Bertrand Russell, P. A. Schilpp, *The Philosophy of Bertrand Russell*, La Salle, Illinois, 1944, p. 287f.

66. *On Faraday's Lines of Force, Scientific Papers*, vol. 1, pp. 156–229. For the bearing of Clerk Maxwell's own ideas on Faraday's theories, see pp. 156ff; and for Faraday's reaction, see Campbell and Garnett, *op. cit.*, pp. 288f, 520f.

67. *A Treatise on Electricity and Magnetism*, vol. 2, (529) p. 177.

68. See the illuminating discussion of Faraday's work and thought by William Berkson, *op. cit.*, pp. 1–125.

69. Campbell and Garnett, *op. cit.*, p. 239.

70. *Scientific Papers*, vol. 1, pp. 451–513; and see Ivan Tolstoy's helpful presentation, *op. cit.*, pp. 66–78.

71. *Scientific Papers*, vol. 1, pp. 467ff, and note his triumphant result 'that *light consists in the transverse undulations of the same medium which is the cause of electric and magnetic phenomena'*. The italics are Clerk Maxwell's, p. 500. See also *A Treatise on Electricity and Magnetism*, vol. 1, (95a) p. 124 for the appropriateness of partial differential equations.

72. *Scientific Papers*, vol. 1, p. 486; cf. I. Tolstoy, *op. cit.*, p. 122.

73. W. Berkson, *op. cit.*, p. 170. Cf. *A Treatise on Electricity and Magnetism*, vol. 2, (831), p. 470: 'The attempt which I then made to imagine a working model of this mechanism must be taken for no more than it really is, a demonstration that mechanism may be imagined capable of producing a connexion mechanically equivalent to the actual connexion of the parts of the electromagnetic field.'

74. *Scientific Papers*, vol. 1, pp. 527–597. See my new edition of this work, Scottish Academic Press, Edinburgh, 1982.

75. Clerk Maxwell insisted that though his work has references to mechanical phenomena, they are to be understood 'as illustrative, not explanatory', for they are adduced merely to assist the mind of the reader in understanding the electrical phenomena. 'In speaking of the Energy of the field, however,' he added, 'I wish to be understood literally.' *Ibid.*, p. 564.

76. 'This velocity is so nearly that of light, that it seems we have strong reason to conclude that light itself (including radiant heat, and other radiations if any) is an electromagnetic disturbance in the form of waves propagated through the electromagnetic field according to electromagnetic laws.' *Scientific Papers*, vol. 1, p. 535. This is the decisive statement of the discussion from p. 534 to p. 580. See also vol. 2, p. 771f.

77. *Ibid.*, p. 564. See also *A Treatise on Electricity and Magnetism*, vol. 2, (568–9), pp. 211ff.

78. See W. Berkson, *op. cit.*, pp. 172, 176.

79. *Scientific Papers*, vol. 1, pp. 554ff; and see *A Treatise on Electricity and Magnetism*, vol. 2, (604–617) pp. 247–257.

80. Albert Einstein and Leopold Infeld, *The Evolution of Physics from Early Concepts to Relativity and Quanta*, Clarion edit., New York, 1938, pp.

143, 146. See also A. Einstein, 'Clerk Maxwell's Influence on the evolution of the Idea of Physical Reality', in *James Clerk Maxwell. A Commemoration Volume 1831–1931*, Cambridge, 1931, p. 71f. This is retranslated as a Foreword to my edition of *A Dynamical Theory of the Electromagnetic Field*.

81. *A Treatise on Electricity and Magnetism*, vol. 2, (555) p. 200f; (831) p. 470.
82. A. Einstein, *op. cit.*, p. 69f.
83. H. Hertz, *Electric Waves*, 1879. See W. Berkson, *op. cit.*, p. 213ff.
84. Reference to this is made in an unpublished letter from Clerk Maxwell to Sir William Thomson (as Lord Kelvin was then) in Glasgow University Library, to which my attention has been drawn by Prof. Sir John C. Gunn, *Kelvin Papers M 17*. The letter is dated Oct. 15, 1864. See also *A Treatise on Electricity and Magnetism*, vol. 2, (865) p. 494, for Clerk Maxwell's rebuttal of *a priori* objections to his dynamical interpretation or theory.
85. *James Clerk Maxwell. A Commemoration Volume 1831–1931*, Cambridge, 1931, p. 62.
86. Campbell and Garnett, *op. cit.*, 393f, 460; *Scientific Papers*, vol. 2, pp. 375ff, 481ff.
87. This was the expression Clerk Maxwell is reported to have used on his deathbed, Campbell and Garnett, *op. cit.*, p. 416.
88. *Ibid.*, p. 135.
89. *Ibid.*, pp., 236ff, 244.
90. The relation of the movement of light to time had already been pointed out to Clerk Maxwell by Faraday, Campbell and Garnett, *op. cit.*, p. 520. Cf. *A Treatise on Electricity and Magnetism*, vol. 2, (861) p. 490.
91. *A Treatise on Electricity and Magnetism*, vol. 2, (561) p. 205. See above at note 58.
92. *Ibid.*, (862–866) pp. 490ff; Campbell and Garnett, *op. cit.*, p. 380.
93. *Scientific Papers*, vol. 2, 'Ether', pp. 763–775. Tolstoy remarks of Clerk Maxwell that 'he never took models of ether seriously, preferring to use them as mere analogies – as a kind of scaffolding which could later be discarded'. *Op. cit.*, p. 129. Olson has pointed out, rightly, that the Scottish realist tradition in philosophy had already rejected the hypothesis of ether along with its epistemological rejection of intermediary ideas as unnecessary, *op. cit.*, pp. 42, 51f, 170ff.
94. A. Einstein, *Relativity. The Special and the General Theory*, New York, 1961, p. 49.
95. Campbell and Garnett, *op. cit.*, pp. 321ff; cf. 415f, 418f, 422f.
96. *Ibid.*, p. 323.

CHAPTER VII

Christian Theology in the Context of Scientific Change*

IN HIS influential work, *The Structure of Scientific Revolutions*, Thomas S. Kuhn has drawn a rather sharp distinction between the process of normal science concerned with problem-solving within the paradigms of a mature scientific community and the emergence of major scientific discoveries when paradigms are under attack and are subject to change. His concern is to make clear the depth and radical nature of revolutionary advance in our controlling concepts, which he can speak of in terms of a 'gestalt switch' or a 'conversion experience'.[1] A revolutionary change of this kind is probably not such a sudden or unstructured event as Kuhn would like to make out[2], but it is the translation of the change into real terms that counts, and that takes rather longer.

An enlightening example of what happens is provided by the treatise of Copernicus, *De Revolutionibus orbium coelestium*, which was published in 1543 by Andreas Osiander with a preface explaining the formal value of the work as offering the best way to calculate the revolutions of heavenly bodies, but without claiming that it constituted a physical description of the nature of things. It was only when that claim was made by Galileo in 1616 and the

* Reprinted from *Pluralisme et Oecuménisme en Recherches Théologiques. Mélanges offert au R. P. Dockx, O. P.*, by Y. Congar *et al.*, 1976.

mathematical formalisation was translated into natural philosophy and presented as valid in real terms, that the scientific revolution really began to bite – and then the fat was in the fire! That is to say, it was 73 years after the publication of *De revolutionibus* that the radical implications of the new theory began to be realised and worked out in such a way that it transformed the foundations of our knowledge of the universe.[3]

Something like that has been taking place in our own day. In 1905 Einstein published several essays of epoch-making significance, bearing on relativity theory and quantum theory, which initiated changes that have been transforming the whole perspective of modern science, but only now, more than 70 years later, are we coming to terms with the implications of these changes for fundamental epistemology, affecting every area of human knowledge. Admittedly there is a difference between what happened in the 73 years after 1543 and what has been happening since 1905, for modern science itself has not been content with a merely formalist or operationalist acceptance of Einstein's theories but has sought progressively to develop them as physical descriptions of nature – although it is only in the last few years with startling developments in high energy physics that quantum field theory has been moving beyond a merely statistical account of 'phenomena' towards a description of physical reality in its inner structure irrespective of the observer.[4] Nevertheless, the comparison between what happened post-Copernicus and what has been happening post-Einstein remains valid in this respect that there is still a serious gap between what has been taking place in the foundations of pure science and the principles of knowledge with which we operate elsewhere, especially in the human and social sciences.

Up to a few years ago, when I put to scientists and philosophers of science questions as to the nature of science and scientific method, they almost invariably gave me answers derived from an obsolete positivist outlook, such as one still finds formulated in well-known text-books by Hempel, Nagel or Feigl. When I asked them specifically about Einstein's thought I tended to get the regular answer, 'We accept Einstein's scientific achievements, but not his philosophy or his epistemology'! And yet on deeper probing the scientists, at any rate, tended to admit that the way in which they formulated their concepts of science and scientific method did not really correspond to the actual way in which they made their scientific discoveries. In other words, they admitted to an anomalous state of affairs between their heuristic advances in knowledge of the universe and the paradigmatic framework, together with the methodological rules abstracted from them, which they had come to take for granted. Although they are now changing rapidly, philosophers of science particularly have tended to operate with the old dualisms between primary and secondary qualities or noumena and phenomena, and to be trapped within the epistemological disjunction of the theoretical and empirical ingredients of knowledge which has had such a fatal influence on European thought.

Let me set out the problem that faces us in terms of the paradigmatic shape of mind that developed in the 18th and 19th centuries within the framework of the Newtonian system of the world and its sharp distinction between absolute mathematical time and space and relative apparent time and space. Here on the one hand we have a masterful analytic habit of mind which carved up the universe into discrete particles or bodies in motion in such a way that they could be connected together only in terms of their external relations; and so there arose the mechanistic conception of the universe which has so cruelly fettered the human spirit. Here on the other hand, in contrast to classical science which tended to reduce everything knowable upwards into abstract timeless essences, we find a regular tendency to reduce everything knowable downwards into observable phenomena; and so there arose the normative conviction that we have no knowledge of things in themselves but only knowledge of things as they appear to us. With Newton himself scientific knowledge involved a massive objectivity, for absolute mathematical time and space, by reference to which as an inertial system, all knowledge of the phenomenal world is controlled and reduced to order, were identified with the divine sensorium: that is to say, it is the mind of the Almighty Creator which gives and maintains the inherent order, regularity and stability of the universe, thereby making it accessible to our objective rational inquiry. But when Kant transferred absolute time and space from the mind of the divine Creator to the mind of the human knower, it could not but be held that the human intellect does not draw its laws from nature but imposes them upon nature. Thus we have the emergence of the paradigmatic conviction that we can understand and verify only what we ourselves can construct and shape for ourselves, for it is our knowing of phenomena that gives them their intelligible form and imposes any meaningful order they may have for us extrinsically upon them. Such is the attitude of mind that has come to permeate our Western culture, not least the human and social sciences, and of course the technological society within which they function, but also within which the Christian Church is bound to communicate its message and interpret it to the contemporary world. Here an insidious sociology of knowledge tends to replace epistemology and a social ideology substitutes for theology.

The fatal bearing of this paradigmatic shape of mind upon modern theology is particularly evident at its most sensitive point: knowledge of the historical Jesus Christ. If it is the case that we do not know things in themselves but only in their external relations as they appear to us; if we can understand only what we assimilate into the circle of our own preconceptions and interpret as having meaning for ourselves insofar as we endow it with our own intelligibility, then we can know nothing of Jesus as he is in himself in his own truth or personal reality, but only what the earliest Christians appeared to make of the phenomenon of Jesus as they clothed it with patterns of significance to suit their own spiritual needs and even created 'historical events' upon which to hang those patterns of significance. I say 'appeared to make of the phenomenon of Jesus', for on the same principle we cannot really grasp any objective content in their knowledge, but can only seek through some symbolic reinterpretation to let what they did become a focus of meaning for ourselves. Hence no research can ever penetrate into the truth of Jesus independent of the controlling structures of meaning imposed upon him from the self-understanding of the early Church. We may indeed be able through clever analysis to discern something of the various layers of 'theologising' embedded in the literary tradition interpreting the phenomenon of Jesus, but in the nature of the case it will not be possible even in the final analysis to reach anything beyond constructions out of the religious consciousness of the earliest witnesses. What is more, if event and meaning are originally disparate, as all this assumes, then the more spiritually or theologically rich a fact is in its literary presentation by the early Church, the further we are removed from the original bare events which, *ex hypothesi*, have no inherent or controlling significance of their own. That is to say, 'Jesus himself' is ultimately only a chimera which inevitably eludes our grasp, for he is completely submerged in the piety of the early Church and irretrievably lost in the objectifying interpretations of the Gospel handed on to us in the New Testament writings. That is the recurring dénouement of the quest of the historical Jesus which for a hundred and fifty years has been carried on within a framework of radical dualism of fact and meaning, or empirical and theoretical components of knowledge, necessarily creating an unbridgeable gulf between the original Jesus and the theologising tradition of the Church. Moreover, such a procedure inevitably predetermines the results of historico-critical research from the very outset, not because of the historico-critical method itself, but because that method is not carried far enough through radical questioning into the preconceptions controlling its deployment, and above all into the axiomatic assumption that at all stages it is man's knowing of phenomena which gives them the intelligible shape and structure in which their meaning is claimed to lie.

It can hardly be insisted strongly enough, however, that, at least so far as the pure sciences are concerned, this whole way of thinking has collapsed, for the dualist principles of knowledge upon which it rested have had to give way in a profound epistemological revolution to another and more concrete way of thinking in which empirical and theoretical components are found to be inextricably interwoven from the very bottom. Here the basic facts or events with which we have to do in the universe, in any area of rational inquiry, are found precisely as facts or events to be shot through and through with their own intrinsic significance, and therefore may be understood and interpreted aright only in terms of their interior structure or inherent intelligibility. A major step in the transition to this new outlook came with the work of Max Planck when he developed the first exact determination of the absolute magnitude of atoms and showed that the structure of nature was governed by the universal constant h, for that signified considerable success in penetrating through the phenomenal to the *real*. The effect of this achievement, as Einstein has pointed out, was to shatter the whole framework of classical mechanics and electro-dynamics and to set science the fresh task of finding a new conceptual basis for all physics.[5] Yet it was with Einstein himself that the really decisive advance, affecting the first principles of knowledge, came, in his establishment of mathematical invariances in nature irrespective of any and every observer, enabling us to grasp reality in its depth. This advance was reinforced and carried further in the development of general relativity which carries with it the ontological indivisibility of matter and structure in the space-time metrical field, and thus also the epistemic unity of being and form in our scientific understanding of the universe. These advances have proved quite decisive, not only because they completed the dethronement of 'the mechanistic universe' begun by Clerk Maxwell's explanation of the electromagnetic field, but also because they broke through and overturned the phenomenalist and positivist conception of science stemming from Kant and Mach, and established the objective intelligibility of the universe, independent of our perceiving and conceiving of it.[6] Thus the paradigm of scientific activity which has permeated so much of our western culture, in accordance with which we start with 'neutral' or 'uninterpreted' observational phenomena, derive our concepts by way of logical abstraction from them, and elaborate scientific theories as convenient functional agreements between these concepts and observational phenomena, has crashed. In evaluating Einstein's achievement in this respect F. S. C. Northrop has written: 'This means that the positivistic theory that all theoretical meanings derive from empirical meanings is invalid. Furthermore, the thesis that the theoretically designated knowledge gives us knowledge of the subject matter of science and of *reality*, rather than merely knowledge of a subjective construct by a neo-Kantian kind of knower, confirms the thesis that the thing in itself can be scientifically known and handled by scientific method. Thus *ontology* is again restored, as well as epistemology, to a genuine scientific and philosophical status.'[7]

The discovery of the indissoluble unity of structure and substance, or of form and being, and not least the primacy of the inherently invisible, intangible structure of the space-time metrical field, has profound and immense implications for all human knowledge, for every human inquiry is carried on within the spatio-temporal structures of the contingent universe which are the bearers of its rational order. Moreover, the rejection of all radical dualism, ancient or modern, brings about an epistemological state of affairs in which a massive new synthesis is in process of emerging. Not only is science, as now pursued in accordance with the nature of things – κατὰ φύσιν – and therefore in terms of the natural coherences latent in the universe, a development and refinement of our ordinary experience and behaviour, rather than an increasing abstraction from them, but the ever-widening divergence between the special sciences, and not least the deep cultural split between the sciences and the humanities, are in process of being overcome from below in the very foundations of our knowledge of the universe. This applies no less to the relation between theological science and the other sciences, physical or human, for theologians also, like the scientists, pursue their inquiry within the contingent intelligibilities of space and time with which the Creator has endowed the universe including man himself. Since Christian theology is pursued not in terms of a God-man relationship, but in terms of a God-man-world, or God-world-man relationship, theological knowledge is bound to be closely related to the knowledge of the universe as the created medium of space and time through which God makes himself known to us, if only because God by his creation has placed man within the universe as that constituent element in it whereby the universe comes to know itself, as it were, and thus unfolds its latent structures and intelligibilities under the process of human inquiry and interaction with the universe. This is not to say that theological science and natural science can be treated in exactly the same way, because each, as is scientifically demanded, seeks to develop and express its knowledge in accordance with the nature of the field in which it is engaged in inquiry. The natural scientist inquires into the intelligible structures of contingent existence, to which indeed man himself belongs, while the theologian inquires of God himself the Creator of the universe and the Source of its contingent rational order, to which, again, he himself belongs. Thus theological and natural science both have their own proper objectives to pursue, but their work overlaps, for both operate through the same rational structures of space and time, as we have seen. While each develops specific modes of inquiry and verification conformable to the nature and direction of its distinctive field, each is what it is as a movement of human inquiry because of the profound coordination between human knowing and the space-time structures of the creation. It is the deeper understanding of that coordination today which has helped to bring about such a change in our conceptions of both science and theology, and thus of the interrelation between theological and natural science.

The purpose of this chapter, however, is not to discuss the interrelation of theology with the various sciences, physical or human, or indeed with natural science in general, but rather to allow theological science to face up to the kind of questions that have been forced upon us in our deeper knowledge of the universe in its latent objectivities, not least with respect to the epistemological foundations of theological inquiry. Theology must learn to do its own work within the revolutionary changes that have been going on in the foundations of knowledge, but to do that in such a way that it remains rigorously faithful to the nature of its own proper object, God the Creator and Redeemer of the world, and to the field of his revealing and saving interaction with man in the space-time universe in which he has planted man in order that man as such, creature of earth, may worship and have communion with him as his heavenly Father. At no point, then, can theology build upon the foundations of natural science or seek to accommodate itself to natural science and the changes that take place in its development, but what it can do, and must do, is to see what, *mutatis mutandis,* the revolutionary changes going on in our knowing habits of mind have to say about the kind of changes theology must make in its own field and on its own ground, as it learns to shake free of the false dualist principles of knowledge which have so insidiously influenced its pursuit in the past, principles to which Christian theology would never have succumbed had it been as faithful to its own scientific objective within its own distinctive field as it ought to have been and to the material content of God's self-revelation in and through the Incarnation of his Creator Word in Jesus Christ.

What do these revolutionary changes in epistemology, and in particular the rediscovered unity of form and being, mean for Christian theology? We are not concerned here primarily with the material content or doctrinal substance of theology but rather with the way in which we are bound to think theologically when we operate consistently with the indissoluble relations between structure and substance in the field of inquiry, and therefore in conformity with the deep interlocking of theoretical and empirical ingredients in the material content of theology. In answering this question we shall take our starting-point from three of Einstein's epigrammatic 'sayings' with which he was wont in characteristic fashion to throw into sharp relief certain decisive issues.

1. 'GOD DOES NOT PLAY DICE'[8]

This is the most well-known of Einstein's *logia*, but it has perhaps been most often misunderstood. He was apt to make this statement in his opposition to what he considered to be quixotic or random elements in contemporary quantum theory, e.g. the so-called 'uncertainty principle', and by way of declaring his own belief in a world of law and order which objectively exists. It was not intended to express 'determinism' which, as Pauli showed in a very significant letter to Born in 1954, Einstein energetically rejected.[9] Rather was it intended to insist that even in quantum theory we cannot rest content with anything less than structural field-laws through which we offer rigorous scientific description of the intrinsic orderliness of nature at the micro-physical as well as at every other level of reality. In other words, 'God does not play dice' formulates the fundamental belief, to which Einstein found himself driven more and more, in the objective intelligibility of the universe, independent of our conceptual construction. This is not to say that this objective intelligibility is to be construed in mechanistic concepts, or in the closed continuum of cause and effect especially when that is expressed by a geometry of rigid relations between bodies independent of time. Rather is it an objective intelligibility in the dynamic structures and transformations in the flow of space-time reality so extensive in its range that we can apprehend it only at relatively elementary levels, and only through what we may call 'open structures' even though they are mathematically precise in their formalisation.

'God does not play dice' imports, therefore, a concept of order, not simply as a regulative principle in the Kantian sense but as a state of affairs independent of us. The universe is so inherently orderly that it is accessible to our rational investigation in its inner constitutive relations, while in so far as the scientist allows his inquiry to be controlled by that immanent comprehensibility in the universe he may, to a measured degree, penetrate to a knowledge of things in themselves and grasp reality in its depth. That this is a way of thinking which breaks through neo-Kantian phenomenalism and observationalism in which the human knower is limited to the regulative and objectifying forms of his own thought-processes, is evident, for example, in the enormous advances of astrophysics in which we reach an orderly and reliable understanding of the universe that can be carried back through time, without loss of its significance and validity, to a state of affairs millions and millions of light years before the emergence of any sentient creature, let alone man. Here we have the emergence of a massive objectivity which, while valid independent of the 'observer', does not discount the knowing human subject, for he finds himself discovering and compelled to acknowledge an objective rationality governing nature which, precisely in knowing, he knows to reach beyond what he can reduce to forms of his own understanding.[10] In fact, the recognition of such a transcendent rationality, over which he has no control, is now discerned by the scientist not only to be essential to pure science but to human rationality as such.[11]

It hardly needs to be pointed out that such a view is much more congenial to classical Christian understanding of the relation of God to the world he has made than the positivist outlook which rests upon the bifurcation of nature into mind and body, subject and object, and the mechanistic conception of the universe to which that gave rise. It is in fact Christian teaching about creation and incarnation which produced the concept of contingent intelligibility upon which all modern science now rests, while it is the transcendence and oneness of God, the creative Source of all rational order, which give unity, identity, objectivity and comprehensiveness to the space-time medium in which we and all created reality are bracketed together in one world. We cannot pursue that train of ideas further now, but must content ourselves with noting the implication of the rediscovered unity of form and being for our understanding of God's self-revelation and self-communication to us within the spatio-temporal structures, objectivities and intelligibilities of this world. Dualist epistemologies, resting upon the model of visual perception, undoubtedly make havoc of divine revelation, for they are so restricted to the description of things only as they are related to ourselves that they cut off the appearances of things from their objective ground, and interpret them as symbolic representations which have meaning for us in so far as they evoke or occasion certain experiences within ourselves. Thus the New Testament revelation is subjected to a radically symbolic interpretation in terms of our human, moral and social responses, in rejection of any objective act or word of God, or any real communication of his own *self* in the incarnation. In such a context the New Testament is treated only as a record of the beliefs and experiences of the early Church, and Jesus Christ is reduced to a status of secondary significance and interpreted in terms of the symbolic objectification of a primitive religious and moral consciousness. What is really primitive, however, is precisely this pre-scientific way of thinking in pictures and images on the model of visual perception, that is, in terms only of a subject-object relation in which we cannot escape from ourselves – in the last resort this reduces all theology into some form of anthropology. In genuinely scientific thinking, however, while symbolic representation retains an essential place, we are concerned to penetrate into the objective coherences and structured interrelations of things in themselves – that is, into object-object relations in which our subject-object relations are transcended and controlled from beyond themselves by reference to the ontological structure of the realities being investigated. This transition from primitive to scientific thinking is one in which we move from *mythos* to *logos,* from image to inner logic, from subjectivity to objectivity. Now when we do that, we move away from the old observationalist and phenomenalist approach to the historical Jesus, which inevitably loses him, to a profoundly Christological approach which transcends cosmological and epistemological dualism alike in an understanding of Jesus Christ as God's *self*-communication to mankind within the space-time structures, objectivities and intelligibilities of our created existence. Far from being violated by the coming of God himself among us in this way, these structures, objectivities and intelligibilities are in fact creatively established and confirmed in their human, creaturely and contingent reality as they could not be otherwise. In other words, the sheer humanity of Jesus, far from being a mask or a symbol of a divine reality detached from it, is found to be the constitutive form of God's self-giving to us in indissoluble union with himself, and is maintained as such in its perfect integrity and reality as humanity. In Jesus Christ God has revealed himself and imparted himself to us within the space-time continuum of this world in such a way that he is inherently in himself what he is toward us in Jesus and what he is toward us in Jesus he is inherently in himself. Here then, in the *homoousion* and the *hypostatic union,* to use the classical terms, there is discerned an indissoluble unity of form and being in the material content of God's self-communication to us in Jesus Christ, which constitutes the ground and the justification for the unity of form and being in a rigorously scientific approach to our understanding of him. The God who reveals himself to us in Jesus Christ is a God who does not play dice with us, for the pattern of his self-revealing, the order of his love and grace manifest in the incarnation of his Son, is one which objectively exists and is dynamically operative in his own eternal Being.

2. 'GOD DOES NOT WEAR HIS HEART ON HIS SLEEVE'[12]

If 'God does not play dice' stands for Einstein's profound conviction that there is immanent in the universe an ordered regularity of all events, 'God does not wear his heart on his sleeve' stands for the no less profound conviction that the real secrets of nature, the reasons for that order, cannot be read off the patterns of its phenomenal surface. That was, apparently, a conviction he had already reached as a child when he first examined a compass and found that the determined behaviour of the needle did not at all fit into the nature of events in his direct experience. 'Something deeply hidden had to be behind things.'[13]

This was not to say that Einstein was concerned to look for hidden causes detached from, and of a different category from, the ordered regularity of things we experience in our everyday world, for he was just as concerned to reject 'occult' causes as Bacon or Newton, and indeed was more concerned to reject the 'occult' than they if only because he rejected the kind of dualism upon which the occult thrives.[14] Einstein's concern was rather to penetrate into the underlying ontological structure of the ordered regularity of things, to which the phenomenal patterns of that regularity are coordinated, by which they are controlled, and in reference to which they are to be accounted for. It must be frankly admitted that the pattern of events manifest on the observed surface is always relative to the observer, his private sensations and his particular stance in time and space – that is after all the Galilean principle of relativity – but, on dualist assumptions, that means that we will never be able to reach knowledge of the real or external world. If we reject dualism, however, and operate with the inherence of form in being, then a different procedure must be adopted. Here we have to do with the inner imageless constitutive structure of things, which is invariant through all relativity for the human knower, and which cannot be grasped by relativist observational means, but only by intellective penetration or theoretic insight. While outward shape on the surface of existence remains observable and imageable and is variant for every observer, the invisible and imageless ontological structure remains constant and invariant for all observers. As such it provides the objective frame underlying the observable variations correlated with it, and therein constitutes the integrative force of their order on the phenomenal level, i.e. even of their surface connection as appearances. To grasp nature like that unitively in its objective depth and inherent relatedness, and in such a way as to do full justice to the differences and relativities of observational experience without allowing them to disintegrate into pluralistic relativism, is what science is about. But it does mean that we have to think in a dimension of ontological depth in which the surface of things is coordinated with a deep, invisible, intelligible structure, and thus think empirical and theoretical, phenomenal and noumenal levels of reality conjunctively together, if we are really to reach knowledge of things in accordance with their distinctive and constitutive nature. 'God does not wear his heart on his sleeve.' Really to know is to be in touch with a depth of reality which has the capacity for disclosure beyond what we can anticipate or imagine.

There is an obvious application of this to our knowledge of Jesus Christ which reinforces the finding we have already reached as to the necessity of a proper Christology if we are not after all to lose him in the relativities of man's religious and cultural responses. Jesus Christ is not to be understood by trying to fit him into the surface regularities of other phenomena or by interpreting his decisive significance by reference to establishable observations and deduction from them, but only by penetrating into the non-observable, intelligible reality in such a way that we grasp Christ in his wholeness and inherent force – that is, only as we penetrate into his essential *logos* constitutive of his incarnate actuality. Here above all we have to learn the discipline of thinking conjunctively together his human-historical and his divine-eternal aspects, and thus to think of him from the start as at once human and divine, one indivisible whole reality. It is the prevalence still of obsolete dualist assumptions that makes people approach the fact of Christ either from his human, empirical side, in the hope of deducing concepts about him of divine import, or from his divine, eternal side, in the expectation of discerning the relevance of his saving power to human existence; but the effect of such a bifurcation is to reproduce again the heretical tensions between ebionite and docetic ideas of the past which have proved both damaging and sterile. However, if we abandon those dualist assumptions and attempt to approach the fact of Christ as an indivisible whole, in order to let it disclose itself to our inquiry out of its own ontological depth, then we find ourselves understanding him *theologically* in the light of his own intrinsic significance, and discover that the divinity of Christ belongs to and undergirds the sheer irreducible fact of Christ even in his human actuality, just as much as the intelligible structures of space-time, which are imperceptible and intangible, belong to the everyday world of actual and visible events, and account for what they are even in the observational variations in which we cannot but experience and describe them. A scientific theological approach of this kind does not operate with 'picturing models' built up from observational phenomena, but with 'disclosure models', i.e. with rational structures in our knowing of Christ which are correlative to the self-disclosure of God and which are forced upon us by the inner relations of the one God who meets us and saves us in Jesus Christ as Father, Son and Holy Spirit. That is to say, God's self-communication to us in and through the incarnation penetrates into the objective and ontological structures of our human existence in the space-time medium of this world in such a way that it sets up within it the laws of its own internal relations and our rational understanding takes on the imprint of what it comes to know, the triune reality of God himself. Thus the Christological approach inevitably moves from what is known as the economic Trinity of God in his revealing and saving activity in history to the ontological Trinity, for God is in himself inherently, antecedently and eternally what he is toward us as Father, Son and Holy Spirit. In this way we penetrate into the deep objective structure of God's self-communication to us in Jesus Christ in such a way as to discover that the doctrine of the Trinity constitutes the basic grammar of theological understanding with reference to which all aspects of God in his relation to the world are to be construed. Here in the Holy Trinity we have the ultimate constitutive relations in God himself, the fundamental 'Constant' upon which the intelligibility and objectivity of all our knowledge of God finally repose, invariant through all the relativity of human knowers. Without the unifying simplicity and objectivity of that 'Constant', we lapse back into the abstractions of dualism in which a serious disjunction opens up, not only between natural knowledge of the one God and revealed knowledge of the triune God, but between kerygma and dogma, for then the revelation of God in Jesus Christ becomes detached from its ontological structure in the incarnation of the Logos and a serious decomposition of both kerygmatic and dogmatic form takes place – which is precisely the sad story of much modern theology as it has become trapped in the fatal dualism of the empirical and theoretical components of knowledge.

3. 'GOD IS DEEP BUT NOT DEVIOUS'

This is my rendering of Einstein's intriguing *logion: 'Raffiniert ist der Herrgott, aber boshaft ist er nicht'.*[15] If 'God does not wear his heart on his sleeve' is intended to express the idea that the secrets of nature cannot be read off its phenomenal surface, 'God is deep but not devious' expresses the complexity and subtlety yet ultimate simplicity and reliability of the universe. That is to say, the immanent order hidden behind the intricate and often baffling interconnections which we find in the universe is essentially trustworthy, for in spite of all that might appear to the contrary when we come up against sets of events for which there seems to be no rational explanation, the universe is not arbitrary or evil. God does not play tricks with us.

This conviction relates to Einstein's discovery that 'light has a unique metaphysical status in the universe'[16]. If all bodies in motion are defined with reference to space and time, all space and time are defined with reference to light. Undefined by reference beyond itself, light is the great constant, with reference to which all else we know in nature is relationally known and defined, and upon which we can invariably rely, and that holds good in spite of the fact that astrophysical exploration of the universe as far as we can reach through space and time raises problems for us which may appear intractable to the laws of physics.[17] Throughout all the dynamic, multivariable structures which pervade the universe of bodies in motion, somehow the constancy of light with its unique metaphysical status supports the conviction that 'God does not play tricks with us', i.e. that there is an immanent order in the universe of the inviolability of which we remain totally convinced, for apart from it the universe would nowhere be accessible to rational inquiry and we ourselves who are creatures of space and time belonging to the same universe could not be capable of rational thought or behaviour of any kind. Thus while in the logical sense such an order in the universe is neither verifiable nor falsifiable, it remains the most persistent of all our scientific convictions for without it there could be no science at all: hence we do not believe that there is or could be anything that can ultimately count against it. To employ another theological paraphrase, in Einstein's vein, 'God does not let us down'.

However, this kind of immanent order, dynamic though it is and compatible with multivariable forms of existence and life throughout the universe, cannot but cause serious difficulties for theology if it is generalised to comprehend all human existence, for it cannot account for evil, pain, error and sin, that is, for disorder and irrationality in the world, which, face to face with God's self-revelation in Jesus Christ we know to be in conflict with his divine will and love. Certainly theology is, and can be pursued, only within the medium of space and time, and therefore only through the spatio-temporal structures of the natural order which it shares with all human rational inquiry, for it is through that medium that God makes himself known to man and through that medium that man is summoned to respond to God's self-revelation, and therefore theology must respect the spatio-temporal structures of the natural order, and not least the objectivity and constancy of those structures which God has given them through the status of created light within the universe, for all this belongs to the covenanted steadfastness with which God continuously sustains the creation in its contingent being and intelligibility. Nevertheless, theology is not grounded upon the natural order of things, but is grounded ultimately upon the transcendent Logos or uncreated Light of God, and takes its form from God's interaction with man in the space-time track of the universe as he brings his creative order to bear upon him in such a way as to intersect the disorder and irrationality which have somehow irrupted into his existence in the form of evil, pain, error and sin, and to redeem human, and indeed all creaturely, being for the perfect will and love of the Creator. Far from interfering or conflicting with the created order of things – for that has come from God – God's creative interaction gives it a deeper level at which it is fulfilled and thus establishes it, and wherever disorder may manifest itself there he is at work in his creating and redeeming purpose restoring it to order and goodness beyond anything it is capable of in itself. Hence theological activity can be pursued by men, who are themselves constituents of the created order, only by thinking the levels of the created and the creative orders conjunctively together. That is why theological statements are properly not without empirical correlates in our space-time creaturely reality and are therefore consistent with the multi-levelled structures of the universe as they become revealed to our scientific inquiry, even though they are grounded beyond in the transcendent rationality of the living and loving God who is the Creator and Sustainer of the whole universe of space and time and the Source of its contingent rationality.

The fact that theology is concerned with God in this way, in the interaction between his transcendent rationality and contingent rationality, or his uncreated Light and created light (whether physical or mental), means that theology cannot but regard the objective structures and regularities that are disclosed in the advance of scientific knowledge as essentially open, stable though they are, to a transcendent Source toward which they contingently point by the very nature of their intelligibility which demands completion beyond itself, even though that pointing by reason of its contingency is unable to terminate upon that Source. Hence it is understandable that theology cannot but regard the unique metaphysical but finite status of light, and the order it involves in the universe, as 'reflecting' through all its immense difference the infinite status of the uncreated Light and Law of God, with reference to which all finite realities and intelligibilities are relationally and dynamically to be defined.[18] It is also understandable that in thinking conjunctively in this way of created light and uncreated Light, theologians should hold to their belief in the transcendent Order and Law of the living God, the Father Almighty, the Creator of all things visible and invisible, in spite of everything that may appear to count against it. Strange as it may at first appear, the steadfastness of that belief in the face of evil, pain, error and sin, which are admittedly so baffling, irrational and disorderly, is not damaged but reinforced by them, just because they are contradictory to the will and love of the heavenly Father. In other words, it is precisely because they believe so persistently and unshakeably in the transcendent Order and Law of God, in the constancy and invariance of his holy Love, that theologians find their faith rebelling against the presence of evil, pain, error and sin wherever it is to be found in the world. But of course the real and actual ground of that faith is in Jesus Christ, the incarnate, crucified and risen Son, who is the unreserved *self-communication* of God to man in the very midst of his darkness and stupidity where evil and disorder are so deeply entrenched in his existence; for that means that God has not held himself aloof from us in our dark and terrible experiences, the self-inflicted hurt and unappeasable agony of pain and guilt in which we are entrapped. God has given nothing less than himself to us there, and brought the complete negation of his holy Love to bear upon our disorder,[19] thus revealing to us that the ultimate order that prevails invariantly through all the relativities of our human experience in evil, pain, error and sin, is the Love of God. That is to say, there is no irrational enigma behind the creation, but only the divine order of divine Love. Above all the passion of Christ insists – and this is backed up by the pledge of God's own being incarnate in him – that, come what may, this divine order of divine Love will finally prevail throughout all space and time, for he who made the terrible Cross to be saving power of God is able by the same Cross to make all things work together for good to those who love him, and nothing will ever be able to separate them from the love of God. The God who confronts the world in the crucifixion of his Son is deep, but never devious! 'God is Light and in him is no darkness at all'. He does not deceive us, but remains forever constant and invariant in the perfection of the Law of his own eternal Being, and as Creator and Consummator of the universe, he is at work setting up within it an invincible order of love which is a creaturely reflection of his own. Of course there remains a great deal in the world that baffles us and challenges our faith, not least the terrible irrationality and stupidity which have somehow overtaken the creatures God has made, together with the monstrous suffering of the innocent, in animal as well as human life, which we dare not minimise; but in the revelation of the constancy of the Light and Love of God we have been given the ultimate centre by reference to which we may find our way through the enigmas and labyrinths of our perplexities, waiting for that glorious end when there will be a new creation with the final Advent of Jesus Christ our Lord.

NOTES

1. *The Structure of Scientific Revolutions*, pp. 121, 150. Kuhn appears to rely rather heavily upon the thought of Michael Polanyi – see especially *Science, Faith and Society*. 1946, new edition 1964, and *Personal Knowledge*, Aberdeen Gifford Lectures of 1951–2, published in 1957 (cf. p. 172f.).
2. See Israel Scheffler, *Science and Subjectivity*, 1967, pp. 74ff.
3. See Sir Edmund Whittaker, *Space and Spirit*, 1946, pp. 53ff.
4. This is precisely what Einstein had persistently demanded of quantum theorists – see Max Born, *The Born-Einstein Letters*, 1971, *passim*.
5. A. Einstein, *Out of My Later Years*, 'Max Planck in Memoriam', p. 209, New York, 1950.
6. A very clear statement of Einstein's view of the relation of the concepts of physics 'to a real outside world . . . independent of the perceiving subject', is given in an essay sent to Max Born, *The Born-Einstein Letters*, pp. 168–173. While Einstein's demand in quantum theory for 'a more complete and direct' description of reality, i.e. irrespective of the observer, clashed with quantum theory as then advocated, it is becoming increasingly evident that his demands for hard objectivity are being met. Cf. here, M. Bunge (editor), *Quantum Theory and Reality*, essays by Karl Popper, 'Quantum Mechanics without "The Observer"'; and K. Popper, *Objective Knowledge*, the chapter on 'Epistemology without a Knowing Subject', pp. 106ff.
7. P. A. Schilpp (editor), *Albert Einstein: Philosopher-Scientist*, p. 407 (italics mine).
8. Max Born, *The Born-Einstein Letters*, pp. 149, 199.
9. *Ibid.*, pp. 221ff.
10. See the opening chapter of *Personal Knowledge*, where Michael Polanyi works out some of the implications of relativity theory for a fresh understanding of objectivity, pp. 3–17; and see further, ch. 3 on 'Order', and *Scientific Thought and Social Reality*, edited by F. Schwartz *(Psychological Issues*, vol. VIII/no. 4, Monograph 32, 1974), chs. 4, 5, 7–9.
11. This point is powerfully argued by Polanyi in *Science, Faith and Society*, 1946, new edition 1964.
12. See F. S. C. Northrop, *Man, Nature and God*, 1962, p. 209f.
13. P. A. Schilpp (editor), *Albert Einstein: Philosopher-Scientist*, p. 9.
14. Dualist thought 'gets rid' of the 'occult' only by reducing everything to phenomenal or material reality.
15. Cited by J. Bernstein, *Einstein* (Fontana, 1973), p. 61, who translates it more literally, 'God is sophisticated, but not malicious'. Cf. the reported variation of this Einsteinian saying: *Gott ist listig, aber nicht hinterlistig*.
16. See F. S. C. Northrop, with reference to a conversation with H. Weyl in 1927, *Man, Nature and God*, 1962, p. 206.

17. The question must be raised whether our use of 'infinites' in these calculations does not involve the same kind of idealisation as Euclidean geometry which falsifies our apprehension of the real four-dimensional world. If so, the problems that face us may not be due to the nature of structures in the real world so much as to a process of abstraction in our regulative equations.

18. It is highly significant that classical patristic theology developed this way of thinking of God in terms of light; while all things are known through their illumination by light, light is to be known only in terms of itself, in its self-shining, like God. Nor is it surprising that it was classical patristic theology which, with John Philoponos, developed the first physics of light, as also a 'modern' notion of 'impetus', and translated into physical terms the relational views of space and time which grew out of its understanding of the creation and incarnation.

19. This is not to imply that God's Love is negative, but that by being purely, wholly, exclusively Love, it negates what is not-love.

CHAPTER VIII

Newton, Einstein and Scientific Theology*

EVERYTHING about us today tells us that we live in a world which will be increasingly dominated by empirical and theoretic science. This is the world in which the Church lives and proclaims its message about Jesus Christ. It is not an alien world, for it is in this world of space and time that God has planted us. He made the universe and endowed man with gifts to investigate and understand it. Just as he made life to produce itself, so he has made the universe with man as an essential constituent in it, that it may bring forth and articulate knowledge of itself. Regarded in this light the pursuit of science is one of the ways in which man excercises the dominion in the earth which he was given at his creation. That is how, for example, Francis Bacon understood the work of human science, as man's obedience to God. Science is a religious duty, while man as scientist can be spoken of as *the priest of creation,* whose task it is to interpret the books of nature, to understand the universe in its wonderful structures and harmonies, and to bring it all into orderly articulation, so that it fulfils its proper end as the vast theatre of glory in which the Creator is worshipped and praised.

* Eighth Annual Keese Lecture delivered at The University of Tennessee at Chattanooga, 26 April, 1971.

Nature itself is dumb, but it is man's part to bring it to word, to be its mouth through which the whole universe gives voice to the glory and majesty of the living God.

That is the universe of space and time in and through which God has revealed himself to man, and it is in and through that universe, as it comes to view under human inquiry, that we are surely to develop and formulate our knowledge of God. The natural scientist and the theologian are both at work within the space-time structures of that universe, the natural scientist inquiring into the intelligible structures of contingent existence, to which man himself belongs as a constituent element in the universe, and the theologian inquiring of God himself the Creator of the universe and the source of its created rationalities, to which man also belongs. Theological and natural science each has its proper objective to pursue but their work inevitably overlaps, for both operate through the same rational structures of space and time; while each develops modes of inquiry and verification in accordance with the nature and direction of its distinctive field, each is what it is as a movement of human inquiry because of the profound coordination between human knowing and the space-time structures of the creation.

It is the deeper realisation of that coordination which we have reached in our own times that has effected a profound change in our understanding of what science is about, and thus inevitably of the relation between natural science and theological science. There are many people who still find it rather difficult to speak of theology as a science or even of theology and science in the same breath like that. If theology is only a subjective movement of life and thought and if science is equated with technology or is regarded as merely an instrumentalist activity, then of course that would be understandable, but it is precisely the kind of bifurcation in thought that gives rise to that disjunction that has now collapsed under the advances of science itself. Thus the problems that many people have in relating theology to science or in thinking of theology itself as a pure science, operating on its own ground in its own distinctive field, appear to come from a rather obsolete notion of science tied up with a dualist outlook upon the universe.

What then is modern science about? Consider the astonishing complexity and richness of nature as it has become disclosed to us through the advances of the special sciences: all this demands of us a deeper and more comprehensive grasp of science than that into which we have been forced within the concept of a mechanistic universe and the rigid instrumentalism to which it gave rise. This is nowhere more evident today than in biology, where the great break-through for which we have been hoping has been obstructed in advance through reductionism into mechanistic concepts. Nature must be courted, not imposed upon. We must allow it to develop and flower under our investigation, if we are really to know it in accordance with what it is, and not simply along the lines of our tormenting distortion and twisting of its subtle patterns and deep underlying structures. Nature is to be explored and understood only through developing empirical relations grounded in its own inherent connections, for it does not yield its deepest secrets to the kind of inquisition we impose upon it within artificial and alien mechanisms. In other words, science is not something to be set against our ordinary and natural experience in the world, but is, on the contrary, a development and refinement of it, a deeper and deeper penetration into the rational order with which we already operate in normal behaviour within the universe. Thus the objective of science in every field is to discover the relations of things and events at different levels of complexity, and to develop our understanding and expression of them in such a way that their real nature becomes progressively disclosed to us. What we are concerned to do is to connect things and think their interrelations – hence the importance of generating appropriate modes and systems of thought, as open and simple as possible, through which the distinctive kind of relation that obtains between the things we investigate can come to view and the specific form of order it embodies can be exhibited. And so we have the double task of penetrating into and determining again and again a new kind of connection and of lifting up our minds to a new level where we can apprehend and bring the new kind of connection to appropriate formulation.

One of the chief characteristics of modern science is that we have now learned to operate with the integration of *form* and *being* in laying bare the dynamic structures and transformations in the flow of space-time reality. This is the immense significance of field theory and of the way in which pure science, e.g. in field physics, has had to move beyond the abstractive procedures of positivist science, or to treat them only within certain methodologically imposed limits. That is to say, here we operate with an objective comprehensibility in the nature of things that is independent of our perceiving or conceiving of them, as Einstein used to say. This is particularly evident in the development and implications of relativity theory in which the empirical and theoretic components of scientific activity have been coordinated in such a way as to effect a fundamental change in the basic structure of physics and an equally fundamental change in our understanding of the structure of the universe. Now with the recovery of the unity of form and being (which the artifical mechanisms of Newtonian science had torn apart) there take place also profound changes in *the modes of rationality* we develop, in *the nature of the cognitive instruments* we have to use, and in the *procedures of verification* that are forced on us from the nature of that into which we inquire. We are still in the midst of this transition from Newton to Einstein, for not a little of our science, and not merely the social sciences, have been slow to adjust themselves to this revolutionary change, with the result that considerable disorientation and tension are everywhere evident in our western culture. We are not concerned at the moment with the problems that arise out of this dislocation in culture, but with the nature of the scientific revolution and its implication for theology. It will help us to see something of what is going on, however, if we probe a little into the mutations of thought that lie behind it.

We may start with the Reformation when a considerable change in the structure and method of theology took place, in an attempt to break free from the rigid thought-forms of mediaeval scholasticism in order to set theological science squarely upon its own proper foundations. It was characteristic of this theology, as found for example in works of John Calvin, that theologians were concerned to elucidate and order their understanding of God solely out of his own self-revelation, and therefore in accordance with the inner principles and connections found to operate in the field of God's interaction with man and the world, and not in accordance with external authorities or preconceived principles. Theology of this kind inevitably called in question the relevance of structures of thought abstractly derived, e.g. from sense experience, and constituted into an independent conceptual system on its own, and thus it resisted any attempt to interpret actual knowledge of God, deriving from his Word and Spirit, within the epistemological framework which such a system already involved, on the double ground that it would do violence to the material content of knowledge of God and sin seriously against scientific method.

At the same time, and not unconnected with this movement of change in Christian theology, the new science that emerged out of the Renaissance took a similar line, in its determination to understand nature out of itself alone and not in accordance with final causes or *a priori* assumptions. It was essentially empirical, *a posteriori* science that declines to prescribe in advance how we are to know in abstraction from what we seek to know, but insists that the nature of the realities being investigated must be allowed to reveal to us the appropriate forms in which they are to be grasped and known. Thus the new science was dedicated to the exploration and understanding of the created universe on its own evidential basis and in accordance with its own interior principles, and so it set itself to the task of finding ways in which nature could be persuaded to reveal its deep underlying connections and of grasping and formulating them in 'laws'. It was in this way, for example, that Newton came to formulate his celebrated 'laws of motion'.

It is significant that it was to *physics* pursued in this way that the term *dogmatic science* seems first to have been applied, i.e. the kind of knowledge which is forced upon us by the nature and structure of reality as it comes to light under our inquiries, to which we give positive assent, so to speak, under the moral commandment of the universe itself, and are obliged to affirm as having universal validity. It was the positive character of this knowledge and its formulation in 'laws of nature' that the expression *dogmatic* was designed to signify. It was taken of course from the old Greek distinction between the *dogmatikoi* and the *skeptikoi* developed in the New Academy, and nowhere more clearly set out than in the work of Sextus Empiricus known to us as *Adversus Dogmaticos*. In contrast to the 'sceptics' who were concerned only with academic questions, i.e. the kind of questions that do not lead to affirmations, the philosophers and scientists (they were identical in those days) and the 'mechanists' (or engineers) were dubbed 'dogmatics' for they were concerned with the kind of questions that do yield positive answers and thus contribute to the advancement of knowledge. That is the sense in which the expression 'dogmatic' was applied to the new science in its determination to put to nature the kind of question which would yield positive results, and thus develop a mode of scientific inquiry in which authoritarian pre-conceptions and merely academic or sceptical questions would equally be set aside. It was after being applied to physics in this way that the expression *dogmatic science*, or *dogmatics* came to be applied to the new positive theology which came out of the Reformation.

Before we go further, it will be worth our while pausing to consider the new kind of question that was now being asked, and the positive nature of the affirmation to which it led. This was the *interrogatio*, rather than the *quaestio*, i.e. an interrogative, rather than a problematic, form of inquiry. It was Lorenzo Valla who came up with this first. He wanted something more than the kind of question that had been traditionally asked in the West after Boethius, which was directed at untieing a knot in some tangled piece of knowledge that we already have. In the mediaeval mode, this proceeded by posing problem questions, drawing distinctions, and by a logical process of argumentation for and against, straightening out the lines of thought from the premises to the conclusions: but all that this seemed to succeed in doing was to clarify knowledge that we already have. What Valla wanted was a mode of inquiry in which questions yield results that are entirely new, giving rise to knowledge that we cannot derive by an inferential process from what we already know. He found that kind of question in the works of the Latin Stoic lawyers and educators like Cicero and Quintilian: that is, for example, the kind of question employed in a court of law where documents, witnesses, states of affairs are interrogated directly and openly, without any prior conception of what the truth might be, so as to let the truth itself, the whole truth and nothing but the truth, come to view. It was that interrogative kind of questioning that Valla directed to historical investigation, and it yielded almost at once the startling knowledge that some of the famous mediaeval papal decretals were forgeries. Valla then suggested its wider application, and its use as what we would call 'a logic of scientific discovery' – his term was *ars inveniendi,* which he contrasted with the *ars diiudicandi*: logic as the art of finding out things rather than merely logic as the art of drawing distinctions and connecting them together. He called therefore for an active inquiry (*activa inquisitio*) to be applied in the development of new knowledge. Valla injected this into the Renaissance study of law, and other thinkers followed him, such as Rodolph Agricola of Heidelberg and John Calvin of Geneva, although Calvin was also influenced by his own teacher of Renaissance law, Alciati. Calvin applied it to the interpretation of the Scriptures, and thus became the father of modern biblical interpretation, but Francis Bacon applied it to the interpetation of the books of nature, as well as to the books of God, and became the father of modern empirical science, not of course that he was himself a great scientist – he lacked the mathematics for that – but he conceived of the empirical method which was to become so tellingly important. Now it is highly significant that several of the greatest men of science, apart from Bacon, such as Copernicus and Galileo, also took their early studies in Renaissance law and became scientists by learning to put the interrogative question to nature in the same way as it had been put to history and literature by others.

Open inquiry of this kind, however, gave rise to positive affirmation as its natural correlate. Precisely by allowing things to disclose themselves to us unobstructed by our prescriptive patterns of thought, it made room for the kind of knowledge that is forced upon us by the nature and structure of reality, which we must affirm, and which it would be irrational for us not to affirm: thus open questions and positive concepts are epistemically correlated. That is why, as we have seen, the new science became so conscious of its dogmatic character. In order to elucidate that further, it may be enlightening to draw upon an analogy developed by Michael Polanyi. Communication theory defines a noise, in contrast to any distinctive series of signals, as a random sequence of sound, conveying no information, message or meaning.. A tune, on the other hand, for example the song of the Baltimore Oriole, or the Italian Nightingale, is a distinctive series of signals with a pattern which signifies something or conveys definite information such as the identity of the singer. Now any single, identifiable message is ideally represented by only one configuration of signals, but the opposite holds for a noise – no significance whatsoever is attached to any group of signals that are a mere noise, for the chance sounds which compose it could well have been quite different. In contrast to that, however, once we have recognised a series of signals or a sequence of events as orderly and meaningful, we cannot think that it might just as well have been otherwise, as Polanyi says, so that we are forced to affirm it with universal intent.

This is what happens when we recognise an intelligible pattern or an underlying order in nature: we affirm it positively and with a necessary exclusiveness. That is why we operate with a minimum principle in the formulation of natural laws. It is in this connection that C. F. von Weizsäcker refers to de Fermat's principle that light takes the shortest path between two points. When we apply that to the formulation of a natural law, we find one possible path forcing itself on us as the actual one, while the others are thereby stamped as really impossible and unentertainable. That is the exclusiveness of a natural law, where we have to do with a structure of reality which we can conceive only in one way, and which we have to conceive in that way in accordance with the nature of things. That is not to question the fact that there are usually several different ways of representing a natural law, but to claim that the structures thus represented have to be thought and framed in our concepts in accordance with their inherent or material logic. Natural laws of this kind, as A. N. Whitehead reminds us, are the *dogmas* of natural science.

It was in this sense that scientific theology after the Reformation came to develop its *dogmas,* positive assertions forced on us by the nature of the realities into which we inquire, and which by their objective structures we are compelled to affirm. We think theologically only as we have to think in accordance with the nature of things, and in consonance with the *interior principles* that become disclosed in the field of our inquiry.

What are these principles of the new science? How did Newton, for example, regard the *principia* which he made use of in his celebrated *Philosophiae Naturalis Principia Mathematica*? They are not to be understood in the Aristotelian sense of *principia,* that is, as fixed premises from which we proceed by logical argumentation. They are not the linear principles or axioms used in the traditional logico-deductive or logico-inductive processes, for that whole approach is now set aside in an attempt to find a way of penetrating into a field of experience which will lay bare its inner structure. But as Newton discovered, that requires the development of appropriate rationalities or cognitive instruments by which the field can be grasped in its depth and through which the scientists can distinguish and articulate its interior principles. It was for this purpose that Newton invented and elaborated the differential calculus – a discovery which he shared with Leibniz, but with which, unlike Leibniz, he was able to coordinate the theoretic and the empirical elements of knowledge of the universe in such a way as to bring to light and formulate the laws of motion. And so the elaboration of variational principles have had their place in physics ever since.

This represents an enormous advance in our understanding of the universe and in the basic procedure of science, but fundamental problems began to arise in the whole fabric of Newtonian science and in the Newtonian universe. These came partly from the phenomenalism initiated by Galileo and developed through Locke and Kant, and partly also from the confluence of Newtonian and Cartesian thought, and are of such importance for the development of scientific thought from Newton to Einstein that we must pay some attention to them.

(a) The first has to do with Newton's concept of absolute space and time, although the difficulty to which it gave rise took a long time to appear. For Newton space and time, which he linked to the divine 'sensorium', formed a vast envelope that contained all that goes on in the universe, inertially conditioning events and our knowledge of them, without itself being affected by them – i.e. it was independent of all that it embraced, and in that sense 'absolute'. Thus space and time, everywhere homogeneous and isotropic in character, constitute an inertial system, the point of absolute rest, by reference to which all our knowledge of the universe is derived and formulated. Together with the particle theory of nature, this inevitably gave rise to the idea of the mechanistic universe and the static concepts that go along with it, which have dominated the

whole of western science for two or three hundred years. It was within this outlook upon God and the universe, and with concepts of this kind, that Protestant theology developed, or perhaps we should say, lapsed back, into scholastic rationalism.

(b) Interwoven with all this was the elaboration of science by way of abstraction from observational experience and the quantitative organisation of phenomenal data for pragmatic ends. Together with the split between subject and object, knowing and being, and the notion of 'representative perception', to which the new phenomenalism gave rise, this led more and more to an emphasis upon abstractive concepts and their logico-deductive manipulation in the formulation of scientific theories or hypotheses. Newton's claim that he invented no hypotheses but deduced them from observation played into this rationalistic positivism, now rapidly developing in European science, which operated on the one hand with a logical bridge between concepts and experience, but disclaimed on the other hand any metaphysical claims as to the relation between its 'working hypotheses' and being. Thus the way of abstraction from observational experience ends up by tearing such a gap between knowing and being that, far from being allowed to provide any independent control over our knowing, being becomes progressively alienated from it by the merely pragmatic or technological nature of our concepts and systems. And so abstractive, positivist science on its part becomes more and more trapped within the artificial structure of its own conventions.

(c) We must now take into account David Hume's radical criticism of the principle of causality. This had the effect of depriving science of any valid foundation in necessary connections obtaining between actual events and of leaving it with nothing more reliable than habits of mind rooted in association. Something had to be done therefore to provide science with a stable structure. This forced Kant to take up the question as to the conditions under which valid knowledge is possible, and to develop regulative principles within which Newton's laws of motion could be given unassailable formulation. What Kant did, in effect, was to transfer absolute space and time from the divine sensorium, which contains and inertially conditions all that God has made, to the mind of man, where it constitutes once again an inertial system conditioning all that the human mind grasps or contains without being itself modified by experience. This was the so-called 'Copernican revolution' in which the human mind is thought of as constructing knowledge out of phenomenal realities, i.e. in which the intellect does not draw its laws out of nature but imposes its laws upon nature. Thus the science which began by putting its question to nature, humbly in the form of a servant, as Bacon expressed it (following Calvin's method of theological inquiry), ends up by putting its question to nature in the prescriptive mode of the judge who demands of the prisoner at the bar that he answer the question strictly in accordance with the stipulations under which it was formulated. It is thus the form in which the question is put that determines the answer that is received. In this way Kant played an essential part in the development of the idea that man is himself the creator of 'the scientific world' and of the equation of science with technology. All it needed was a replacing of the Kantian *synthetic a priori* with an evolutionary explanation of the 'preconceptions' through which science organises our observational concepts for the Machian brand of positivism to arise, with its rationalistic functionalism and its complete disjunction of form from being.

Other problems also cropped up in the history of science after Newton, deriving from the Enlightenment, such as the failure to take into account certain destructive tendencies at work in the human mind which, important though they are, need not detain us now. Sufficient has been said to show that the whole trend of this development had the effect of restricting science within the rigid structures of a particulate view of nature, and within modes of thought that were tied down to sensed experience of particulars upon which logico-deductive operations were carried out. Within this development the concepts of *principia* and *hypothesis* suffered a serious lapse from the change that came over them in Newton's thought, although as we have seen, he contributed to this: indeed it was forced upon him by the mechanistic system which he built up, in which *principia* operating from a point of absolute rest tended to take on the very character of fixity which they had in the rejected Aristotelian science. Yet it is difficult to see how Newton and his successors could have operated otherwise, so long as they were dominated by an epistemology of perception, for then some static or mathematical space and time had to be postulated in order to deliver knowledge of the universe from its relativism for perceivers and thus to emancipate it for the kind of universal and objective validity demanded by science.

More and more, however, the mechanistic universe proved unsatisfactory. This was made particularly clear after the discovery of the electromagnetic field and the failure of classical science to account for it in mechanistic concepts. It was the assumption of the existence of an inertial system conditioning our knowledge as well as causing events that proved so obstructive, for in the nature of the case it could not cope with experimental results that conflicted with observation, and this became particularly difficult in the Kantian reinterpretation of scientific knowledge, as even Ernst Mach discerned. Then of course came the chance discovery of four-dimensional geometry and with it the realisation that the geometrical structures of classical physics could not be detached from changes in space and time with which field theory operated. The time was ripe for another enormous stride forward in which science broke out of the enclosure of the mechanistic system and its static concepts and fixed *principia,* which came with Einstein through relativity theory and the new axiomatic geometries of space and time. This step forward involved a step back to Newton in a detachment of his postulational thinking from his claim to have deduced theory from observational data, and so Einstein followed the method of Newton in the 'free invention' of a new cognitive instrument for deeper penetration into the intelligible order of the universe. It was 'free' in the sense that it was not reached under logical control from fixed premises, and it was 'invented' under the pressure of the nature of the universe upon his intuitive apprehension of it. Thus, taking his cue from Newton's differential equations, and from Maxwell's use of partial differential equations in field theory, Einstein developed a new mode of rationality known as *mathematical invariance.* This had the effect of breaking through Kantian phenomenalism and Machian positivism, and of establishing a genuine *ontology* in which the scientific mind was at grips with objective structures and the intrinsic intelligibility of the universe. This involved a radical change in outlook upon the universe, for it meant a rejection of dualism, and a way of thinking of the universe in its inherent unity of form and being. For that reason 'mathematical invariance' has two senses, referring to the cognitive instrument through which the mind penetrates into the structure inherent in nature, and referring also to the invariant structure in nature which is irrespective of any or every observer. The epistemic coordination of these is forced on us by the kind of unity between the mathematical and the physical so evident in the four-dimensional geometries of space and time.

Here once again we have a revision in the notions of *theory* and *principia.* 'Theory' is no longer to be understood, as with the positivists, as a convenient arrangement of our observational concepts for certain pragmatic or technological ends, involving an economy of cognitive organisation that has no 'metaphysical' relation to any order inhering in nature; that is to say, it is not simply a provisional 'working hypothesis'. On the contrary, 'theory' is now understood in its original sense as *theoria,* a 'speculative' penetration into the structure of things, a refined 'lens' through which we see into the underlying order of nature or rather allow it to disclose itself to us. *Principia,* on the other hand, are not fixed but fluid axioms. They do not constitute the initial A B C of our knowledge from which other content is derived, but are cognitive instruments in the axiomatic penetration into the objective comprehensibility of the universe. As such they are developed only in and through processes of interrogation and discovery and are not known beforehand (except perhaps in a subsidiary way by some of the greatest minds). We are not concerned here, then, with axioms in the old sense of fixed premises or principles in which we argue from certain accepted positions to necessary conclusions, as in Euclidean geometry. What we have here are open flexible structures used postulationally, and therefore with fluid revision the further they penetrate into and lay bare the 'inner logic' of the field under investigation. And in so far as they succeed in revealing basic rational structures in the universe, they force upon us claims as to their validity, and we realise that we 'invented' or came upon them because they came at us from the side of the universe itself, compelling us to formulate them as 'laws' through the astonishing correlation between our human thinking and empirical reality. Once we have penetrated into those mathematical invariances and harmonies of the real world we cannot think that they might just as well have happened otherwise, for they are thrust upon us as belonging to an intelligible order independent of us and reaching out far beyond our knowing of them. That is why we find ourselves having to make affirmations about the universe beyond the range of their immediate evidential basis, convinced that we are in touch with an underlying order of inter-connections that is of universal validity.

There is another feature of scientific concept and statement brought to light by relativity theory which must be noted, the relation between the objective structures of reality and our representations of them. The theory of relativity cannot be construed in positivist terms as a merely provisional arrangement of our ideas, for that would reduce it to relativism, which is so often the way in which it is understood in the social sciences. On the contrary, relativity theory refers to an objective relatedness in the universe invariant to any and every observer, but for that very reason it necessarily relativises (Einstein did not use this word here) *our* representations of it. There is an invariance in the universe which we are forced to affirm with an exclusiveness and a universality, which does not allow it any provisional character, but there are various ways of representing that invariance, and therefore various points at which axiomatic penetration into that invariance can be achieved. It is because we are concerned here not with the kind of picturing model thrown up by an epistemology of perception but with a disclosure model, that the cognitive instrument we use precisely in so far as it is appropriate directs us away from its own representation to the objective invariance we discern through it. The model and its representation will always be open to further and further refinement, and in that sense are of a provisional character, but they are what they are through their coordination to an invariance that is not of a provisional kind. Indeed the very fact that we can offer various representations of such a structure in the universe, without making any difference to what we apprehend, reveals that it is so objectively deep that it remains invariant to our representations of it – although such representations, of course, must be appropriate or faithful in the way they serve the disclosure of the objective invariance. Thus while the theory of relativity forces us to distinguish between variant and invariant elements in our scientific concepts and statements, it also makes clear that the variant elements are what they are through their relation to the invariant. This distinction between the invariant and the variant, and this way of relating them to each other, are of great importance for the advance of science in coping with the destructive and obstructive elements in human thought rooted in man's self-centredness, particularly evident in technologically oriented knowledge, for they check man's tendency to impose his own utilitarian schematisms, and his own technocratic ideologies, prescriptively upon nature, including humanity; but they are also important for they enable science to take account of the provisional character of scientific representations insisted upon by Ernst Mach, without the positivist disjunction between thought and being or science and ordinary experience and without the reduction of physical laws to convenient conventions and the nominalist dogmatism to which that way of thinking gives rise (e.g. such as came out of 'the Vienna Circle').

I have spent some time in tracing the movement of scientific thought from Newton to Einstein in order to exhibit the way in which modern science has come to proceed, for it is fundamentally with the same kind of procedure that we are concerned in *scientific theology*. Here too we reject logico-deductive argumentation from fixed *principia*, and try to emancipate thought from static concepts and mechanistic systems; and here also we are concerned with a profound reorientation in man's knowledge which leaves epistemological and cosmological dualism behind in operations that have to do with the primordial unity of form and being. Consequently scientific theology, no less than natural science, is concerned with the discovery of appropriate modes of rationality or cognitive instruments with which to enter into the heart of religious experience, and therefore with the development of axiomatic concepts with which to allow its interior principles to be disclosed, and in that light to understand, as far as we may, the rational structure of the whole field of God's interaction with man and the world he has made. If the task of pure science in every field is to inquire into the relations of things and events at different levels of complexity, and to develop our understanding and representation of them so that their real nature becomes progressively revealed to us, that is precisely the objective of scientific theology. Its task is to bring to view the *new and distinctive kinds of connection* that obtain in the relation of God to man within the space-time structures of the creation, and to generate, under the objective pressure of the divine self-revelation, appropriate modes and systems of thought, as open and as simple as possible, through which those distinctive connections can come to expression in our human representations of them, and yet to do that in such a way that the constancies of the divine economy, invariant for any and every believer, stand out in their distinction from and are yet served by, the variant formulations and interpretational systems which we develop in the progress of our inquiry. Thus theological concepts and statements have a feature similar to that implied in relativity theory, for they refer to what is greater than we can ever conceive, and are themselves relativised precisely by the revelation of that transcendent reality which they serve. That is why it belongs to the precision of theological statements that they fall short of the majesty and glory of God, for they are appropriate only as they point beyond themselves in such a way as to distinguish themselves as human variables coordinated with the divine invariance. As Søren Kierkegaard once said, in a rather different context, we must learn, before God, to relate ourselves absolutely to the absolute and relatively to the relative: error may arise either through relating ourselves relatively to the absolute or absolutely to the relative. It may be added, however, that when we do relate ourselves absolutely to the absolute, we find ourselves relativised by it.

This way of thinking, through following essential clues impressed upon us by reality, and by way of postulational and axiomatic penetration through the unity of form and being into the inner logic or orderly relations inhering in any field of inquiry, is not so new in theological as in natural science. Let us take some historic examples.

Athanasius in the fourth century. In his first book, *Contra Gentes,* Athanasius set himself to clear the ground for a scientific Christian theology by sustained argument with the thoroughly dualist thought of contemporary Greek culture. In rejecting cosmological dualism and the notion of the logos as a cosmological principle, for the Christian notion of the Logos or Son by whom God created the universe and through whom he interacts with it in redemption, he had to find a way of thinking out the Christian faith in its profound unity of form and being. That he set out to do in the subsequent book, *De Incarnatione,* and to grasp the kind of inner connection or logic revealed in creation and redemption. This was neither a causal nor a logical connection for it did not have that kind of necessity. In the process of his inquiry Athanasius found ways of 'extending' his thought into the inner movement of the divine love, and came up with what he called the pattern or structure of grace, which had its own kind of compulsion or logic deriving from the nature of God and his 'philanthropy'. And it was in the light of that logic of grace that he expounded the interrelation of creation, incarnation and redemption, and went on to lay the scientific foundation upon which the theology of the Christian Church has rested ever since.

Anselm of Canterbury in the eleventh century. Influenced by Athanasius in the East and Hilary in the West, Anselm rejected the method of deducing theological truth from fixed premises, even if they were derived from the Holy Scripture or the authoritative pronouncements of the Catholic Church. The task of theology properly begins where biblical citations end, with understanding the realities to which those citations refer, and that means grasping them in their inner or underlying connections, for only in that way could theological statements rest upon the truth itself. A scientific theology, he held, could not be satisfied with anything less than that. Thus in the *Cur Deus Homo* Anselm insisted that even Jesus Christ must not be treated like a fixed principle, or a logical cypher, from which to extend formal logical connections and thus to build up a system of necessary truth. And so Anselm, setting Christ treated like that aside *(remoto Christo)*, developed a way of penetrating into the heart of God's interaction with man in incarnation and atonement, in order to bring to light the inner logic of the truth *(ratio veritatis)* or the necessary reasons *(rationes necessariae)* through which we are compelled to think truly or rightly in accordance with the actual way which God has taken in revealing himself to us and saving us. The 'necessary reasons' do not refer to any logical or causal necessity, but to the kind of rational compulsion under which our minds fall when they are open to the inner order of the truth itself. It is highly significant that in developing scientific theology in this way Anselm found he had to distinguish several levels of truth, each with its own inherent logic *(ratio veritatis)*, each level opening upward toward the level of the Supreme Truth, the creative ground of them all. Here, undoubtedly we have a remarkable advance in scientific theological thinking, not followed unfortunately by mediaeval theologians who soon afterwards lapsed into a way of thinking, on the model of traditional geometry, in which they deduced theological concepts from biblical and ecclesiastical statements and worked them up into coherent logical systems. But Anselm had at least one great weakness, his inability to cope with the ingredient of time in theological statements.

Kierkegaard in the nineteenth century. In *The Philosophical Fragments* Kierkegaard turns aside from any attempt to reason precisely from fixed axioms, but selects a starting point which he hopes will carry his thought into the very heart of things where he can get a grip upon its distinctive pattern or order. He does this by throwing a contrast between Christ and Socrates in which he finds his thought forced to concentrate upon the *movement of the eternal in time.* Just where Anselm was weak, Kierkegaard succeeds in penetrating into the inner logic of the incarnation as bound up with temporal movement *(kinesis)*, but this raises the basic question as to the appropriate mode of the reason with which to grasp the movement of the truth. And so a hundred years ahead of his time Kierkegaard devised a way of thinking by abandoning a point of absolute rest and moving kinetically along with the truth in order to understand it. This is similar to what Einstein was to call 'kinematics', but here it would be more apposite to speak of it as a kinetic mode of the reason. Quite evidently to grasp the action of God in creation or incarnation a cognitive instrument needs to be created which will do it justice; but to think the creative and redemptive acts of God through the formal or discursive reason would distort understanding of it, for it would necessarily think away the dynamic movement essential to it – and its real inner logic would escape us. This is not unlike the problem that was to face quantum mechanics in our own century, with its demand for a quantum logic in which the geometrical and dynamic aspects of things are coordinated: without that kind of cognitive instrument it will hardly be possible to determine the kind of rational order underlying behaviour of quanta.

It should now be evident, even from these three instances of classical thought, that modern theology has much to learn from the past, but in view of the course of western theology during the last three hundred years in which it has come to expression within the Newtonian universe, that we stand today at the point of transition, where we need to carry through the same sort of advance in theology as we have seen at different stages in the movement of modern science from Newton to Einstein, from particle theory to field theory, from differential quotients to mathematical invariances, from a mechanistic system with its static concepts to the dynamic but objective structures or transformations that are now basic to scientific knowledge of the universe. Just as it is impossible to construe nuclear interaction in terms of classical dynamics or the old logic of determinacy that goes with it, or to apprehend the distinctive organismic operations with which we have to do in biology by reducing them merely to physicochemical processes and the kind of mathematical complexities they involve, so it is just as impossible to understand the distinctive kind of dynamic and ontological interaction, with which we are concerned in the field of relations constituted by the God-man-world manifold, either within a framework built up by abstraction from sensed images and relations or within a system elaborated through formal logical operations which by their very nature bracket off time and action from proper consideration. Just as today we require a quantum logic and a biologic if we are to advance much further in these fields of scientific inquiry, so we need a *theologic* if we are to have the kind of genuine breakthrough that modern theology needs.

Where, then, does modern theology stand today?

Perhaps that question cannot be answered better than by characterising the work of Karl Barth, by far the greatest theologian of the modern era, as a massive attempt to carry historical theology forward by thinking into each other the contribution of the Fathers and the contribution of the Reformers. The Fathers were concerned to ask questions as to the *being* of God in his acts, and in so doing laid the foundations for the doctrine of God and for Christology. The Reformers devoted themselves to questions as to the *acts* of God in his being, and thus concentrated the attention of Protestant thought upon the saving activity of God in history, upon atonement and the historical Jesus. But the Patristic understanding of the being of God in his acts suffered considerable change within mediaeval dualism, when being became detached from act and was inevitably interpreted differently, e.g. in terms of an Aristotelian rather than the patristic concept of 'substance'. This gave rise to the ontology and static constructs of scholastic thought, which the modern world at the Renaissance and Reformation left behind in its attempt to grapple with the dynamic and the contingent. Reformation theology, on the other hand, also suffered considerable change, for within the radical dualism of Newtonian and Cartesian thought its concentration upon the acts of God in his being led to the detachment of the saving acts from his being, and ran out into the sand of functionalism and timeless events. The loss of ontology proved quite fatal, for Protestant theology rapidly dissolved into the phenomenology and sociology of religion, and thus became trapped in the general disintegration of form which is the end-product of our social positivism. Over against that whole development, Karl Barth's dogmatics is to be appreciated as a gigantic attempt to overcome the radical dualisms that beset mediaeval and Protestant theologies, and to think into each other the being of God in his acts and the acts of God in his being, in a thoroughgoing integration of the ontic and the dynamic, and then in the light of the inner organic connections that come to view, and the fundamental grammar of God's self-revelation as Lord, to reinterpret the whole of Christian theology by setting it more squarely upon its proper foundations.

What Karl Barth has attempted to do in theology, then, is not unlike what several great physicists have been attempting in the development of a general field theory which will bring together and transcend the corpuscular and undulatory theories of light. But to say that is to indicate that Barth has brought classical theology to much the same point where natural science now stands poised. The problem of physics today, as Richard Feynman has pointed out, is that while it has been able to determine a number of fundamental laws, and to discern things that are common to these various laws, it has not yet been able to understand the connection between them. It may well be that in this respect Karl Barth has carried his theological thinking somewhat further than contemporary field physics, for one of the outstanding features of his dogmatic science is the way in which he has been able to unfold it with architectonic structure and beauty, indicating that he has penetrated rather deeply into the underlying organic relations in our understanding of the God-man-world manifold. The question must be raised, however: How far is this at the expense of holding theological concepts and statements apart from physical concepts and statements? Or, how far has Barth really succeeded in overcoming the besetting dualism of western theology? Is it possible to do that without at the same time altering the whole outlook of man toward himself and the universe, and therefore without radically reconstructing the very basis of our western culture? Certainly these questions make it clear that the theological and the natural and human sciences must advance together, but the fact that they do now stand poised together for this kind of universal advance is one of the most exciting features of our times.

Let me indicate, however, two points where it is clear that we must advance through and beyond Barth.

(1) If we are to take as seriously as Barth himself did the relation between the incarnation and the creation in God's creative and redemptive interaction with the world, then a closer relation must be established between natural theology and revealed theology. Karl Barth rightly attacked traditional natural theology as constituting an independent conceptual system on its own, and therefore as constituting the prior and prescriptive framework within which revealed theology could only be distorted and misinterpreted. He attacked it on a double ground: from the actual content of positive knowledge of God which called in question prescriptive forms derived from ground on which actual knowledge of God did not arise – the effect of that he held, was to split the concept of God into two, evidenced by the sharp division in mediaeval theology between the tractate on the one God and the tractate on the triune God; and also from the side of rigorous scientific method which will not allow such a bifurcation between prior epistemological structure and empirical content. But for these same reasons, which presuppose a rejection of deistic and epistemological dualism, the theoretic and empirical components of our knowledge of God in and through the space-time structures of the creation must be brought together. There is a close parallel here to the advance of physics in its relation to geometry, as Einstein has expounded it. Euclidean geometry was pursued as an independent theoretic system, antecedent to physics, but that has proved an idealisation which falsifies our understanding of the real world when applied to it. But with the discovery of the four-dimensional geometries of space and time, geometry is brought into the heart of physics and pursued in indissoluble union with it. There it becomes, as Einstein said, a kind of natural science, for its structure changes, but it remains geometry and constitutes in that organic relation with physics its epistemological structure. Similarly, I would argue, natural theology must be brought within the heart of positive theology, where of course its structure will change, for then physical statements and theological statements will be intimately correlated. This means

that positive theology will change also, for it will have to be pursued in indissoluble relation with the space-time structures of the creation, which in a different way are explored by natural science. It is then through such an integration and reorientation of natural and positive theology that we will be able to overcome the dualisms that have undermined theology from below, and fragmented it in the tragic manner of modern times, but to speak of such an integration and reorientation is to speak of the task of scientific theology.

(2) While Karl Barth has succeeded as no one else has for many centuries in opening up the whole vista of theology and revealing its profound simplicities and elegant connections, he did not succeed in 'inventing' (in the sense of the term as we have used it of Einstein), and probably did not even attempt to 'invent', the appropriate cognitive instrument or instruments through which we may bring to light and represent for ourselves the profound harmonies and symmetries of the divine grace in which is enshrined the inner logic of God's creative and redemptive operations in the universe. Historical theology has never even come up with an instrument corresponding to the four-dimensional geometries of space and time which have played such an astonishing role in the advance of our scientific knowledge of the created universe. But this is the task of the future. It will be far more difficult to come up with something like this in theology than in any natural science, but only if we are able to come up with it, will we finally be able to overcome the dualisms we have been speaking of; not, to be sure, to become engulfed in some kind of monism, for the synthesis of the future will be altogether different – that we can already see: it will be a synthesis of new structures, hierarchically ordered in multiple levels, and infinitely open to the transcendence of the living God. That must also be the task of a thoroughly scientific theology.

In concluding this lecture, let me indicate quite briefly the consequences of such an advance. It will mean a profound clarification and simplification of the whole corpus of Christian theology. The more profoundly we penetrate into the ultimate 'logical basis', or 'economy' of theological knowledge (to borrow some of Einstein's favourite concepts), the more clearly we will be able to discern the inner core of basic concepts and relations from those which are of only temporal or peripheral significance, and which will inevitably wither away as convenient conventions thrown up by this or that period of theological advance but which have only time-conditioned and fleeting cultural significance. Christian theology will then emerge immensely stronger, radically simpler, yet its profound universality will come to view in such a way as to bring compelling conviction from its own inner force and validity. Theological science rigorously pursued in this way will inevitably have a unifying effect throughout Christendom, and thus acquire an ecumenical significance which it has not had since the seventh century.

CHAPTER IX

Natural Theology in the Thought of Karl Barth

THEOLOGIES may be divided into two distinct types which, for the purpose of this chapter, may be called 'interactionist' and 'dualist'. By an interactionist theology I mean one in which God is thought of as interacting closely with the world of nature and history without being confused with it, and by a dualist theology I mean one in which God is thought of as separated from the world of nature and history by a measure of deistic distance. Obviously there are degrees of closeness and distance, while their extremes tend to pass over into each other. Thus a theology in which God is thought of as so transcendentally other that he cannot be the 'object' of our knowledge, as in the thought of Schleiermacher, can only acquire content through constructions out of our immanent religious consciousness. Nevertheless a working distinction between interactionist and dualist theologies may serve a useful purpose in helping us to get into the heart of the problem.

The theology of Karl Barth, not least for his uncompromising rejection of natural theology, has frequently been criticised for its deistic dualism in which God as 'wholly other' is set completely over against the world of nature and history. There are certainly *prima facie* grounds for this judgment, when we consider Barth's early stress upon 'the infinite qualitative distinction' between God and man, eternity and time, which he took over from Kierkegaard, not to speak of the influence upon him, directly as well as indirectly through Herrmann, of Kant's critique of the traditional arguments for the existence of God. Convinced that the subordination of evangelical Christianity to 'Cultural Protestantism', and the appalling loss of depth and meaning that even *God* had for the prevailing theology, were due to the assimilation of God to nature and of revelation to history, and thus the reduction of theology to anthropology, that had been going on since the end of the eighteenth century, Barth determined to call a halt to it by tearing up the Protestant synthesis and creating such a *diastasis* between God and man, that God could really be recognised as God in the sheer majesty of his divine nature and in his absolutely unique existence and power, while man, disenchanted of his pretended divinity, could be free at last to be truly and genuinely human. Then also such a boundary line would appear between Christianity and the Church's institutional and cultural involvement in the structures of the world, that the Gospel could be heard as *Gospel,* and its message could be brought to bear upon the world in all its power and newness as message *from* God *to* man. The achievement of this distance or separation of the divine from the human led Barth to conceive the relation between grace and nature, revelation and religion, in such a dialectical and diacritical way, that he could be trapped into speaking of God as everything and of man as nothing, which appeared to cast such a slur upon the creation that he was accused of Marcionism as well as deism. To do Barth justice, however, it must be said that his stress upon the infinite qualitative difference between God and man was intended to throw into sharp relief the fact that while there is no way of man's own devising from man to God, there is indeed a bridge between man and God created through the invasion of God in his Godness into time and human existence and his activity within them. That is to say, his emphasis upon the transcendence of God was not upon some abstract and distant deity but precisely upon the impact of the mighty living God upon man and therefore upon his nearness to man in the midst of nature and history, i.e. upon what Barth was to call 'the humanity of God'. Nevertheless, in his eagerness to speak of the divine intervention 'plumb down from above' in such a way that it did not fall under the disposal of man or minister to his Promethean self-assertion, Barth made use of analogies like the tangential relation or mathematical point, and in so doing he tended to develop a 'timeless eschatology' and to construe the divine activity exclusively in terms of the *event* of grace, but this in turn provoked the charge of theological 'occasionalism'.

There is certainly a deep and persistent problem in Barth's thought here which cannot be glossed over, one that has its roots in an *Augustinian and Lutheran dualism*. He owed it not simply to a residual influence upon him of Wilhelm Herrmann of Marburg, but to his fascination with the young Luther whose thought was then being brought to light in the new *Lutherforschung*. It was from Luther that he took the mathematical analogies mentioned above, and from Luther, as well as from Kierkegaard, that he derived not a little of his dialectical-paradoxical language which he used with such force in his early writings. It was the Augustinian dualism lying behind all this that helped him to develop the brand of existentialism that is found in several editions of his *Commentary on Romans,* and it was into a form of this that he tended to be flung back as he sought to combat the kind of synthesis (Augustinian-Thomist) between the divine and the human advocated by the Jesuit theologian Eric Przywara through the notion that all being is *intrinsically* analogical, for it was precisely that synthesis in its romantic Protestant form which Barth held to be the source of the corruption at work in German theology for nearly two centuries. In the course of these debates with Romans and Lutherans, Barth became more aware of the subtle dangers of Augustinian thought, not only in its inherent dualism but also in its notion of grace which through its ingredient of Neoplatonic participation in the divine could be used to bridge the gap between God and nature. It was, of course, this element in the thought of Przywara and others that had been allowed to corrupt the conception of analogy found in St Thomas Aquinas, and set Barth off in a wrong slant against it.

Although vestiges of this dualism persisted in Barth's thought, most notably in his understanding of the sacraments, his theology even at this early stage became quite definitely of the interactionist type. This is particularly evident at three points. (1) Barth's break-through to a profound objectivity and a new realism in his interpretation of the Biblical message. A decisive influence upon him here was the teaching of Johann and Christoph Blumhardt in whom Barth found 'astonishing and unheard of objectivity in the matters of God'. This was in stark contrast to the religious subjectivity that characterised pietism and liberalism alike, and that constantly gave rise to a dualism between inwardness and history. For Barth, God is present with us and acts upon us in the world and in history in the fullest and most real sense. His objectivity is not simply that he is there, over against us like the overwhelming reality of being itself, but that he encounters us and acts upon us as the creative Source of all being, as the Lord God, objecting to and resisting any attempt on

our part to subdue his divine Reality to some form of our own
subjectivity even by way of explaining his Reality or proving his
existence abstractively from the side of our own autonomy or
self-understanding. As Barth sees it, therefore, it is upon the sheer
objectivity of the living God which will not allow us to consider his
Being apart from his Act that any natural theology which proceeds
by abstracting from God's activity must invalidate itself. (2) His
recovery of the Reformation understanding of the Word as
grounded eternally in the personal Being of God. This imported
such a oneness between God's Word and his Act, backed up by his
own Being, that the operation of the Word, alike in creation and
redemption, in kerygma and in sacrament, was conceived as God's
decisive interaction with what he has made, sustaining its ontological relation with himself, while calling forth from man a reciprocal
relation in which true human response in knowledge and obedience
is upheld in its freedom and grounded in his own divine Reality.
For Barth this conviction that God is Word in his own eternal
Being, and that in his Word God's own Being personally com-
municates himself, had to call in question the validity of any
knowledge of God's Being reached apart from his Word. We
cannot steal knowledge of God in some sort of third-personal way,
behind his back, as it were. Just as God's Being cannot be abstracted
from his Act, for God is he who he is in his Act, so his Being cannot
be abstracted from his Word, for he is who he is in his Word. Thus
any natural theology would have to establish itself on the ground of
a dualism between God's Being and his active Word, while an
interactionism grounded in the unity of Being, Act and Word in
God would have to question whether such a natural theology ever
reaches the real God whose living existence includes his speaking
and acting. (3) The immense significance of the Incarnation to
which Barth seems to have awakened through study of the Church
Fathers. If we are to take seriously the fact that God became man in
Jesus Christ, really became man once and for all, without of course
ceasing to be God, then must we not ask what that imported for
God himself? Does it not mean that to all eternity God has ceased to
be God only, since he has taken up human nature into himself and
maintains it there to all eternity, so that there is no God for us now
except this God who is exclusively bound to Jesus Christ? If God
himself is untouched in his own Being by the Incarnation, does that
not mean that in the ultimate analysis he must be thought of as
having held himself aloof from us, and does that not throw grave
doubt upon the nature of his interaction with us? When at this point
mediaeval theology, taking its cue from Peter Lombard – *deus non*

factus est aliquid – was prevented by *a priori* presuppositions as to the impassibility of God from taking seriously the *'became* flesh', or *'was made* man', of the Incarnation, was it not in the last resort resiling into a dualism or even into some form of deism? On the other hand, if we do take the Incarnation seriously, i.e. without lapsing into monophysitism or Nestorianism, how can we avoid the implication that, whatever happened before the Incarnation, now that it has taken place, God is nowhere to be known apart from or behind the back of Jesus Christ? If the Incarnation means that the eternal Truth of God has entered time and for ever assumed historical form in Jesus Christ, how can we know that Truth except by entering ourselves into historical relation to its incarnate reality in time? And if once we have come to know God in his own living Reality in Jesus Christ, how can we go on maintaining the validity of a natural knowledge reached independently of revelation without driving a deep wedge between the God whom we claim to know by nature and God's own living Reality in the Incarnation? Thus Barth's understanding of the Incarnation as the Truth of God incarnate in space and time, encountering us objectively in Jesus Christ, had the unavoidable effect of calling in question any idea that the truth about God arises within us, out of the depth of our memory or self-consciousness, and any idea that God as he really is can be reached through detached, timeless reasoning, independent of God's self-revelation in history, after the fashion of the traditional proofs for his existence. But above all, it had the effect of destroying those elements of dualism in his own thought which had provided ground for the charges of deism, Marcionism and occasionalism levelled against him.

How then are we to describe Barth's attitude toward natural theology?

Whatever may have been his earlier views, when he was doubtless affected by the Kantian critique of the possibility of the knowledge of God within the limits of the natural reason, Barth quickly left them behind to take up a very different position on the ground of actual knowledge of God based on his Word. Here as he looked out from within the perspective of Christian theology upon natural theology he did not reject the existence of natural knowledge or commit himself to any metaphysical refutation of it, but found himself trying to understand it as something that is 'impossible' and that nevertheless 'exists', i.e. something that exists in opposition to the actual knowledge of God mediated through his Word, and which must therefore be called in question by it as illegitimate and invalid in so far as it claims to be knowledge of God as he really is. Natural theology is not a phenomenon that can simply be brushed aside, for it has a strange vitality in virtue of which it persists in the history of human thought. Barth explains this vitality as that of the natural man, for natural theology as such arises out of man's natural existence and is part of the whole movement in which he develops his own autonomy and seeks a naturalistic explanation for himself within the universe. It must therefore be taken seriously and be respected as the natural man's 'only hope and consolation in life and death' which it would be unkind to take away from him in his natural state. Nor is it something that can or should be combated on its own ground, for as soon as one attempts to do that one has thereby conceded the ground on which it rests, namely the autonomous existence of estranged and sinful man. That is to say, the claim to a natural knowledge of God, as Barth understands it, cannot be separated out from a whole movement of man in which he seeks to justify himself over against the grace of God, and which can only develop into a natural theology that is antithetical to knowledge of God as he really is in his acts of revelation and grace.

From this point of view the danger of natural theology lies in the fact that once its ground has been conceded it becomes the ground on which everything else is absorbed and naturalised, so that even the knowledge of God mediated through his self-revelation in Christ is domesticated and adapted to it until it all becomes a form of natural theology. Barth reached this judgment through extensive examination of the history of German Protestant theology which is extremely difficult if not impossible to refute. Moreover he felt this to be reinforced through his analysis of the contemporary situation immediately before and after Hitler's rise to power, for what appeared to lie behind that upsurge of paganism in a Christian country was the domestication and absorption of Christianity into the romantic depths of German nature and culture. This explains why Barth was so angry with Emil Brunner's mediating pamphlet 'Nature and Grace', for to those fighting the battle of resistance in Germany it appeared to fortify the basis on which the so-called 'German Christians' were advocating conciliation with the Nazi régime, and why Barth was no less sharply opposed to those misguided Roman theologians who adduced St Thomas' dictum, *gratia non tollit naturam sed perficit et complet,* as supplying theological grounds for the concordat between the Vatican and Hitler – grace, it was argued, does not destroy German nature (blood and soil) but perfects and fulfils it! It seemed to Barth that not simply the purity but the very existence of the Christian Church was at stake in the conflict with the natural and ideological theology of the Nazis. Subsequent events have surely justified Barth in his uncompromising stand against that sort of naturalisation of the Christian message. On the other hand, there seems little doubt that in the debate Barth was sometimes trapped, for example in his arguments with Brunner, into dealing with natural theology on its own ground, which did not help to clarify the real issues.

Of course the actual ground upon which Barth claimed to stand in his attitude to natural theology was the grace of God in Jesus Christ: from that standpoint the setting aside of all natural theology appeared as a corollary of *sola gratia*. This is an argument from the *exclusiveness* of Jesus Christ, the Way, the Truth and the Life, apart from whom there is no way to the Father, but it is also an argument from the exclusive nature of Christ's vicarious sacrifice, for in his death and resurrection God has done something for us which we could not do for ourselves, in reconciling us to himself. When perceived in its epistemological significance, this means that we are unable to achieve through our natural powers and capacities the cognitive union with God which true knowledge of him requires. If we are to know God we need to be redeemed from our mental alienation from him, renewed and reconciled in our minds, and adapted by divine grace to his Reality. The fact that God himself had to become man in order to break a way through our estrangement and darkness, and work out a way of bringing us back to himself through the saving life and death and resurrection of Christ, not only precludes us from entertaining other possibilities of a way from man to God but actually invalidates them all. Moreover the completeness and comprehensiveness of God's saving act in Christ mean that divine grace does not operate by patching us up, or adding to our natural capacities what we lack, but by setting our life on a wholly new basis. This is why Barth insists that in face of the Cross of Christ we are bound to say that all natural theology perishes at the point where the knowledge of the one and only God is gained in the face of Jesus Christ and by the renewing of men in the Holy Spirit. It is important to note, however, that even here Barth is not denying the possibility or the existence of natural theology, but pointing out that it is undermined, relativised and set aside by the actual knowledge of God mediated though Christ. Just as when we are justified by the grace of God in Jesus Christ all our natural goodness is set aside, for we are saved by grace and not by our own works of righteousness, without there being any denial of the existence of natural goodness, so here, in the epistemological relevance of justification by grace, our natural knowledge is set aside, for we know God through his own grace and not by our own efforts of reason, without there being any denial of the existence of natural knowledge.

It is sometimes argued that Barth excludes natural theology only in the name of Biblical revelation and faith in Christ and not on epistemological grounds. But this is hardly true, for Barth does develop a very powerful epistemological structure in the heart of his theology which through its intrinsic integration with the material content of our knowledge of God in Christ can allow no place for an *independent* natural theology in the body of theology proper or even as a preamble to the faith. Certainly Barth does not fall into the category of the Roman fideists whose views were condemned by the first Vatican Council, for he does not reject natural theology on the ground of any rational scepticism and then have recourse to some sort of traditionalism; nor does he reject it, like Bultmann, on the Gnostic thesis put forward by Basileides, that we cannot know what God is but only what he is not; nor again does he reject natural theology in virtue of a strain of Neoplatonic agnosticism, such as even infected the thought of St Thomas and still makes many modern Thomists ultimately take refuge in a non-conceptual relation to God. In no sense is it our reason despairing of itself that carries us over from God's incomprehensibility but only God's revelation of himself which is not thwarted by our littleness or incapacity. Thus, Barth argues, it is not by proceeding along any *via negationis*, but only on the ground of our positive rational knowledge of God, in which we really know God through God and know him to be *quo maius cogitari nequit,* as St Anselm expressed it, that we are forced to acknowledge that all our natural knowledge of God falls far short of his Majesty and misses the mark of his Reality. It is the actual content of our knowledge of God, together with the rational method that inheres in it, that excludes any movement of thought that arises on some other *independent* ground as ultimately irrelevant and as an inevitable source of confusion when it is adduced as a second or coordinate basis for positive theology.

We would fail to understand Barth quite seriously if we did not appreciate that his struggle with the problem of natural theology is also a struggle for rigorous scientific method in theology. It is worthwhile pointing out here how far removed Barth is from the preoccupation of continental Kantians with *Erkenntnislehre*, i.e. with the development of a philosophical epistemology in abstraction from fields of actual knowledge in this or that science. Whenever Barth engages in polemical debate with 'philosophy', he is not concerned in any way to dispute the necessity or relevance of logic and metaphysics, but to attack the erection of an *independent* (and naturalistically grounded) *Weltanschauung* within which, it is claimed, Christianity must be interpreted if it is to become understandable in the modern world, and more frequently, to attack the erection of a masterful epistemology, elaborated *independently* of actual theological inquiry, which is then to be applied prescriptively to knowledge of God. In his rejection of this kind of 'philosophy' Barth stands shoulder to shoulder with every proper scientist who insists on the freedom to develop scientific methods appropriate to the field of his inquiry and to elaborate epistemological structures under the compulsion of the nature of things as it becomes disclosed to him in the progress of his investigation, all untrammelled by *a priori* assumptions of any kind. *A posteriori* science involves rigorous methodological questioning of all preconceptions and presuppositions and of all structures of thought independent of and antecedent to its own processes of discovery. Form and content, method and subject-matter, belong inseparably together, but form and method are determined by the nature of the content and subject-matter. Hence epistemologies properly emerge, through *pari passu* conformity of our understanding with the nature of the object, toward the end of scientific inquiries rather than at the beginning, and cannot therefore be detached to constitute some kind of preunderstanding or allowed the kind of priority from which it could dominate the object. Rather do they develop out of the inherent intelligibility of the object and serve its verification in our understanding. This is why Barth makes so much of the epistemological implication of justification by grace alone, for it forces upon us a relentless questioning of all our presuppositions, prejudgments and *a priori* authorities, philosophical or ecclesiastical, in such a way that in the last resort we are thrown back wholly upon the nature and activity of God himself for the justification or verification of our concepts and statements about him. The doctrine of justification thus appears to be the point in Christian theology where it becomes most evident that scientific objectivity and theological truth coincide. Certainly it is at that point that Barth's exclusion of natural theology is seen to rest on the two-fold ground of theological content and scientific method. His attitude to natural theology is governed, then, not only by God's intelligible self-revelation but by the rational structure of the knowledge to which it gives rise in our faithful understanding of it.

From this perspective it becomes clear that what Barth objects to in natural theology is not its rational structure as such but its *independent* character, i.e. the autonomous rational structure which it develops on the ground of 'nature alone' in abstraction from the active self-disclosure of the living God. In point of fact, however, the rational structure for which natural theology strives, but which it does not really reach and only distorts from its independent stance, can be reached within the understanding of faith and comes to light as we inquire into its objective ground in God himself. That is why Barth can say that *theologia naturalis* is included and brought to light within *theologia revelata,* for in the reality of divine grace there is included the truth of the divine creation. In this sense Barth can interpret, and claim as true, the dictum of St Thomas that grace does not destroy nature but perfects and fulfils it, and can go on to argue that the meaning of God's revelation becomes manifest to us as it brings into full light the buried and forgotten truth of the creation. In other words, while knowledge of God is grounded in his own intelligible revelation to us, it requires for its actualisation an appropriate rational structure in our cognising of it, but that rational structure does not arise within us unless we allow our minds to fall under the compulsion of God's being who he really is in the act of his self-revelation and grace, and as such cannot be derived from an analysis of our autonomous subjectivity.

It may help to make Barth's position clear if we borrow an analogy from the relation of geometry to physics. Although this is not an analogy which Barth himself uses, it is one which I have discussed with him and which he approved as a way of setting out his own thought. Since the rise of four-dimensional geometries which have brought to light a profound correlation between abstract conceptual systems and physical processes, geometry can no longer be pursued simply as a detached independent science, antecedent to physics, but must be pursued in indissoluble unity with physics as the sub-science of its inner rational structure and as an essential part of empirical and theoretic interpretation of nature. As such, however, its character changes, for instead of being an axiomatic deductive science detached from actual knowledge of physical reality it becomes, as Einstein said, a form of natural science. Similarly, with the rejection of an independently thought-out epistemology, on the ground that method and subject-matter are inherently connected, natural theology can no longer be pursued in its old abstractive form, as a prior conceptual system on its own, but must be brought within the body of positive theology and be pursued in indissoluble unity with it. But then its whole character changes, for pursued within actual knowledge of the living God where we must think rigorously in accordance with the nature of the divine object, it will be made *natural* to the fundamental subject-matter of theology and will fall under the determination of its inherent intelligibility. No longer extrinsic but intrinsic to actual knowledge of God, it will function as the essential sub-structure within theological science, in which we are concerned to develop the inner material logic that arises in our inquiry and understanding of God. Looked at in this light Barth's exclusion of an *independent* natural theology assumes a formidable scientific character, for surely no genuinely scientific inquiry can let itself be controlled by an independent logical structure even by conceding to it any claim to constitute an indispensable precondition or precomprehension for the inquiry in question.

It should now be clear that the position Barth has adopted in regard to natural theology involves the complete rejection of any deistic disjunction between God and the world of nature and history, together with the split in our concept of God to which such a disjunction inevitably gives rise. Instead of holding two conceptual systems, that of natural theology operating with premises outside of faith, and that of revealed theology operating with premises within faith, Barth is committed to one coherent framework of theological thought that arises within the unitary interaction of God with our world in creation and Incarnation. In place of a dualism, however, he works with a polarity of ontic and noetic structures resulting from the divine interaction, and indeed with an analogical correspondence between the inner intelligibility of the given reality, the Being and Truth of God, and the rational structure immanent in our understanding of him, the latter being imposed upon us by the self-revelation of God and grounded through it in the 'necessity' or objective rationality of God himself. That is to say, we can operate only with reasons that arise on the actual ground we are investigating, within the limits of the noetic structure required by the nature of the given object. Hence in rigorous scientific theology there can be no exercise of a noetic rationality according to a necessity or law of its own, without its being conditioned and backed up by an ontic necessity or intelligible basis in the object of knowledge – to do that would be to become guilty of an arbitrary movement of thought, i.e. what Barth claims to detect in an *independent* natural theology.

This reconstruction in his understanding of theology was reached by Barth finally through his epoch-making study of the thought of St Anselm, and worked out in volume two of his *Church Dogmatics*. The task of theology, as he now saw it, was to penetrate through the inner and necessary relation between our knowledge of God and the inherent rationality of the truth and being of God, to God himself as he really is. In the course of this there emerges, as St Anselm rightly claimed, the properly grounded proof of theological knowledge, which is certainly compelling for those who have entered into an empirical relation with God through faith, but which ought to command rational respect even from unbelievers for the validity and force of its logical structure.

This calls for a comment and two questions. Since the task of theology is finally to penetrate, in some measure at least, into the objective rationality of God himself, even though when we do that we are more than ever aware of him as *quo maius cogitari nequit*, the really fundamental issue is the doctrine of *God*. How then does Barth think of the *ratio veritatis* (in Anselm's sense) of God's supreme being which ultimately determines and shapes our knowledge of him? And how does Barth relate the rational structure in our understanding to the objective structure in God's revelation of himself to which it answers? Both these questions bear upon the nature and function of natural theology when it is included within the body of positive theology.

Barth's answer to the first question is already given in his doctrine of the Trinity which he understands not simply in an economic, or in a social sense, but essentially in an ontological sense. God is triune in his own eternal Being. The root of the *doctrine* of the Trinity is found in his revelation of himself, in which he makes himself the object of our knowledge, and remains in the mystery of his being transcendently, indissolubly Subject whom we can never get behind or master, but is nevertheless sovereignly free to be with us and in us as the One through whom he makes himself known. Revelation means that we know God out of, and in, and through himself, as Father, Son and Holy Spirit who coinhere in one another in a living communion of mutual love and personal modes of being. The *ratio veritatis* of his revelation is however the *ratio veritatis* of the Trinity, for he is antecedently and inherently in his own eternal being what he is toward us as Father, Son and Holy Spirit. That is the *ratio veritatis* that determines and shapes true and faithful knowledge of the divine being wherever it arises.

Then comes Barth's counter-question. If God in himself, and as we know him to be in his acts of grace and revelation, really *is* Father, Son and Holy Spirit in his own eternal and undivided being, then what are we to make of the validity of an *independent* natural theology that terminates not upon the triune being of God, i.e. upon God as he really is, but upon some being of God in general? Does it not really miss the mark, by abstracting his existence from his act, and so by considering one aspect of his Being apart from his other aspects? However, if natural theology is included within the body of our knowledge of God as he really is, must it not be correspondingly trinitarian in its structure, and indeed precisely as trinitarian constitute the inner sub-structure of all sound theology?

How are we to assess this? Barth has certainly shown, with a power unrivalled since the days of high patristic theology, that to know God is to know him as Triune, that the doctrine of the Trinity belongs to the fundamental groundwork of theological knowledge, and that trinitarian thinking constitutes the basic grammar of theological knowledge. In consistency with this Barth has worked out on the one hand a doctrine of creation which, as Dr Hartwell has pointed out, is 'intrinsically trinitarian in its ontology', and on the other hand a doctrine of the Incarnation of the Word in which the *vestigia trinitatis* appear in the creaturely and worldly forms which God has assumed in his revelation. However, if we are to take as seriously as Barth claims to do the unitary interaction of God with our world in creation and Incarnation, there must surely be a closer connection between the conceptualities of theological science and those of natural science than we find in Barth's thought. He has, I believe, pointed out to us the right direction in which to travel, but did he himself actually travel along it very far, or think it out adequately enough?

There is undoubtedly an enormous problem here which we may indicate by comparing briefly the positions of St Augustine and St Thomas. St Augustine did attempt to develop the trinitarian structure of Christian theology by showing how intrinsic it is not only to the mutual relation which God has established between us and himself through his Word, but to the basic constitution of the human soul which bears *vestigia trinitatis* within its creaturely existence as such. Augustine worked, however, with a radical dualism between the intelligible and sensible worlds, so that he could achieve this trinitarian correlation between the Creator and the creature only through incorporating into his thought a powerful element of Neoplatonic participationism and a corresponding theory of enlightenment. St Thomas rightly rejected both ontologism and illuminism, and set himself to overcome the dualism by developing the Augustinian concept of supernature to bridge the gap between God and the world, and by building up, with the help of the *philosophia perennis,* a realist and unitary basis for the knowledge of God. However, since for St Thomas all human knowledge is grounded in sense experience he was forced to reject any notion of intuitive knowledge of God for an abstractive knowledge of him, and thus to develop an autonomous natural theology with its own logical structure powerful enough to claim universal validity and to commend itself to the *Gentiles*. That this was not given an entirely independent status is clear from the fact that he did not regard it as achieved through the unaided reason and developed merely philosophically, but as achieved only through reason already adapted to God by his grace, and therefore to be included within his *theology*. Nevertheless, it is a natural theology which abstracts from God's activity and in the nature of the case can only reach as far as the Being of God in general and *in abstracto*. The effect of this in the last resort was to drive a wedge between the being of God as such and his triune being, and so it remains open to the damaging charge of Barth that it imports a split in the concept of God. Moreover an abstractive natural theology of this kind tended to reinforce the latent Augustinian dualism in St Thomas' thought between God and the world through a more Aristotelian notion of the impassibility and changelessness of God, while the fact that this natural theology with its claim to universal validity was treated as a *praeambula fidei* opened the way for revealed theology to be interpreted on its basis and then domesticated within the thought-forms of the *philosophia perennis* which it employed.

The rise of a powerful natural theology once again in the seventeenth and eighteenth centuries, this time within Protestantism, and within the dualist framework of knowledge that resulted from Newton's notion of absolute space and time independent of the events and processes that take place within their all-embracing envelope, not to speak of the Cartesian isolation of subject from object, would seem to reinforce the judgment that natural theology emerges and flourishes within a deistic breach between the being of God and the world he has created, while its abstraction from God's activity in the world serves to harden the breach. The distance between God and man was considerably wider in Protestant than in Roman natural theology, especially when the concept of supernature fell away, with the result that here more than in mediaeval thought Christianity was interpreted on the ground of a religious and philosophical *a priori* and so became domesticated within the thought-forms of the prevailing philosophies.

The position adopted by St Thomas was more profoundly rooted in divine revelation, so that in spite of a division between two sources of knowledge and the division in the doctrine of God it implied, his natural theology was more firmly correlated with the body of theology proper, and thus has endured the test of history rather better than that of the English empiricists or German idealists. In spite of its problems St Thomas' achievement was to establish the fact that if knowledge of God is to be actualised in us it requires a rational counterpart to it in our structured understanding of it, firm enough to merit philosophical analysis and consideration on its own. How far has Barth appreciated this and how far does he really get to grips with it? Has he succeeded in carrying the discussion beyond St Augustine and St Thomas in offering a solution to their problems? That brings us to the second question mentioned above: How does Barth relate the rational structure in our understanding to the objective structure in God's revelation of himself to which it answers? In order to get an answer to this question we shall have to ask how Barth relates the reconstruction of our understanding that takes place under the impact of divine revelation to the understanding of the natural man considered on his own.

We may take as our starting-point the problem of how, in view of the fact that justification by grace calls in question and sets aside our natural goodness, Barth relates the Christian life to natural goodness, or Christian ethics to general ethics. If there is no relation at all between them, does that not plunge us into a chasm of meaninglessness? That is why Barth, like St Thomas, can insist that grace does not destroy nature but perfects it, for the reality of divine grace includes the truth of the creation and brings it to its fulfilment, and why he finds it so important to work out a doctrine of creation that is trinitarian in its ontology, and to establish the close relation between the Incarnation and the creation through the Son of God become man, 'by whom all things were made'. This means that behind the question of the relation of Christian ethics to general ethics, and our question of the relation of Christian theology to natural theology, or rather to the rational structure immanent in natural theology, there lies the basic question as to the relation between the 'new man' in Christ to 'man' as such, the 'good creation' of God. Let it be granted, as surely as it must be, that the self-justification of the natural man is excluded and therefore the use of an independent natural theology to fortify him in his self-explaining autonomy over against the grace of God, but this does not mean that we can leave hanging in the air, as it were, the truth of human and creaturely rationality, for on Barth's own showing it must be brought to light and fulfilled within the context of grace. Does Barth, then, actually work this out so far as the rational structure of our *human* understanding is concerned in its relation to the reconstruction of that understanding which befalls man in grace? It must be admitted that at this decisive juncture

Barth draws back, apparently out of anxiety lest the old corruption through naturalistic fallacies, which worked such havoc in the history of Protestant theology, should be given any chance to come back, and tends to restrict the relation between them to the *event* of grace without developing, at any rate in any adequate way, the ontology of the creaturely structures which it assumes. But is this failure not at the expense of a conceptual gap between theological dogmatics and our understanding of created existence, rational as well as physical, and may not this be a reason why Barth's own immense achievements in the advance of pure theology lack the appreciation they deserve?

A penetrating and creative critique of Barth along these lines has been elaborated in recent years by Fr Henri Bouillard of Paris, in two works of outstanding importance (*Karl Barth,* 1957, and *Connaissance de Dieu,* 1967, Eng. tr. 1968, from which the following citations are made). In the process of his discussion Bouillard concedes not a few of Barth's substantial criticisms of natural theology, and moves very close to him while disengaging the real point of Barth's critique from some misunderstanding of Roman theology on his part. He agrees with Barth that we cannot know God except through God, on the foundation of Biblical revelation and through faith, but insists that we must add that it is *we* who know God. While the objective foundation of faith resides in divine revelation, 'the subjective foundation of its possibility resides necessarily in us; otherwise it would not be our certainty. The possibility of the natural knowledge of God is the transcendental condition of the knowledge of faith' (p. 39f). In other words, the very knowledge of faith includes a natural knowledge capable of being demonstrated in a 'proof'. According to the thesis of Professor Bouillard, therefore, 'philosophical reflection offers to the Christian the means of making explicit the natural knowledge implied in faith and of thus experiencing, through a critical process, the certitude that the God in whom he believes is indeed his God and that this belief is not a dream' (p. 61). Regarded in this way natural theology constitutes 'the rational intra-structure of Christian theology' (p. 62), which does not necessarily precede the knowledge of faith, but 'is necessarily implied by the rational condition of man' (p. 40). However, when Bouillard speaks of this natural theology as an *a priori* and links it with Bultmann's 'prior understanding' or 'precomprehension', he seems to be confounding a *logical* with an *epistemological a priori*. This is one of the major confusions that Barth sought to clear away from theology in his struggle for rigorous scientific method. Moreover, when Bouillard admits, rightly, that neither the knowledge of the Incarnation nor that of the Trinity is included in a determined way in the *a priori* of the natural knowledge of God, he seems to be forced back into that damaging division in the concept of God's being which Barth exposed; but he does defend himself by arguing that to envisage an aspect of God's being apart from the Trinity of his work in revelation and reconciliation is a legitimate 'methodological abstraction' provided we do not simply rest in it. This does not seem to me to be a sufficient answer to Barth, for it does detach the structure of natural theology from any ground in the being of God as he really is. If the natural theology that operates abstractively in this way is only 'a non-formalised knowledge' (p. 29), or 'an open-ended structure which faith comes to fill in its own way' (p. 62), then it is not after all necessarily implied in the knowledge of faith. How then can it be regarded as 'a rational intra-structure' that is the subjective counterpart to the objective ground of faith in God's own being?

Fr Bouillard's brilliant critique of Barth compels considerable assent, but it is not without its own problems. Nevertheless it does become evident through his discussion that the gap between his thought and that of Barth is very narrow, and this is exciting, for it is an indication that Reformed and Roman thought are in the process of converging at this point, to the benefit of both of them. Yet it is also evident that the gap that remains at this crucial point where we are concerned with the fundamental structure of Christian theology will not be closed until Reformed and Roman theologians devote far more attention to the *nature* of the epistemological and logical structures that arise in theological inquiry and are thrust upon us from the intelligible reality of God's own eternal being.

CHAPTER X

Truth and Authority in the Church*

L ET ME begin by setting out the position for which I wish to argue in ten interrelated theses on truth.

1. The truth is that which is what it is and that which discloses what it is as it is. The concept of truth enshrines at once the reality of things and the revelation of things as they are in reality. Truth comes to view in its own majesty, freedom and authority, compelling us by the power of what it is to assent to it and acknowledge it for what it is in itself.

2. The truth of God is that he is who he is and that he reveals who he is as he is. The truth of God is the self-subsistent being of God in which he is open to himself in his being he who he is, and in which he reveals himself to us as he is in his own reality. In himself God is only light. There is no darkness or deception in him. What God is towards men he is eternally in himself, and what he is in himself he is faithfully towards men. He is truth and keeps truth for ever, and as such is the source and standard of all truth.

3. The truth of God for us is the unconcealment of God in his own majesty, freedom and authority. He confronts us with himself in his *autousia* and *autexousia,* in the prerogative of his own truth, in the power of his own self-evidence, in the light of his own being.

*Lecture read to L'Académie Internationale des Sciences Religieuses in L'Institut Catholique de Paris. on May 27, 1969.

He is truth who cannot be mastered by us but who does not remain closed to us. We know him truly under the compulsion of his being what he is and by his nature must be, and under the light of his truth which is his divine being coming to view and becoming in our understanding and knowledge of him what he is consistently in himself and in all his relations with us.

4. In God *logos* and *pneuma* are not separated from *ousia* and *physis* or therefore from *alētheia*. It is through God's Word and Spirit that we know God evidently in his own being and according to his own nature, and are enabled to conceive of him in terms of the *intima locutio* in God himself, and therefore in his own eternal reality. *Fides esse nequit sine conceptione.* Since there is no non-conceptual knowledge of God, the proper distinction is not between apophatic and kataphatic knowledge of God, but between kataleptic and kataphatic conceptuality in our knowledge of him.

5. Truth and truthfulness, *Wahrheit und Wahrhaftigkeit,* require to be distinguished, the truth itself from the truth of relation. We owe it to the truth to be truly related to it. Truthfulness is an openness to the truth and a right orientation in accordance with the nature of the truth. While truthfulness involves an analogical relation to the truth, the truth itself always retains ontic priority, for it is what it is in its own reality before it is recognised by us, and what it is in itself is the compulsive ground of our recognition of it and the inexhaustible source of our conceiving it. There is a vast difference between *veritas est adaequatio intellectus ad rem ad extra* and *veritas est adaequatio rei ad intellectum*.

6. The truth of being and the truth of statement require to be distinguished. It is impossible to picture how a picture pictures what it pictures, without reducing the reality pictured merely to a picture of it. No more can we state in statements how statements are related to being, without reducing the relation of statements to being entirely to statements. To attempt to do this is to resolve the truth of being into statements about it. Hence we must distinguish between *vera propositio* and *veritas propositionis,* and maintain a true relation between a statement about the truth and the truth itself. It does not follow that because a statement about the truth must be distinguished from the truth of being to which it refers, it is not objectively grounded in that truth. Even if we cannot argue from the statement itself to the reality to which it directs us, and in which it is intelligibly grounded, nevertheless the reality shows itself and thrusts itself upon us in accordance with its own nature.

7. Scientific theology operates with different levels of truth. The basic distinctions to be observed are those between the level of the

truths of statement, the level of the truths of created being, and the supreme truth which God is in his self-subsistent being. These levels cannot be flattened out without loss in objective depth and in universality of range. But within the organic structure of scientific elucidation we operate with different logical levels, where each level is open to the level above it through propositions not decidable within itself, but necessary to its consistency, and which are decidable only within the wider logical level with which it is coordinated in an open translogical relation. Because the concepts on one level are analogically related to the concepts on another level, not through any one-to-one correspondence between them, but through the coordination of the complete levels by which they are defined, they are nevertheless conceptually analogated even though the representational contents they enshrine do not correspond to their referents across the levels.

8. Scientific theology also operates with a stratification in the totality of its concepts and relations in which there is a distinct hierarchy of truths. On each level there arise secondary and even tertiary theological conceptions which are necessary for the system of our thought and which derive their significance through theoretic connection with our primary concepts close to experience. But these primary concepts, belonging to different logical levels, are graduated to form a hierarchy of truths in which some are more basic and central than others through their direct and intuitive relation to the fundamental datum of revelation or the divine object of our knowledge and experience. Through this stratification of concepts and levels scientific theology penetrates into the primordial unity constituting the 'natural' intelligible basis of our knowledge of God, which results in an immense clarification and simplification of its whole structure. In proportion as that basis comes to view in its ultimate economic simplicity, it becomes apparent that some intermediate levels are only of a methodological nature, and that many of the conceptions they carry, necessary as they may have been in the process of theological development, must eventually disappear as temporarily expedient but ultimately irrelevant abstractions. Thus the profundity and richness of our theological understanding is proportionate to the economic simplicity or paucity of its foundational concepts and the universality of their range of enlightenment.

9. Theological formulation takes place through a movement of interpretative and explanatory penetration into the inner intelligibility of the divine revelation, in which we allow our human thoughts to be moulded pliantly and obediently by the truth itself and thus to

take their basic form from the inner locution in the very being of God. In this movement of understanding the divine revelation we do not operate with a criterion of truth lodged in the subjects of the human interpreters (whether as individuals or as the Church), for we are thrown back objectively upon the truth of the Word of God which forces us to call in question all our preconceptions and prejudgments as it declares itself to us in the present. In theological formulation we do not operate with definitions of the truth that are regarded as its necessary extensions, but with statements that serve the truth in its own inexhaustible reality and intelligibility, in such a way that they become progressively refined media through which the truth imprints itself more deeply upon our minds in its own self-explication and power. Since the ultimate truth of theological formulations does not lie in those formulations as such, but in that which they serve, they are truthfully related to the truth only when they make clear that they are relativised by the truth. The fact that they fall short of the truth is an essential element in their propriety and precision.

10. Since the truth of God is known in its own self-light and in its own self-evidence, by the act of God in the Word and Spirit of his own being, and therefore on the ground of its own authority, we do not need to posit a special illumination or a special infusion of grace, independent of the truth, for its right reception and expression. Neither in knowing nor in formulating the truth may we invert our active reason or active tradition into an authority over the truth, for then we would confound the truth of being with our articulation and expression of it. Authorities do arise in our understanding and in its development in the Catholic Church as methodological necessities and decisive organs in the clarifying and checking of our expression of the truth, and in the achievement as far as possible of objectivity and universality, but they fall into secondary place before the actual disclosure of the truth in its own right, relativised by its absoluteness. The truth of the divine being always breaks through the forms of thought and speech by which we serve it, for it retains its own majesty, freedom and authority over us. Through its exaltation over all other authorities it makes us free to know it finally out of itself and by grace alone, and demands of us an obedience that transcends our respect for the authoritative institutions of the Church, necessary as they are in the historical mediation of the truth to mankind.

These ten theses are not meant to be understood as theses in the scholastic sense, calling for counter theses, so that an argumentation may be developed in which we operate with clear-cut *distinctiones*. Rather are they theses that are thrust forward from a field of continuous connection and which cannot be abstracted from that field of connection without change of intention or distortion. As set out here these theses are naturally and necessarily connected, in that they overlap and flow into one another, so that they cannot be sharply divided. Nevertheless a real progression of thought is intended as we move through them from the first to the last. My main intention in these theses has been to express as strongly as possible the *truth of being,* and along with the truth of being the *referring function* of language, and especially of course the referring function of theological statements. When that referring function is damaged or broken the semantic intention of statements suffers badly, and we are inevitably thrown back upon ourselves to supply their meaning, that is, from some sort of self-understanding on the part of those who make the statements.

For an instance of this in the history of thought we may turn to the late Middle Ages as it gave way to the Renaissance. Under the impact of a distinctive philosophy of logic and language, the so-called *via moderna* as it was pursued by Occam's successors, the referring function of language was severely damaged, so that thought tended to move in one of two directions: on the one hand, it tended to develop into moralism, such as we find in the writings of Erasmus in the high Renaissance, but on the other hand, it tended to develop into a rather extreme form of nominalism, the so-called *logica sermocinalis* of the terminists. We have been witnessing a counterpart to that in our own time when once again the referring function of language has suffered severe damage, and people are thrown back upon themselves to supply the meaning. This is evident on the one hand, in existentialism which corresponds in its way to the moralism of the Renaissance, and on the other hand, in the linguistic philosophy which corresponds to the nominalism and terminism of the late mediaeval period of thought. These two aberrations are twins: they belong together because they have each derived from the broken relation of semantic reference to objective reality. Today, however, we find this outlook so widely spread that it has seriously affected other aspects of our life and thought, not least art and music which manifest everywhere serious disintegration of form.

The reason for this phenomenon, the corroding or refracting of the referring function of language, in late mediaeval as in modern times, is evidently to be traced to a radical dualism pervading thought, loosening or even detaching its relation to objective reality. Earlier forms of this are apparent in the classical philosophy of the high Middle Ages and in the classical philosophy of modern Europe, in the developing notions of representative perception, i.e. of images and ideas 'in the middle' which are the immediate terminal points of our apprehension, *objecta mentis* distinct from external objects in the real world. Behind that epistemological dualism, of course, lay a thoroughgoing cosmological dualism, in mediaeval times the Ptolemaic cosmology and in modern times the Newtonian cosmology. We are not to explore the effect of those dualisms upon theology, but it will be sufficient to note that they did involve a dualism between the intelligible and the sensible which had considerable impact upon the history, life and thought in the Church. That is nowhere more evident than in the fourteenth and fifteenth centuries, when a disastrous dualism began to open up in the heart of theology: it was due in part to the teaching of the Occamists, but also, and not least, to a massive revival of Augustinianism, when the old dualism between the intelligible and sensible realms came back with such force that the physics and metaphysics of Aristotle fell under sharp criticism: and the great mediaeval synthesis began to fall apart. There can be little doubt that this Augustinian form of dualism poured out of the Middle Ages into the world of the Renaissance and the Reformation – nowhere is that more evident perhaps than in the Lutheran distinction between the two kingdoms of faith and sight, gospel and law, and so on. But it is important to see that this Augustinian dualism characterised the whole of Protestantism, and lay behind the development of European thought after the Reformation. Of special significance was the radical form it took after Kant and his sharp distinction between things in themselves and things for us, which has also had its considerable effect in the development of modern Roman thought. I think especially here of the obsession with the phenomenological approach to knowledge, whether we take that in its Protestant form which undoubtedly gave rise to the main tendencies in Protestant biblical exegesis, or in its Roman form which lies behind a good deal of the reinterpretation of St Thomas from Maréchal to Karl Rahner. Whether we take this development in its Protestant or in its Roman forms, we find modern theology thrust back upon the same epistemological problems. The religio-cultural tradition, the ecclesiastical character, and the theological style, may all be somewhat different, but it would not be difficult to show how close neo-Protestant and neo-Roman theology really are to each other. Some of us, indeed, who have been struggling to lead Protestant theology out of its nineteenth-century reduction to a form of anthropology and to set it on more adequate scientific foundations, cannot help but discern in the so-called 'new theology', e.g. as advocated by some of the *Concilium* theologians, something like a relapse into the mistakes of nineteenth-century Protestantism, of Schleiermacher and the Hegelians particularly.

It is rather disturbing, I think, to find in some of our Roman friends an obsession with what is called the *non-conceptual element* in theology. This is something that we Protestants can understand, especially in the post-Kantian tradition, with its cultivated contrast between the noumenal and the phenomenal and its severe refraction of conceptual relations with God. But Protestant and Roman positions in this respect both go back to the same basic assumptions and problems that derive from the late mediaeval world. Let me point to one common factor only: the tendency of Augustinian thought to take flight from this world into another world above and beyond space and time altogether. In spite of all the attempts to tame this in Thomism and various forms of Aristotelian thought, mediaeval exegesis was persistently *oblique*. In Occam's language, it was concerned with the *intentio obliqua*, rather than the *intentio recta*. Looked at from this point of view, Occam's emphasis upon second intentions, rather than primary intentions, was not so widely removed from the emphasis in mediaeval exegesis upon the figurative rather than the literal sense of Holy Scripture. Behind both lay the same presupposition: a radical dualism that deflected direct conceptual relation with God and the referring function of statements. Once that happens, you are cast back upon second intentions in logic and oblique meaning in language. That is the basic root of so many of our problems in exegesis, in the allegorical exegesis of late patristic and mediaeval times and in the moralistic and existentialist exegesis of modern times. It is not difficult to trace the history of the concern for the *intentio obliqua* over against the *intentio recta*, from Occam to Erasmus, from Erasmus to Dilthey, and from Dilthey to Bultmann. Take away the style and idiom of modern philosophy, and it becomes evident that existentialist exegesis and allegorical exegesis operate on the same basic assumptions and have the same problems. Thus I feel sure that, from the philosophical and epistemological point of view, theologians will more and more agree that much modern exegesis of the New Testament does not differ in principle from the allegorical exegesis of the Augustinian tradition, and that as we look back upon allegorical exegesis with a little pathetic ridicule, so they in the days ahead will look back upon modern existentialist exegesis with the same sort of pathetic ridicule because it was oblique and rejected the *intentio recta*.

I have not discussed the other movement of thought that developed in the late Middle Ages, the nominalist and conventionalist views of language and statement everywhere apparent in the terminism or linguistic philosophy of those times. We have distinct parallels to this also in the modern world, and where more than in the Anglo-Saxon schools of philosophy? The direct connection between modern and mediaeval language philosophy is not so easy to draw, because of the rise of modern science which is concerned primarily with direct intentions and with the objective reference of our statements to the universe, but it would not be difficult to show that the same basic assumptions lie behind both forms of language philosophy which lead them to replace thinking of real connections in the objective world with thinking the connections between statements, and thus to reduce the major problems in the last analysis to linguistic problems. It is to this temptation that many theologians have succumbed especially in the English-speaking world, but behind it all lies a severe refraction in conceptual relations with God, resulting in a conceptual letting go of God and a denial of the cognitive nature of theological statements. But if in Britain this manifests a preoccupation with logic, it is a first cousin to the continental preoccupation with phenomenology, for in both the same epistemological dualism has determined their fundamental orientation.

My concern in these theses on truth is to point in a very different direction: away from the radical dualisms that thrust us either into some form of oblique existentialism or into some form of oblique linguistic philosophy, because in theology, as in any pure science, we are concerned primarily with direct intention and with the referring function of statements and propositions. This applies as much to biblical hermeneutics as it does to theological dogmatics. Let me turn then to the actual theses and offer some explanation of them.

1. The first three theses, or rather sets of theses, are concerned primarily to set out the truth of being, and, as will be evident, I have used for this purpose language that comes from the Fathers, early Mediaevals, including of course Augustine and Anselm. It seems to me that in this Christian tradition we have a flowing together of what one might call the Hebraic notion of truth with the Greek notion of truth. By the Hebraic notion of truth I mean that which is concerned with the consistency and faithfulness of God who reveals himself to us in such a way that what he reveals stands in a relation of absolute fidelity to what he is in himself. But this is combined with the Greek notion of truth which relates to the reality of things,

their *alētheia* or *physis*. This is evident in the thought of St Augustine, who spoke of truth as that which is and which shows itself to be what it is, but it is developed in the thought of Anselm and Grosseteste in their superb treatises on truth. Behind this lie not only certain aspects of Plato's concept of truth which were taken up by some of the Fathers, for example by Clement of Alexandria, but which have often been neglected, but also, aspects of the teaching of Aristotle in *Metaphysics* G and the *De Interpretatione* 18, which played an important part in the mediaeval world. However, here we have a problem of interpretation, due to the fact that on one side of his teaching Aristotle held a fully realist notion of truth, as the truth of being, but then on another side of his thought, for example in the *Metaphysics,* he developed a more intellectualist and dialectical concept of truth. This duality is clearly reflected in the teaching of St Thomas Aquinas, although in the last analysis he seems to have held a more intellectualist than a realist concept of truth.

In the thinking of the Fathers, then, and not only before Augustine, two aspects of truth appear to me to have been fully and beautifully woven together to constitute what was the main tradition of the notion of truth right up to St Anselm. It was this that many of the mediaeval treatises *De veritate* discussed. I think it should be noted at this point that we cannot really understand the language of the Fathers by reading back Latin Aristotelianism into them. For example, we cannot understand *physis* by reading *natura* back into it, nor can we properly understand *hypostasis* by reading it as *substantia*. In some of the fragments of Clement of Alexandria, to whom I have already referred, where we are given some very clear definitions of what *physis*, *alētheia* and *hypostasis* are, we discern a way of thinking very different from that which tended to develop in a more intellectualist way later on. Many modern scholars are, I think, still far from appreciating what went on in Alexandria in those early centuries, when the Fathers hammered out their basic theological concepts and terms, not only in the literary culture of their day, but in the midst of the most advanced scientific achievements of the ancient world, and not least, if the extant fragments of Anatolius are anything to judge by, in the light of an advanced philosophy of science *(hē epistēmonikē theōria)*. It is when we compare the concepts and terms used by these Fathers, from Clement to Athanasius, for example, with what we have in the scientific manuals and treatises that survive, that we find them operating in theological science with tools basically similar to those with which the physicists and mathematicians and engineers or 'mechanists' had equipped themselves for their own research. I mention this, as it gives us a very different slant on early Christian theology from that which tended to supervene when this scientific orientation fell away and a more psychological and logical approach took its place, e.g. with Augustine and Boethius.

As I understand the patristic concept of truth, as it developed in these ways, *alētheia* or *veritas* is that which is what it is and what it discloses itself to be. The primary emphasis here is on the sheer reality of things, but it takes in the notion of 'unconcealment' (as Heidegger has called it), that is to say, the fact that the truth shines in its own light in its own evidence and forces upon us an assent and a consent in relation to it. This is a point where we find Aristotelian and Stoic language put to good use by the Fathers: I refer to *pistis* and *sygkatathesis*, and *hekousia sygkatathesis*, which they employed to speak of the faith or assent, or willing assent, which is forced on us by the self-evidencing and self-manifesting reality of things. This was applied equally in natural science and in theology, but in accordance with the different *physis* or reality in each field, that is in accordance with the nature of reality which manifests itself in the Christian religion and in accordance with the nature of the reality that manifests itself in the fields where natural science engages in inquiry. This meant that there was basically one way of knowing, so that the Fathers even in the 4th and 5th and 6th centuries could speak of genuine knowledge as *kata physin*, according to the nature of things. Knowledge *kata physin* applies to God, and it is the nature of God that determines the appropriate way we are to know him. In this terminology *kata physin* was the equivalent of *alēthōs*: or *kat' alētheian*; *alētheia* and *physis*, and in this respect also *ousia*, were basically the same. It is, then, in terms of this classical patristic orientation that I have tried to set out a general approach to truth in thesis *one*.

2. In thesis *two*, this is applied to our thought of God. He is himself the truth who reveals himself as he is and who remains faithful to what he reveals of himself. Here the Greek concept of the openness of truth and the Hebraic concept of the consistency of God are brought together, as indeed they had already been brought together in the New Testament. This God who does not deceive us in any way, he who keeps faith and truth, he who keeps covenant with us, is himself the source and standard of all truth. In other words, truth is here seen as the truth which God is in his own eternal being, and the truth which he shines upon us from and through himself.

3. In the *third* thesis, I have tried to apply this to our knowledge of God, by following the same basic patristic and early mediaeval

tradition. The distinctive language of the Alexandrian theologians is used to speak of the freedom, authority, and prerogative of God as himself the truth. These are the terms *autousia* and *autexousia,* which together with other words such as *autologos, autobasileia, autodikaiosunē, autoagapē, autodoxa,* were attempts to speak of God in a way appropriate to him in the unity of his word and person, his being and act, and so on. Face to face with God, we are up against the ultimate truth of being in God's own self: it is only as we are cast upon him in this way, as the ultimate Source of all truth who is not closed to us but who by his nature is open to us, that we may know him truly, for then we know him under the immediate compulsion of his own being, in the power of his self-evidence.

This brings us to a point that needs further discussion, and which affects, perhaps, more those who have been deeply influenced by the teaching of St Thomas. To use Anselmic language: when we really know God we know that we know him under the compulsion of his being who he is and what by his nature he must be; we know him truly under the light of his truth which is his divine being coming to view and becoming in our understanding and knowledge of him what he is consistently in himself and in all his relations with us. Perhaps I may be allowed to indicate the point that needs to be discussed by referring to the distinction drawn by Duns Scotus between a *voluntary object* and an *involuntary object.* When I know an involuntary object like this hand of mine, it compels me, as it were, *per modum causalitatis* or *per modum entis* to know it in accordance with what it actually is, but when I know Père Dockx who is next to me I know him not as an involuntary object – he is that also of course in so far as he is a physical being – but as a voluntary object. That is to say, he is a personal agent, and is as such the object of my knowing, but I may know him in this way only in so far as he *freely* and *willingly* gives himself to be known by me, and in so far as I *willingly* know him. At this point, medieval thought was in line with the Stoic emphasis upon *hekousia sygkatathesis* or willing assent. That is to say, knowledge here involves a moment of the will. But Duns Scotus went on to show that even when a moment of the will is involved in our knowing, in relation to one another or in relation to God, when the other reveals himself to me, within that voluntary relationship, my mind still falls under the compulsion of what is there – and it is that which is finally compelling, and finally self-evidencing. It is this second point that is sometimes forgotten or omitted in Thomist thought. We recall that St Thomas himself taught that that to which the understanding gives assent does not move the understanding by its own power but by the influence of the will; but then he also went on to say that the intellect assents to something, not through being sufficiently moved to this assent by its proper object, but through an act of choice, i.e. because it is enough to move the will but not enough to move the understanding. This detachment of the understanding, even in the assent of faith, from the self-evidence of God in his own being and truth, means that in the last resort faith has to rest upon moral grounds and operate only with an indirect relation to the *autousia* and *autexousia* of God. In the nature of the case this opens up a gap between faith and its object which is occupied by an *authority other than the truth of being*. This was bound to create difficulty as soon as a more direct relation between the understanding and its object opened up in natural science, as began to happen with William of Occam, so that the hiatus between faith and reason that opened up in the later Middle Ages cannot be blamed simply on Occam, who in the realm of faith and theology held, with St Thomas, to an indirect relation between the understanding and the immediate compulsive evidence of its object. Certainly both Thomas and Occam stand in marked contrast to Anselm at this point in his doctrine of *necessitas,* i.e. the compulsive ground of understanding in the truth of the divine Being.

In view of this teaching of St Thomas, namely, an indirect relation in the assent of faith to its object mediated through the will, and a refraction in its conceptual relation to the self-evidence of God, in view, then, of St Thomas' resiling from the truth of being in the full sense, one must venture the question – however shocking it may sound to Thomists! – whether this did not lead into a voluntarist, and, in spite of itself, into a nominalist direction. If this were the case, it would help us to understand why even in the Council of Trent it was a nominalist theology that was predominant even though St Thomas' *Summa* was laid on the high altar!

I have raised the problem of mediaeval theology with the truth of being in this way because it helps us to see the deep affinity between it and the problem of neo-Protestantism. I refer here to the refraction in the conceptual relation of faith to its object which developed with and after Kant, when because of the alleged non-evidence of its object faith was moved to assent through the will, so that its understanding of God was made to rest on moral grounds. But once a gap is opened up in this way between the understanding and its proper object and the will is allowed to move in to assist the understanding in giving assent, then sooner or later some form of the active intellect or active reason comes on the scene and there takes place a shift in the basic notion of truth, in which the *adaequatio intellectus et rei* is understood less as *adaequatio intellectus ad rem ad extra* than as *adaequatio rei ad intellectum*. That was, it seems to me, the difficult change that happened in mediaeval thought, and which has certainly happened in Protestant thought: but when that takes place, it is in the last analysis we who control and manipulate what we know, and as Kant used to say, make it the object of our thought. This is certainly the manifest tendency in Protestant and Roman phenomenological theology, in which theology tends to be converted into some form of theological anthropology. Moreover, as I see it, the movement in Roman theology from Maréchal to Rahner which brings St Thomas and Kant together, instead of overcoming Kantian phenomenalism serves rather to bring out the latent phenomenalism in Aquinas, and thus accentuates the retreat from the truth of being.

When we consider this problem of mediaeval theology with the truth of being in the light of the teaching of St Anselm, it becomes very apparent that the root difficulty lies in the admission of a *non-conceptual element* in our basic knowledge of God. I can understand why some great modern Thomists, and theologians as open-minded as Schillebeeckx, are tempted to take refuge in this non-conceptual relation, if only in order to cope with the hard kataphatic conceptualism evident in some of the more difficult pronouncements of the Curia. But that is certainly no way out of the problem. Rather must we penetrate back into the truth of being and find in its inner structure the source of our conceptions of it, and at the same time discern the bi-polar nature of the conceptuality which arises in this way. This is a conceptuality rooted and grounded in the objective intelligibility of reality, but incorporating also a subjective counterpart, since it is after all we who conceive, think, formulate and our knowledge of God grounded upon his own self-evidence is not cut off from the fact that it is, *deo dante et deo illuminante, our* knowledge of him. However, when the relation between these two poles of conceptuality is snapped by the importation of non-conceptual elements, then serious problems inevitably arise. Let me refer again to that particular problem I located in the teaching of St Thomas about the assent of faith: our minds know the truth as they assent to it, but since the object is not sufficiently compelling of itself to our understanding, we require some kind of *lumen infusum* or some kind of *gratia infusa* or indeed *fides infusa,* which then comes, as it were, from behind in order to enable us to assent to the truth in spite of its non-evidence. But this is not to evade the problem of conceptualism, for it becomes more fideist and authoritarian, since the conceptual dualism in our relation to the truth is maintained and assent is demanded through the submission of the will to what is not evident to the mind rather than through a direct yet willing assent to the truth of being. Here, then, the refraction between the understanding and the truth brought about by the introduction of a non-conceptual relation is overcome in a roundabout way through an infused grace motivating assent. Sooner or later, however, that roundabout way is bound to collapse, and then thought breaks apart, and tension arises between authoritarian pronouncements of truth and the consciences of the faithful. As I understand it, that is a basic problem today in the Roman Church, for both the theologians of the Curia and the advocates of 'the new theology' still rely on St Thomas' analysis and solution of the problem, and neither side has thought through profoundly enough the relation between our conceiving and the inherent intelligibility of God in his own self-evidencing reality. Hence what I am asking of both Roman theology and Protestant theology, which in different ways share the same basic problem, is to take more seriously the *truth of being*.

4. This brings me to the main point of thesis *four,* that in the biblical and early patristic doctrine of God, the divine *logos* is not separable from the divine *ousia*. Let me indicate the significance of this by referring to the important little book *De verbo mirifico* published by Reuchlin early in the sixteenth century and officially examined by the University of Paris in view of its suspected orthodoxy. In it Reuchlin had attacked the prevailing mediaeval tradition, for the most part Augustinian and Thomist, which interpreted the *logos* of God mainly in terms of vision and intellection, and argued that when the Nicene concept of the *homoousion* is applied to Word become flesh, it must be agreed that the Word is eternally inherent in God *as word*. In this way Reuchlin sought to establish a more realist understanding of the *verbum dei* in its incarnate and revealed forms, which had important implications for biblical interpretation and theological understanding. According to the Augustinian-Thomist tradition, however, word in God must be taken ultimately in a metaphorical sense. While St Thomas was unwilling to go as far as St Augustine in equating the divine Word with the shining of the divine light or the divine vision, he was nevertheless in such deep agreement with St Augustine that he could persistently attack St Anselm for distinguishing *dicere* and *intelligere* in God. Thus in the last resort St Thomas seems to have thought of the Word of God not as word but as the form of the divine intellection, an act of God which takes the form of what we mean by word in his relation to us. For St Anselm, on the other

hand, Word inheres in the very Being of God in the form of Speech, and so he could speak of the *intima locutio apud summam substantiam* to relate it to the *ratio veritatis* inherent in God as the Supreme Truth. Moreover, Anselm related this more closely – though still perhaps deficiently from the point of view of Greek patristic theology – to the Spirit of God. Thus it is through his Word and Spirit that we may know God evidently and compellingly in his own Being and according to his own Nature. And because the *intima locutio* inherent in God himself, the object of our knowledge, is the creative ground and source of all *locutiones rerum* inherent in the truth of created beings, we can both conceive of God and speak of him truly in ways that are grounded in himself, even though he transcends all our conceiving of him. It is for this reason, then, that St Anselm could reject a non-conceptual relation to God: *fides esse nequit sine conceptione.* There can be no knowledge of God, no faith, which is not basically conceptual, or conceptual at its very root, and therefore there is no non-conceptual gap between God's revealing of himself and our knowing of him. Far from meaning that knowledge of God in his eternal Being is captured within the grasp of our creaturely concepts, this means that the human concepts which arise in faith under the creative impact of the speech of God are grounded beyond themselves in the *ratio veritatis* of the divine Being.

5. These concepts of the truth of being in God must themselves be true. Hence theses *five* and *six* are devoted to *truth* and *truthfulness,* since it is important to keep in view a proper distinction between the truth of God himself and a true relation between our minds and the truth of God. At this point I have a problem with Küng's provocative book, *Wahrhaftigkeit,* for the way in which his thought runs between *Wahrheit* and *Wahrhaftigkeit* makes me ask whether he does not need to think out more carefully the relation between truthfulness and truth, and between true statements and the truth of statements. In clarifying this distinction, St Anselm found that he had to distinguish between several different levels of truth, the truths of statement and the truth of signification, the truth of created being (the *veritas essentiae rerum,* as he called it) and the Supreme Truth; and insisted that the relations between these several levels, in the order I have mentioned them, are all open upward towards the Supreme Truth and are not reducible downward. It will be sufficient for us to note, following St Anselm, that the truth is such, whether we find it in created being or in the divine being, that it lays us under a debt: we owe it to the truth to be truly related to it. Thus truthfulness is seen to be an openness to the truth and a

right orientation towards it in accordance with the nature of the truth. While truthfulness involves an analogical relation of reference back to the truth of being, the truth of being itself always retains ontic priority, for it is what it is in its own reality before it is acknowledged by us, and what it is in itself is the compulsive ground of our recognition of it and speech about it. It is thus part of the truthfulness of true concepts and true statements that they distinguish themselves from the truth itself which has laid them under obligation to it, and that they direct us away from themselves to that truth as the 'cause' of what they are.

6. In developing further the need to distinguish between the truth of being and the truth of statement, in thesis *six,* and to indicate the problem that arises when we confuse them with each other, I have adapted some language of Wittgenstein's about the relation between pictures and what they picture. No more than you can picture in a picture how a picture pictures what it pictures, without reducing everything to a picture, can you state in statements how statements are related to being, without reducing everything to statements – yet that is precisely, I suggest, what both realists and nominalists in different ways tried to do. Now if those who posit a non-conceptual element in our knowledge of God are thereby intending to safeguard an empirical relation to the divine Being, in the recognition that you cannot convert true relation to being simply into a statement, then that would seem to be very right. I can appreciate that, for there is no knowledge of God or of the universe which does not comprise both an empirical as well as a theoretical component. But this is not what the positing of a non-conceptual relation actually means to most people who want a break in our conceptual relations with God in order that they may not subject him to the control of our conceptions and formulations. However, the effect of such a break in our conceptual relations means that instead of terminating upon God himself as their rational ground, our concepts bend back and terminate upon our own consciousness, so that in the last analysis it is our own self-understanding which is the criterion of their truth or falsity: they never get beyond what the mediaevals called the *objecta mentis.*

A similar problem seems to arise in the thought of philosophers like Wittgenstein and Heidegger. Both of them are concerned to break up the hard structure of concepts and statements in order to allow the reality of things to 'show through', although they were concerned in rather different ways with the relation of language to being. Heidegger insists that he is not an existentialist, and that his main concern is with *Sein* or being, and claims that his analysis of existence is with a view to breaking up false ontologies, in order to open up the way for being and truth, *physis* and *alētheia*. But it seems to me that in point of fact he does tumble over into existentialism, since he too works finally with a non-conceptual relation to being. He has some fine things to say about the problem created through the secession of *logos* from *physis,* but since *logos* does not inhere in being and being cannot therefore be conceptually grasped, the only way Heidegger can think of letting being disclose itself to him is through a non-conceptual leap on his part into nothing: but then he can only fall back upon himself and his own self-understanding, as surely as an arrow shot up into the air falls back to the ground.

Wittgenstein had rather similar problems. He too made very important contributions to modern philosophy, not least in his analysis of the function of language, and certainly in his later thought he stands apart from many of his would-be followers, but it would be difficult to absolve him from serious mistakes that keep on cropping up in the various stages and forms of the linguistic philosophy, and not least the inveterate nominalism that is evident in the substitution of 'linguistic statements' for 'physical state-ments', or in the reduction of empirical relations to the relations of statements. But let it be granted that both Wittgenstein and Heidegger intended something different: to penetrate through the fixities of language patterns, in order to make room for sheer reality, or what I have called the truth of being. If that is the case, we can well learn from their intentions as well as their mistakes about the need to distinguish the truth of being from the truth of statement, for unless the truth of statement is grounded beyond itself in the truth of being it can quickly replace the truth of being altogether. It does not follow, because a true statement about the truth must be distinguished from the truth of being to which it refers, that it is not objectively grounded in that truth. Even if we cannot argue, as both Wittgenstein and Heidegger remind us, from the statement itself to the reality to which it directs us, nevertheless the reality shows itself and thrusts itself upon us in accordance with its own nature: but statements can serve that disclosure of reality only if they themselves are grounded intelligibly in it. Were that not the case, we would have only poetry and no science.

It may be worth noting at this point that one way of becoming a nominalist is to become an extreme realist. If our statements are absolutely adequate to the object, how can we distinguish the object from statements about it? This was, of course, pointed out long ago by Plato, with rather different language, in the *Cratylus*. Assuming that language has a real *(physei)* and a mimetic relation to reality *(alētheia tōn ontōn)*, the more our terms *(onomata)* become exact images or replicas *(eikones)* of the reality of things, the more inevitable it is that they should be mistaken for that reality and become substitutes for it. Thus if they are to perform their denotative function adequately, directing us to reality beyond themselves in such a way that there takes place a disclosure *(dēlōsis)* of reality, they must have, as it were, a measure of inadequacy in order to be differentiated from that to which they refer. In other words, the realist *(physei)* relation of language to being *(alēthia tōn ontōn)* requires to have at least a dash of conventionalism (a relation *thesei*), or perhaps even of nominalism, about it, in order to be truly related to the truth. For true statements to serve the truth of being, they must themselves fall short of it and be recognised as such, for they do not possess their truth in themselves but in the reality they serve.

This is a lesson that we theologians have to learn again and again. It is surely in that light that we may see the immense significance of the distinction drawn by Pope John XXIII at the outset of the Second Vatican Council, between the substance of the faith and our formulations of it. That does not mean that formulations of the faith are not objectively grounded in the substance of the faith, and its inherent intelligibility, and therefore it does not mean a halt to scientific theology. That is to say, to distinguish between the substance of the faith and the Church's formulations of it, does not mean (as it seems to have been interpreted in some quarters) that our thought can be allowed to run off in an oblique direction, into some so-called kerygmatic or existentialist theology, without rigorous attention to the grounding of our thought in the inner structure of the faith, and therefore without raising the question as to the truth or falsity of our concepts and statements.

In the four theses that remain, I have tried to apply these issues we have been discussing to the scientific elucidation and organic structure of theology. The main points of each thesis have been set out at greater length, for that seemed needed in order to show how questions of statement, analogical relation, interpretation and authority function in the development of scientific theology. But since they are set out more fully in these paragraphs, my comments upon them may be relatively shorter.

7. In theses *seven* and *eight*, I take up again the need for different levels of truth and concept which had been projected in the thought of Anselm and Duns Scotus, and set out their translogical relations and hierarchical structure, within which questions of analogy and truth are to be elucidated. The basic distinctions to be observed are

those between the levels of truth of statement and the truth of created being, and then between these and the Supreme Truth which is God in his self-subsistent Being and in his own transcendent Rationality. These levels cannot be flattened out without loss in objective depth and in universality of range. In order to indicate the problem to be considered here, let me point once again to the thought of St Thomas. As I understand it, he began in his early days by considering the analogical relation in terms of relations or of proportionality. Thus the relation between God and his being was compared in its likeness and unlikeness with the relation between man and his being on another level, but without of course involving any reciprocation in this comparison, and the analogical relation was construed not only in terms of proportions but proportionalities. But the more rigorously this was thought out in a scientific way, and that meant in those days thinking *more geometrico,* the more closely the levels had to be brought together, since classical mathematics and Euclidean geometry do not operate with levels of proportion and the relations between them. St Thomas was clearly nervous of employing the mathematical concept of proportion in any strict way, and it is not surprising that the stress on proportionality began to fade out. On the other hand this *more geometrico* way of thinking made it all the more important to introduce a real refraction in the relation between our conceptions and the transcendent Being of God in order to prevent the projection of our creaturely images and ideas into God – hence the importance for St Thomas of a powerful element of Pseudo-Dionysian apophaticism. This meant a valuable change of emphasis in St Thomas' notion of analogy, as having to do not with relations in concepts themselves, but with their referring back to, or their intending, the reality of God beyond their power to grasp it. This greater measure of objective depth introduced into the structure of theology opened up the way for a return to something like the Anselmic hierarchy of different levels, and that seems to have been the intention of Duns Scotus in his notion of different *gradus cognitionis de deo* in which every lower level is directed to the supreme level *(ultimus finis)* as its goal in God. Of course, if these various levels are flattened out on to one and the same level and the terms they employ are treated as terms in the same logical calculus, then contradiction and absurd univocities result – which is what has happened not infrequently in Thomist misinterpretations of Duns Scotus.

It is much the same problem we are faced with today, especially in attacks from the linguistic philosophies, when again and again they examine theological, and indeed metaphysical concepts, and treat them as if they were on the same level as the concepts we work with in our ordinary natural experience and speech, and then profess to find them meaningless. That is to say, by flattening them all out on to one and the same level, they point to the absurd contradictions and impossibilities that they involve when all the time the fault is theirs in a serious confusion not only of logical types but logical levels. We would have much the same problem if we attempted to convert statements in nuclear physics to the kind of statements we use in classical physics, forgetting that classical physics is but a limiting case of nuclear physics, and that here we operate with different levels of connection which cannot be redacted into one and the same level without absurd contradictions and paradoxes. A cognate error to this is made by many continental theologians who attack objective thinking in theology as though it were merely objectifying thinking, and accuse it of projecting creaturely concepts into God and of introducing impossible contradictions, when the real confusion is theirs, in mixing different languages and levels of thought. It is not my intention to examine and expose these pseudo-problems here, but rather to indicate the immense importance and indeed necessity of learning to think in theology in terms of coordinated levels of thought, much as we have been forced to do today in the exact sciences.

It is, I believe, when we elucidate theological concepts and relations in terms of a hierarchic structure of inter-related levels of thought, that we can determine problems of analogy and of the truth-reference they involve more clearly and exactly today than it was possible in classical or mediaeval times, because of what we have learned not least through the mathematicians who have had to clarify the relations of symbolic and linguistic levels of thought. I have in mind here particularly some of the main points advanced by Frege and Gödel.

In any science today we normally work with three basic logical levels of thought, and by science I mean any real field of knowledge pursued in a rigorous and organised way: the level of ordinary statement and connection appropriate to everyday rational experience, the level of rigorous, scientific statement where we are concerned with elucidating objective structural relations, and a third level which we may call the meta-scientific level where we treat of intricate epistemological and logical connections. These various levels are coordinated together in such a way that each level is open to the other and translogically related to it at certain boundary points – that is, to use Gödelian language, where the system of statements or the calculus contains certain statements which are not decidable on that level, but are decidable on another level, within a wider logico-deductive or logico-syntactical system to which they also belong. But on that level, likewise, there are certain statements which are not decidable within it but only from within the system of another and higher level. This coordination of levels, considered purely *theoretically*, could, of course, go on *ad infinitum*, but normally we operate only with three or perhaps four such levels – more would be empirically and scientifically meaningless. The Gödelian theorems show that in order to be consistent each level must be incomplete, or in other words that the consistency of any one level depends on its translogical coordination with another level to which it is open. This is a very remarkable achievement in thought which has been universally accepted, but there are three implications of it that I would like to note, especially. (a) Structures of thought coordinated in this way are necessarily open structures, always incomplete in themselves, but orientated beyond themselves; (b) the different levels in which these structures are found constitute a hierarchy, as Bertrand Russell has shown, which is open upwards and not downwards; and (c) statements are normally tested and controlled from two coordinated levels, but because the structures are open upwards and not downwards, there can be no reductionism.

It is, I believe, within this open hierarchical structure of levels of thought, that we are able to cope with the problem of analogy and truth-reference, in a way that our predecessors were not able to do. The main point to remember is that there is no one-to-one or point-for-point correspondence between the concepts on one level and their counterparts on another level, but they are analogically related through the translogical relation between the different levels to which they belong and by which they are defined. For example, there is no one-to-one correspondence between human fatherhood and the Fatherhood of God, for in each case the term 'father' is defined and has its logical truth-reference in the level of thought to which it properly belongs or in the syntactical system in which it is used, so that the way in which human fatherhood is analogated to divine Fatherhood must be through the way in which the levels in which they are respectively defined are coordinated as wholes. The concept of human fatherhood is thus an open structure of thought with more than a logical truth-reference in the system in which it is employed, but with an analogical truth-reference above and beyond itself to a higher level of concepts upon which it depends for its meaning and consistency even on its own level. On the other hand, the concept of the Fatherhood of God which is defined by the supreme level is in the nature of the case not open to any reduction to or definition from below, although the structure open from below through its analogical and translogical reference is necessary for *our* apprehension of the divine Fatherhood. At the same time the representational content of what we mean by a human father does not as such correspond to anything in the divine Fatherhood, although it is conceptually coordinated with it in this open way through the hierarchy of levels.

Perhaps I may be allowed to refer back for a moment to the difference of view between Duns Scotus and the Thomists. The latter misunderstood Duns Scotus when they accused him of the error of univocity in the way he spoke of God and man. The point Duns tried to make is that if you speak of the Being of God and the being of man on one and the same logical level, by which these terms are defined, and are therefore treating terms like 'being' merely in their second intentions in a single syntactical system, that is, in their logical truth-reference only, they are used univocally, but if you speak of the Being of God and the being of man on different logical levels, and thus think of them as related not logically but metaphysically, then you think of them analogically and not univocally. What Duns was attacking here was the tendency to flatten out statements about God and statements about man on to one and the same level, when contradictions inevitably arise. It cannot be claimed that Duns Scotus saw his way clearly through these problems, but his insistence that theology must operate on different levels was very sound. This way of thinking has now fortunately been opened up for us, and theologians may use it with considerable profit in a scientific clarification of forms of human thought and speech about God.

8. If it is granted that scientific theology today must operate with a stratification in the totality of its concepts and relations in which there is a distinct hierarchy of levels, then there must also be a *hierarchy of truths* as defined in terms of those different levels. It is the question as to the theological status of those truths that is raised in thesis *eight,* together with the question as to the differentiation between truths and truths which the very concept of hierarchy involves.

Let me begin my comments by taking once more an analogy from mathematics, in which we operate with different levels of equations and relations, as in our multiple algebras. On each level there are basic concepts which have been developed from the ground of empirical experience through, it may well be, several other levels, and through that coordination they are applicable to existence. On any one level, however, we may elaborate our logico-deductive operations in such a way as to derive a host of equations and relations which are consistent with the basic concepts on that level but which may have no applicability to existence whatsoever. In so far as they have no applicability to existence, they are useless for real science, so that when the elaboration of concepts beyond the point of applicability to existence or scientific relevance is reached, their multiplication becomes a game. Sometimes of course concepts are developed in this sort of way without any concern for their scientific relevance, but which are later discovered to have application to existence, e.g. Hamilton's quaternions. It is not always easy, however, to discern when the elaboration of concepts in this way is simply a game, perhaps a very clever game, but in itself scientifically valueless. On the other hand, it is often the case that, only when our conceptual connections are extended far from their original base, are we able to clarify the significance and relevance of our *basic concepts*. Once that clarification has been achieved, however, the extension of conceptual connections beyond the point of applicability to existence which brought about that clarification is halted, while the concepts elaborated become expendable, and are cut away.

Something similar to this takes place in theology within the stratification of levels of which I have been speaking. Our theological concepts are developed in whole fields of connection in order to make the basic concepts clear, but when we have done that many of the ideas elaborated in that process become expendable. Thus on each level there arise secondary and even tertiary theological conceptions which played a necessary part in developing the scientific structure of our thought, but while some of them are still needed for the organic connection of our concepts, and maintain their significance through their service to the basic or primary concepts close to the centre of our Christian faith and experience, others became expendable once their particular function has been fulfilled, and cannot but obstruct further development and obscure the whole structure if they are retained. The application of what is called 'Occam's razor' is just as necessary in theology as in any other pure science: the multiplication of entities or conceptions beyond necessity is to be rejected.

Two further comments on this process need to be made. (a) If we insist out of some form of naive realism that there must be a one-to-one correspondence between our theological concepts and reality, then as we develop our conceptions by deducing them from basic concepts, we are tempted to posit corresponding realities for them which they do not really have. Some of our basic ideas do have empirical correlates of that kind, although as we have seen that correlation must be construed through the coordination of the different levels; but other concepts are only what we might call 'theorems' or relations posited to connect up basic concepts with each other, and do not have empirical correlates. They have to be treated as conjunctive concepts within the system which as a whole does have empirical correlation, but not as having distinct entities to which they refer. Let me illustrate this from the doctrine of grace. At one stage it appeared necessary to distinguish between several different kinds of grace, in order to make clear certain basic conceptions, but to posit different entities corresponding to them, hypostatised realities of this or that grace, would involve us in the guilt of an unscientific multiplication of entities as well as conceptions. Hence it becomes necessary not to treat all our conceptions as if they were of the same kind or of the same status in the theological structure – some concepts have only peripheral significance, and some have only a transient function to perform, and that should be clearly recognised.

(b) Because we are concerned in theology with the interaction of God with us in time and space, theology inevitably and rightly involves a profound historical development. It is then in this connection also that we must consider the theological status of our concepts, and not least the distinction between primary, secondary, tertiary concepts, and transitory notions or mere theorems. It is also important to see, however, that the different levels that arise in the stratified structure of Christian theology have not infrequently a close relation to different stages in the historical development of our thought. Thus certain theological conceptions, even of a basic kind, were thrown up in the process of historical development clothed in forms that were conditioned by a particular culture, but which are now in need of clarification. As they have come down to us they have been shaped by a conceptual system which it was found necessary to use at the time, and were defined in that system in such a way that they were connected to transitory conceptions. But now those transitory conceptions have fallen away, so that the theorems that helped to define them must be altered, otherwise they can only obscure and distort the basic conceptions they were originally defined to serve. Let me suggest that 'transubstantiation' is a concept of this kind, designed to express the Church's understanding of the real presence of Christ in his body and blood in the Eucharist. And let me grant that at a certain stage of theological development the concept of the real presence had to take this theoretical form, defined within a system of ideas mainly of an Aristotelian kind. But once we have reached through 'transubstantiation' a clearer and deeper understanding of the real presence of Christ, then, should not the concept of transubstantiation in its old mediaeval form give way or be allowed to take a more adequate form through which what was intended, and is now more clearly grasped, may be expressed? To perpetuate 'transubstantiation' as if that form of the conception had a point-to-point correspondence with the real presence, would surely involve a serious misunderstanding of what 'transubstantiation' used to convey even in classical mediaeval thought.

What I am suggesting, then, is that the application of this understanding of the stratification in the totality of our theological concepts, and the hierarchy of truths which that involves, to the historical development of Christian doctrine, would enable us to carry through a much needed scientific clarification in the whole corpus of the Church's thought. Moreover, it would help to deliver our understanding from being held captive to statements and notions of the truth which, however compelling they were in their field of reference at the time, have served our grasp of the truth so well that now they have to be criticised or relativised, or at least reshaped, in the light of it. A procedure of this kind would provide us with a progressive development in theological understanding in such a way that we would be continuously committed to the truth of being as it outruns the statements that are brought from time to time to serve it, and are thus thrown back upon the inherent authority of the substance of the faith in face of our formulations of it in such a way that we are delivered from an authoritarian nominalism in which immutable formulations are clamped down upon the mystery of God in his self-revelation. Is that not how the concept of the hierarchy of truths, incorporated into the constitutions of the recent Vatican Council, actually took effect, although with not a little caution, in its deliberations? I think particularly here of *Lumen Gentium*. Thus what the hierarchy of truths seems to mean in operation as well as in scientific discussion is, that in the progress of believing inquiry the basic and central concepts are thrust forward more and more into their commanding position, close to the heart of the faith, as manifestations of its very substance, while other concepts, important and necessary as they may be, fall towards peripheral significance, and some actually fall away altogether after having fulfilled their transitory functions. As this happens, there inevitably takes place a considerable clarification of

Christian doctrine, through radical simplification and profound unification.

It is not so easy for the Church as such to carry that through very rigorously, for by its nature it embodies, and carries over from the past into the present, a vast development of tradition, but what does help the Church very considerably is well coordinated activity with the body of its theologians whose purpose it should be to serve the fundamental datum of divine revelation. Through this stratification of concepts and levels, scientific theology seeks to penetrate into the primordial unity constituting the 'natural' intelligible basis of our knowledge of God, with a view to the clarification and simplification of the whole structure. In proportion as that basis comes to view in its ultimate economic simplicity, there is bound to take place a powerful unification of understanding grounded on the substance of the faith which carries with it at the same time a universality of range in which the whole Catholic Church is objectively involved.

9, 10. In the last two paragraphs, theses *nine* and *ten,* the questions hitherto set out and discussed, in regard to truth of being and truths of statement, are applied to problems of authority that arise in the interpretation of the divine revelation and in the functioning of Church institutions. It may well help us at the start to draw a couple of distinctions: between *primary* and *secondary* authority, and between the *authoritative* and the *authoritarian.* According to biblical teaching, all authority *(exousia)* derives from God himself. He alone is the primary or ultimate authority, but there are secondary authorities, or delegated authorities, whose function it is to serve his supreme authority, and they function authoritatively when they serve the divine authority in such a way as not to obscure it but to let it appear in all its ultimate prerogative and majesty, and to be acknowledged as such. However, when these secondary authorities arrogate to themselves the authority delegated to them, thus constituting themselves authorities in their own right, then they become perverted, the 'authorities of darkness'. Thus instead of serving the ultimate authority which brings freedom, they exercise an authoritarian tyranny which demands unreasoning submission. It is in this light that the New Testament presents the unique authority of Christ, which is characterised by an astonishing authoritativeness, over against the authority of the Scribes and Pharisees, which is merely authoritarian and enslaves the consciences of men. It is in a similar light that the authority of the law is presented, for example, by St Paul. The law derives from God, and behind it stands all the divine majesty and holiness, and it is the function of the law to reveal and serve the divine majesty and holiness. But, owing to the dialectic of sin, the law tends to become an authority in itself, and as such even to become 'the strength of sin', for it exercises such an authoritarian tyranny over the consciences of men that it enslaves them and separates them from direct relation to God. Regarded in this autonomous status, as an independent authority on its own, the law becomes a 'demonic' authority from which we are redeemed only through the blood of Christ. The important thing for us to notice in this biblical teaching is that even the divinely promulgated law, and the divinely appointed institutions such as the Temple authorities, could both become entangled in a situation where, instead of being authoritative they have become authoritarian, and instead of ministering to the ultimate or primary authority of God they have usurped it and come to play a 'demonic' role.

I would like to suggest that it is the same basic issue with which we are concerned in the distinctions between the truth of being and the truths of statement, and between the truths of created being and the truth of the Supreme Being. The truths of statement are what they ought to be when they serve the truth of being, and the truths of created being are what they ought to be when they serve the Supreme Truth. The hierarchical structure of levels of truth which we have been considering means that all truth of statement and all truth of created being serve the Supreme Truth, for they are all under obligation to that Supreme Truth, while the Supreme Truth cannot be brought under obligation to, or under the control of, the truths of created being or the truths of statement. But when this structure becomes inverted, then we attempt to subordinate the Supreme Truth to the truths of the creature and his statements, and we become entangled in a perverted authoritarianism in which we impose the preconceived patterns of our own self-understanding upon the divine revelation, and we clamp down our own independent human formulations upon the substance of the faith.

Theses *nine* and *ten* are designed to clarify these problems with a view to obviating any betrayal of our trust, whether we are called as interpreters and teachers of the Word of God or as churchmen engaged in exercising the magisterium of the Church. In interpreting and explaining as far as we can the datum of God's self-revelation to mankind, and in guiding and directing the minds of the faithful into right relations with the Truth of God and right understanding of the substance of the faith, we ourselves are rightly related to God only as we serve his divine majesty, freedom and authority, in the absolute prerogative of his own truth, in the divine power of his own self-evidence, and in the pure light of his own Being – that is, in such a way as never to transfer the centre of authority from the objective revelation of God to ourselves, and never to mask the authoritative majesty of God by an authoritarian exercise of our calling to serve him in the Church.

If St Anselm and St Thomas were correct in their analysis of the word *intelligere,* as *intus-legere,* then what we do in the interpretation of the Holy Scripture is to penetrate understandingly into it in such a way as to read within it the *veritas* underlying its many outward expressions, and it is the same method, as both St Anselm and St Thomas insisted, that we must adopt in the interpretation of theological statements in order to bring to light the *veritas fidei.* As St Thomas put it: 'we have to investigate the root of the truth *(debemus investigare veritatis radicem)* and know how what is said is in fact true *(scire quomodo sit verum quod dicitur)* – otherwise we may be assured that something is as it is, but acquire no real knowledge or understanding and depart empty'. Such a movement of inquiry involves intelligent reflection and explanatory reasoning, but as St Anselm used to insist, it must be a humble process of inquiry into the reason of things *(quaerere rationem quomodo sit),* and that takes place as we allow the *veritas* to come to view in its own inherent *ratio,* so that our judgments and statements about it are formed under its own authority *(auctoritas veritatis).* Let me express this in a different way. In such a movement of inquiry we may well have to construct a scientific instrument, or set up some scientific apparatus, but precisely for the disclosure of what is different from it, the objective structure in the object of faith, and therefore we must beware of imposing the scientific instrument or apparatus upon the object of faith. Thus the very questions we ask, and the criteria we employ, and the statements we have to make in the prosecution of inquiry, must all serve the truth in its own authority and intelligibility, in such a way that they all become progressively refined media through which the truth imprints itself more deeply upon our minds in its own self-explication and power. It is therefore as we allow the truth itself to retain its own majesty, and decline to transfer the source of authority from the truth itself to ourselves that we find objective and compulsive ground for agreement.

This takes us back to the crucial question as to whether the assent and consent of the faithful to the truth rests *directly* upon the truth of God in its own self-light and self-evidence, or whether it is *indirectly* induced through some special illumination or some special infusion of grace, independent of the truth, enabling the faithful to receive or accept the truth. It is the latter which opens the way for an authoritarian exercise of the magisterium, but the former which invites an authoritative exercise of the magisterium in serving the inherent and ultimate authority of the truth itself. Thus if the truth of being is given its rightful priority and prerogative over all truth of statement, that does not mean any relegation or even depreciation of the magisterium, but the grounding of it upon what St Anselm called the *solida veritas* itself.

In every science there inevitably arises a structure of tradition and authority, without which it could not advance: they are methodological necessities and decisive organs in the clarifying and testing of our understanding and expressing of the truth, and in the achievement as far as possible of objectivity and universality, but they rightly fall into secondary place before the actual disclosure of the truth in its own right, and are therefore constantly relativised by the priority of that truth over them. That is how the scientific conscience operates. It is not otherwise in the Church of Christ where we have to do with the majesty and authority of God himself as the Supreme Truth. And so genuine authorities arise in the historical Church, theological and ecclesiastical authorities, appointed by God to serve his own majesty and authority, and thus to be instruments in guiding and testing the understanding of the faithful, and in the achievement as far as possible of objectivity and universality; but just because they are appointed to serve the majesty and authority of God himself they necessarily fall into secondary place before him, that God himself may be all in all, and his truth may retain unprejudiced and uncompromised its own absolute prerogative over all conscience in Christ. Thus the exaltation in the Church of the ultimate authority of the Supreme Truth over all other authorities creates freedom for the faithful, for it makes us to know the truth finally out of itself and by its grace alone, and demands of us an obedience that transcends our respect for the authoritative institutions of the Church, divinely appointed though they may be, and necessary as they prove to be in the historical mediation of the truth to mankind. On the other hand, it is only as these institutional authorities in the Church are rigorously subordinated to the majesty and authority of the Supreme Truth, that they evoke and gain the respect that is due to them, for then they are not authoritarian tyrants over our conscience but authoritative instruments of the Truth that makes us free. The rule of authoritative representation is clearly exhibited in the New Testament teaching about the Spirit of Truth who does not speak from himself, i.e. out of his own authority, but speaks only what he hears from another. That is the Spirit of Truth who informs all authentic magisterium in the Church, directing it away from itself to the one Truth of God revealed and incarnate in Jesus Christ, in order that it may serve that Truth in such a way that it is allowed to retain its absolute priority over all the Church's teaching. Thus the exercise of the Church's magisterium in witnessing to the Truth of God must take the form indicated by John the Baptist at the beginning of the Gospel:

'He must increase, I must decrease.'

CHAPTER XI

*Immortality and Light**

TO RISE from the dead and live in the age to come is the appointed destiny of the children of God. In that continuing personal life they are like angels and can no longer die, for as children of the resurrection they are children of God. He is the God, not of the dead, but of the living, for in him all are alive. That was the message of Jesus handed down to us through the Evangelists as an essential part of the Gospel. Jesus did not speak of an 'immortality' which depends on the natural force of the soul to resist the corruption of death, but spoke instead of a life-relation with God which cannot terminate for it is anchored beyond our mortal existence in the ever-living God himself. He preferred to speak of this as 'eternal life' which is freely given by the heavenly Father to his children on earth and which, far from ending with death, results in a resurrection to a fullness of imperishable life in God.

Jesus Christ is presented to us in the Gospel, however, not merely as a teacher about eternal life, but as the actual embodiment of the Life of God in our humanity. Hence he constitutes in his own life, death and resurrection the saving intervention of God which brings an end to the power of death and mediates a new resurrected existence for mankind. In St John's Gospel this is expressed by the

*The Drew Lecture on Immortality delivered at Spurgeon's College, London, November 1980.

teaching that just as God the Father has Life in himself, so he gives the Son to have Life in himself and thereby to be the fountain of the life for others. In the midst of our mortal existence Jesus Christ is himself the Resurrection and the Life. All who believe in him may share his divine Life and its resurrecting power, so that when they die they will not perish but pass from the darkness of death into the light of an unending personal life with Christ in God.

Throughout the New Testament there is a rich theology of eternal life, with various distinct but complementary emphases in the epistles of St Paul, St Peter and St John, and in the Apocalypse, in which the teaching given in the Gospels is developed in the light of the redeeming passion and resurrection of Christ. My concern in this lecture, however, is not to work that together into a coherent doctrinal form, but to discuss certain basic elements in it from a particular perspective to which attention is not usually given, except in some well-known Christian hymns, namely, the relation of immortality to light.

I propose to do this by taking as a basis for discussion two passages from St Paul's first and second letters to Timothy, and proceed by way of comment and elucidation of the relevant points.

The first passage is from I Timothy 6. 12–16.

> Fight the good fight of faith; take hold of eternal life to which you were called when you made the good confession in the presence of many witnesses. In the presence of God who gives life to all things, and of Christ Jesus who in his testimony before Pontius Pilate made the good confession, I charge you to keep the commandment unstained and free from reproach until the appearing of our Lord Jesus Christ; and this will be made manifest at the proper time by the blessed and only Sovereign, the King of kings and Lord of lords, who alone has immortality and dwells in unapproachable light, whom no man has ever seen or can see. To him be honour and eternal dominion. Amen.

The second passage is from II Timothy 1. 8–10.

> Do not be ashamed then of testimony to our Lord, nor of me his prisoner, but take your share of suffering for the gospel in the power of God, who saved us and called us with a holy calling, not in virtue of our works but in virtue of his own purpose and grace which he gave us in Christ Jesus ages ago, and now has manifested through the appearing of our Saviour Christ Jesus, who abolished death and brought life and immortality to light through the Gospel.

The basic ideas, and of course the language, which the Apostle deploys in these passages, are familiar to us from the whole range of the Biblical tradition, from the Old Testament as well as the New Testament, in which life and light are brought closely together. We may point to the thirty-sixth Psalm as typical: 'With thee is the fountain of life; in thy light do we see light'. God himself is Life and Light in an absolute sense which infinitely surpasses our comprehension, but as such he is the ultimate creative Source of all life and light, making alive and enlightening what he has made in accordance with his purpose of love and grace. In this respect the distinctive feature of the Gospel is that this divine Life and Light have become manifest to us in an incarnate form in Jesus Christ. As the living God himself among men he quickens and enlightens all whom he brings into relation to himself, and grounds their creaturely life and light in the uncreated Life and Light of God.

I

'God alone has immortality and dwells in an unapproachable light.' This is the major premise, so to speak, of everything that must be said here. God alone is unceasing and self-sufficient in his power to live, eternally existing in himself in a way that is beyond all comparison and infinitely surpasses our power to comprehend. He is by nature underived, without beginning and without end. Immortality belongs to him, and to him only, as the natural or intrinsic property of his being. As the one and only God he is the transcendent Creator and Lord of all. Everything that is, in heaven or earth, owes its existence to him, for he freely created it out of nothing and sustains it in its existence by the power of his eternal being. The whole universe of visible and invisible realities is radically contingent in its existence and nature, for it need not have come into existence and has no inherent force to continue in existence: it depends entirely upon the beneficent will of God.

It is in the light of this doctrine of the eternal God and his creation of the universe out of nothing that the question of human immortality must be considered. If to be divine and uncreated is to be intrinsically immortal, then to be creaturely and human is to be intrinsically mortal. Quite evidently this applies to our physical existence, for our bodies come into being and then crumble away and cease to exist as such, but does this apply to what we call the 'soul' or the rational self? Does the human soul enjoy life and light in virtue of any natural power of its own which makes it eternally durable throughout all the changes and ravages of time and therefore finally impervious to the corruption of death? The Christian view, however, is that the soul is a creature no less than the body. It came into being out of nothing through the creative will of God, so that like everything else in the universe it is naturally contingent and perishable, liable to dissolve back into nothing. Considered in itself, the soul can only pass away: it is intrinsically mortal and not immortal.

The extant literature of the Early Church reveals that this Christian doctrine of God and his relation to the universe which he has created and continues to sustain out of nothing soon came into a head-on collision with Greek thought at two significant points which bear upon our theme. It was a general tenet of Hellenic thought that the world was not created by God but was the embodiment of divine reasons, the eternal forms which are the ground of its intelligibility. It was also assumed by Hellenic thought that there is a radical dualism between the intelligible and the sensible, or between form and matter. While the actual world was recognised as composed of form and matter, form was held to be the divine, intelligible element, the definable timeless essence of things which makes them what they really are, but matter was held to be no more than the sensible element which is only fleetingly and accidentally related to reality as its appearance. Greek thought identified the real with what is necessarily and timelessly true, and discounted the sensible or material as deficient in rationality or merely contingent and accidental. It was this combination of ideas which prevented the emergence of what we call empirical science, for in refusing to accept the full reality of matter or the rationality of the contingent, it restricted scientific knowledge to the realm of necessary truths of reason and changeless geometrical forms utterly detached from space and time. A genuine science in our sense could not have arisen until those fundamental tenets of Greek thought were destroyed, and that is precisely what happened with the Christian doctrine of God and his relation to the world. The doctrine that God has freely created the universe out of nothing and endowed it with a created rational order of its own, implied the full reality of matter and the rationality of the contingent. Matter and form are here regarded as equally created out of nothing and as inseparably unified in one contingent rational order pervading the whole universe. The creation of matter out of nothing meant that it had to be treated as contingent reality, and not as unreal; and the creation of form out of nothing meant that it had to be differentiated from God's uncreated rationality as contingent rationality. It is not surprising that this Christian doctrine of creation was attacked as 'impious' and 'atheistic', for within the framework of Greek thought about God and the world it could only mean that God, from whom all rational form and reality derive, was himself created out of nothing.

This was the context in which, following the teaching of the New Testament, the Christian Church had to think out the notion of human immortality. Christian and Greek thought alike operated with the basic idea that to be immortal is to be divine, and to be divine is to be immortal. But Greek thought identified the divine with the rational, i.e. with what is timelessly and necessarily true. And since the soul was held to be the rational part of man, it argued for the immortality or the divine incorruptibility of the human soul – and that idea was underpinned by the ancient Orphic religious idea which pervades Greek mythology that the soul is a spark of the divine temporarily imprisoned in the body. In that event death could only mean the happy release of the soul from its entanglement in the darkness and irrationality of matter or contingent existence.

That notion of immortality was not open to Christians, as early Christian theologians like Justin Martyr, Athenagoras, Theophilus and Irenaeus were not slow to point out, for the human soul is creaturely and not divine, and if it is rational that must be regarded as a creaturely rationality utterly different from God's eternal uncreated rationality. The decisive factor in the argument, however, lay not simply with the doctrine of creation out of nothing which Christianity shared with Judaism, but with the doctrine of the incarnation. On the one hand, the doctrine of the incarnation as the personal embodiment of God's eternal *Logos* (which at the moment we may think of as the divine Reason or Rationality) in a particular creaturely being, shattered the Greek idea that the divine Logos is immanently embodied in the universe as its necessary rational order, and demanded a radical distinction between the uncreated Rationality of God and the created rationalities of the cosmos. On the other hand, the fact that in Jesus Christ God's own eternal Logos had become man, assuming physical contingent matter into union with himself, implies that the physical creation far from being alien to God is actually accepted and affirmed by him as real even for God, which has the effect of obliging us to cherish the material world of space and time as God's good creation and to respect its created order as the realm in which he has purposed to manifest his divine love. The doctrine of the incarnation, together with the doctrine of creation out of nothing, implied a radical distinction between God and the creature, between uncreated and created rationality, but it also had the effect of unifying the sensible and intelligible, or material and rational elements, in created realities, which changed the understanding of human nature. Instead of the soul and the body being regarded as antithetical, they were regarded as complementary, so that, to borrow an expression from James Denney's 1910 Drew lecture, man was understood as the body of his soul and the soul of his body. That was bound to affect the whole notion of human immortality, and it did, for it meant that a Christian understanding of man's continuing personal life after death has to take the body into its basic equation.

Before we turn to that, however, let us note that while on the Christian view the soul like the body is intrinsically mortal this does not mean that it must die. The creaturely soul is utterly contingent, for it depends upon God for its existence and its creaturely continuity. If it is to survive human death it must depend likewise on the creative and sustaining power of God who only has immortality and who only is the source of life. That is to say, human immortality can only be conceived as a gift of God's grace within a relation between the creature and God which God will not terminate but brings to a fruition in what the New Testament calls 'eternal life'. The soul can be put to death, as Jesus said, and warned us that that is something to be feared much more than the death of the body; but Jesus himself came to set man's relation with God on a wholly new basis of grace and love in which eternal life will be the very order of his human existence.

II

Let us return to the point that, as God made him and gave him life, man is at once body of his soul and soul of his body. It is in that unity and wholeness of his human nature that God sustains him in being as man, and, in spite of the fact that he is essentially creaturely and perishable, brings him into a relationship with himself in which man's life need not cease but may continue without end. In this case the Christian is bound to look upon death with a horror unknown to the Greek or Oriental who thinks of the end of his physical existence as the release of his spirit, for the death of the body threatens his dissolution and therefore his survival as a human person. Life after death for the Christian must involve a recreation of his whole human nature as soul of his body and body of his soul, that is, a resurrection of man in his ontological integrity as man.

The situation is seen to be much more serious, however, when we recognise that death as we human beings now experience it, is rather more than the kind of death we find in nature around us, when for example a living organism perishes and disintegrates in the dust. Death as we human beings know it is more than 'natural corruption', St Athanasius argued in the De Incarnatione, for there is lodged in the heart of it the threat of divine judgment upon human sin and evil, which intensifies the power of corruption in human death far beyond its natural force (3–5). As Georges Florovsky wrote in his Harvard essay on 'The "Immortality" of the Soul':

> The burden of sin consisted not only in self-accusations of human conscience, not only in the consciousness of guilt, but in an utter disintegration of the whole fabric of human nature. The fallen man was no man any more, he was existentially 'degraded'. And the sign of this 'degradation' was man's mortality, man's death. In separation from God human nature becomes unsettled, goes out of tune, as it were. The very structure of man becomes unstable. The 'union' of soul and the body becomes insecure. The soul loses its vital power, is no more able to quicken the body. The body is turned into the tomb and prison of the soul. And physical death becomes inevitable. The body and the soul are no longer, as it were, secured or adjusted to each other (*Collected Works*, III, pp. 221f).

In this event the resurrection of man to eternal life in his wholeness and integrity as man must involve the act of expiatory atonement which deals decisively with human guilt and its divine judgment, and thereby destroys death by taking away its fearful sting. But it must also be a positive act of salvation in the ontological depths of human existence in which man's very being and nature are recreated and established in a life-relation with God which can never perish.

That is precisely the theme of the second passage which I have chosen as a base for our discussion here, salvation by grace which God 'has manifested through the epiphany of our Saviour Christ Jesus, who abolished death and brought life and immortality to light through the Gospel'. In the incarnation of his Son God has laid hold of our disintegrated and decaying human existence in such a way as to penetrate into the inner core of its corruption in death and destroy its power and at the same time to regenerate and reintegrate the human race through a life-giving bond of union with himself. Patristic theology was surely right, therefore, in stressing the fact that he who became incarnate in Jesus Christ was none other than the Creator Word of God through whom all things were made and in whom all things visible and invisible subsist and are held together. That is to say, the incarnation of the Creator within the conditions and structures of our space and time existence had an ontological effect upon the whole creation, and in particular upon the whole structure and life of the human race which would otherwise have disintegrated into nothingness under its own corruption and the divine judgment upon its evil. That is the staggering significance of what the New Testament calls the *epiphaneia* or *parousia* for it involves a vast *palingennesia* (regeneration) of humanity and ultimately a new heaven and a new earth. All this is not to detract in the slightest from the fact that in Jesus Christ God has come into our world in an acutely personal and personalising way which reestablished and secures and intensifies individual personal relation with God, but in so far as we take seriously the fact that Jesus Christ is the Creator Word of God himself in indissoluble ontological union with creaturely human existence, we are bound to reckon with the fact that every man irrespective of who he is, what he does or believes, subsists and coheres as man in Jesus Christ the incarnate creative ground of his being. That is to say, we have to take seriously the fact that since the incarnation human nature has been set on a new basis in relation to God who only has immortality. That is the irreducible ontological ground for our hope of immortality, an immortality which is the gift of God's grace but which he has eternally secured for us in Jesus Christ. Let us explore this a little further, in three respects.

(a) Central to this Christian hope is the oneness between Jesus Christ the incarnate Son and God the Father. In technical theological terms what is at stake here is what the Nicene-Constantinopolitan creed called the *homoousial* or *consubstantial relation* between Jesus Christ and God or what the Chalcedonian Council spoke of as the *hypostatic union* between the divine and human natures in the one Person of Christ. If that bond does not ultimately hold, if Jesus Christ is not really one in being and agency with God the Father Almighty, the Maker of heaven and earth and of all things visible and invisible, if he is not himself God of God and Light of Light, then the Christian hope is finally and utterly empty – the message of the Gospel has no substance to it. The forgiveness of Jesus is merely the transient word of a human creature without any ultimate validity, the deeds of Christ in life and death are merely transient episodes with no more than moral or symbolic significance at the most. But if Jesus Christ really is one in being and agency with God the Father, then everything he said and did for us and our salvation has ultimate validity and reality. Where has this been more concisely or clearly expressed than in the Fourth Gospel? 'My sheep hear my voice, and I know them and they follow me. And I give unto them eternal life, and they shall never perish, and no one shall snatch them out of my hand. My Father who gave them to me, is greater than all, and no one is able to snatch them out of my Father's hand. I and my Father are one' (John 10. 27–30).

(b) No less central to the Christian hope are the passion and resurrection of Christ, but they are the passion and resurrection of the incarnate Son and Word of God through whom all things were made. The whole incarnate penetration of God into our fallen and corrupt humanity which has brought upon itself the divine judgment presses toward its culmination in the crucifixion and resurrection of Jesus, for it is through the atoning sacrifice of Christ on the Cross that the fearful division between God and man and man and God is healed in what the Bible calls 'propitiation'. The gracious drawing near of God to man and the incredible assumption of man into union with God in the incarnation is brought to its consummation in the death of Christ when the consubstantial oneness or hypostatic union in Christ's relation with God the Father, far from disintegrating, asserts its power in the midst of the perdition and dereliction of death thereby vanquishing death and destroying its power, and issuing in the resurrection not only of Jesus Christ himself but of the whole human race ontologically subsisting and cohering in him, the Head of the new creation. Who can plumb the fearful depth of what took place in the passion of Christ, when God incarnate cried out in desperate anguish in his struggle with the powers of darkness made obdurate by his own righteous judgment against them? The Cross tells us that God is not a God who holds himself aloof from mankind in its self-inflicted agony of guilt and violence and ontological pain, but has come into the midst of all that we are in our state of perdition in order to bring healing and reconciliation and renewal. Our salvation derives from and depends on the unreserved *self*-giving of God for us on the Cross when through incarnate atonement he undid sin and guilt in the depths of human being, destroyed death and brought life and immortality to light in the resurrection of Jesus Christ from the grave, the First-Born from the dead, as St Paul called him.

Let St Peter summarise this Gospel for us. 'Blessed be the God and Father of our Lord Jesus Christ, who according to his great mercy begot us again unto a living hope by the resurrection of Jesus Christ from the dead, unto an inheritance incorruptible and undefiled and that does not fade away, reserved in heaven for you, who are guarded by the power of God through faith unto a salvation ready to be revealed in the last time' (I Peter 1. 3–5).

(c) This brings us to the third point I wish to note: the future consummation of our hope in Christ. Both of the basic passages which I have adduced from St Paul's letters to Timothy speak of our salvation and participation in eternal life or immortality in connection with the *epiphany* of Christ, which, as I have already noted, is equivalent to the other New Testament term *parousia*. It is highly significant that both terms refer to what we call the first

advent of Christ and his second advent – the New Testament does not use either term in the plural, as though there were more than one *epiphaneia* or *parousia*, for the advent presence of God in Jesus Christ in whom Deity and our creaturely humanity are brought into hypostatic union once and for all reaches from the birth of Jesus to his coming again to judge the quick and the dead. That is to say, the incarnation is not a transient episode in the economy of salvation, for the Kingdom of Christ shall have no end, as the Creed expresses it. We live, as Justin Martyr once expressed it, *in the midst of Christ's parousia (Dialogue with Trypho, 52)*. This has to do with the fact that the incarnate coming and presence of the Son of God affected, as we have seen, the whole structure and existence of the human race, and not simply isolated individuals. But it also means that individuals who believe in Christ and participate in the *paling-ennesia* of what took place in him from his birth to his resurrection share that experience with others, and enter into its fullness only as the saving renewal of the incarnation, passion and resurrection of Christ are finally actualised in the human race as a whole, and all things are gathered up in Christ the Head of the new creation. Here we have to do with the tension between what some scholars have distinguished as the 'realised' and 'futurist' elements in the Christian hope.

Let me focus attention only on one particular aspect of this: the astonishing fact that within the one indivisible epiphany or advent of the incarnate Son of God, the 'moment' when each of us dies and goes to be with Christ is somehow identical with the 'moment' when Christ will come again to judge and renew his creation, for in a real ontological sense those who die in Christ are already risen with him. That is something we find very difficult to understand owing to the refraction of time as we experience it in the world which Christ has already redeemed but which is eschatologically in arrears, as it were, in the enjoyment of its inheritance in Christ. We have to reckon here, however, with something like a 'relativity of simultaneity' which relativity theory has brought to light and which seems to contradict the common sense notions which we generate within the split space and time of our everyday experience. Thus Einstein found he could maintain the constancy of light in all uniformly moving systems by the novel idea of assigning two different but equally real times to the same event. I do not wish to argue from relativity theory in physics or cosmology to a solution of the problem we have in Christian theology of understanding temporal experience in Christ when in him the age to come telescopes back into this present age in such a way that in Christ we live simultaneously in two ages or times, the on-going present and the future which comes to meet us, but only to suggest that this analogy from our scientific understanding of the behaviour of light in the physical universe may help to make a very difficult notion a little more understandable for some people today. The primary theological point to get clear, however, is the ontologically and temporally indivisible nature of the one epiphany or advent of the incarnate Son of God in whom all men and all ages are held together, without any detraction from real differences between different individual experiences or times. It is because we are resurrected together with Christ, and are indeed already risen in Christ that at the return of Christ to judge the quick and the dead and make all things new we meet up with an event that has already overtaken us. It is the ontological bond in Christ who has taken up our space–time into himself through incarnation and resurrection which constitutes the indestructible ground of our life eternal with Christ in God. To be in Christ is to be in him who *is* the Resurrection and the Life.

III

There is one final point we must discuss, the place of Christian confession, testimony or witness to which both of our basic passages from I and II Timothy refer. Let me recall the words. From I Timothy:

> Fight the good fight of faith; take hold of eternal life to which you were called when you made the good confession in the presence of many witnesses. In the presence of God who gives life to all things, and of Christ Jesus who in his testimony before Pontius Pilate made a good confession, I charge you to keep the commandment unstained and free from reproach until the appearing of our Lord Jesus Christ . . .

From II Timothy:

> Do not be ashamed then of the testimony of the Lord, nor of me his prisoner, but take your share of suffering for the gospel in the power of God, who saved us and called us to a holy calling, not in virtue of our works but in virtue of his own purpose and grace which he gave us in Christ Jesus ages ago . . .

At an earlier point we noted that through the incarnation of the Creator Word of God all that Jesus Christ did in life, passion and resurrection affected the very existence and nature of the human race and indeed of the whole creation. In the incarnation all things are gathered up, reintegrated and restored to their true ground and reality in Christ who has the primacy over all things and in whom all things consist. In a fundamental sense, therefore, the ontological regeneration and restoration of humanity has already taken place in Christ, so that as Patristic theology could argue, the general resurrection of all men follows from the resurrection of Christ the Head of the new creation as surely as in the process of physical birth the body follows the head. How, then, are we to think of individual resurrection in relation to the general resurrection, or the resurrection of believers in relation to the resurrection of all men, the righteous and the wicked alike?

Athanasius reminds us that in his incarnation the Son of God had a twofold ministry to fulfil. He was sent both to minister the things of God to man and to minister the things of man to God. That is to say, Jesus Christ had a Godward task to fulfil as man, as well as a manward task to fulfil as God. Granted that the whole act of condescension and humiliation which the incarnation represents is a sheer act of God's love in which the *self*-giving of God must be accorded the primacy, nevertheless the role of the human Jesus within that was absolutely essential, for it was precisely *as man* that God came in Christ to work out our salvation. Quite fundamental to the human side of his activity was the good confession which Jesus Christ made before Pontius Pilate. His human testimony or witness before God as well as before man was intrinsic to the whole course of his vicarious obedience as the Servant of the Lord and as such belongs to the very substance of our salvation in him. To partake of that salvation is to share with Christ Jesus in the confession which he himself made, for it is to be yoked together with him in the very exigencies and conditions of our human life which he came to assume and in assuming to heal and save. Not to share in the good confession of Christ, not to take up his cross and follow him, to be ashamed of his testimony and to resile from the call to die with Christ, is to contradict the very salvation and resurrection in which we are all involved through Christ's incarnational assumption of us into himself. No rejection or unbelief on our part can undo what Christ has done on our behalf or can undo the all-decisive impact of his passion and resurrection on our human existence, so that we are quite unable to cut ourselves off from the resurrection of all men, the just and the unjust, at the last day. But neither does participation in the resurrection depend on any act of will or decision on our part or upon our own effort in fighting the good fight of faith. As we had nothing to do with our natural birth, we can do nothing to effect our rebirth in the Spirit. We are not saved or regenerated in virtue of any activity of our own, whether it be contrition, personal decision, witness or confession, for what saves and regenerates us is the activity of Jesus Christ in his vicarious life and obedience, in which we are called to share through the grace of God. Even when we are commanded to lay hold on eternal life, what counts is not our feeble grasp of God in Christ but his almighty grasp of us within which our grasp of faith is enclosed and faithfully sustained. That Jesus Christ really took our place in the human responses of knowing, believing and worshipping God, of repenting, obeying, laying hold of eternal life or bearing testimony, is something that many people find it extremely hard to accept, ready as they may be to accept that God acts on their behalf in Jesus Christ, for somehow they want to reserve what they conceive to be an element of their own independence or freedom for themselves. But are they not thereby substituting their own faith and their own personal response in the place of Christ's which he offered to the Father on our behalf, and is that not a way of finally setting the Man Christ Jesus in his saving mediation aside, and indeed of declining to let him take our place completely and unreservedly? All this, of course, is not to detract in any way from the freedom he gives us or the obedient response he demands of us as his children, but to give them their full value, for it is only within his all-embracing and undergirding faithfulness in giving himself unreservedly for us in the totality of our human being and life that we are genuinely and spontaneously free in our response, for then they are rendered unconditionally in answer to unconditional grace. We cannot forget the parable Jesus told to the effect that when we have done all that it is our duty to do, we are still unprofitable servants. In other words, we are saved or justified by grace alone and not by *any* works that we do.

In spite of the fact that in God's gracious assumption of our human nature in Jesus Christ all men without exception are involved, in spite of the fact that Jesus Christ bore all the sin of mankind, including the sin of unbelief, so that when he died all died, and in spite of the fact that all men are included in his vicarious resurrection, the New Testament tells us that at the last day a division will become manifest as people are separated from one another, much as sheep are separated by a shepherd from goats. And that final judgment, as Jesus insisted, will involve a discrimination that will take us all by surprise. While God's saving grace, and with it the gift of the resurrection, is extended equally to all irrespective of their worth in such a creative way that their human being is not allowed to lapse back into nothingness but is sustained and reinstated before God, nevertheless it seems clear that not all will enjoy the fruit of the resurrection or the blessedness of eternal life in God. In the last day, as Jesus taught, when the dead hear the voice of the Son of Man summoning them to go forth from the grave, for some people that will mean a resurrecting to judgment. Here we are confronted with something that is quite inexplicable, which surely has to do with the irrationality of evil. Whatever else evil may be it entails a radical discontinuity, a break in our relations with God, which cannot be rationalised away through the continuities of logical explanation. The fact that atoning reconciliation between man and God was accomplished as God himself became incarnate and penetrated into the fearful chasm of our death and its separation from God showed that the chasm of evil was quite abysmal or bottomless. Only the utter self-giving of God in the indescribable anguish of the dereliction of the Cross could save us – that is the measure with which God has measured the enormity of evil and its discontinuity. The Gospel does not offer us at any point an explanation of evil, or therefore of the fact that when face to face with the unreserved love of God and its unconditional grace, there are evidently people who finally refuse what God has done on their behalf.

Let us look at the problem from the perspective of the fact that God *is* love, and that all he has done for us from creation to redemption and will do in the consummation of all things is his ceaseless and total self-giving in love. In his love God gives himself impartially, equably, unconditionally to all alike, to the just and the unjust, the believing and the unbelieving, the good and the wicked. It is precisely because he does not withhold his love from the unbelieving or the wicked that his love opposes their unbelief or their wickedness, and that the relation of love into which he gratuitously assumes them resists the strange will of the sinner to isolate himself from God. Thus it is precisely the love of God which judges the sinner, while the unconditional nature of the self-giving of God in love even to the wicked can only mean his unconditional judgment. Since God *is* love, he can no more cease to love than he can cease to be God, and since his unconditional love is his unconditional self-giving he can no more restrict that self-giving or withdraw it in any way, than he can diminish or contradict the love that he eternally is. Moreover, since the self-giving of God in Love to mankind has once and for all been enacted in the incarnation, passion and resurrection of his Son in Jesus Christ, he can no more withdraw from the final consummation of his purpose of love or therefore from actualising the final judgment of his love upon a recusant sinner than he can undo the incarnation or go back upon the atoning sacrifice upon the Cross. In the last resort, therefore, it is by this Man, Christ Jesus, that God will judge the quick and the dead, for all judgment, as the Fourth Gospel expresses it, has been committed to him. Part of what baffles us in this state of affairs is the fact that the unrelenting out-pouring of God's love upon the sinner continually sustains him in being even in the midst of his ultimate refusal of that love and its judgment of him.

Now let us turn back once again to our chosen passages from St Paul's letters to Timothy, in which the relation between the immortal God and the human creature is spoken of in terms of *light*. Here we operate with a distinction between uncreated and created light and between uncreated and created immortality. Just as the uncreated Light of God enlightens us in Jesus Christ, so the Immortality of God immortalises those whom Jesus Christ through his incarnate epiphany brings into a saving relation with himself. Just as Immortality and transcendent Light are one in God, so for us to be enlightened by God in Jesus Christ is to be given life and immortality. This relation between life and light, as we have already had cause to note, is common to the whole biblical tradition. But let us now think of it especially in relation to Jesus Christ, the real Light whose coming into the world enlightens every man with the light that is the life of men. That is to say, Jesus Christ is not like John the Baptist, only a reflection of or a witness to the Light, but is himself the actual Light of God embodied in humanity. As such he is the Light of the world, who certainly penetrates into our darkness, even into the fearful darkness of death, but far from being extinguished by it, he destroys death and brings life and immortality to light through the Gospel.

Let me restrict our consideration of this to two points which bear upon our immediate theme.

1. In Jesus Christ the eternal, uncreated, unapproachable Light of God which no man can see and live, has embodied itself amongst us in the form of a human life. It is not only that the human life of Jesus was so drenched with the Light of God that it was utterly translucent with divine purity and holiness, but that the life of Jesus was itself the form God's Light has graciously taken in order to enlighten mankind. In Jesus Christ the uncreated Light of God adapted itself, so to speak, to dwell with frail, mortal man without consuming him, but in Jesus frail, mortal human nature has been adapted to receive the Light of God dwelling in it in such a way that it was made alive with the very Life of God. This does not mean that in Jesus Christ the uncreated Light of God overwhelmed or replaced the created light with which he was endowed in his

humanity, but that in him uncreated and created light were united in such a way that neither was impaired or diminished through relation to the other. Nor does it mean that in Jesus Christ the eternal Life of God substituted for his human life, but that in him divine and human life were united likewise in such a way that neither was impaired or diminished through relation to the other. It is as such that Jesus Christ is presented to us in the Gospel as both the Light and the Life of the world, the life-giving Light and the enlightening Life of mankind.

2. It is as such that Jesus Christ will judge the quick and the dead in the consummation of his epiphany – and there is no other Judge, for God has committed all judgment to his Son. That is to say, there will be no final judgment behind the back of Jesus, for as the incarnate embodiment of the Light and Life of God he constitutes in his own life, passion and resurrection both the ultimate Judge and the ultimate criterion by which judgment will be carried out. It is precisely as Jesus, and only as Jesus, that God will judge mankind at the last day. Just as in all his providential dealings with mankind, God sends the rain and makes the sun shine upon the just and the unjust alike, so throughout the whole course of redemption and in its consummation in the last day God has shown and will show the same impartiality of his grace toward the just and the unjust, the believing and the unbelieving, as he bears upon them by his enlightening and quickening power. Then, we are told, the just will shine forth as the sun in the Kingdom of their heavenly Father, but nothing like that is said of the unjust. Although there is no darkness in God somehow the Light of God mediated in and through Jesus Christ bears upon the unbelieving and the recalcitrant in such a way that darkness results. According to the Evangelists this is precisely what happened already in the earthly ministry of Jesus when the seeing were made blind by his Light. That is the strange paradoxical result to which Jesus once referred in the words, 'If the light that is in you is darkness, how great is that darkness'. That is how, I believe, we are to understand the final judgment when there will emerge into the open the division that takes place, in their interaction with the Light and the Life that are Jesus Christ, between the children of light and the children of darkness. It seems that while we cannot contribute one iota to our salvation, we are able, not to undo the love of God or the unconditional gift of his light and life to us, but to become so locked up in ourselves that the Light of God in Jesus becomes the fire of a consuming judgemnt and even the ultimate Love of God a kind of hell to us.

Now by way of conclusion let us focus attention once more on the *epiphany* of our Lord and Saviour Jesus Christ, in which all our hope for eternal life is rooted and pledged. Far from being some sort of manifestation of God's presence timelessly and tangentially bearing upon the human race from outside, the epiphany is the actual personal presence of the living God with all the fullness of his eternal Light, Life and Love, intersecting the course of human history and penetrating into its ontological ground in such a way as to heal the breach between the creature and the Creator and reconcile man to God, anchoring our human existence in the ultimate Reality of God the Father Almighty. Utterly divine and transcendent though it is, therefore, the incarnate epiphany of God in the birth, life, crucifixion and resurrection of Jesus Christ is also space–time reality. It is real historical event that does not crumble away into the dust of oblivion, for God has negatived within it the corrupting force of evil and death so that it persists throughout all space and time as live imperishable reality, pressing toward the ultimate point when God will creatively and redemptively gather up and bring to its final consummation the activity of his grace in the return of Jesus Christ to judge the quick and the dead and make all things new. As such the epiphany is yet to be unveiled in its fullness both as a transcendently divine event and as an essentially historical event, in what St Paul has called its 'proper time'. That is to say, everything that the Christian Gospel tells us about the hope for personal, immortal life is bound up with the final Advent of Jesus Christ which must be given its full space–time reality as an event of basically the same nature as the resurrection of Jesus Christ from the grave. But what took place intensively there in Jerusalem will unfold in all its extensive reality, embracing the whole universe in a new heaven and a new earth. That is the divinely appointed destiny of the created universe, and it is within that destiny that each of us will enter upon the inheritance prepared for us, in Jesus Christ in God.

INDEX OF NAMES